D1229721

Widening Horizons in Creativity

ANOTHER BOOK BY THE SAME AUTHOR

Scientific Creativity: Its Recognition and Development.
Selected Papers from the Proceedings of the First, Second,
and Third University of Utah Conferences.
EDITED BY Calvin W. Taylor and Frank Barron.

Front Row: Taylor, Torrance, Drevdahl, Clark, Leary, MacKinnon, Guilford, Sprecher, Wight

Second Row: Westcott, Jablonski, Hyman, Datta, Fiedler, Parnes, Gamble

Third Row: Roberts, McRae, Mednick, Levine, Holland, Beittel

Fourth Row: Astin, McPherson, Mullins, Brust, Barron, Elliott, Ghiselin (Harmon was not present)

Widening Horizons in Creativity

The Proceedings of the Fifth Utah
Creativity Research Conference

EDITED BY

Calvin W. Taylor

Chairman of the Utah Conferences
and Professor of Psychology
University of Utah

JOHN WILEY & SONS, INC., NEW YORK · LONDON · SYDNEY

To L. L. Thurstone,
Uncle Will, Aunt Lizzie,
and my University of Chicago days.

Preface

This volume presents the report of the fifth (1962) national conference in the Utah creativity research conference series. The secluded, scenic setting at Mount Majestic Lodge and Manor, high in the Wasatch Mountains at the Brighton, Utah, ski resort, proved to be an inspiring site for such a conference.

This report consists of five parts, with the first part containing two historical reports of interest to the creativity movement. Although Professor Arnold Toynbee was unable to accept our invitation to attend this conference, he very generously allowed us to use, as the first chapter, his insightful description of the vital role of creativity in history. We are also grateful to Corbin Gwaltney and the Editorial Projects for Education for permission to use Toynbee's challenging paper and to Paul Cracroft for indispensable assistance in this matter. Furthermore, we are fortunate in having the permission of Mrs. Thurstone to use L. L. Thurstone's provocative and farsighted paper on creativity and scientific talent as the second historical report. This paper was presented a decade ago as a result of my invitation to Professor Thurstone to participate in a National Research Council meeting on criteria of success in science. It is evident in this article that he was an astute forerunner in his thinking on creativity, in the same way that he was years ahead in numerous other topics in psychology, as those of us who received doctoral and other training under him have clearly recognized.[1]

[1] Professor Thurstone was undoubtedly interested in creativity throughout his career and accomplished basic research and developed techniques underlying much of the total creativity research effort. In addition to his own creativeness, he had the experience for a period (after completing his undergraduate degree in engineering) of being a research assistant to Edison. Shortly after presenting the paper reprinted in this book, he initiated a General Motors-supported project directly on creativity but died before he was able to realize the fruits of his own creativity project.

The remaining parts of the book consist of the proceedings (including discussions) of the entire conference, which are presented almost verbatim. Part II includes seven chapters under the general head'ng of Creative Process Studies, a distinctive feature of this book. Part III contains reports of progress in research on education and the development of creativity. Part IV consists of important studies on criteria and predictors. These studies entail multiple measures of creative performance and numerous psychological characteristics found to be correlated with creative performance. Part V, the last section, reports on creativity studies in special fields and settings, such as architecture, visual arts, public relations, advertising, and industry.

Since the welcome of the University's Academic Vice President, Daniel J. Dykstra, to those at the conference was so appropriate, the essential portions of his remarks will be quoted:

A university means many things to many people. To the uninitiated, it means a place to spend vast sums of money. Also to the uninitiated it means a place where impractical people exchange impractical points of view. I suppose there are some who in justification of this position would point to this conference as Exhibit A. To many, a university is a place where people pick up weird notions about religion or about politics; to them, it is a place to be shunned and avoided.

To the initiated, however, a university is an institution dedicated to the transmission of information, to the exchange of views, to the development of the appreciation of the arts and sciences. I think that the reason I am especially pleased to welcome you here is that this particular conference helps promote all three objectives. You gather to transmit information from one to another, to explore new ideas, and to be concerned with creativity in the sciences, in the arts—in fact, in all fields of knowledge. To me all this is highly important, and thus I wish this conference all possible success.

On behalf of the University of Utah I want to thank the National Science Foundation for making both this conference and the entire conference series possible. I think that it is a wholesome thing in a society like ours to have a source of funds in support of activities and endeavors where the major objective is in the realm of ideas.

A brief description of the conference series seems to be warranted. Each of the first three Utah research conferences, held in 1955, 1957, and 1959, included nearly twenty carefully selected researchers whose work provided the substance of each conference. Every participant reported on his latest research project, with rather full discussion periods following each report. For each conference approximately one thousand copies of the complete report and discussion were reproduced essentially verbatim in multilith form by the University of Utah Press. When these three conference reports were out of print, thirty papers selected from them were published by John Wiley & Sons, in a single volume entitled *Scientific Creativity: Its Recognition and Development.* Frank Barron assisted me in editing that book.

After the first three large conferences, it seemed wise to produce a stocktaking report, with the help of a small group selected from the most active researchers in the field. A group of six worked out a review designed to interpret and evaluate creativity research knowledge; some of the most promising leads and most urgent needs for further research were emphasized. We met for three days in June 1961, in a conference which differed from the others in the series, since it involved only a small group who summarized research findings to date rather than reporting and discussing only our latest research. The contributors were John Holland, Paul Torrance, Joseph McPherson, Hubert Brogden, Thomas Sprecher, and I, with J. P. Guilford, Anne Roe, and Frank Barron serving later as senior reviewers. Work on the book *Creativity: Progress and Potential* (McGraw-Hill), which emerged from this small fourth (1961) conference, actually continued from 1960 through 1963, with participants working individually and in pairs on the final report.[2]

The five main contributors to the 1961 report served with me as the steering committee for the 1962 conference. This fifth conference was announced in *The American Psychologist* several months before it was held. All psychology departments with graduate programs also received a special letter asking them to inform us of any workers in the field of creativity, either in their department or elsewhere. This letter was a follow-up to a copy of the 1959 report, sent to psychology departments at the suggestion of those attending the 1959 conference, especially Mullins and McPherson. We were able to distribute the 1959 reports through a supplemental contribution of $300 from the Dow Chemical Company.

We accumulated a list of all persons nominated by the departments of psychology in the United States and Canada, of all who had been nominated for previous conferences in the series, and of those others nominated by the steering committee and other valuable sources (including some previous steering committee members). In all about 200 persons were nominated by one or more of these methods. From these nominees the steering committee selected the final participants: those judged most likely to make the best contributions at the conference and thereby to advance our knowledge as far as possible from where

[2] Other background information and acknowledgments on the Utah creativity research conferences are contained in the prefaces to the 1955, 1957, and 1959 conference reports (published by the University of Utah Press); in the history and acknowledgments as well as the preface to *Scientific Creativity: Its Recognition and Development;* and in the preface to *Creativity: Progress and Potential.*

it was in the 1961 stocktaking report. Following the pattern established at the second conference, we invited a few observers to listen to the conference, primarily because their organizations displayed exceptional interest in activities in the field of creativity.

We varied slightly from the pattern of the first three conferences by not having subgroups meet the last day on crucial subtopics in creativity. Instead we had five observers report briefly on their work, with each report becoming a chapter in this book (Chapters 14, 15, 20, 24, and 25). A subgroup of observers added their collected reactions to the conference (Chapter 28). The names of these observers are mentioned in the latter chapter, wherein each one describes briefly his interests and efforts in creativity.

As stated in our first (1955) report, after research conferences of this type, which have an "inner circle" of participants, it seems wise to make the essential findings and ideas presented at the conference available to as wide an audience as possible. Creativity is, after all, a large but embryonic field, filled with unknowns. A serious difficulty arises whenever any individual attempts to judge, from his subjective and limited perspective, the future worth of every idea expressed. This becomes necessary whenever summary reports containing "only the ideas which are more valuable" are prepared. Some of the best ideas in research conferences may be strange, unexpected, and unorthodox to many current researchers, who might feel more comfortable and be more "efficient" if only the more orthodox ideas and approaches were reported.

To avoid biased reporting, we decided, with strong conviction, to publish an essentially verbatim report of each conference, if at all possible. The discussion, which was usually spontaneous and free flowing, was transcribed from tape recordings as it actually occurred, whether during the course of a report or after its completion. The essence of the discussion was retained so that every idea expressed could be made available to all interested persons not in attendance. After the initial transcripts had been typed, the entire conference was audited in an attempt to correct and complete the transcription—a difficult process we called "prooflistening." The transcribed paper and the discussion pertaining to it were sent to each participant, who then edited and returned them. He was also asked to add to the total bibliography every research study cited in his report, in addition to a list of what he considered to be the five or six other best readings in creativity. It is satisfying to know that similar full reporting has been accomplished for each of our large research conferences.

In each of the conference reports, our goal has been adequate communication both of the ideas expressed and of the searching spirit so fully displayed. In some cases, hopefully, the tentative nature of early thinking has also been communicated.[3]

As indicated in my own report at the first (1955) conference and in our further research on the relations between communication abilities and creative abilities, we believe that many problems are involved in the attempt to report scientific information so that it will have the greatest impact on researchers and others. One idea is that essentially the same scientific information could be presented in quite different styles. Our experience suggests that reporting of live discussion among leading researchers is one of the more provocative styles.

To indicate when the discussion changed from one person to another, two symbols have been utilized in this book. These appear at the beginning of a paragraph; appearance of a new symbol signals a change of person.

S The speaker giving the report is doing the talking; **S** is also the author of the chapter.

C A participant, otherwise unidentified, is making a comment or raising a question; **C** refers to any discussant.

There are two main reasons for not identifying the participant in each exchange. First, the attempt to identify accurately each participant's exchanges would have been a heavy burden, especially since these were lively, spontaneous exchanges. We did not want to lose the spontaneity by requiring a formal pause and announcement of each person's name before he could enter the discussion or make any remark. Second, we believe that a good scientific idea must ultimately be able

---

[3] To our knowledge, no one has made a study to determine whether the more formal parts or the live discussion parts of a report have more creative material in them per unit of publication space. We feel that discussion material serves both to provoke more thoughts in the minds of readers and to show them how crude or how well-grounded is the subject matter being presented. During a conference I attended, one of the participants suggested that the material finally used in the written volume might prove to be less creative and refreshing than those comments which for some reason were omitted. This criticism, however, could not be leveled at this fifth Utah creativity report (nor at the first three), since nearly all the discussion was transcribed and published. We strongly suspect that the lively, unexpected discussion in the Utah reports is one of the main reasons these reports have been virtually self-propelling. In fact, students in creativity seminars have repeatedly remarked that they felt they could step right into the discussion as they read the transcribed reports. They indicate also that they realize from these discussions that even the experts are largely guessing in many spots, so they too feel they have a right to enter into the discussion with their own ideas. Consequently, we doubt that a teacher could teach solely by authoritarian means if his students had textbooks with such discussion materials.

to stand on its own merit, regardless of whether it came from an authority or from a person as yet unknown. In Chapter 9, however, we did identify all participants in a spontaneous discussion that arose on process versus products in creativity. Consequently, extra effort was required to name every discussant and to give each a chance to edit his own discussion before we put the chapter into final form.

We also think that there is merit in an accurate description of the manner and sequence in which things occur in scientific work. Therefore, we have tried to give a clear, complete presentation of what occurred in this research conference. At the same time, we are probing into complex and unwieldy areas that deal with numerous characteristics, some of which appear to be almost intangible, such as intuition and the various stages in the complex creative process.[4]

[4] The growing awareness of the importance of both accurate reporting and more subtle, complex inner processes is well illustrated by the following excerpts from the 1962 presidential address of Carl B. Allendoerfer to the Mathematical Association of America. "This outline of mathematics, however, is accurate only for a mature theory which has essentially been embalmed in textbooks. . . . Surely, this is not the way in which it was invented. Indeed, we usually perform the magical feat of building the fifth story of our structure without first establishing a foundation or even thinking about the first four stories. We start at both ends and the middle and only after decades of effort bring forth the beautiful, logical, and polished gems which we dangle before our students. It is no wonder that students are baffled by the very idea of doing research in mathematics.

"Let me describe briefly the process of mathematical discovery. Beginning with nature, we seek to find as many relationships within it as we can. If we can systematize these, we do so, but a lack of organization of our material does not keep us from pushing forward. On the basis of what we have observed, we guess theorems and use these to derive other theorems. Immediately we rush to apply these back again to nature and proceed headlong if our predictions are successful. Axioms, logic, and rigor are thrown to the winds, and we become intoxicated with our success and open to dreadful errors.

"This process is called 'intuition' and its nature is a matter of the greatest conjecture, in spite of the writings of several of our most distinguished colleagues. The successful unraveling of this process would be a major contribution to the understanding of the human mind. But, it is by this means, explained or not, that the great majority of mathematical theorems are first discovered. The products of this intuitive discovery are frequently wrong, usually unorganized, and always speculative. And so there follows the task of sorting them out, weaving them into a proper theory, and proving them on the basis of a set of axioms. It is at this stage that the mathematical model is likely to be constructed. The details of this process go in our seminars and in our discussions in the corridors of meetings like this, but almost never appear in print. Hence the inner circle of creative mathematicians have the well-kept secret that in a great many cases theorems come first and axioms second. This process of justifying a belief by finding premises from which it can be deduced is shockingly similar to much reasoning in our daily lives, and it is somewhat embarrassing to me to realize that mathematicians are experts in this art. . . .

"As I turn now to the reform movement in the teaching of mathematics, let me

In this conference series, we have been interested primarily in understanding the fundamental nature of creativity and its characteristics, after which we will know better how to develop and encourage it and how to establish an optimum environment for its nurture. The first steps are to learn all we can about what it is and how to build measures to identify it, so that we can formulate sound educational, environmental, and other programs designed to be more favorable to creative talent.

As illustrated in this collection of papers and in the previous reports at the Utah conference series, it has been demonstrated that useful research has been done on many different aspects of creativity, from the elementary schoolroom through the universities into various research installations, professional activities, and industry. Consequently, there is no longer any question that fruitful creativity research can be done. In fact, at this relatively early period of serious scientific research, there are already a great number of leads to pursue. Naturally we hope that this report will have the catalytic effect upon research and action programs which considerable evidence suggests the previous Utah reports have had.

During the conference series we rotated the steering committee each time to insure a high percentage of top creativity researchers being nominated and selected to participate. There has been a deliberate attempt to have researchers representing various behavioral sciences, education, the physical and biological sciences, and the arts.

In all, a total of 55 different nationally selected participants in the conference series has presented over 80 individual research reports in various subareas of creativity. These totals do not include the contributions of Toynbee and Thurstone in the historical reports herein, nor those of the many observers who attended and participated in subgroup reports and in some of the discussions.

I want to acknowledge the farsighted type of support provided by NASA (Robert Lacklen and Allen Gamble, monitors) and by the Air Force Office of Scientific Research (Rowena Swanson, monitor) which has enabled us to give much needed time and thought to our own creativity research studies on NASA and Air Force scientists and to further analyses of these data (as reported in Chapter 16).

The invaluable assistance of many local persons in the formation, operation, and recording of the conference is gladly acknowledged. Their "behind-the-scene" activities freed the participants to focus prac-

---

first discuss intuition. It is here that the learning process must begin, for in some sense the student must follow the path by means of which mathematics developed in the first place. . . ." (Carl B. Allendoerfer, "The Narrow Mathematician," *The American Monthly*, Vol. 69, No. 6, 1962, 461–469).

tically their entire attention upon the conference topic and discussions. Robert Ellison, Victor Bunderson, Gary Cooley, Tony Jacobsen, Mac Richards, Chandler Cook, Lorraine Loy, Ken Wodtke, and Clifford Abe performed many functions in the staging and recording of the conference. Those who helped in the arduous task of transcribing the first draft of the reports and the initial revisions of these drafts from the tape recordings included Allison Day, Marianne Cram, Joyce Nilson, Ada Lund, Madge Nickell, Karen Rynio, Susan Smith, Sally Meik, Elaine Stuart, Barbara Mortensen, and Elizabeth Knight. Tony Jacobsen assisted me in overseeing this vast transcription and editorial revision work and the prooflistening connected with it. Stanley Mulaik, Lynda Clemmons, and Robert Ellison gave assistance in the editorial work on the manuscript. Barbara Mortensen, Nancy Taylor, and Stephen Taylor helped in the production of the final report for this NSF Project #G14667. The excellent typing of the final report and manuscript was done by Connie Jensen, who also organized and edited the final bibliography, helped in proofreading, and otherwise gave more assistance than anyone else on the final manuscript for this book. She and Frank Williams helped with the index.

The staging of a conference of this type and the preparation of an almost verbatim final report cannot be accomplished without valuable contributions and cooperation from many people. Most important of all, the participants deserve many thanks for their reports and their many lively and friendly exchanges. I cannot overemphasize the point that the fruitfulness of the conference hinged primarily upon the contribution of the participants, who brought a rich background of scientific training and research experience to bear upon the difficult problem of creativity and its many ramifications. It is to their credit that they had also found many new approaches to this complex problem.

I appreciate the interest of the National Science Foundation in giving financial support to both this conference and to all of the previous conferences. I acknowledge the excellent guidance of Robert Cain, who has served as the NSF monitor over the grant for both this conference and the smaller stocktaking conference held before this one, and I am grateful also to Thomas Mills for his general guidance on the total project. I was glad to have Milton Levine serve again as the NSF representative at this conference.

In summary, it has been a distinct pleasure to work and associate with all those in any way connected with this total project. The responsibility for any shortcomings in this venture belongs to me alone.

CALVIN W. TAYLOR

Salt Lake City, Utah
September 1964

Contents

xvii

part I Historical Reports

chapter 1 Is America Neglecting Her Creative Minority?[1]

Arnold Toynbee, Royal Institute of International Affairs

S America has been made the great country that she is by a series of creative minorities: the first settlers on the Atlantic seaboard, the founding fathers of the Republic, the pioneers who won the West. These successive sets of creative leaders differed, of course, very greatly in their backgrounds, outlooks, activities, and achievements; but they had one important quality in common: all of them were aristocrats.

They were aristocrats by virtue of their creative power, and not by any privilege of inheritance, though some of the founding fathers were aristocrats in conventional sense as well. Others among them, however, were middle-class professional men, and Franklin, who was the outstanding genius in this goodly company, was a self-made man. The truth is that the founding fathers' social origin is something of secondary importance. The common quality that distinguished them all and brought each of them to the front was their power of creative leadership.

In any human society at any time and place and at any stage of cultural development, there is presumably the same average percentage of potentially creative spirits. The question is always: Will this potentiality take effect? Whether a potentially creative minority is going to become an effectively creative one is, in every case, an open question.

The answer will depend on whether the minority is sufficiently in tune with the contemporary majority, and the majority with the minority, to establish understanding, confidence, and cooperation between them.

[1] Reprinted with permission of both the author and the Editorial Projects for Education (Corbin Gwaltney, editor).

The potential leaders cannot give a lead unless the rest of society is ready to follow it. Prophets who have been "without honour in their own country" because they have been "before their time" are no less well-known figures in history than prophets who have received a response that has made the fortune of their mission.

This means that effective acts of creation are the work of two parties, not just one. If the people have no vision, the prophet's genius, through no fault of the prophet's own, will be as barren as the talent that was wrapped in a napkin and was buried in the earth. This means, in turn, that the people, as well as the prophet, have a responsible part to play. If it is incumbent on the prophet to deliver his message, it is no less incumbent on the people not to turn a deaf ear. It is even more incumbent on them not to make the spiritual climate of their society so adverse to creativity that the life will have been crushed out of the prophet's potential message before he has had a chance of delivering it.

To give a fair chance to potential creativity is a matter of life and death for any society. This is all-important, because the outstanding creative ability of a fairly small percentage of the population is mankind's ultimate capital asset, and the only one with which Man has been endowed. The Creator has withheld from Man the shark's teeth, the bird's wings, the elephant's trunk, and hound's or horse's racing feet. The creative power planted in a minority of mankind has to do duty for all the marvelous physical assets that are built into every specimen of Man's nonhuman fellow creatures. If society fails to make the most of this one human asset, or if, worse still, it perversely sets itself to stifle it, Man is throwing away his birthright of being the lord of creation and is condemning himself to be, instead, the least effective species on the face of this planet.

Whether potential creative ability is to take effect or not in a particular society is a question that will be determined by the character of that society's institutions, attitudes, and ideals. Potential creative ability can be stifled, stunted, and stultified by the prevalence in society of adverse attitudes of mind and habits of behaviour. What treatment is creative ability receiving in our Western World, and particularly in America?

There are two present-day adverse forces that are conspicuously deadly to creativity. One of these is a wrong-headed conception of the function of democracy. The other is an excessive anxiety to conserve vested interest in acquired wealth.

What is the proper function of democracy? True democracy stands for giving an equal opportunity to individuals for developing their unequal capacities. In a democratic society which does give every individual his fair chance, it is obviously the outstandingly able individual's moral duty to make a return to society by using his unfettered ability in a public-spirited way and not just for selfish personal purposes. But society, on its side, has a moral duty to ensure that the individual's potential ability is given free play. If, on the contrary, society sets itself to neutralise outstanding ability, it will have failed in its duty to its members, and it will bring upon itself a retribution for which it will have only itself to blame. This is why the difference between a right and a wrong-headed interpretation of the requirements of democracy is a matter of crucial importance in the decision of a society's destiny.

There is at least one current notion about democracy that is wrong-headed to the point of being disastrously perverse. This perverse notion is that to have been born with an exceptionally large endowment of innate ability is tantamount to having committed a large prenatal offence against society. It is looked upon as being an offence because, according to this wrong-headed view of democracy, inequalities of any and every kind are undemocratic. The gifted child is an offender, as well as the unscrupulous adult who had made a fortune at his neighbours' expense by taking some morally illegitimate economic advantage of them. All offenders, of every kind, against democracy must be put down indiscriminately according to this misguided perversion of the true democratic faith.

There have been symptoms of this unfortunate attitude in the policy pursued by some of the local educational authorities in Britain since the Second World War. From their ultraegalitarian point of view, the clever child is looked askance at as a kind of capitalist. His offence seems the more heinous because of its precocity, and the fact that the child's capital asset is his God-given ability, and not any inherited or acquired hoard of material goods, is not counted to him for righteousness. He possesses an advantage over his fellows, and this is enough to condemn him, without regard to the nature of the advantage that is in question.

It ought to be easier for American educational authorities to avoid making this intellectual and moral mistake, since in America capitalists are not disapproved of. If the child were a literal grown-up capitalist, taking advantage of an economic pull to beggar his neighbour, he would not only be tolerated but would probably also be admired, and public opinion would be reluctant to empower the authorities to curb his activities. Unfortunately for the able American child, "egghead" is as damning a word in America as "capitalist" is in the British welfare state; and I suspect that the able child fares perhaps still worse in America than he does in Britain.

If the educational policy of the English-speaking countries does persist in this course, our prospects will be unpromising. The clever child is apt to be unpopular with his contemporaries anyway. His presence among them raises the sights for the standard of endeavour and achievement. This is, of course, one of the many useful services that the outstandingly able individual performs for his society at every stage of his career; but its usefulness will not appease the natural resentment of his duller or lazier neighbours. In so far as the public authorities intervene between the outstanding minority and the run-of-the-mill majority at the school age, they ought to make it their concern to protect the able child, not to penalise him. He is entitled to protection as a matter of sheer social justice; and to do him justice happens to be also in the public interest, because his ability is a public asset for the community as well as a private one for the child himself. The public authorities are therefore committing a twofold breach of their public duty if, instead of fostering ability, they deliberately discourage it.

In a child, ability can be discouraged easily; for children are even more sensitive to hostile public opinion than adults are, and are even readier to purchase, at almost any price, the toleration that is an egalitarian-minded society's alluring reward for poor-spirited conformity. The price, however, is likely to be a prohibitively high one, not only for the frustrated individual himself but for his stepmotherly society. Society will have put itself in danger, not just of throwing away a precious asset, but of saddling itself with a formidable liability. When creative ability is thwarted, it will not be extinguished; it is more likely to be given an antisocial turn. The frustrated able child is likely to grow up with a conscious or unconscious resentment against the society that has done him an irreparable injustice, and his repressed ability may be diverted from creation to retaliation. If and when this happens, it is likely to be a tragedy for the frustrated individual and for the repressive society alike. And it will have been the society, not the individual, that has been to blame for this obstruction of God's or Nature's purpose.

This educational tragedy is an unnecessary one. It is shown to be unnecessary by the example of countries in whose educational system outstanding ability is honoured, encouraged, and aided. This roll of honour includes countries with the most diverse social and cultural traditions. Scotland, Germany, and Confucian China all stand high on the list. I should guess that Communist China has remained true to pre-Communist Chinese tradition in this all-important point. I should also guess that Communist Russia has maintained those high Continental European standards of education that pre-Communist Russia acquired from Germany and France after Peter the Great had opened Russia's doors to an influx of Western civilisation.

A contemporary instance of enthusiasm for giving ability its chance is presented by present-day Indonesia. Here is a relatively poor and ill-equipped country that is making heroic efforts to develop education. This spirit will put to shame a visitor to Indonesia from most English-speaking countries except, perhaps, Scotland. This shame ought to inspire us to make at least as good a use of our far greater educational facilities.

If a misguided egalitarianism is one of the present-day menaces in most English-speaking countries to the fostering of creative ability, another menace to this is a benighted conservatism. Creation is a disturbing force in society because it is a constructive one. It upsets the old order in the act of building a new one. This activity is salutary for society. It is, indeed, essential for the maintenance of society's health; for the one thing that is certain about human affairs is that they are perpetually on the move, and the work of creative spirits is what gives society a chance of directing its inevitable movement along constructive instead of destructive lines. A creative spirit works like yeast in dough. But this valuable social service is condemned as high treason in a society where the powers-that-be have set themselves to stop life's tide from flowing.

This enterprise is foredoomed to failure. The classic illustration of this historical truth is the internal social history of Japan during her two hundred years and more of self-imposed insulation from the rest of the world. The regime in Japan that initiated and maintained this policy did all that a combination of ingenuity with ruthlessness could do to keep Japanese life frozen in every field of activity. In Japan under this dispensation, the penalty for most kinds of creativity was death. Yet the experience of two centuries demonstrated that this policy was inherently incapable of succeeding. Long before Commodore Perry first cast anchor in Yedo Bay, an immense internal revolution had taken place in the mobile depths of Japanese life below the frozen surface. Wealth, and, with it, the reality of power, had flowed irresistibly from the pockets of the feudal lords and their retainers into the pockets of the unobtrusive but irrepressible business men. There would surely have been a social revolution in Japan before the end of the nineteenth century, even if the West had never rapped upon her door.

The Tokugawa regime in Japan might possibly have saved itself by mending its ways in good time if it had ever heard of King Canute's ocular demonstration of the impossibility of stopping the tide by uttering a word of command. In present-day America the story is familiar, and it would profit her now to take it to heart.

In present-day America, so it looks to me, the affluent majority is striving desperately to arrest the irresistible tide of change. It is attempting this impossible task because it is bent on conserving the social and economic system under which this comfortable affluence has been acquired. With this unattainable aim in view, American public opinion today is putting an enormously high premium on social conformity; and this attempt to standardise people's behaviour in adult life is as discouraging to creative ability and initiative as the educational policy of egalitarianism in childhood.

Egalitarianism and conservatism work together against creativity, and, in combination, they mount up to a formidable repressive force. Among American critics of the present-day American way of life, it is a commonplace nowadays to lament that the conventionally approved career for an American born into the affluent majority of the American people is to make money as the employee of a business corporation within the rigid framework of the existing social and economic order. This dismal picture has been painted so brilliantly by American hands that a foreign observer has nothing to add to it.

The foreign observer will, however, join the chorus of American critics in testifying that this is not the kind of attitude and ideal that America needs in her present crisis. If this new concept of Americanism were the true one, the pioneers, the founding fathers, and the original settlers would all deserve to be prosecuted and condemned posthumously by the Congressional committee on un-American activities.

The alternative possibility is that the new concept stands condemned in the light of the historic one; and this is surely the truth. America rose to greatness as a revolutionary community, following the lead of creative leaders who welcomed and initiated timely and constructive changes, instead of wincing at the prospect of them. In the course of not quite two centuries, the American Revolution has become worldwide. The shot fired in April 1775 has been "heard round the world" with a vengeance. It has waked up the whole human race. The Revolution is proceeding on a world-wide scale today, and a revolutionary world-leadership is what is now needed.

It is ironic and tragic that, in an age in which the whole world has come to be inspired by the original and authentic spirit of Americanism, America herself should have turned her back on this, and should have become the archconservative power in the world after having made history as the archrevolutionary one.

What America surely needs now is a return to those original ideals that have been the sources of her greatness. The ideals of "the organisation man" would have been abhorrent to the original settlers, the founding fathers, and the pioneers alike. The economic goal proposed in the Virginia Declaration of Rights is not "affluence"; it is "frugality." The pioneers were not primarily concerned with money-making; if they had been, they could never have achieved what they did. America's need, and the world's need, today is a new burst of American pioneering, and this time not just within the confines of a single continent but all round the globe.

America's manifest destiny in the next chapter of her history is to help the indigent majority of mankind to struggle upwards towards a better life than it has ever dreamed of in the past. The spirit that is needed for embarking on this mission is the spirit of the nineteenth-century American Christian missionaries. If this spirit is to prevail, America must treasure and foster all the creative ability that she has in her.[2]

[2] The late President John F. Kennedy, in his address on October 22, 1963, to the National Academy of Sciences, likewise spoke of the potential values of creativity: "As we begin to master the potentialities of modern science we move toward a new era in which science can fulfill its creative promise and help bring into existence the happiest society the world has ever known."

chapter 2 Criteria of Scientific Success and the Selection of Scientific Talent[1]

L. L. Thurstone; University of North Carolina

S   As I understand the purpose of this meeting we are to discuss two separate but related problems. I am glad to have the opportunity to express my ideas on these two problems.

1. Several important fellowship programs have been under way for quite a number of years, and it should be possible to look into the old records, the original application blanks, testimonial letters, and other supplementary data to ascertain whether the successful men could have been selected from the data that were available at the time they were appointed. I assume that we are dealing here primarily with post-doctoral fellowships as in the National Research Council fellowship program and the National Science Foundation program.

In making a study of the records of these men when they were appointed in comparison with their later performance in scientific work we must, of course, deal with the criterion problem. By this we mean the appraisal of the relative success of these men during the five or ten years after they completed their fellowship year.

[1] Paper presented November 14, 1953, at a conference on criteria of success in science, conducted by the Research Advisory Committee of the Office of Scientific Personnel, National Academy of Sciences–National Research Council. The editor of this book was then the director of the research program to which this paper was addressed. This early-dated paper is included because of its accurate forecast of the problems, methodologies, and findings to be encountered in research on creative scientific talent.

10

2. Another related problem is to formulate some hypotheses that might be investigated in studying some new methods of selection which can eventually be evaluated against future criteria of success. I shall try to make a few suggestions also on this aspect of the larger problem that is before us.

During the past few years there seems to have been a tremendous increase of interest in the problem of selecting creative talent in various fields. There have been a number of conferences of various groups on the problem of selecting creative talent in science and engineering. Some of them have been especially concerned with selection to identify the innovators and inventors. Other conferences have been concerned with creative talent in the field of leadership and administration. It is fortunate that this very fundamental problem is attracting a good deal of attention by men in responsible positions because there is no question that the creative talent in our population is one of our principal national assets. It is high time for us to do something aggressive in the identification of creative talent in various forms and in the subsequent training and encouragement of such talent.

Let us turn first to the problem of identifying in some more or less objective way the degree of scientific success of the former holders of postdoctoral fellowships. One naturally thinks of membership in elective scientific societies as one criteria. Election to Sigma Xi would hardly qualify in this category, especially in those universities where it is more or less routine practice to elect all graduate students in the science departments to Sigma Xi. This criterion varies considerably from one field to another so that it would have to be appraised more or less informally. In considering election to various societies we should note the age at which election takes place. Or perhaps we should indicate rather the number of years after the doctorate at which such election takes place. Promotion to a full professorship or to associate professorship and the age at which such promotion takes place can be considered as one index. This index must be considered in relation to the average age at which men attain the rank of associate professor or full professor in the college concerned. It is to be assumed that all of these indices will be summed in some appropriate manner. We might inquire also at what age the student was starred in *American Men of Science*.

One naturally turns to the publications as indicative of a man's scientific productivity. The number of publications is worth something, but this criterion must often be discounted because it is not uncommon practice to paraphrase a doctor's dissertation in a number of separate papers. It is very common for young men who have had good scholarship during their student days to stop producing entirely after the doctorate. It might be worth while to ask how many publications a man has produced in the first five years after the doctorate. In suggesting a point like this we recognize merely that a man is probably worth a little more if he has written several papers in the first five years than if he has produced nothing at all.

It is customary for a fellowship applicant to submit letters of endorsement from senior men in his field. When I read such letters I always interpret them in terms of my judgment of the men who write them. A single letter of definite endorsement from a man in whom I have confidence is worth far more than enthusiastic letters from a dozen men whose judgment I know nothing about. I assume that this is universal with all of us. In studying letters of recommendation from men in each field of science there might be an opportunity to study not only the applicants but also the batting average of the men who wrote the letters of recommendation. It might be a good idea to publicize the fact that a study of this kind is being made. It might be announced, for example, that all letters of recommendation will be checked against subsequent performance of the applicants so that the judgment of the endorsers will be subject to review. This could constitute a cumulative record for the endorsers of fellowship applications. If teachers knew that they were themselves to be rated eventually as to whether their recommendations are worth anything, the recommendations might increase in validity. At any rate, it is inevitable that the judgment about a candidate will be influenced by the reputation of the men who endorse him.

In studying the relative success of the former fellowship holders it might be worth while also to study the relative success of their teachers during the postdoctoral fellowship years. I should like to suggest a hypothesis that could be investigated in terms of the reports of the postdoctoral students. One might investigate the extent to which the sponsor's investment of his own time in the training and development of a student is related to the student's subsequent success. Courses are certainly not enough at the postdoctoral stage. It is quite likely that those fellowships will be most fruitful where the sponsor invests a good deal of his own time and effort in the training of the young men who are entrusted to his supervision.

Next I should like to suggest what would be for me a very important aspect of the appraisal of an applicant. When I look over the documents and letters about an applicant for a fellowship or assistantship, the most important thing that I look for is some evidence that the applicant has done something scientific and original on his own initiative. I prefer that it be something original that was not assigned by any teacher. It should be something that had nothing to do with course grades. It should be something that the applicant did simply because he wanted to. If there is no evidence of such effort on the part of the applicant, either in his own statements or in the letters of recommendation, then I find myself more or less indifferent. I would not insist that such evidence be directly related to the particular field of specialization in which the student wanted to major. What I am looking for is some indication of originality, creativeness, and initiative that shows some spark of imagination. It is much easier to extract evidence of this kind quite informally in an interview than in the formal letters of application for an appointment.

While on the subject of the interview I should like to suggest another hypothesis in the selection of creative talent in science. Lead the conversation to something bizarre and different and propose something that is a little queer. If a student responds immediately with a clear proof that the new idea is all wrong, then the negative suggestibility is not a good sign. I would rather gamble on a student who toys with a queer idea to see what the world would be like if it were really so.

In appraising the relative scientific success of former fellowship holders we could ask about ten creative men in each special field of each science to nominate the most promising younger men in their field. Then I would discount somewhat the cases in which men nominate their own students. Nominations that are made in this way could be taken as indices that the young men are successful.

Next I should like to mention what seems to be the principal handicap in the selection of creative talent in all fields including science. I have in mind the typical committee scene where everyone is glaring at transcripts of grades in fellowship appointments. Grades do not tell the story, especially if we are looking for creative talent.

In dealing with an applicant who has a straight A record I like to ask a pet question, namely: "Is there any evidence there that this man has ideas?" I have seen situations where this question seemed to be considered out of order. When we encounter a straight A record in a fellowship application, we can be pretty sure that the applicant is intelligent and perhaps very bright. In the absence of other evidence, such a transcript might be indicative of intellectual docility. I have known several such cases where the applicants really did have creative talent even though there was no evidence of it in the application. I have also seen other cases of this kind where the student had good grades but was unable to think of a dissertation problem, to say nothing of thinking about a problem that really had some originality. My point is that in addition to the scholarship record we should look for evidence of creative and original work, and we should encourage the applicant somehow to reveal it.

We should make studies not only of the scholastic average but also of the dispersion in the grades in order to ascertain whether students who will later be successful in science can be somehow differentiated from those who are less successful. I recall a controversy some years ago when I was examiner for the college at The University of Chicago. We gave scholarship examinations covering the four divisional fields, namely, physical science, biological science, social science, and the humanities. The question was how the scholarships were to be awarded. The rule at that time was that scholarships were awarded to those students who accumulated the largest number of points over the four divisions. My contention was that we would probably be selecting a larger proportion of future leaders in the various fields if we required a minimum standard in each of the four divisions to assure communication with the student at the university level. In addition we should give special preference to those who showed outstanding performance in some one division. In this way I thought we would be more likely to find the future successful writers, composers, physicists, mathematicians, and biologists, and perhaps also some students who might eventually help develop the social studies as real sciences. The matter was discussed for some time, but I was overruled. I should like to repeat my former recommendation that we require a minimum attainment over a fairly general field to assure communication with the student at the university level. Fellowship appointments should be given to those who show outstanding performance in some one field which will probably be their lifework.

Outstanding creative talent is sometimes associated with outstanding performance in several fields. Such individuals are extremely rare. We are more likely to find the future successes by looking for indications of outstanding performance in some one field.

In recognizing the great dispersion in the mental profiles of creative people in different fields of work, the least that we can do is to test each candidate for the primary mental abilities with research tests that have been developed by a number of men who have worked on the isolation of components of intelligence. A dozen or more cognitive components in human endowment have been isolated so far, and nobody knows whether scientific talent is closely associated with any of these components. It would be fairly simple to try to experiment to ascertain whether creative talent in science is associated with any of the primary cognitive functions that are already known. If such should be the case, the study would be of great value.

Another hypothesis is that creative talent in science may be associated with characteristics of personality and temperament in addition to the cognitive or intellective functions that may characterize such talent. In fact, it may eventually be found that the essential characteristic of creative talent is the association of certain mental abilities with certain personality traits. With this in mind we should investigate the personality self-rating schedules for what they may be worth in this connection.

For the past three or four years several psychologists have been working on the development of objective tests of personality. These are very formal objective laboratory procedures some of which have shown clear relation to certain personality traits. As far as practically feasible, these tests might be tried on certain groups of young scientists for later appraisal as to whether they have any predictive value.

Another hypothesis that might be worth some empirical inquiry is whether creative talent in science is associated with artistic interests of some kind. It has been my impression that those students who have creative talent seem to be rather frequently interested in some of the fine arts. This is only a hunch and it may be a false lead, but it should be fairly simple to make some preliminary inquiry about it in the selections of fellowships for scientific work. I believe it is a fact not generally recognized that creative scientific work is largely artistic in character.

If a number of indices of various kinds are found to be positively related to creative talent in science as distinguished from scholarship in the ordinary sense, a check list of such characteristics might be prepared and later correlated with subsequent creative work in science.

The Educational Testing Service in Princeton has accumulated vast records of graduate students who have been selected by their examinations. It would be interesting to know whether any validation studies have been made against criteria of creative talent in science. By this time there may be quite a number of scientists of national reputation who took those examinations when they were students. A follow-up might give some clues about what they were like as students and by which they might have been differentiated from less successful candidates. It would seem to be possible to prepare the proper kind of reading comprehension examinations that would be especially adapted for young science students. We can be pretty sure that such examinations would be concerned with the ability to read to learn exactly what is said rather than with mere speed of reading.

The Westinghouse Science Talent Search Program has been going on for some years. Some follow-up studies might be made of the students who were selected for scholarships. In such a follow-up study we should be very careful not to pay too much attention to college grades. We should look, rather, for creative work of which there might be evidence even during the undergraduate course.

In the search for scientific talent something must be done to find such talent in the back woods. At The University of Chicago it has been rather frequently remarked that many of our best graduate students come from colleges that are entirely unknown. The endorsers of those students are probably often also unknown. An effort must be made to discover the scientific talent that is undoubtedly lost every year in the relatively little-known schools. Statistically speaking, the number of undergraduate students who contact outstanding men in science is quite small compared with the talent that is available among undergraduate students. I should like to suggest that some creative scientists might be induced to interview science faculties even in the smaller colleges in search of superior scientific and creative talent. At first the appraisals might be quite informal, but the effort might yield a good crop of promising talent.

Finally, I should like to make the suggestion that the selection of young men for fellowships be done by a committee of men who have themselves discovered something in science. They should not just be men who are personally acceptable as teachers and counselors. The committee should consist of men who are themselves obviously creative in science. They might have a good chance of identifying creative talent among the youngsters. Perhaps a number of senior men in American science can be induced to contribute some time to such a project in the hope of discovering early some of the stars in the next generation of American science.

part II Creative Process Studies

chapter 3 A Creative Process
Check List:
Its Development and Validation

*Brewster Ghiselin, Roger Rompel,[1] and Calvin W. Taylor,
University of Utah*

S   The Creative Process Check List or, as it has alternatively been called, the Check List for Scientists is one of many instruments that were used in a research project completed in 1961 at the University of Utah on conditions relative to the productivity of Air Force
scientists.[2] The Check List was devised as a means of collecting data
of introspection that we thought might prove useful in predicting productivity and creativity in scientists. We reasoned that if, as we believed, the essential product of creative work is a new configuration
formed within the mind, an order of ideas or images either augmenting
or restructuring human insight, then creativity must be understandable,
in one of its aspects, as behaviors effecting significant and original
transformations in the organization of consciousness. We surmised
that, as each scientist made or tried to make such transformations, the
more successful scientist would experience and observe a different pat-

[1] The second author was serving as a predoctoral research fellow (5F1 MH 17,
388–2) of the National Institute of Mental Health at the University of Utah during
the time he was involved in this research, 1961–62.

[2] The final technical report of the entire project by Calvin W. Taylor, William R.
Smith, Brewster Ghiselin, and Robert Ellison is entitled "Explorations in the Measurement and Prediction of Contributions of One Sample of Scientists," *Report
ASD-TR-61-96*, Aeronautical Systems Division, Personnel Laboratory, Lackland
Air Force Base, Texas: April 1961. vi + 62 pp.

tern of behaviors than would the less successful. If we were right, the character of the pattern of experience observed thus by the scientist would be significantly related to the degree of his success.

There is only one way of observing configural innovation immediately as it occurs in the subjective sphere, and that is through introspection. We wondered how much the scientists we had been studying had observed in this way and if they could remember and report accurately what they had perceived. If we could not provide them experimentally with opportunities for further observation, perhaps we could assist their recall. There seemed little doubt that they could supply us with usable material. We reflected that many creative people, including scientists, have given significant accounts of their subjective experience in production, reporting it either in writing or by word of mouth, and independently or in response to an interviewer.

But for our purposes these modes of report were not satisfactory. We needed for analysis and measurement a body of statements that would be strictly comparable with one another. Not even the structured interview could provide sufficient control, especially of the subjects' terminology. A check list recommended itself to us as both manageable and reliable. Our research in several areas had demonstrated the dependability of various instruments of self-report, check lists among them, as means of measuring ability and predicting success in performance. A check list presenting in random order a group of terms permitting alternative ways of referring to the phenomena that we were investigating would constitute a linguistic schema, by means of which we could compel any number of subjects to use a common language and a common method in reporting upon a specified area of their experience. The information thus gathered could be projected as a complex of dimensions measurable in various ways.

In determining what phenomena to explore, we were guided by Ghiselin's criterion of creativity: the idea that creative production is essentially "an origination of significant order in the subjective sphere," the shaping for the first time of some part of that "universe of meaning"[3] in terms of which men understand their world and themselves. We concentrated upon that crucial moment of performance, within the whole action, when a new configuration of insight is formed and brought into focal clarity. We asked ourselves first what happens, and what terms

[3] Brewster Ghiselin, "Ultimate Criteria for Two Levels of Creativity," in *The Second (1957) University of Utah Research Conference on the Identification of Creative Scientific Talent*, Calvin W. Taylor, Principal Investigator, Salt Lake City: Univer. of Utah Press, 1958, p. 150; also in *Scientific Creativity: Its Recognition and Development*, edited by Calvin W. Taylor and Frank Barron, New York: John Wiley & Sons, 1963, p. 42.

can indicate what happens, in the configural field just before a new order is realized in it, and at the instant of realization, and immediately after. As for what may occur altogether outside the field of attention, the worker must be ignorant of it. Yet we thought it might be intimated through the character of the feelings that accompany developments in the configural field. And thus we were led to ask, secondly, what the affective concomitants of the observed configural events might be and what adjectives could characterize them. We found some answers in the literature reporting phenomena of the kind we were investigating. Many of the most authoritative introspective explorations of production —production presumed to be creative—are much concerned with the character of the worker's attention, its clarity or vagueness, for example, and with the quality of his feeling. These and other such reports supplied adjectives for the list and influenced selection of the referents which the terms in our list point to.

A central problem in constructing the Creative Process Check List was semantic. The items of the list must indicate complex and elusive subjective states by means of rather ordinary words. The subjects must be presented with the vocabulary of a miniature language, very limited in extent yet precise and diversified enough to represent their experience justly. Above all it was necessary to avoid the guidance of response through repelling it with derogatory terms or tempting it with flattering ones. Such terms as "creative" and "inspired" were omitted both for this reason and because their meaning was felt to be too loose and large. While exercising these precautions, we tried to approximate the vocabulary of intelligent and experienced workers in a variety of fields, and we supplied enough synonyms to permit expression of shades of meaning. The subject might choose, for example, in indicating a state of attention unconstricted by definite configurations, any one or all of several epithets: Whitehead's "muddled," Einstein's "vague," or others such as "chaotic" and "confused." Freedom of response had to be preserved if the pattern of responses given by each subject was to provide dependable indications of his experience. Yet some limits had to be imposed if patterns manageable in research were to be found.

To obtain separate reports on two different kinds of phenomena, we divided the Check List into sublists: List A, States of Attention, and List B, States of Feeling. It was administered to research scientists in the form of two parallel lists of adjectives. Each item was followed by three spaces within which the subject was required to place a check if he chose the adjective as an appropriate description of his experience *before*, *during*, or *after* his act of grasping (or shaping) a new insight, solving a problem, or otherwise bringing a new order into being within the field of his consciousness. The adjectives for *List A* were as follows: focused, diffused, vague, fixed, fluid, narrowed, ranging, inclusive, shifting, vacant, confused, static, expanded, wandering, orderly, scattered, clear, chaotic, contracted, muddled, wavering, intense, variable, faint, jumbled, fluctuating, dazzled, unconfigurated, arrested, configurated, sharp, characterless, dispersed, steady, scanning, and searching. The adjectives for *List B* were these: tense, happy, uneasy, calm, annoyed, excited, serene, sad, cool, inspirited, exalted, frightened, restless, satisfied, feverish, delighted, indifferent, relieved, impatient, depressed, eager, nervous, pleased, anxious, confused, lost, expectant, peaceful, exhausted, dulled, empty, depleted, enriched, pressured, pressed, full, disturbed, troubled, and disorganized.

In devising List A, we were guided by the assumption that certain of the designated states of attention, and combinations and sequences of states, are favorable or unfavorable, either absolutely or partially, at different stages in the scientist's effort to produce new insight. Similarly, in designing List B, we assumed that certain readily observable phenomena, the scientist's feelings and patterns of feeling at various stages in the process, can indicate important concomitants (perhaps organic conditions or developments) in themselves too obscure or complex for observation, which are favorable or unfavorable for production. Support for these more specific hypotheses was drawn from records of introspection made by all sorts of creative workers, and from the findings of various experimental studies.

Our idea, for instance, that a high degree of definiteness and stability, of "order," in the field of the worker's attention opposes the appearance of the unforeseeable new insight constituting a creative production is sustained by authoritative testimony and by research findings, old and new. More than fifty years ago, Henri Poincaré put forward the idea that "disorder . . . permits unexpected combinations":[4] that is, disorder—the opposite of inhibitory order—permits the appearance of new configurations of insight. Paul Valéry's later remarks about disorder paralleled Poincaré's:[5] "For the fact is that disorder is the condition of the mind's fertility: it contains the mind's promise, since its fertility depends on the unexpected rather than the expected, depends rather on what we do not know, and because we do not know it, than on what we know." These references may remind us of Frank Barron's recent reports of experimental evidence that original and creative people show strong preferences for disorder in a considerable range of circumstances.

[4] "Mathematical Creation," in *The Creative Process*, edited by Brewster Ghiselin, New York: The New American Library, 1955, p. 42.
[5] "The Course in Poetics: First Lesson," *The Creative Process*, p. 106.

In his article "The Psychology of Imagination," based largely upon his own research and that of others directed by Donald MacKinnon at the Institute of Personality Assessment and Research, Barron has expressed his conception of this tendency in the creative personality as follows:

> The truly creative individual stands ready to abandon old classifications and to acknowledge that life, particularly his own unique life, is rich with new possibilities. To him, disorder offers the potentiality of order.[6]

Support for our second hypothesis, that feeling may be indicative of favorable or unfavorable conditions in creative production, appears in the context of the statement of Paul Valéry quoted above: "The mind can always feel in the darkness around it the truth or the decision it is looking for, which it knows to be at the mercy of the slightest thing, of that very meaningless disorder which seemed to divert it and banish it indefinitely." Suggestive rather than highly precise, this statement nevertheless strongly emphasizes the connection of specific feelings and modes of feeling with the essential process of creative production, the bringing into being of a configuration augmenting or restructuring the configural organization that constitutes the universe of meaning, or of understanding, in terms of which we envisage ourselves and the world.

For scoring the Creative Process Check List, two independent methods were used, one theoretically determined, the other empirically. The latter was a statistical item analysis. The rationale and results of these two methods of scoring will be presented in the following section.

RESULTS OF A THEORETICALLY DETERMINED SCORING METHOD

In preparing a system for scoring the Check List for use in the Air Force research project, our procedure was to weight the various patterns of responses positively for the favorable states and combinations of states of attention and feeling, negatively for the unfavorable. Our method of scoring List A is described briefly in the following paragraphs.

To designate the significant states of the configural field or of developments within it, we selected four terms, explicitly defined them, and determined what adjectives or combinations of adjectives in the list must be regarded as referring to the areas of meaning they delimited. The first of these concepts, *determinacy*, or determinateness, configural firmness and clarity, we took to be indicative of the state of attention when the consciousness is focused—that is, strongly occupied by a configuration of any kind. Thus determinateness, the quality predominant in the configural field in focused attention, may indicate either the preoccupation of the mind with matter blocking further developments, or

[6] *Scientific American*, 1958, 199, No. 3, 164.

its illumination by insight just achieved. If it were the prevailing condition, or were evident in full force, at the first stage of the process reported in the Check List, there would be reason to believe that the worker's behavior was unpromising. Even though the process concluded, as all those reported in the Check List would conclude, in the production of some new insight, its beginning in a state of narrowed and fixed attention would suggest an operation of slight scope, a minor adjustment or refinement within a body of insights already mastered in its general organization, rather than a major reconstitution of perspectives. At stages beyond the first, evidence of strongly focused attention would have other significance.

The other concepts of our scoring system for List A were as follows: *breadth*, indicating, in general, span of consciousness, inclusiveness in envisaging matter of any kind, or range or variety in the activity of envisaging it; *flexibility* or easy, swift, and free movement from one configuration or group of configurations to another, or from one stage of attention to another; and *indeterminacy* or indeterminateness, in its extreme a complete absence of forms in the field of consciousness, but typically an indefiniteness in the configuration or configurations presented, whether describable as elusiveness or as disorder, as faintness and evanescence or as an unmanageable complexity of conflicting intimations.

A striking illustration of the need for indeterminacy appears in a comment made by one of the writers studied by Barron.[7] This writer remarked that in the moment when he was actually producing, at the instant of forming new insights, he was "almost unconscious." If a writer were completely unconscious while producing, his behavior would be utterly automatic. If he were "fully conscious" it might be that the use of peripheral, unfocused materials would be inhibited by the configurations in the focus of attention.

The final step in preparing to score List A was to devise a scale of values expressing our conception of the relative fruitfulness, at each stage of production, before, during, and after, of the conditions and behaviors designated by our four terms singly or in combination. We felt, and have reason still to feel, as subsequent discussion will show, that we knew pretty well on the whole what to score positively or negatively. But the difficulty of giving a precise weight to the significant items and combinations of items was extreme, and clearly it was not overcome.

In devising a means of scoring List B, in which the scientists recorded

[7] Presented with permission of Frank Barron.

their stages of feeling, our method was similar. But we proceeded with less certainty. We assumed that strong anxieties would tend to inhibit the full play of imagination, that inhibition would increase anxiety, and that conversely the stronger emotions of pleasure would accompany free and rich imaginative activity and would be particularly marked during and just after the flooding of the mind with new light. We guessed that such epiphany must rather exalt and delight than perturb and depress.

During the tentative development of our scale, we tested its validity against the records of some subjects in our sample of scientists whom we knew best, particularly those whose performance was least in doubt and whose communication with us during interviews about their experiences in working had been most full, frank, and illuminating. We did not change our scale to conform to these findings but used them rather to correct our theoretical understanding, insofar as they seemed to cast light upon it. Correction of the scale was made upon the basis of such enlargements of insight as we could stimulate by these and all other means at our disposal.

We found that it was possible for the originator of the test frequently to infer, with considerable accuracy, from the Check List and interpretive score alone, the characteristic performance of men in the sample whom he had not interviewed and whose records he had not studied, but who were so well known to another member of the research team that he could estimate the success of the inference. In short, the data given and organized thus for scoring often sufficed to give a suggestion of the kind of person we were dealing with.

When the Check Lists were scored, after use with a battery of other potential predictors administered to a group of over one hundred scientists at the Air Force Cambridge Research Center, the results were somewhat disappointing. List A, States of Attention, yielded no significant validity coefficients whatever, among seventeen possibilities. List B, States of Feeling, was found to correlate significantly with only two of seventeen measures of the contributions of scientists which we had obtained through an extensive program of research, and these were not the criterion measures which we had regarded as definitely indicative of creativity.

The seventeen measures, or criteria, were as follows:

Productivity in written work, mainly completing paper work.
Recent quantity of research reports.
Quality (independent of, or as distinguished from, originality) of research reports.
Originality of written work.

Scientific and professional society membership.

Actual quantity of work output as judged by peers, supervisors, laboratory chiefs.

Creativity rating by laboratory chiefs (higher-level supervisors).

Overall performance.

Likableness.

Visibility of the scientist.

Recognition for organizational contributions.

Status-seeking, organizational-man tendencies.

Current organizational status.

Contract-monitoring load.

Peer ranking of productivity as a scientist.

Supervisory rating of drive-resourcefulness.

Supervisory rating of creativity.

A significant degree of correlation with the States of Feeling list was found for two somewhat related criterion measures: the visibility of the scientist in the organization (the degree to which he was widely known as a person or by name) and the degree of his recognition for organizational contributions (a potentially creative contribution to the organization). The correlation with the former measure was .23. With the latter, it was .37. This correlation defined the most clearly valid characteristic obtained for the latter criterion.

Considering the meagerness of positive results, we suspected that our methods of scoring, or of interpreting the data of the scores, might be at fault. The fact that some correlates had been found encouraged us to think that the data already obtained might yield significant results if subjected to various further kinds of treatment.

RESULTS OF AN EMPIRICALLY DETERMINED SCORING METHOD

To test the possibility that the scoring might be more at fault than the instrument itself, a comprehensive statistical item analysis was conducted in which all 225 items of the Check List were correlated in turn with each of the 14 first-order criterion factors (the other 3 criteria— the last 3 in the above list—were initial criteria, not factored criteria). During this initial validation of the Creative Process Check List, point-biserial correlations for all the Check List adjectives (at each of the three stages—before, during, and after) with the 14 first-order criterion factors were obtained. A complete version of the procedure and results, which are presented briefly below, can be found in Rompel's thesis (1962).

First the items of the Check List which had been checked by 8% or more of the scientists were determined. Then, for each of the 14 criteria in turn, those of the items thus retained which had point-biserial correlations with that criterion of .20 or more were given a scoring weight of $+1$ or -1, depending on the direction of the correlation. Next, each Check List marked by an individual in the sample of 100 scientists was scored with the keys constituted by the 14 sets of adjectives thus empirically determined, and the scores obtained in this way for each scientist were correlated with the criterion scores in terms of which the characteristics of the specific scientist had been estimated in the contract research for the Air Force.

The results of this empirical validation were much more encouraging than the results of scoring with the two theoretically determined keys had been. These empirically keyed scores from the Creative Process Check List yielded initial validities ranging from .34 to .69, with a mean validity of .48 for the 14 first-order criterion factors. Half-sample cross-validities were understandably lower because of the small sample size (half-sample $N = 50$).

Thus the Creative Process Check List has yielded significant results, despite the fact that because of great variability in the number of items checked by respondents it did not lend itself very well to the statistical analysis described above. Some sizable validities were obtained for each of the 14 criterion factors. In general, it may be said that nearly all the adjectives on the lists were checked by some of the scientists and nearly all were significantly correlated with one or another of the 14 criterion factors, often with several of these criteria. These results show that the hypotheses which directed the shaping of the instrument must have had more than a little pertinence and validity. Evidently the Creative Process Check List has potential for selecting scientists in accordance with a specific criterion.

ADJECTIVES CHECKED BY TWO KINDS OF SCIENTISTS

The Creative Process Check List appears potentially valuable also for differentiating among scientists according to their relative standing as expressed in terms of the various criteria.

A second-order factor analysis by Rompel (1962) supplied 6 second-order criterion factors which were found to account for the 14 first-order criterion factors. Of these second-order criterion factors, the two with the largest factor loadings are of particular interest in this context (see Table 1). The first of these factors is a measure of general creativity; the second is a measure of material recognition and success. They are essentially distinct from each other. The second-order "general creativity" factor was distinguished primarily by 3 first-order factors: creativity ratings by high-level supervisors, originality in written work, and quality of research reports. The second-order "material success" factor was distinguished primarily by the first-order criterion factors of current organizational status, likableness, visibility, and recognition for organizational contributions.

TABLE 1

Rotated Second-Order Factor Pattern

First-Order Factor	Second-Order Factor	
	General Creativity	Material Recognition and Success
7 Creativity rating by higher-level supervisors	.50	
4 Originality in written work	.40	
3 Quality of research reports	.23	
13 Current organizational status		.69
9 Likableness		.59
10 Visibility		.43
11 Recognition for organizational contributions		.41
14 Contract-monitoring load		.21
1 Productivity in written work	.41	.35
6 Actual work output	.32	.46
8 Overall performance (ten supervisory ratings)	.28	.43
5 Scientific and professional society membership	.22	.37
2 Recent publications		
12 Status-seeking, organizational-man tendencies		

From the independence of these two second-order criterion factors it must be inferred that, as a rule, the individual scientist (in representative research centers) can be described either as primarily creative or as primarily materially successful—one or the other but not both. The individual scientist who is both creative and materially successful is an exception, according to our findings. Likewise, the scientist with a very low degree of both creativity and material success is an exception.

TABLE 2

	Before	During	After
Attention	diffused wandering* wavering*	steady scanning searching	clear intense configurated*
Feeling	restless pressed	tense happy* calm* delighted enriched* excited	calm* pleased* delighted

Examining a classification of subjective experience reported by these two relatively different kinds of scientists, we shall see that they can be differentiated on the basis of how they describe their creative processes at successive stages. For the following analysis the introspectively determined descriptions were broken down into two categories, as shown in Tables 2 and 3. Each table represents statistical tendencies rather than a single uniform pattern checked by every scientist in the sub-

TABLE 3

	Before	During	After
Attention	focused ranging confused wandering* wavering* variable jumbled sharp	intense	diffused fixed configurated*
Feeling	tense calm nervous	happy* calm* nervous expectant enriched*	happy calm* excited exalted satisfied relieved pleased* full

group. Table 2 shows the adjectives which the "creative scientists" (those *high in creativity and low in material success*) checked consistently and which attained statistical significance.

The adjectives which were checked by the "materially successful scientists" (those *low in creativity and high in material success*) and which met the standards of consistency and significance are listed in Table 3.

Although it is apparent from the common (asterisked) items in the two tables that there is some overlap among the words checked by the "creative" and by the "materially successful" scientists, more differential than assimilative adjectives can be observed. Both sorts of adjective will be examined more closely in the two following subsections.

States of attention

Before the culminative moment of creative activity, the creative scientist evidently experiences, like his professionally more successful colleague, a degree of flexibility, of movement, in his imaginative activity ("wandering," "wavering"). But although the successful scientist reports also some "ranging," suggestive of still greater freedom of movement, and some liberating incertitude (expressed in "confused" and other adjectives), these favorable indications are severely qualified by an adjective of contrary purport, "focused," which is reinforced by the adjective "sharp." The adjective "focused" implies also an even more adverse characteristic: constriction of view, lack of breadth and inclusiveness in vision, at the moment when vision ought to be most open to all relevant possibility. For focus is concentrative and preclusive. Thus the adjective "diffused," the opposite of "focused," indicates an enormous advantage for the creative scientist, whose experience it characterizes.

During the moment of his shaping a new insight, the creative scientist experiences a state of attention he describes as "steady," "scanning," and "searching," terms indicative of controlled and active pursuit of illumination. The professionally successful scientist reports only "intense" attention, less suggestive of activity than of concentration or of suspense in expectation or contemplation.

Immediately after his shaping of new insight, the creative scientist's attention is "clear," "intense," and "configurated"—evidence that his effort has culminated in exact and vivid apprehension. The professionally successful scientist's report of "fixed," "configurated" attention is equally the evidence of attainment. Perhaps his report of "diffused" attention at this stage may be taken to indicate some vague wonder, surmise, or redirection of the mind toward further adventures. Or it may indicate sheer relaxation.

Judging only by these similar characterizations of their attention at this final state, one cannot distinguish clearly between the two kinds of scientists. Since both have reached their goal, production, the quality of their products alone could differentiate them at this point. In order to see the difference exhibited in the data of the Check List, we would have to look also to the antecedent stages and consider the whole pattern thus constituted.

It may be observed that, in general, the results of the statistical analysis of List A of the Check List tend to substantiate the theory which guided construction of the instrument. The use by the creative scientist of such words as "diffused" and "scanning" to describe the earlier stages of his attention would seem to support the hypothesis that great scope and activity of thought, fostered by avoidance of persistent focus upon configurations, even to the point of admitting real instability and disorder, favors origination of significant insight, the sort that this kind of scientist has had to produce in abundance in order to qualify as "creative." The use by the less creative (but materially successful) scientists of such adjectives as "focused" and "sharp" to describe the earliest of the three stages of attention likewise tends to support the notion that a high degree of definiteness and stability in the field of attention opposes the development of new insight, at least of such quality and in such quantity as to earn for the producer the epithet "creative."

States of feeling

A considerable degree of differentiation is discernible also in the descriptions of states of feeling by the two kinds of scientist. The creative scientist reported feeling "pressed" and "restless" before the moment of insight in the creative process, whereas the successful scientist reported feeling "nervous," "tense," "calm." Exigency, impulse, and unsettled urgency are intimated in the report of the former, moods and emotions in the report of the latter. The contrast, between incited energies and excited sensibilities, is highly suggestive. The feelings of the creative scientist call for activity, for performance. Those of the successful scientist call, if for anything, for relief.

Less difference is apparent at the next stage. The creative scientist reported feeling "tense," "excited," and "delighted" during the shaping of new insight; the successful scientist reported feeling "nervous" and "expectant." Since significant numbers of both groups also reported that they were "happy," "calm," and "enriched," the difference between the groups is not very great. Nervousness implies more agitation and probably more anxiety than does tenseness, however. The adjective "delighted" seems to indicate more rewarding activity or attainment, possibly a greater nourishment and fulfillment in the enriching experience, than does "expectant."

Immediately after the moment of insight, the creative scientist felt "delighted," the successful scientist felt "relieved," "satisfied," "exalted," "full," and "excited." Both were "calm" and "pleased": the latter betrayed perhaps some traces of perturbation, prior or present.

Interpretation of this evidence must be tentative. Yet it appears that the creative scientist is challenged and stirred when faced with a problem and is unequivocally rewarded by mastery. The less creative scientist, on the other hand, apparently tends often to be threatened by a problem and occasionally to feel, besides pleasure in mastery, relief from his temporary insecurity when he has solved it. This interpretation is supported by information obtained in the use of a biographical inventory on NASA scientists (Taylor and Ellison, Chapter 16) which suggests that scientists are dominant and aggressive and have a desire to master the world about them independently.

FURTHER POTENTIALITIES OF THE CREATIVE PROCESS CHECK LIST

The Creative Process Check List appears to be a promising research instrument for investigation of the psychological processes of scientists. It also appears likely to prove useful as a predictor of scientific accomplishment. These inferences, mainly from the results of the analysis which has been described, are enough to justify further exploration of the potentialities of the instrument for scientists and for others.

It seems probable that a higher degree of validity in the Check List would have been demonstrated by the statistical analysis if certain adjectives of virtually identical meaning (for example, "confused," "muddled," and "jumbled") had been treated as one in analysis of the data, in accordance with the practice anticipated in forming the Check List. This absorption of synonyms by one and another equivalent term would have reduced considerably the variety of adjectives, through a legitimate generalization, and at the same time it would have increased the incidence of items checked often enough to be significant for statistical use.

Other procedures for dealing with the plethora of adjectives are possible. The approximately synonymous adjectives might be grouped into subscale scores or into combined sets of items for item analysis. Still another promising procedure would be to factor-analyze the Check List to form suitable groupings of items and to produce empirically determined subscales. By such means, and by dropping from the list in a later administration some other adjectives that were checked extremely rarely, the Check List might be adapted to the requirements of statistical practice and be made to attain its full potential usefulness.

More radical adaptation might well be considered also. Possible new formats for the Creative Process Check List include pair comparison or forced choice and the combination of words into phrases. New items in phrasal form might represent meanings that could not be so precisely expressed by a single adjective. The possibilities for improvement of the instrument are hardly to be delimited by present insight.

chapter 4 Empirical Studies of Intuition

Malcolm R. Westcott, Vassar College

S   Though there may be some echo-like features to my remarks, I think that I am talking from a different part of the canyon. Basically I would like to discuss three things: first, an issue in the philosophical discussion of intuition which is one of the heritages we have from philosophy and from the history concerned with this problem; second, some studies which are relevant to the problem of intuition and which arise in slightly different areas of psychology; and, finally, my own research in the area.   I would then like to tie these together and discuss how the various research efforts appear to converge.

Intuition has been talked about by philosophers much more than it has been studied by psychologists.   A great portion of this philosophical discussion is reviewed by Wild (1938), and he finds that it splits rather cleanly on a couple of points.   The point that I want to cover particularly concerns the processes which are involved in the gaining of an intuition.   The issue is whether they are normal sensory processes— that is, something amenable to psychological analysis—or whether they are abnormal, nonsensory processes, presumably processes which would not be amenable to psychological analysis.   Wild cites some thirty-odd views on this issue and tabulates a vote; he finds that philosophers go two-to-one for the abnormal, nonsensory view of intuition.   If we as psychologists accept this opinion we are stripped of our weapons to attack the problem of intuition; we cannot use any of our hard-won notions of intellectual and cognitive processes.   On the other hand, we may elect to throw the rascals out, and consider intuition as a special

34

case of some other, more familiar psychological processes. We can then bring all of our concepts in the areas of intellectual, cognitive, and emotional processes to bear on the issue.

In spite of our fairly necessary and basic disagreement with the majority of philosophical views a thread runs through all the philosophical discussions of intuition which makes it possible for us to be relatively congenial at a gross level. At this gross level, the phenomena which are described, while not always identical, certainly share in a consistent element. It is generally conceded that, when an individual intuits, he reaches a conclusion, a synthesis, a formulation, a solution to a problem or whatever it might be, without being aware of the basis on which this conclusion or synthesis is erected. This is a view of the event of intuition which is quite commonly held by mathematicians, musicians, artists, and psychologists as well as philosophers. We can share this view that "an individual reaches a conclusion without knowing how he did it" without being obliged to grapple seriously with the issue of whether the absence of support is apparent or real. As empirical scientists we are committed to our notions of intellectual and cognitive processes and to the sensory way of knowing things, and can operate successfully on the premise that the absence of support of conclusions in an intuition is only an apparent absence.

This assumption readily leads us to invoke unconscious thought processes which parallel or at least are analogous to more ordinary thought processes. While this assumption of analogous processes does not explain anything, it stakes out an area for questioning—an area *within* psychology which should be called upon to deal with problems of intuition. From this point of view, then, we can set up an appropriate situation in a laboratory, or we can look for certain kinds of events in the natural world which we will call intuitive events. The defining characteristic of the situation seems to be that an individual reaches his conclusion, solution, formulation, or whatever, without being aware of how he reached it. This does justice, I think, to the historical philosophical notion of intuition and does not do violence to other views.

It is certainly true that in talking about intuition, just as in talking about creativity, it is possible to define it in any way one wants to as long as the definition works. I have paid some attention to what philosophers, mathematicians, artists, and musicians have said. Philosophers have worried about this much longer than psychologists have. The definition seems to be a suitable one for experimental purposes and at the same time to do justice to the philosophical views.

Among the definitions offered by philosophers, there is one other point of contention which could well come up with psychologists. It need not become a problem, however. That is the question of whether an intuition must be right or if it may be wrong. Many philosophers feel that intuition, in order to be properly called an intuition, must be successful, correct, proper, valid, whatever term you care to use. However, if we set up a situation in a laboratory where an individual can reach a conclusion on inexplicit bases, his conclusion may be correct or it may be incorrect. We can study these two aspects of the phenomenon separately in the laboratory, whereas it is unlikely that we would be able to study them thus in the natural world. When we are wrong we generally forget it; no one writes an essay entitled "My History of Bad Guesses." In the laboratory, however, we can study the unawareness of the thinker concerning the basis for his conclusion, and the accuracy of the conclusion, as separate empirical events.

Several kinds of experiments have been carried out which can be addressed to this problem. Some of them have been called studies of intuition; some of the experimenters have used the term "intuition," but most have not. Only two of those whose studies I am going to discuss have used the term "intuition." Others have spoken of insight, or of unconscious concept formation, and one that I am going to describe used neither term and was principally concerned with transfer of training. I would like to discuss several of these experiments; and while I don't propose that this will be an exhaustive treatment of the field, it will serve to display at least a rough sampling. I will then go on to tell about the kind of research that I am doing on this issue.

The first experiments that I will discuss are those referred to by their authors or others as studies of insight and/or unconscious concept formation. There are two, in particular, I want to describe, principally because they are not very well known. The first is by Pickford, in 1938. He told his subject that he would be shown a series of straight-line polygons, and that the subject was to indicate from the very beginning whether the polygon being shown at any given time belonged in or out of a preselected category. Each time he responded, he was given feedback as to his success. He was to indicate his basis for judgment as soon as he knew the principle involved. Pickford noted that the level of success typically rose above chance for some time (though not a particularly long time) before the principle could be correctly stated. In this experiment, the principle was the inclusion of a right angle in the positive polygons. Pickford interpreted this result as indicating that the subject was utilizing the principle before being able to verbalize it. Is this simple demonstration a suitable representation of the notion of intuition described above: the reaching of a correct conclusion on the basis of an unconscious principle? Operationally, "unconscious" is synonymous with "preverbalization." I submit that it is formally suitable, but the content in this situation appears to be a bit trivial.

Another experiment similar in nature, but analyzed in more detail, was carried out by Snapper for an undergraduate honors thesis at Harvard in 1956 under Eric Heinemann. To my knowledge it has never been published. The procedure was essentially the same as in the Pickford study, except that the subject was instructed to sort a series of cards, some 400 or more, no two of which were identical. The cards had multiple borders, crosses, stars, circles, etc., on them, all in different numbers and colors, with corners cut off, notches out, and so on. They were to be sorted with reference to a sample card pasted on the front of the positive box. Each card was to be placed in the box with the sample card on the front, or tossed into the reject bin. Again, with each card, the subject was told "right" or "wrong." The rather stringent success criterion which had to be met was 25 successive correct sortings. Since the number of trials was much larger in this study than in Pickford's, and the principle more obscure, the curve of increasing success stretches out more obviously. Fifty-two subjects were used and the data are described as showing, for 6 of the subjects, a curve of slowly increasing success up to criterion, which looks like a simple learning curve. For 13 of the subjects, a typical insight curve results, with a sharp jump occurring after some trials; the remaining 33 subjects failed altogether.

The subjects who reached criterion in small cumulative increments took, on the average, fewer trials to do so than did the subjects who reached it by insight. An inquiry afterward revealed that those who showed a sudden spurt of insight were able to state the principle involved, while those who attained criterion slowly could, as a rule, offer no sensible reason for their correct sortings. From some of these subjects, the proper principle could be slowly and painfully extracted; with others, no amount of encouragement or coercion could make them admit that they knew how they were doing the task. With further pressure eventually all offered statements, but the statements did not often square with the facts. A further observation was that these who operated on the nonverbal basis which I am willing to call "intuitive" approached the entire task in a much more relaxed and casual way than did the others. The verbalizers actively worked out successive hypotheses and tested them, using great series of trials to do so, and after rejecting each, moved on to another.

This experiment, rather than relying on the notion of unconscious concept formation or unconscious thought processes, is interpreted as being the fairly direct result of operant conditioning of a sensory-motor discrimination response, some subjects interposing language responses, some simply letting reinforcement have its effects, others being essentially unaffected by reinforcement.

Here, again, we have a small group of subjects reaching a conclusion, a judgment, a solution to each trial, without being able to state how they have done it. Is this intuition in the same form as it appears in major breakthroughs in mathematics, physics, or psychology? Again, I submit that it has the rudiments of exactly the same process. This is the only experiment of this kind with which I have been in contact in which the principle involved in this sorting or discrimination has *never* become explicit for some of the subjects. They have been successful in doing it but have never, within the experimental situation, been able to verbalize the underlying basis for the final response. Although we can get performances without so-called awareness, in most of the other experiments, subjects eventually get the idea. In this experiment there was a group which never got the idea explicitly.

Perhaps a look at another, more complex situation will help to consolidate the questions in this area. A device known by the name of the Psi Apparatus, alternately called the Logical Analysis Device, allows subjects to press buttons which give information in the form of blinking lights about the properties of the circuit inside. From this information the subject's task is to make a center light go on by means of the proper sequence of button presses. A single problem takes about an hour, since the device is quite complicated. Here, an individual can proceed to gather information of an analytic sort, combine it synthetically, and eventually reach a solution to the problem. It is possible to study the efficiency of each of these operations by means of an attached event recorder which records what question was asked when and what was done subsequently. One can determine how many times the subject asks the same question of the device, how many unnecessary questions are asked, how the information is used, etc. By carrying out an analysis of subjects' performances on this device with a parallel analysis of patterns of autonomic activity in the subjects while working on the device, Blatt (1960, 1961) explored variations in cardiac activity associated with problem-solving behavior.

Efficient problem solvers on this device, that is, people who asked the fewest unnecessary questions (ideally, one can get away with no unnecessary questions, but no one does), showed marked change in cardiac activity at three points during the problem-solving process: (1) when all the necessary information had been gained, (2) when their behavior shifted from primarily analysis to primarily synthesis in terms of the kinds of button pushing they were doing, and (3) as they approached the final solution. Inefficient problem solvers did not show these marked shifts at the autonomic level.

In an inquiry afterwards, subjects who showed these changes in their internal responses were not able to report that they had felt them, or that they were aware of the changes in their cognitive activity. These physiological changes in arousal, while not explored in the other laboratory studies, seem to have been particularly important in the anecdotal study of intuition. Quite in contrast to Blatt's study, where subjects were unable to report this arousal, a wild excitement, followed by a sudden flash, is an extremely common element in autobiographical reports of intuitions, of insights.

Blatt interprets these findings in a psychoanalytic framework and considers these autonomic responses to be primary process events— primitive kinds of responses—and the whole operation of affect in cognition to be at the preconscious level. The two groups of subjects did not differ in their own evaluations of their involvement, but the efficient problem solvers considered the task more in terms of "fun" than did the inefficient problem solvers.

Efficiency and inefficiency are somewhat correlated with time, but there is a tremendous amount of overlap between the two groups in the amount of time taken. A subject can go a great length of time in this task without asking any questions. This does not make him inefficient, however. There are some, whom I call organ players, who just sit there and beat on this thing. Some others ask a question and then sit and think.

I would like to go on to another kind of study on which I was requested particularly to report. This is a study by Lorraine Bouthilet for a Ph.D. dissertation at Chicago in 1948 under Thurstone. Its characteristics are very similar to those of the other unconscious concept formation experiments except for its title. Bouthilet called it "intuitive thinking." She gave subjects some training series and test series, 20 pairs—that is, 20 training series, each of which was accompanied by a test series. The training series consisted of paired associates. The pairing was based entirely on the principle that the associate was made up of letters contained in the stimulus word, each of which was seven to nine letters long. There were 40 associate pairs in a list, and they were exposed to the subject once at two seconds per exposure. The subject was given instructions comparable to normal paired-associate tasks. After going through a list of 40 paired associates pretty quickly, the subject was then flipped over to the test section for that series and was told:

On this test there are 40 stimulus words, and after each one follows 5 words.

You are to pick out the one which is the associate from the other page. Do not be surprised if you see words which look unfamiliar because in going through a list as long as this and as quickly as this, you are surely going to forget some of them. But do your best and check every one, even if it looks completely unfamiliar.

Some of the words were completely unfamiliar because in the test series only half of the words listed were the words which had appeared in the training series. The other half were different words which the subject had not seen before. However, for each stimulus word on the test series the associate was made in exactly the same way as in the training series. The associate for these new words was made up of letters contained in the unfamiliar stimulus words. The principal concern Bouthilet had was which words the subjects selected as associates to these unfamiliar stimulus words. The principle here was that the subjects would go ahead and do better than chance on these, operating on the basis of a principle of the associate being contained in the stimulus words. It was hypothesized that this principle would be gained unconsciously without the subject's awareness and that the subject would proceed to get better and better with more and more training. The results looked very much like the Pickford results. There were 20 trials because there were 20 test series. The only measurements actually included in the analysis of the data are the performances on the test series of unfamiliar words. The curves go along and do rise above chance before the point at which the subject states the principle. In this case, each subject eventually did state the principle. The curves rise rather rapidly; that is, over the course of two or at the most three test series, at some point in the 20 trials, they go from slightly above chance or at the chance level up to 100%. This is an experiment of the same sort as Pickford's, but, I think happily for history, it is called "intuition."

C   May I register an illustration of individual differences? When I looked at those curves in Bouthilet's dissertation, I did not see that they rose particularly or that they demonstrated intuition. This is all inspection. You look at those curves and there appears to be some gradual improvement; I could interpret it as just chance fluctuations.

S   I think that Bouthilet did not claim that these fluctuations over the first few series are improvements. My impression is that what she was pointing to is the fact that the curve does not go directly from chance to 100%. There are one or two steps on the way up. They come very fast, though. I think that these are the points of intuition that she is talking about.

C   No, I meant that she was talking about the slopes and thought that there was some gradualness to the rise. I thought that there wasn't.

I think that her experiment is right, but she didn't demonstrate it with enough data.

S I think it is worth pointing out that although we speak of these as experiments they are not experiments in the classical sense; they turn out to be repeated demonstrations of this kind of phenomenon going on.

Without attempting to integrate these findings yet, let me say simply that it seems evident that people can operate in a very successful fashion, making complex discriminations and important shifts in behavior without awareness of what they are doing or the fact that any change has taken place. It appears that there are, at least in some cases, changes in affect accompanying these changes in overt behavior, and that the entire operation can go on without any awareness by the subject.

It is my personal feeling that these studies are relevant to the investigation of intuition, and they have repeatedly brought us face to face with the fact that intuitive events can be studied in the laboratory. We often study, for analytic purposes, events which may seem trivial in the grand scheme of things, and I believe that we need, for example, autonomic studies and behavioral shift studies of great artists and poets, mathematicians and scientists; we need studies of unconscious concept formation among chemists in the field of chemistry, among architects in the field of design, etc. Some day we may have them.

I wish that I could say that my own research fills the gap I have just mentioned, but it does not. It is concerned with individual differences in the tendency to make intuitive judgments and with the success of these judgments in solving problems. Individual differences in these tendencies and capacities are studied as they relate to other variables of the individual's life—various kinds of intellectual success and patterns of personality and attitudes.

First, let me describe the experimental situation in which my own studies are carried out. A subject is presented with a series of 20 problems to solve, and the information necessary to solve each is available in small quantities. The subject is instructed to *solve as many problems as possible using as little information* as possible. The actual format of the problems has gone through several modifications but at present consists of a masonite board with 20 rows of slots in it. Beneath each slot is a piece of information which I call a "clue," and each clue is covered by tinfoil, which can be punched out with a stylus. The *clues must be taken in the sequence given*. When the person reaches what he feels is the answer, he records it on the answer sheet.

C This is like the tab test used in studying troubleshooting behavior.

S Yes. The assumption is made that the less information the sub-

ject takes before attempting a solution the greater is the intuitive compo-
nent in the act of solving the problem. It is not assumed here that the
principle on which the solution is based is entirely unconscious, but
rather that the subject may make a judgment at a point in time when
several alternatives still remain. The task consists of series problems,
either numerical or verbal, and analogy problems, either numerical or
verbal. All four kinds are represented. Success is also evaluated, and
a solution is scored correct if an individual reaches the same conclusion
that is almost universally reached when all the information available
is used. The instruction is that you are to include on the answer sheet
that answer which would be appropriate if you had opened the entire
sequence of clues. That is, you must take account of both the informa-
tion you have seen and the information you have not seen.

C   Isn't there a risk-taking factor here?

S   Yes. In this situation, intuition is the process of using little
information to reach a conclusion which is generally reached on the
basis of significantly more information. A one-shot success may be, of
course, a good guess; but consistent success represents, in this frame-
work, intuitive problem solving. There are individual differences in
these performances.

C   On the answer sheet do you give the subjects a choice of right
answers?

S   No. They have to supply the answer. With the analogy prob-
lems, the first half of an analog is present, but they have to provide the
answer.

C   Do you distinguish between the time it took for the intuitive act
and the act of inserting the answer?

S   No. I record only how much information has been taken. I've
been playing a little with another form which attempts to get the sub-
jects' tentative solutions en route as they arrive at them and are willing
to report them, but I have no data to present yet.

C   In that the subject might have an idea of what he wants in the
way of information but has to take what he gets, isn't this a kind of
grab-bag situation?

S   You might say that. The subject is instructed to carry out a
certain task and is told what is a good performance and what is a poor
performance. He opens the information and gets what I have been
willing to give him.

In some other papers, I demonstrated that there are individual differ-
ences in both the tendency to make these intuitive leaps and in the
tendency to be successful. At the same time, these two performance

variables are not related; that is, an individual may be high or low on information demand and still be either high or low on the dimension of success. The correlation between these two does not differ significantly from zero. These findings were replicated on five different samples of college students, and I am confident of their stability.

Having established these facts to my satisfaction, I inquired concerning what differences there might be in the individuals representing the four extreme types of problem-solving performance: (1) those who require little information and are consistently successful—the true intuitive thinkers; (2) those who require significantly more information than the average but are also markedly more successful—the steady, hard-working problem solvers; (3) those who demand a great deal of information but are unable to solve the problems—individuals possibly blocked or unduly rigid or confused; (4) finally, those who ask for little information and then *leap to failure*—persons who are unsuccessful intuiters, possibly desperate, or committed to the long shot at whatever cost. For experimental purposes, these groups are selected as being at least 1 S.D. high or low on both scoring dimensions. From one pool of 195 subjects, I was able to identify 10 intuitive thinkers, 22 careful successes, 20 careful failures, and 17 intuitive failures. The intuitive thinkers are consistently rare, but the others are about equal in numbers.

First of all, the personality and attitude scales which I used were selected on several grounds: they were readily available, some of the data were already in, and they purported to measure impulse expression, flexibility, and manifest anxiety. Specifically the scales were the FL scale and the IE scale from the Vassar College Attitude Inventory (Sanford, Webster, and Freedman, 1957) and the Taylor Scale (Janet Taylor, 1953). These scales failed to discriminate very successfully any of the groups from any others. Again, on several samples, academic success also failed, as did verbal and mathematical aptitude tests from the College Entrance Board, and professors' ratings on a variety of things.

On the other hand, an item analysis of the personality-attitude scales showed that there were some consistent differences among the groups, and it was possible to extract items which characterized each of these four kinds of problem solvers. I found the high information demanders, regardless of success, to be characterized by items which I interpret as reflecting caution, conservatism, compliance, and a relative unawareness of their inner states. In contrast, the low information demanders appear to be moody, introspective, unconventional, and quite tensely involved in what they are doing. Within each of these groups, there were individuals who had solved problems successfully and individuals who had shown a singular lack of success. I would like to describe these subgroups next.

Among the high information demanders, those who are highly successful do not seem to be as rigidly committed to conservatism and compliance; they appear to be willing to question things, and they show some awareness of themselves. The unsuccessful ones appear to be defensive and rigidly moralistic. Here it seems that success may serve to mitigate the conservatism reflected in high information demand; or, on the other hand, a softened conservatism outside this situation may lead to greater success.

Among low information demanders—the moody unconventional subjects—the successful and the unsuccessful are differentiated by items which do not quite match the statistical reliability of the other differentiations but which are very meaningful psychologically (working only at the 10% level instead of at a lower 5% level). The successful ones are comfortable with themselves and unafraid, while the unsuccessful ones appear to be depressed, desperate, hopeless, despondent. These findings are replicated on three separate groups of Vassar students and appear to be quite stable. Though these latter subjects don't do any worse in college than others, they look pretty bad to me. It strikes me as if I have a clinical scale of depression. Some of these results were reported at the Eastern Psychological Association (Westcott and Ranzoni, 1962).

Another approach to description of the ways in which these different types of thinkers view their worlds is through a self-concept study, based on an adjective check list. These are the words they have checked to describe themselves. The intuitive thinkers, regardless of their success check such words as "headstrong," "quick," "demanding," "sharp-witted," "independent," and "inventive" more often to describe themselves than do the nonintuitive thinkers (those who require a lot of information). This latter group uses such words as "kind," "modest," "cautious," "shy," "conscientious," and "patient" more frequently than does the former. I have not yet had a chance to differentiate the various levels of success within each group. It is a fairly slow process, and the subgroups become progressively smaller.

It seems that a fairly clear and consistent picture of the intuitive as compared to the nonintuitive thinker is emerging, at least at the extremes. I am continuing my study of these extreme subjects through individual interviews. The first round of interviews is complete now but as yet unanalyzed. I see extreme differences in the subjects, though I don't know what groups the subjects belong to when I interview them.

When the interviews are analyzed this summer, I will try to put the whole thing together.[1]

There is another way in which we are attacking the same problem of intuitive thinking at an earlier developmental level. Several of my students have been involved for the past two years in studying the performances of students in nursery school, fourth through eighth grades, and college on a task involving fragmented pictures. There are several series of pictures, each series containing several pictures of the same object, with each picture more nearly complete than the one before it. The task is to identify the object pictured as early in the series as possible. We have found individual differences in this performance which correlate only slightly with intelligence test scores; the performances are stable; and we find that the older subjects do better and are less variable than the younger ones. It is interesting that apparently exactly the same pictures can be used, with different degrees of discrimination and reliability, over the entire range of subjects from nursery school to college. On this task the subject can guess as often as he wants. I'm sure this brings the point of first guess much closer to the beginning of the series than in the problem-solving task—the subject doesn't get the feeling of burning his bridges.

Let me just go back and review the three kinds of studies I have mentioned. First, the studies which are explicitly called studies of unconscious concept formation require an individual to learn a principle and then put it to work in making decisions, without the prior intervention of a verbal statement or awareness as to the basis for decision; the observations arising in such experiments are interpreted as representing unconscious thought processes or the simple result of operant conditioning. Second, the study of autonomic responsiveness parallels changes in cognitive activity, both of which go unobserved by the subject; the hypothesis may be held that these autonomic changes are in fact the cues which lead to the cognitive changes, and that these occur only in efficient problem solvers. Finally, there are my own studies of the tendency to leap early or late, on the basis of little or much information, the tendency to be successful or unsuccessful in such attempts, and the study of some personality and attitude correlates of such performance.

I would like to attempt to tie these various findings together with the aid of some material presented by Mosher at the Eastern Psychological Association meetings in 1962. He described the procedures by which

[1] This analysis, as well as an integration of all the personality material, is now available: M. Westcott and Jane Ranzoni, "Correlates of Intuitive Thinking," *Psychological Reports*, 1963, 12, 595–613 (also as Monograph Supplement, 5-V12).

individuals at different ages gather information and use it in solving a 20-question type of problem. Roughly, the younger children, 6 years old, asked very specific questions, concrete ones, leaping toward a complete solution (and usually missing it) in one move. Older children (8 to 11) asked greater and greater proportions of what he calls "constraint-seeking questions," questions which progressively narrow the field of possible solutions. This appears to be a developmental change, and one which is of particular interest to a group working with Suchman at Illinois. These people describe their work as studies of inquiry training; it is concerned with teaching children to ask successive constraint-seeking questions in various areas of science to narrow in on the problem, and subsequently on the solution.

These constraint-seeking questions appear to be one's best bet when faced with a problem-solving task in an unfamiliar area. They serve to delimit the field progressively and keep it manageable. But it is often true that the area in which one is being faced with a problem is not completely foreign. It appears that over a period of time, in contact with a given body of knowledge or inquiry, one gains constraints which become automatic, probabilistic in nature, and likely to be unconscious or unverbalized.

In high-level, sophisticated problem solving, there are many of these constraints on one's question-asking behavior, constraints which are not explicitly sought and found in the immediate situation, but which come from a long and varied acquaintance with question asking and information gathering in the immediate area and in related areas. It is my feeling that these additional constraints both contribute to and detract from efficient problem solving, and make up at least one of the multiple hinges upon which intuitive thinking swings.

It is important to note that many of these built-in constraints are probabilistic in nature, and they do not always hold. They are not rigid rules but may be used as rigid rules. They may provide not only constraints but also constrictions. Perhaps the most important prior constraint concerns the circumstances under which an individual follows or does not follow the dictates of another probabilistic constraint. An individual, having arrived at a point in education, training, and experience where he has a great many useful probabilistic constraints, may be faced with circumstances under which the breaking of these probabilistic rules is the most crucial step toward a major solution of a major problem.

Perhaps what we are referring to when we speak of intuition is the process of leaping beyond constraint-seeking questions to a more primitive form of behavior—that represented in children—the leap to a specific solution when many alternatives still remain.

The various studies cited indicate that this leap may indeed be a primitive type of behavior, represented in the 20-question situation in the youngest group of children. If interpreted as nonverbal operant conditioning, it is as common in subhumans as in humans; if interpreted within a psychoanalytic framework, it derives from primary process and autonomic responses; it is accompanied by personality and attitude patterns which represent a relatively unsocialized and guilt-free relationship to the world.

Through traditional education and discipline of cognitive processes, we explicitly attempt to remove growing children from their primary process and from their unsocialized, nonverbal levels of behavior. There may be only a very few among us who can look at the world with that renowned "eye of a child," or who can regress in the service of problem solving and in fact reach conclusions in much the way children do— without explicit evidence, on the basis of nonverbal cues, by breaking constraints, by intuition.

These various approaches to the problem of intuition all have consequences beyond their immediate results; all of them yield further hypotheses; all of them, I believe, contribute to what may be our first psychological understanding of the phenomenon of intuition.

C   I think that it is unusual for us to have a man here from Vassar, but I don't think that it is unusual for a man from Vassar to be studying intuition.

S   A look at the psychological literature indicates that it is unusual for anyone to be studying intuition.

C   A marketing concern in San Francisco has written me, indicating that they have described the intuitive person from their experience and that they see a great similarity between this intuitive person and our descriptions of the creative person. In our exploratory study of troubleshooting behavior, we found some consistency of performance per troubleshooter. I was wondering whether you had thought at all about the next step in your potential sequence of events. We sensed another phenomenon when people finally leaped to a conclusion or decided that they were ready for a conclusion. If they missed and still hadn't solved the problem, one tendency was then to turn it into a guessing game instead of returning to seek further information before they made their next leap. Do you have anything along this line?

S   No, but I would predict this kind of behavior from people who use little information and are wrong. From the evidence that we have, the kinds of personality items which they check "true" are: "I have diarrhea once a month or more," "At times I think I am no good," "Sometimes I am embarrassed and break out in a sweat," "I shrink when facing a crisis or a difficulty." These are people who apparently have little fortitude to face up to things, and if they shoot early and quickly and are unsuccessful, conceivably they just go back and thrash about.

C   We had some impression that a large number of them—not just a special few—stayed in a guessing game about "trouble location" instead of returning to an information-seeking phase before making a next leap.

C   I have some information about Suchman, since you mentioned him. I think that he has a different view of this intuitivity from what you have. He takes his children, these sixth graders he works with, and gives them rather complicated problems, and they play games such as twenty questions. What he tries to do is put them through a training program so that they learn to ask better and better questions to discover scientific principles underlying an observed phenomenon. He finds that his bright children are the ones who indulge in these intuitive leaps, but this gets them into trouble. The problems are rather complex, and they jump too fast. They hit upon a hypothesis too early, and then they are chained to it and have trouble. He finds that the biggest problem he has with these bright children is to break down this intuitive leap and to get them first to assemble their information and then to go ahead systematically without leaping too soon.

S   The leaping is an earlier, more primitive form of behavior.

C   The point is, though, that I think you were making almost the reverse implication: that one of the problems in education is that it is too successful in keeping people from leaping.

S   I certainly was. I am suggesting that hopefully we can come full circle to where an individual does have built in a great many constraints which he gains only by moving in this slow progressive fashion and then can learn to let go of them. I think that we have seen in our own field or in other fields where an individual has offered a solution to a problem, typically a theoretical solution, and ends being chained to it for an entire lifetime, long after the thing has been destroyed. An early leap is often restricting in this sense. If it is right, then that's fine. If it is wrong, the person may be out of luck for the rest of his life.

C   Almost all the items that are answered "true" more frequently by the low-information, unsuccessful group are on the ego-strength scale on the MMPI. It suggests to me that it might be worth your while to analyze these groups in terms of ego-strength scores and also for some implications of hysteria, because if a person is going to behave intuitively, he can get out into left field very fast. He has to have high ego strength accompanying the intuitive tendencies, if you think of intuition as a dispositional tendency and then think of ability to discriminate to be accurate in intuition as a function of some other kinds of traits.

S   Yes. Actually what you are saying supports some hypotheses that I have but have not yet been able to test well in this area. I used what I had on hand and tried whatever I thought a priori might be the most helpful. I did not use the whole Vassar College Inventory.

C   You had more at hand than you realized. The California Psychological Inventory, the MMPI, and the Inventory of Personal Philosophy contribute most of what you have, and further scores could be obtained from them.

C   Is there a convergent intuitive thinking which differs from a divergent intuitive thinking?

S   I don't know, but I would certainly say that everything I have here is convergent.

C   Yes. I was wondering what divergent intuitive thinking would show because it might be an entirely different problem.

S   One could certainly raise this question. I have taken some subjects and said, "O.K., here you go. Do everything out loud." I taped some of these responses. They are almost unmanageable except in terms of an impressionistic assessment. Some subjects will verbalize everything: "Open the first clue there," "All right, there are nine possibilities here that I see, maybe eleven," "Then go on to the next," "All right, that eliminates such and such and such and such." The first clue they use as a stimulus for divergence. Then they begin to hack at that one as they go along. I think that some people do this progressively step by step. They diverge, converge, diverge, converge, and so on. Others, I think, don't do any of this explicitly in the sense that they look at one clue and say: "Eh . . . so that's one," and then they open the next one right away and immediately, without offering any convergence, begin to diverge.

C   Again, our best troubleshooters showed quite different methods of solving their problems. For example, some used an open, obviously logical approach, whereas others used what appeared to observers to be an internal, almost mystical, intuitive movement to the solution.

S   It is clear that there is not any *necessary* flash that occurs. People *can* shoot early without any great confidence. There are probably a couple of groups within each of these four subgroups that I described, and I have to work with them separately to see within my low information-low success group, for example, whether there are people who offer early, reasonable but wrong answers and others who offer principally wrong and unreasonable solutions.

C   In connecting this to the arts, I think that there are some differences in the process. A person can make an early leap and be "way off," or he can do it during the process of a work and incorporate what would be a mistake or an error into the final texture of the thing. This interests me as behavior because often you see a person who is doing too well and needs the risk, in the sense of throwing himself off. I see this as a different kind of process from the type of intuitive thinking you're getting.

S   In the situation that you describe one can conceivably incorporate errors. You might say that the early guesses are occurring on the canvas. They can be modified.

C   They can be drawn in by other attacks, no matter how far off they are.

C   That study isn't different from any typical scientific project, where you can also do a lot of remedial work.

C   But you can remove the traces.

C   In science you can report a mistake, although it is usually reported in different terms.

C   Do you know the story Sean O'Casey tells, in *Inishfallen, Fare Thee Well*, of sitting for his portrait for Patrick Touhy? Poor Touhy was a slow worker and seemed a timid painter to O'Casey. At one point, as Touhy kept fiddling about without putting brush to canvas, Sean got more and more annoyed and finally said, "Aw, chance a stroke, man." (*Laughter*)

C   There is quite an impressive article by Springbett (1957) supporting the phenomena of intuition.

C   There are two other very relevant studies which were done at the Institute of Personality Assessment and Research (IPAR). One was Block and Petersen's (1955), in which they also used various autonomic measures.

C   There is another interesting and extreme anecdote to support the point about incorporating an early leap into your final solution. Humphrey quotes an anecdote about Beethoven, who apparently worked with a scissors and paste method. He would make his first draft and then paste over it as he made his corrections until on one of his works, I forget which, there was a big mound of paper. Later, people studying his creative processes peeled off this paper, layer by layer, and discovered that the final version was identical in every note with the first version. (*Laughter*) He had found the "lost chord."

C   This is true of his *Ninth Symphony*. If you trace it back to an earlier period of his work, the theme of it is heard in an earlier composition.

S Do you know of anything like this in the study of the depth of painting over paintings?

C In some modern paintings you can't order the sequence, and in some you can. In older paintings you can be pretty sure of the additions. But for some moderns, if you got photographs after the artist starts, you could not put them in an order, above chance, I am sure. I've tried it.

C This is a problem for programmed instruction. Recently I had reported to me some results to date of people who had been using some of our tests of creative thinking in connection with pre- and posttests involved in language and arts programmed instruction. They interviewed fifth-grade children, with a minimum IQ of 135, using eighth-grade programmed instruction material. They found that some of them just hated this programmed stuff. They made a split at the median on the total scores on the test on creative thinking and found that all those who hated it were in the top on the high-creative scale. Their gains in a pre- and posttest measure were erratic, so the total gains of the high-creative group were low because some of them were high and some of them were actually as low as zero. Those in the low group made consistent gains—practically all of them made gains of 20 or 30 points, but there was a greater variability in the high group. The first hypothesis about what went wrong is that this programmed material had permitted only very, very tiny leaps, which were disliked by some in the high group.

S A couple of years ago, I read a paper at the Eastern Psychological Association (Westcott, 1960) which described a picture-completion kind of test with fifth- and sixth-grade children in two different schools. We had the teachers rate the children on creativity by whatever standard each teacher wanted to use; then we explored what the standards were and the teachers seemed quite in accord with what we have talked about. The score on this task, which we called "perceptual inference," did an almost perfect job of discriminating between creatives and noncreatives among pairs of children matched on IQ in the same school. This study was replicated this year, but I haven't published the fact that it didn't work a second time, so I'll read it now into the record. The previous results just did not hold up at all. Maybe they will on the next try; I don't know. This is always the trouble with replication.

C Yes, you should never do replication studies. (*Laughter*)

C You talked about the autonomic arousal response in the Blatt study and you mentioned the Block and Petersen study, but I am not too sure exactly what role autonomic responses play in your thinking.

S   I'll hypothesize that these autonomic responses are the triggers for changes in behavior.

C   You mean that they are random fluctuations?

S   They are not random fluctuations, though. I think that the important point is that among the effective, efficient problem solvers the changes are not random. They shoot up. In some of the curves that Blatt presents it looks as if they shoot up before the behavioral shifts occur. In others, it looks as if they shoot up at the same time. Now, I hypothesize the autonomic event as antecedent because I like to. There is no evidence that this is an antecedent any more than that it is a consequence. I think that a more detailed analysis would yield an answer to this question of whether the autonomic response precedes or follows.

C   I'm thinking of doing a study on this.

S   I am a long-time devotee of autonomic responses, and so I consider them as having a central role in intuitive leaps. I am perfectly willing to hypothesize either way, but I think that the experiment, analyzed in a lot of temporal detail, would give you an answer in either direction or in no direction for that matter. You could hypothesize either way, and I prefer to hypothesize that this is causative.

C   At IPAR the form of Remote Associates Test we used was a booklet having two words on the first page. Let's say the answer was "sweet." There might be "cookies" and "sixteen" or "heart" and "sixteen" on the first page, and a person writes his answer down if he can and turns the page. Next there are four words: "heart," sixteen," "tooth," and "talk." Again he writes an answer, and so on until he gets ten given words. The booklet contains about nine pages. Here we can break down the stages of problem solving.

S   This is getting more and more information with successive guesses.

C   I can't see how autonomic responses would be a precedent behavior, though. It depends on your definition of precedents. You would have to at least say that there is an unconscious solution to the problem coming up, and that this causes a relevant response, which, in turn, pushes the solution up a little higher and makes it. . . .

S   I wouldn't feel obliged to say that.

C   I fear that this discussion is leading to where part of the group will be for convergent thinking and the other part for divergent thinking. (*Laughter*)

S   I believe very strongly in the importance of the gut reaction.

C   Providing you haven't taken here a steep leap that's an incorrect one and that you live with the rest of your life.

C   We learned at the first conference that the criterion evaluation of creativity of products may turn out to be essentially a gut reaction.

C   Yes, we started with that—with the thrill up the back of the German patent officer.   Now we're completing the cycle by getting the gut reaction into the predictor side.

chapter 5 An Associative
Interpretation of the Creative Process[1]

Sarnoff A. Mednick and Martha T. Mednick,
University of Michigan

S   The effort to arrive at an understanding of the mechanism of the process of human thought has engaged the energy of every scholarly and artistic discipline. Perhaps the most systematic and enduring formulation has been that of the associationists. Men such as Locke, Hume, James Mill, Bain, and Freud developed detailed theoretical accounts of thinking in associationistic terms. We shall attempt to make use of this approach in accounting for that special variety of thinking, creative thinking.

First, we will describe three associative mechanisms by which the creative process may occur. Second, we will discuss the problem of individual differences in creativeness in terms of an associationistic theory. We will then introduce a test that was devised on the basis of this theory. Finally, we will describe some of the experimental research which has been completed at the University of Michigan. This research was initiated and highly stimulated by a year spent by the senior author at the Institute of Personality Assessment and Research (IPAR) in Berkeley.

We began by carefully reading the statements of manifestly creative individuals concerning their own creative work. One of the first readings was a statement by Lucretius, who labored to point out that creative thinking was not a gift from the gods or some magical talent that some

[1] This research is supported by the Cooperative Research Branch, U.S. Office of Education, Contract 1073.

individuals were blessed with, but simply a product of the reassembling of old knowledge. He pointed to examples such as the mermaid constructed of appropriate parts of fish and woman and the centaur constructed of appropriate parts of horse and man. He felt that these creative conceptions were nothing more than the combining of bits of previously existing knowledge.

Brewster Ghiselin's (1952) anthology on the creative process was a major source of material for our reading. In this book Einstein is quoted as saying, "The psychical entities which seem to serve as elements in thought are certain signs and more or less clear images which can be combined. This combinatory play seems to be the essential feature in productive thought." Andre Breton describes a collage by Ernst as being distinguished by a "marvelous capacity to grasp two mutually distant realities without going beyond the field of our experience and to draw a spark from the juxtaposition." Robert Frost (1962) said in an article in the *Atlantic Monthly*, "Let's put this straight. The coupling [and here he is talking about the coupling of poetic ideas] that moves you, that stirs you, is the association of two things that you did not expect to see associated."

In terms of associative theory the communality in these and other statements can be expressed in the form of a definition of creative thinking. *Creative thinking consists of forming new combinations of associative elements, which combinations either meet specified requirements, or are in some way useful. The more mutually remote the elements of the new combination, the more creative is the process or solution.* We have been advised by a lawyer that this definition conforms very nicely with the federal patent law. This makes it probably the only psychological theory which would stand up in a court of law.

THE MECHANISMS OF THE CREATIVE PROCESS

The basic task in the creative process is to bring together, in some useful fashion, ideas which are usually remote from each other. It follows then that the creative process will be facilitated by any state of affairs which tends to maximize the ideational contiguity of otherwise disparate ideas. Any such state of affairs will increase the probability of a creative solution. We shall discuss three mechanisms which tend to bring about such a state of affairs.

The first of these mechanisms is a classical one, *serendipity*. In associationistic terms we would say that the requisite associative elements are evoked by the accidental, environmental, contiguous appearance of appropriate stimuli. Thus, two unrelated ideas may be brought together in consciousness because objects evoking these ideas co-occur accidentally in the environment. The discoveries of the X-ray process and of penicillin have been ascribed to serendipity. A physicist at Northwestern University makes systematic use of this process. He has cut up the indices of physics textbooks so that he has hundreds of little slips of paper containing facts and theories of physics. He has put these slips of paper into a fishbowl and mixed them up. He regularly draws out two or three at a time to see whether he can find new and useful combinations. When we have described this behavior to other physicists they have expressed no surprise whatsoever but have actually asserted that they have often made use of techniques something like this one.

C   That is a good idea. Things like that are used in certain creativity training programs.

S   Yes, we have been thinking about cutting up some psychology textbooks. (*Laughter*)

C   I don't think that cutting them up would help at all. (*Laughter*)

S   In some cases it would do little harm.

The second method is that of *similarity*. The requisite associative elements may be evoked in contiguity as a result of the similarity of the associative elements, or the similarity of the stimuli eliciting these associative elements. This may occur in certain kinds of poetry, music, and painting where similarities in form, in sound, and in colors are very important. This mode of creative solution may be encountered in creative writing which exploits homonymity and rhyme. The contiguous ideational occurrence of items like alliterative and rhyming associates may be dependent on a factor such as primary stimulus generalization. It seems possible that this method of bringing about the contiguity of associative elements may be of considerable importance in domains of creative effort which are not directly dependent on the manipulation of symbols.

The third method is *mediation*. This is probably the most important mechanism of the three. Here the requisite associative elements may be evoked in contiguity through the mediation of common elements. For example, you pull together ideas X and Z, which ordinarily would never belong together, by the mediation of idea Y, which is associated with both of these. Poincaré, in talking about his development of the Fuchsian functions, says that in discovering their importance he simply combined two different kinds of mathematics which happened to have a similarity in methods of transposition (Ghiselin, 1952). Another good example of the mechanism of mediation occurs in Marianne Moore's poem, "The Monkey Puzzle," in which she uses the striking image of "the lion's ferocious chrysanthemum head" (Moore, 1951). Here we have the two terms "ferocious" and "chrysanthemum" which ordinarily would not occur together in thought. Their creative juxtaposition is made possible by the mediation of the image of a lion's head. An example from psychology is Kohler and Fishback's (1950) idea of relating reactive inhibition and cortical satiation, probably through the mediation of the common associate "tiredness" or "fatigue."

INDIVIDUAL DIFFERENCES IN CREATIVE PERFORMANCE

Let us now attempt to make use of these basic notions to explain the factors which may produce individual differences in creative performance. Just as with the situational factors discussed above, any ability or condition of any individual which serves to bring otherwise mutually remote ideas into ideational contiguity will enhance the probability of creative performance. To begin with, it should be clear that an individual needs knowledge. If the requisite elements are absent they cannot be combined. An architect who does not know about the existence of a certain kind of wood could hardly be expected to use it as the facing for a building.

Of great importance in the matter of individual differences is the concept of the *associative hierarchy*, which refers to the organization of an individual's associations around ideas. We find such organizations to be reliable characteristics of the individual's thinking. In order to define associative hierarchy let us first consider the way associations are organized around ideas. Russell and Jenkins (1954) asked 1008 college students at the University of Minnesota to give a single association to the word "table." "Chair" was the response of 840 of these students. In all, this group of 1008 students produced only 47 different words as associates to the word "table." The response next in popularity after "chair" was the word "food," given by 41 individuals. The remainder of the group produced a variety of responses. Three people actually gave the name "Mabel"; one person responded with "pool." From these response frequencies we can construct an associative hierarchy such as is presented in Figure 1. Because of the sharp drop in the curve which occurs after the response "chair" on the abscissa, we call this a steep associative hierarchy.

In contrast we have data from this same group on words like "comfort." The 1008 students responded with 152 different words to the word "comfort." As it happens, the most frequent response was "chair," given, however, by only 117 people. The next most popular response was "bed," given by 99 individuals; 76 gave "ease," and 71

gave "home."   One person responded with "whisky."   When we plot
these data (Figure 1) we see that the associative hierarchy characteristic
of the word "comfort" is indeed relatively flat.

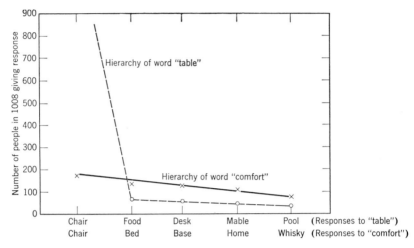

Figure 1   Associative hierarchies for "table" and "comfort."

Individuals as well as words may be characterized as having their
thinking dominated by flat or steep associative hierarchies. Some people
will reliably respond to an idea with its most stereotyped associate.
Perhaps this is what we mean by the notion of the prejudiced individual
or the individual with an *idée fixe*.   Others, reliably, will give more
atypical associates.   Individuals characterized by flat associative hierarchies are unreliable associators.   There is no *single* strong response
so dominant in their thinking that its production can be accurately
predicted.   It will be immediately apparent that it is the individual
characterized as having a flat associative hierarchy who is more likely
to attain a creative solution.   It may be noted as an aside that at this
conference a great deal of attention has been given to paper-and-pencil
attitude and interest measures, as means for studying differences between highly creative and less creative individuals.   These measures
require the subject to report whether he has a negative or positive association to each of a group of test items.   From what has just been said
about the notion of flat and steep response hierarchy, it should be clear
that the less creative individual will be producing reliable data when he
makes responses to the test items.   On the other hand, we would
seriously distrust any content interpretation of the responses of the
highly creative individual, since these are relatively unreliable.   A recent
Ph.D. thesis at the University of Minnesota has demonstrated that

individuals who have stereotyped associations tend to show greater reliability on interest measures such as the Strong Vocational Interest Blank.

(If we may be permitted one more aside, we would like to comment on the use of the Word Association Test in research on creativity and originality. There have been many attempts to measure originality by means of the Word Association Test. Very frequently the researcher will tabulate the frequencies in the population of the responses given by his subjects. Those who achieve relatively low scores are considered highly original. One cannot contest this method in terms of its logic, but in terms of its practicality we believe that it is not ideal. If we wish to test for stereotypy of associative behavior, we have found it most reasonable to use words which *can* elicit stereotyped responses. Thus, if we make use of a word like "comfort" as a stimulus, we cannot really specify what a stereotyped response is because there is none. On the other hand, a word like "table" clearly can elicit a stereotyped response, "chair." In the Kent-Rosanoff Word Association Test there are about thirty words which elicit highly stereotyped responses (words whose primary associates have probabilities of 40% or higher). The commonality score is then simply the number of times the individual responds with the most common or popular response in the population.)

To get back to the main current of this talk, it should be clear that the individual characterized by a steep associative hierarchy would be the one who would achieve a high commonality score on the Word Association Test just described. At IPAR such a Word Association Test was administered to a group of female mathematicians, a group of prominent architects, and a group of research scientists. When we scored the commonality of their associations, there was a very highly significant difference between those who were designated by IPAR as creative and those who were considered less creative. This result held for all three samples. It is of some interest to note that in the sample of forty architects those who showed uncommon associations tended to be judged by the IPAR staff as being less likable. These individuals, the more original individuals, are also rated as being "argumentative, complaining, demanding, dissatisfied, distrustful, fault-finding, impulsive, infantile, irritable, nagging, rattle-brained, rude, slipshod, suspicious, touchy, unfriendly, and whiny." This group of "originals" is rated as *not* being "considerate, cooperative, mannerly, mild, peaceable, reasonable, reserved, retiring, self-controlled, and self-denying."

C I would like to insert one other fact that is interesting. Ravenna Helson did a study of Mills seniors with strong *interest* in creative activity, as assessed by a childhood activities check list. These girls were found to write more original TAT stories than their classmates, to score high on the Barron Verbal Originality Scale and the Barron Complexity Scale, and to be more frequently nominated by the Mills faculty as having outstanding creative potential.   Adjective Check Lists sent to mothers of Mills seniors showed that mothers of girls with strong creative interests described themselves more frequently as irritable and touchy than mothers of other girls and less frequently as adaptable, forgiving, pleasant, and unselfish ($p < .01$). These were self-descriptions by the mothers themselves, not of the girls who were creative.

S   In relating these Adjective Check List results, what I hope to illustrate is that the behavior the individual manifests on the Word Association Test represents a reliable tendency in his thinking.   We find that if he thinks atypically people see him as behaving atypically. Thinking determines the way people make judgments, the way they behave with others, the way they describe themselves on personality inventories, and the way they behave creatively.

The effect of experience on creative ability

The possession of a steep associative hierarchy can be attained by many different pathways.   One of the important pathways is the number of times you have given the same associative response to a given stimulus in a given context.   If you continually think the same thought to the same idea in a given context, you are going to have a steep associative hierarchy for that idea.   This leads to the interesting suggestion that the longer a person has worked in a certain field, the less probable it is that he will come up with a creative solution in this field.   It also suggests that if a person switches his field new discoveries are much more likely to result.   This latter statement should make it clear that the prediction does not hold as a function of chronological age, but only of the age in the field.   It goes without saying that some fields may be more prone to this effect than other fields.

A newcomer can have a very flat associative hierarchy and have just barely enough knowledge to see freshly and clearly where an experienced worker with an extremely steep hierarchy has gone wrong.   From what I have heard, it seems that steep associative hierarchies are acquired extremely quickly in theoretical physics, mathematics, and chess playing.   In any case it looks as though the originality of individuals in these fields quickly depreciates, so that the theoretical physicist is old and ready to be put out to pasture by the age of 25.

WHAT MOTIVE IS REWARDED BY CREATIVE BEHAVIOR?

One of the fundamental questions which we raised at our seminars at the University of Michigan was, Why does anyone make the effort to be creative? It seems like an awful lot of trouble. You can certainly make much more money and lead a calmer and a more tranquil life by not being creative. One direction that our thinking took was the notion that highly creative individuals may be pushed by a *drive for associative novelty*. We would like to clearly differentiate "drive" from "preference." By drive we are referring to a state, akin to hunger, which motivates behavior. In order to test for the existence of such a drive we made use of the fact that when a drive is partially satisfied, it results in a reinforcing state of affairs. Thus if a hungry organism has food systematically delivered upon the exercise of a certain response, this response will increase in probability and will be learned. A hungry rat will learn to press a bar if we continually reward him by delivering food. By analogy we reasoned that, if an individual has a high need for associative novelty and if we present him with associations which are novel, these should reduce his need and should reinforce any behavior in which he has been systematically engaging and which has produced this associatively novel stimulation. Our method (Houston and Mednick, in press) was to take a group of words and type two of them on a card, one above the other. One of the words was a noun, for example, "father"; the other, an adjective or verb, such as the word "black." We presented these words to individuals one at a time with the following instructions:

Call out one of the words on the card; call out the word you prefer at the moment. We urge you to pay attention to what is going on because you will be asked questions about it later.

In pilot studies we found that highly creative individuals (as defined by scores on the test described below) were individuals who typically did not call out nouns but showed a marked tendency to call out verbs or adjectives. Individuals who are not creative tended to prefer the noun member of the pair. Now, if in a T-maze study a rat originally shows a position preference for turning right, you train him to turn left. Since the highly creative individual tended to show a preference for verbs and adjectives, we decided to train him to prefer nouns. When the subject reported a preference for a noun, the experimenter responded with a word which was a highly infrequent or novel association to that stimulus. If the subject responded with a verb or adjective, the experimenter responded with a word which was an extremely frequent association to the stimulus. Novelty was defined simply in terms of associative frequency. Thus, if the subject called out an adjective such as "black," the experimenter responded with the most common response, "white." If the subject preferred a noun like "father," he received an unlikely response like "eggbeater." The novel associations all had an associative probability of less than one in a thousand.

C   Was the response of a particular type of word or noun, or was it an adjective, or was it just an uncommon associate?

S   The response words were not categorized in that way. We don't know.

C   Were the two words paired, comparable in steepness of their associative hierarchy?

S   No. The two words were selected as follows. We equated nouns and non-nouns for number of letters and Thorndike-Lorge probability (that is, the probability of the word's appearance in the written language), and we equated the position on the card for nouns and for non-nouns. In all we presented 160 cards. These 160 trials were broken into four blocks of 40 trials each. In the first block of 40 trials the experimenter gave the most probable association, no matter what word the subject chose. This enabled us to determine the free operant level of noun preference of the two groups. It was on the forty-first trial that the experimenter began to respond with uncommon associates to noun choices. The associative novelty did seem to act as reinforcement for the highly creative subjects. Their tendency to give noun choices increased significantly. What was surprising was the decrease in the number of noun responses manifested by the less creative individuals. This drop was also statistically significant. Perhaps being a low-creative individual means having a drive for more stable and more conventional associations, which are apparently reinforced by the boring comebacks of the experimenter.

I should make one thing clear about this study: when we say associative novelty here, we are referring only to probability of associations. There are many paths to improbability—very funny ones, ones which will rhyme, ones which are somewhat nonsensical, etc. Although we do not hold out much hope, we shall attempt to categorize these responses and evaluate their effect as a function of category.

C   Did you try the opposite approach of attempting to take creative people and deluge them with lack of novelty to see what would happen? I accidentally did this. It was meant to be a control group, and perhaps what you have just said explains the result. We had the subjects go through about ten trials, repeating the same association over and over again to a list of twenty words. What we found was that, when we handed the subjects a problem to work out, instead of being a control group, half of them gave almost no responses, and the others did extremely well. We have never seen such high scores on these problems. Apparently they dived right in just to be doing something other than the dull, boring associative task.

S   Houston is now planning a study where we will give high- and low-creative individuals long, long periods of highly probable responses. (Interspersed among these we will throw in three or four novel associations just so the subjects will know it can happen.) We will follow this boredom period with the conditioning experiment described above. The point is to see whether we can manipulate the need. If we are indeed dealing with a need for associative novelty, then it should be possible to increase it through deprivation and thus enhance operant conditioning.

C   Is the converse of what you are suggesting possible? That is, can you satiate the need for novelty? I was thinking that if you provided a continuously and ever increasingly rich environment for supposedly creative individuals it might actually "turn them off" after a while.

S   Yes, this seems quite consistent with Parkinson's laws; that is, the organization which has just built the beautiful new laboratory is the one which is about to fold. If the environment is too rich, too complex perhaps, it does satiate a need for novelty.

AN ASSOCIATIVE TEST OF CREATIVE ABILITY

We would like to describe a test which grew from this associative theory. In the construction of this test we wished to build a device which not only correlated with creative ability but also actually required the subject to perform creatively at the time of testing. In terms of our definition we wanted the subject to demonstrate his ability to form mutually remote associative elements into new and useful combinations.

The method we utilized was the mechanism of mediation, because we think that this is the most important of the mechanisms. The subjects were required to provide mediating links between a number of unconnected elements. We did not wish that the task require rational, logical, or conceptual ability but sought to have it completely associative. We wish to underline the importance of this aspect of the test. In addition, since the theory intends to be a general theory purporting to explain creative thinking in all areas of endeavor, we attempted to make sure that the materials were not especially relevant or favorable to one discipline or one area of creative performance. We initially thought that we could solve this problem by using material of extremely low familiarity, such as nonsense forms. We quickly found, however, that certain groups (e.g., engineers) were particularly adept in the use of such material, and we eventually dropped the nonsense forms from consideration. We turned to words of very great familiarity in the language, hoping that we could equate familiarity in this manner. We chose very common word pairs, like "ham and eggs," "bed-bug," "pool-hall," "chorus-girl," "week-end." Given these materials, the items almost wrote themselves.

The items consist of three unrelated words; the subject is asked to give one word which can relate the other three. We give the subjects four examples to aid in the communication of the instructions. Here is an example of an item:

White   out   cat

the answer to this item is "house." We have a "White *House*," "out *house*," and "*house* cat." Here are some additional examples:

Item	*Answer*
Wire, chair	Wheel or electric
Flower, Berlin, paper	Wall
Hard, head, boiled	Egg

C   Do the items all depend very much on compound words?

S   Yes.

C   They are all modifiers?

S   I can't think of one thing that would describe them all except that they are associatively related.

C   Is the answer always a word which follows the stimulus item?

S   The answer can go on either side of the stimulus item. We are now doing a study which concerns the question of the determinants of the difficulty of items. One of the factors we are considering is the position of the answer in respect to the stimulus item.

The test in its present form consists of thirty items and is called the Remote Associates Test (RAT). Several forms are now available. The internal reliability of the test is .92. The homogeneity of the items is probably instrumental in producing good reliability.

C   Does this correlate with the functional fixedness problems?

S   We have not done any research correlating these measures. In our first study making use of the test we correlated scores with ratings from design instructors at the University of California College of Architecture on a group of twenty architectural students. These design instructors had known the students for at least one year and had seen evidence of their creativeness in their products. Now, we have no measure of the reliability of the rating, since we received only one rating for each student, but the correlation between the RAT and the ratings was .70. Here is a verbal test and here is architectural performance, and they seem to be somewhat related. In another study using a revision of Donald Taylor's 1957 creativity rating scale, we found that scores on the RAT tests of graduate students in psychology at Northwestern University and the University of Michigan correlated .55. Students at these universities are fairly well known by their research advisors, since they are required to complete some research in their first year under the sponsorship of a faculty member. The number of cases was 42. The Miller Analogies Test had also been administered to some of these students, and this correlated .056 with the ratings. The correlation of the RAT scores with grade-point average was −.12. I might say here that we have found similar correlations between RAT scores and grade-point averages in other samples (Martha T. Mednick, 1963).

Thirty RAT items which were relatively easy and which seemed to be appropriate for elementary school children were administered at the elementary school at the University of Michigan. Polly Mosteller, an art faculty member at Wayne State University, was doing a dissertation with the children at the university school, part of which entailed an evaluation of their creative ability in painting. She has devised a measure of art ability which is extremely reliable. The criteria she used are composed of several separate judgments of artistic ability.

Aesthetic. The overall quality and the total excellence of artistic ability in the field of painting. In obtaining the judgment there were thoughtful and separate considerations of all contributing factors, color, composition, vitality, etc.

Color. The total effectiveness and uniqueness in the quality of the colors. In arriving at the total color judgment, particular attention was given to sensitivity of color relationships, creation of new and unusual colors, and the use of imagination and originality.

Composition. The two-dimensional organization of space. Decisions leading to this judgment give consideration to the utilization of the total painting surface as well as attention to the interrelations of the total space.

Symbolism. Does the house look like a house?

Vitality. Presentation of the art qualities which, when viewed, provide the feelings and experience of movement, vibrance, and strength in contrast with things that are fixed, rigid, and motionless.

Perspective Depth. The creation of a geometric, three-dimensional effect.

Symbolism and perspective depth correlate very highly with intelligence. Mosteller had three well-known local artists go through each of these categories; she reported reliabilities between pairs of the four judges. These reliability coefficients ranged between .68 and .96. The mean reliability coefficient was .82.

C   Is this an interrater correlation?
S   Yes.

The correlation of these easy RAT items with aesthetics was .58, with composition .44, with symbolism −.17, with vitality .41, with perspective depth .13. All but two of these were significant.

Perhaps also of interest in this context is a study which has just been completed at IBM. The RAT was given to a number of personnel at different installations of IBM. The RAT scores were correlated with the number of prizes that had been awarded these subjects in previous "suggestions" competitions. The RAT correlated .44 with the number of prizes the individual had won. What is of special interest is that the investigators also had a score of verbal fluency on these subjects, and this verbal fluency score correlated negatively with the criterion and positively with RAT. When this fluency score was partialed out of the RAT, the correlation of RAT with the criterion was raised to .53.

RESEARCH IN EDUCATIONAL SITUATIONS

When the test was first assembled we administered it to a group of eighty students at MIT and obtained their grade-point average for their first two years of studies. The correlation between grade-point average and RAT score was −.27. At Harvard, coincidentally, we found a correlation of −.27 also between grade-point average and RAT score. We have consistently obtained negative correlations with grades in college. Perhaps in explanation of this, Barbara Miller (1960), in a senior honors thesis at Michigan, found that students with high scores on the RAT get better grades from instructors who are rated as being more flexible as opposed to dogmatic, whereas people with low scores get the same grades regardless of the instructor's characteristics. Walker (1962) found that high school students with high RAT scores show a greater amount of grade variance than do low scorers. The high scorers tend to get better grades in courses that are congruent with their interests. With low scores on the RAT there was no such relationship.

C   I presume that you have not yet done anything about building a nonverbal RAT.

S   No. We are, however, working on a device which we call the CAT (the Conceptual Associates Test). This test is the Guilford Consequences Test in reverse. We administered the Consequences Test to a large group of individuals. Taking the responses which people gave as consequences, we give four or five of these to individuals and ask them to try to guess the cause of these consequences. Performance on the CAT seems to relate very highly to RAT performance. No criterion studies have been done with the CAT.

C   I would like to comment on your RAT. Though I may be wrong,

I doubt that this three-way association test differs very much factorially from one-way and two-way association tests, which tend to be quite similar to each other in factorial composition. If this is true, then we have some puzzles to resolve in terms of findings with these other association tests.

At the 1955 conference, the most promising single test probably appeared to be the Word Association Test, with lively questioning of what scoring method to use in terms of the cut-off level for the "uncommon" responses. Then the result was reported later that the frequency of common responses may be a better score than uncommon responses in terms of predicting creative performance. But in time this test has been seen as not nearly so promising. In fact, we had high hopes for it, too, and used it with three different scoring methods in our study, only to find that only one out of 51 validity coefficients for this one-way Word Association Test was significant in our study of the creative and productive contributions of Air Force scientists. Perhaps we did not use the best scoring system, or maybe your new associates test has better items—is somewhat different factorially—and you know we want to try it out, but all these results together seem to raise some puzzling challenges that need to be better resolved and understood.

S   I must say that we feel very strongly that the RAT paradigm is not merely one involving simple word association. What one measures in the area of simple word association (if you are taking a measure of commonality) is simple originality, not creativity. Originality is probably the cheapest response of which human beings are capable. It is much more difficult to be conventional than to be original. For example, if you pose the problem of how much is 4 + 4, I could answer 1,367,854. I doubt that anyone in the world has ever given this answer before. Thus it is extremely original. However, it is not creative unless it serves some purpose or satisfies some criteria. If in the Word Association Test the subject responds to every word with the names of his relatives, he will probably receive a very high score on originality; however, it is difficult to see how such responding is creative or related to creativity. Thus, in terms of the approach we are taking, a creative response must meet criteria. On the RAT we usually have only one response which is correct. There is a specific criterion evident, which is communicated by the instructions and the samples.

May we conclude by mentioning some of the research which is currently occupying our attention.

1. *Incubation.* We are attempting to study the variables affecting the process of incubation in creative thought. We use the RAT item

paradigm as our problem; we study the effect of rest intervals varying in length and filled in different ways. We have been successful in producing an incubation effect in the laboratory.

2. *Child rearing.* The senior author was involved in an extensive study of child rearing conducted some seven years ago in Cambridge, Mass. The study involved extensive interviews with mothers on child-rearing practices. We are now able to go back to this community, administer the RAT to these children, and relate their scores to the mothers' reports on child rearing.

3. *Determinants of RAT item difficulty.* We are gathering extensive association data on RAT item materials in order to understand better what goes into performance on this test.

4. *Alternate forms.* We are continuing to develop new and improved alternate forms of the test at each level.

5. *Associative behavior.* We are devoting considerable energy to developing a better understanding of associative behavior, especially the differences in such behavior between high and low scorers on the RAT test.

[Mednick then asked the conference group to perform an associational exercise in connection with the word "creativity." Later, after the papers had been scored by J. M. Richards, Jr., in only one of several possible ways, the following report was presented by Mednick.]

S I can only give you now the frequency with which various responses by 24 people were given to the word "creativity." "Originality" or "original" was given most frequently (16 persons); next was "new" or "newness" (10 times); "novel" or "novelty" occurred 7 times. "Unusual" occurred 6 times. Words which were each given 4 times were "inventiveness" and "intelligence." The 7 words which occurred 3 times were "serendipity," "open," "imagination," "flexibility," "different," "discovery," and "adaptive." A total of 24 different words occurred twice, and 360 "unique" words were given only once. With a total of 396 different words, an average of over 16 words was given by each person in two minutes.

So there are a number of people here who think the word "creativity" has something to do especially with originality and newness and unusualness and novelty.

C Maybe you should send each of us a report with this complete list of 396 words so that we will have our speech all prepared whenever anyone asks us what the definition of creativity is.

chapter 6 Creativity and the Prepared Mind:
The Role of Information and Induced Attitudes[1]

Ray Hyman, University of Oregon

S   In this paper I want to describe an experiment where we induce attitudes toward prior information to see how this will affect creative problem solving.

The point of departure for my experimental program is the role of preparation in discovery and innovation.   In the history of scientific and technological discovery, the concept of preparation refers to many things.   Among others, preparation refers to an accumulation of information, to a conceptual schema or particular organization of information, to a sensitivity to discrepancies, to an "attitude of mind," or, at times, to opportunism.

Within this context, the issue that motivates the present study is that for each of these meanings of preparation we can find cases where preparation seems to have helped creativity, and we can find other cases where preparation seems to have hampered creativity.

In the particular experiment that I will discuss we are dealing with preparation in terms of information that we give to people.   The basic question underlying the current experiment can be put this way: Under what conditions does information help you to be creative, and under what conditions does information keep you from being creative?

[1] This particular experiment is part of a larger research program on creative problem solving that is being supported by the General Electric Foundation.

In addition to this basic question, my research is characterized by three other features. In the first place, my approach is experimental. This means, among other things, that I am dealing with *induced changes* in performance. I focus upon creativity as something which can change or be changed within an individual rather than as something that varies among individuals.

In the second place, I emphasize *immediate* rather than remote *determinants* of creative performance. Although I believe that dispositions, personality traits, and stable, long-term factors are important, I also believe that we may be wise to see first how much we can change creative performance by such proximate controls as "hints," "directions," "sets," and other instructional and task variables. Only after we know the range within which we can change performance by these more immediate inputs can we adequately study the contributions of the more remote factors.

Let me give just one of several possible examples of what I mean by this point. I was once talking with a manager of engineering whose company had just lost several million dollars because of marketing a defective machine which later had to be withdrawn from the market. As a result, the company was under tremendous pressure to recover its previous position in a highly competitive market. The manager was worried because in this market, if you do not look ahead and keep generating new patents, you cannot survive very long. Yet his men, 18 design engineers, had not turned out a patent in the past year or so. Like everyone else in the company, their major concern was with current pressures to keep the business out of the red. The manager, in order to change this lack of new patents, first thought in terms of his selection policies. Maybe he had chosen the wrong men. Maybe he should fire some of his present staff and hire new men. One day the thought occurred to him: "Why not first call the men in and tell them what I want?" He called them to a meeting and told them, "Look, men, we need patents, or else we die." The next month his men presented him with several patent applications. And they've been continuing at that rate ever since. One gets the impression that, essentially, the men just looked at each other and said, "Well, if that's what he wants, why didn't he say so?"

There are plenty of other examples that I might also use to illustrate that, in many instances, we may be making a serious mistake in looking for long-range, distant personality and dispositional "explanations" of current creative performance when the major controls reside in relatively transitory, short-term, self-imposed sets or notions as to what is wanted.

The third feature of my research program is its emphasis upon *open-system tasks*. Classical studies of problem solving have limited themselves to closed-system tasks where there is a clearly defined goal and where the subject either succeeds or fails in achieving this goal. Because I am interested in the kind of problem solving that is involved in creative performance in science and technology, however, I believe that we may learn more that is relevant to the issues of preparation and creativity if we study performance in response to tasks where there is no clearly right or wrong answer, where solutions can differ in terms of various degrees of subjective and objective adequacy.

THE TASK

In the present experiment, for example, the task requires the subject to provide us with his best proposal for getting more European visitors to the United States. This open-system task, which we have adapted from one that has previously been used by Donald Taylor (Taylor, Berry, and Block, 1958) provides us with raw data in the form of written essays. We chose this task, after pretesting seventeen possible problems, because our subjects see it as a "real" problem; most of them find it to be interesting; and all seem to have roughly equivalent backgrounds for dealing with it.

PROCEDURE

The basic idea behind the present experiment is this: We expose our subjects, who are 74 male and 92 female undergraduates, to different sets of information; and then we see how this exposure affects their subsequent problem solving. The information we showed our subjects was in the form of four different ideas that other students had suggested as solutions for the Tourist Problem. Some of our subjects were exposed to four rather common ideas, and some to four rather uncommon ideas.

The conditions under which the subjects were given these ideas were a "constructive" and a "critical" condition. The subjects in the constructive condition were given twenty minutes to list as many good features as possible for each of the four ideas. The subjects in the critical condition were given twenty minutes to list as many weaknesses as possible for each of the four ideas. These evaluational tasks not only served to create two different conditions under which the information was absorbed, but also served to force the subjects to think about the information they were given. The tasks also were intended to induce either a positive or a negative attitude toward the given information.

The combination of the two evaluational conditions and the two informational conditions, plus a control condition, resulted in the following five independent groups and treatments:

Group	Treatment
Control	Work on syllogisms for twenty minutes
Constructive-common	List good points for the four common ideas
Critical-common	List weak points for the four common ideas
Constructive-uncommon	List good points for the four uncommon ideas
Critical-uncommon	List weak points for the four uncommon ideas

Immediately after the first part of the experiment, all subjects were given twenty minutes to produce their own solutions to the Tourist Problem. This task was followed by two other problems which were intended to detect transfer effects. As a final task, the subjects rated various ideas that were relevant to the Tourist Problem.

Judged effectiveness

The solutions to the Tourist Problem, after being typed and assigned a random code number, were judged according to a global scale of overall effectiveness. Two judges working independently produced ratings that correlated .76. Although there was a slight tendency for the constructive groups in both the male and the female samples to produce more effective solutions, the differences among the groups were quite small and far short of statistical significance.

Content analyses

The experimental conditions, however, produced significant differences in the content of the solutions. The major differences can be briefly summarized and interpreted as follows.

The constructive groups tended to use the ideas to which they were exposed. In effect, they apparently grafted these ideas onto solutions they otherwise would have produced. In the case of the constructive-common group, the acceptance of the common ideas resulted in solutions only slightly different from those produced by the control group because the four common ideas were ones that this group might have employed anyway. In the case of the constructive-uncommon group, however, the acceptance of some of the four uncommon ideas resulted in solutions that were much more different from those produced by the control group.

The critical groups, on the other hand, showed practically no tendency to employ the ideas to which they were exposed. In the case of the critical-uncommon group, the avoidance of the four uncommon ideas resulted in solutions only slightly different from those of the control group because the uncommon ideas were ones that this group might not have employed anyway. In the case of the critical-common group, the avoidance of the four common ideas resulted in solutions that were greatly different from those of the control group. Not only did these subjects tend to avoid the common ideas, but also they employed ideas that they otherwise might not have brought to bear upon this problem. In the sense of having to come up with responses other than the dominant ones, only the critical-common group seems to have been forced by the conditions of our experiment to indulge in problem solving.

That is the simplest summary that I can give you. Now, if you are willing to say that, when all the groups are equivalent on quality of their solutions and that the group that achieves its quality through the more unusual methods is the more creative, then the constructive-uncommon and the critical-common groups produced the most "creative solutions." In terms of actually doing any work to achieve the solutions, the critical-common group is the only one in this experiment that looks as if it has done any "thinking."

Attitude

After completing the experimental tasks, the subjects rated on their own scale of goodness a set of 13 different ideas which other students had proposed as solutions to the Tourist Problem. Among these 13 ideas were those, both the 4 common and the 4 uncommon ones, which were evaluated by the experimental groups in the first part of the experiment. Although the constructive groups tended to rate the ideas they had evaluated only slightly more positively than the control group, critical groups rated the 4 ideas they had previously evaluated significantly and strikingly more negatively than did the control group.

Contrary to what we expected, this induced change in attitude was highly specific and did not affect the evaluation of the other items. The subjects in each group were equivalent in their ratings on all the other ideas. In other words, the attitudes of the groups that were made more negative toward specific information did not spread to other items of information.

COMPARISON WITH A PREVIOUS EXPERIMENT

The reason why we were looking for, and expected, this spread of effect is because of its occurrence, in a striking way, in an earlier experiment. It is interesting to compare the outcome of the present experiment with that of the earlier study which was conducted with engineers in the General Electric Company (Hyman, 1961). These engineers were participants in the Creative Engineering Program and were considered to be highly creative individuals. (The switch from working with these highly selected engineers to doing research with college sophomores represents one of the most striking qualitative differences between the two experiments.)

Both the earlier experiment and the present one employed the same "constructive" and "critical" conditions for inducing attitudes toward relevant information. In the General Electric experiment, however, we used a task especially designed for engineers—the Automatic Warehousing Problem, where the task was to design an automatic warehousing system that would meet certain requirements.

The major results of the General Electric experiment were that both constructive groups produced solutions that were rated significantly more creative than those produced by the two critical groups. Moreover, the effects of the constructive and critical conditions spread to the solutions of an apparently unrelated problem.

In the present experiment, the effects of the induced attitudes seem to be highly specific and closely tied to the particular information that was evaluated. In the General Electric experiment, however, the effects of the induced attitudes seemed to be less closely tied to specific information and appeared to spread beyond the domain encompassed by the Automatic Warehousing Problem.

Because there are many differences between the two experiments, there can be many reasons for the differences in the nature of the observed effects. If I had to make a guess, however, I would give two reasons as the key ones. The first reason is the difference in preparation that the subjects in the two experiments brought to their respective tasks. The engineers in tackling the Automatic Warehousing Problem were dealing with a problem that was central to their professional interests. Moreover, they had training and experience on various components that would be involved in any solution. The students, on the other hand, in tackling the Tourist Problem were dealing with a problem that was obviously peripheral to their major concerns and present background. They had very little knowledge about the actual conditions behind the current tourist situation.

Consequently, if our experimental manipulations had any effect at all upon the engineer's attitude toward specific ideas about the Automatic Warehousing Problem, we would expect this effect to spread to a wider constellation of interconnected ideas which are associated with the specific ideas evaluated. Since the evaluated ideas involve possibilities and associations more central to the engineers' interests and experience, the effects would also be expected to be fairly central and widespread. Any effects upon the attitudes of students toward specific ideas about the Tourist Problem, on the other hand, would not be expected to spread very far, since the issues involved and the problem itself are more loosely tied to each other and unrelated to associations which are central to the students' everyday lives.

The second reason is the difference in the restrictions imposed by the different tasks upon achieving an adequate solution in the two experiments. The Automatic Warehousing Problem demanded a tightly organized system to meet certain requirements. The possible answers were mutually exclusive in the sense that the proposal of one system necessarily ruled out the proposal of other systems. The Tourist Problem, on the other hand, could be handled by a loosely organized package of ideas for dealing with various subproblems. The acceptance or rejection of any particular idea did not affect the inclusion or exclusion of other possible ideas. In other words, the Automatic Warehousing Problem by its very nature forced the subjects to choose among possible alternatives; the Tourist Problem was less restrictive in that subjects could avoid the necessity of choice by simply including each idea they thought had some merit. I cannot state, at this point, just why I think that this necessity for a final choice may be related to whether the experimental inputs spread or stay specific, but my hunch is that this will turn out to be an important factor. In part, this belief is related to my feelings that "creativity" has more to do with the standards and values which individuals employ for selecting among alternatives than it does with the generating of alternatives.

DISCUSSION OF THE EXPERIMENTS

These experiments as well as the others I have conducted in my program point to a number of potentially significant questions for future research. In this chapter, however, I want to deal with just one question: What must we add to our present experimental approach to produce findings that will more closely bear upon the issue of preparation and creativity? My experiments up to now have been somewhat oversimplified, but they have at least served as an entree into this vast and important area.

One additional ingredient that we are considering for inclusion in future experiments is involvement. As you can guess, subjects vary a great deal in how much they say they are involved and how much time they are willing to devote to our experimental tasks. In the future we plan to concentrate upon the subjects who indicate some involvement with our experimental task.

Once we have assured ourselves that we are dealing with involved subjects, we will try to see what factors in addition to information are necessary to elicit a truly creative solution. One of these additional factors might simply be the matter of time—time to digest, to consolidate, to incubate. Consequently, we plan to stretch the interval between problem presentation and final solution to a matter of days or weeks.

But the most important ingredient, in my opinion, lies in the nature of the task, as has already been suggested by our comparison of the General Electric experiment with the present one. We have to employ open-system tasks that permit creative problem solving to occur. The Tourist Problem as we presented it in this experiment apparently does not allow for creativity. Our subjects were quite consistent in stating that the task demands practical and effective ideas, but not original or creative ones. They seem to be saying that, until the more obvious ideas for solving the Tourist Problem are tried out, we cannot tell whether there is a need for "a more creative approach." I think in retrospect that they are right. It is only when the common ideas are shown to be ineffectual, or if competing goals have to be satisfied, or if some other hurdles have to be overcome, that creativity may be called for. In line with this thinking, we have already started to build hurdles and conflicting goals into the experimental tasks that we give our subjects. The slight evidence that we have accumulated so far suggests that we may be right in surmising that our induced attitudes and informational conditions produce more general effects under conditions where subjects are solving problems with built-in conflict.

CONCLUSIONS

The major contribution of these two experiments, I would suggest, is not so much in what they tell us about preparation and creativity, but rather in helping us to formulate more adequately the questions we might want to ask about prior information and creative problem solving. As highly oversimplified paradigms, they serve chiefly as a way for us to get our foot in the door. Within the context of this approach and with additional modifications such as I have suggested, I feel that we can learn a great deal about the role of preparation and creativity through the experimental method.

C   So far your studies hint in the direction that it isn't the sheer knowledge that a person has, but how he receives, processes, and utilizes it, that may be of importance.

S   I think that I agree with what you are saying. I believe that it is the way we take in or receive information that is important.

C   As I have raised the question to educators of the relation between the amount of knowledge a person possesses and creativity, I find them full of questions and discussion and defensiveness. Would you dare state at this early stage what your implications are for education now?

S   I think the implications are that information has to be taken in with a problem-solving approach or attitude. In some of our procedures we are trying to get our students and engineers to solve problems before they encounter them—to look at new information in such a way that they say to themselves, "How can we use this for other purposes?" In fact, I plan to try to induce phenomena in our experiments that correspond to serendipity; "serendipity" can be thought of, in my usage, as a problem which has already been solved but has not occurred yet. And when it does occur, something in the situation snaps.

C   Would you say that a very general kind of attitude which might be bought by word or deed by formal education is that information is a tool and not an end? Now this would be quite different from something that we have talked about, too. And if we take information as being something which can be used, which I think is one implication of what you are saying, it must be handled in that way. This is quite diametrically opposed to our notion of truth for its own sake. Is that so?

S   I really don't know that it is diametrically opposed.

C   I really don't know way down deep either. But it seems to me that it may be. Our thought is that the mind grows and feeds upon knowledge and information rather than merely getting knowledge for its own sake. Is that right?

C   But Hyman is saying something different: Knowledge should be looked at as something you take in as a food rather than something taken for its own sake.

C   Well, this is a possibility.

C   The Physical Science Study Committee at MIT with Zacharias at the head has used this for the past several years as a basis for completely modifying the course content of high school physics.

S   By "this" you mean a problem-solving course?

C   Yes, making the student think through his problem rather than merely giving him a straight presentation.

S   I am familiar with Suchman's research in which he tries to teach school children to ask questions and to formulate their own hypotheses and discover for themselves the physical principles underlying scientific demonstrations. One practical problem with this approach to teaching is that it takes much more time (and one can cover much less ground) and much better teachers to get it across.

C   But in the physical science course a whole series of films is supplied.

C   The thought which came into my mind was that, when you take in information for truth's own sake, even there it could be for the use of understanding further knowledge. And the other thing I was going to say about this comment you made before about the kind of problems the students have: I talked about opportunity problems and obstacle problems, which are really what you are dealing with here. I think that your last statement is important—to teach the student to meet opportunity problems just as much as obstacle problems, if not more so.

S   By "opportunity" you mean where there is an opportunity to be creative rather than a requirement?

C   This is the more common situation in our society today the way things are, and therefore I think that your experiment is easier with this first problem, the obstacle problem, but that you have to get the other kind, too, for a really solid education.

C   If I read you right—and I am speaking generally—if you have a person encounter a closed system, you can bring about creative thinking when you ask him to become critical about the closed system. If you have an open system you want him to be constructive when he encounters it.

S   I think that we had better make a distinction here. The distinction between open- and closed-system problems is not the same distinction you make between divergent- and convergent-thinking problems. Now divergent-thinking problems, I understand, are problems where the task of the subject is to generate a lot of ideas, not to solve a problem (by providing one final solution). And the convergent-thinking problems are essentially the ones in which the subject has to end up with one solution. He has to choose among alternatives. I think that I am dealing with open-system tasks in the sense that the subjects have to come up with one solution. We don't know what it is; it could be any possibility. In fact, we see solutions that we have never seen before. But the subject has to come up with *one* solution.

C   You said that the subjects run into a lot of common ideas and when they approach them critically they come up with fresh ideas— they move away from the common thinking.

S   That is right. In one of our experimental conditions we get them to critically evaluate common ideas.

C   This would be a common closed system in the sense that all they are running into is old common ideas.

S   I see what you mean . . . a closed system psychologically, not logically.

C   And you approach a closed system critically but an open system more constructively to get fresh ideas.

S   I agree with the first part of what you say, but I am not sure about the second part. I think that there is as much of a problem with divergent thinkers as there is with convergent thinkers in the sense that some people never can converge.   Dollard and Miller say that one of the dangers of inducing people to free-associate, through psychoanalysis or otherwise, is that afterward they may never concentrate on any one problem long enough to finish it.   Dollard and Miller seem to be suggesting that, after you teach people to free-associate and be divergent, you have to supplement this by training them in how to suppress all kinds of other thoughts and to zero in on a solution.

chapter 7 The Relationship of Ego Diffusion to Creative Perception[1]

Frank Barron, Institute of Personality Assessment and Research, University of California, Berkeley

S   The incentive value of novelty and stimulation and the existence of a motive toward spontaneity and self-expression for its own sake have in recent years been demonstrated in a variety of experiments. Primates, for example, will learn difficult tasks simply for the reward of being able to look out a window or to sit where they can see something happen.   Learning will occur in the white rat when the reward is the stimulation of certain cortical centers by electrical impulses passed into the brain through implanted electrodes.   In brief, there is a growing body of laboratory evidence in support of the thesis that novel stimulation is sought for its own sake and can serve as a motive for the development of skills.

This line of experimentation offers serious challenge to the concept of homeostasis, which posits a basic conservative tendency in organisms, a disposition to adopt patterns of behavior that are effective in reducing

[1] The filmed experiments described in this paper were not conducted at the Institute of Personality Assessment and Research, which does not have the necessary medical staffing or facilities for such research, but were carried out independently by the present author and by Sterling Bunnell, M.D.   For a comprehensive account of research in this field, see the article by Barron, Bunnell, and Murray Jarvik, M.D., in *Scientific American*, April, 1964, "The Hallucinogenic Drugs."

The film was not completed as planned, because of the policy adopted subsequently by the Food and Drug Administration of restricting the use of psilocybin and other hallucinogenic drugs for research purposes to investigators sponsored by federal or state government agencies.

the need for counteraction. If homeostasis were the rule, organisms would act always in such a fashion as to produce an equilibrium psycho-physiologically. But these observations point to the need for a more complex and inclusive formulation. There seems to be an essential and continuing tension between the maintenance of environmental con-stancies and the interruption of such constancies in the interest of new possibilities of experience.

The creative process itself embodies this tension, and individuals who distinguish themselves in artistic, scientific, and entrepreneurial creation exemplify vividly in their persons the incessant dialectic between integra-tion and diffusion, convergence and divergence, thesis and antithesis. I have attempted in my own research, employing highly creative people as subjects of study, to understand the specifics of this essential tension in terms of such dualities as intellect and intuition, the conscious and the unconscious, mental health and mental disorder, the conventional and the unconventional, complexity and simplicity.

From these studies I have come to the following most general con-clusion: in the sequence of related acts which taken together as a process result in the creation of something new, there occur consistently a rhythmic alternation and occasionally a genuine resolution or synthesis of certain common antinomies. By this I mean that certain apparently contradictory and contrary principles of action, thought, and feeling, which usually must be sacrificed one to the other, are instead expressed fully in the same sequence, the dialectic leading at special moments to an unusual integration.

Of all the common psychological antinomies, the most basic is that arising from the distinction between self and not-self. This is the beginning of perceptual structure and the most primitive achievement of the ego. Whether things are going on inside us or outside us is the first thing we must get straight if we are to think causally. With that established, we can make discriminations in space and time, we can describe events at specific space-time coordinates, we can give reasons, and we are able to be objective and experience our self as subject, a subject distinct from the world of objects.

In my most recent research in creative perception, I have been explor-ing the consequences of the temporary obliteration or at least attenua-tion of that distinction. Let me introduce the description I am going to give by a single observation drawn from this research, based on the reactions of creative writers, painters, and musicians to the consciousness-altering drug psilocybin, a chemical synthesis of the psychically active principle in the so-called sacred mushroom, *Psilocybe mexicana* Heim, which is used by the Maxatec Indians of Mexico in their religious rituals.

I am not sure what the observation means, but it certainly is relevant to the act of relinquishing the distinction between self and not-self, and I think also to the creative act. The reaction of which I speak is laughter. One might dismiss it, as reports in the psychological and psychiatric literature commonly do, by saying that the drug produces a condition of euphoria in which there is senseless laughing. But I have asked a number of subjects afterwards what they were laughing about, and I have received replies which had in common the notion that the laughing was sheer pleasure in no longer having to maintain what I shall call "the project of the ego." Here is a typical written account, by a painter who incidentally never had heard of Maslow's "peak experience."

Possibly the most important part of the experiment for me was my awareness of a totality and awareness of nothing. Thoughts took on a great reality, and I could sit and enjoy myself thinking. Sometimes the thoughts were so delightful and so real that I would laugh happily over them. While the thoughts took on this reality at the peak point of the experience I felt that I was able to not think. I could sit empty, and then a thought would pulse through my mind. I was never quite sure whether the thought came from—originated—with me or outside me. Many times I felt like a large receiver through which things were passing. I felt as though I were collecting information. This made me extremely happy. My laughter was aboout this happiness and was not in response to what other people in the room had said. . . .

Moreover, it was possible to evoke such laughter simply by asking certain quite sensible questions: the very questions, in fact, which if you can answer them correctly will get you considered sane enough for most purposes, the standard psychiatric questions for determining whether a patient has what used to be called a "clear sensorium." These are the questions: Who are you, where are you, why are you here, what is your name, what day is it? The questions themselves arouse laughter when through action of the drug certain fundamental ego-structures are rendered ineffective temporarily.

I have brought with me to this conference some of the footage of a film which I am now making, showing the effects of psilocybin upon the performance of creative artists while they are under the influence of the drug. I shall show only two of the sessions, one with a ballet dancer who heads a troupe currently doing very original work, and another with a painter. I have with me also some tape recordings of later interviews with the subjects, and perhaps we can listen to at least one of these.

(The film was now shown. The first subject assumed a number of dance positions, and throughout the experience, which lasted some five hours, from 1 P.M. to about 6 P.M., she spoke only when addressed by the experimenter. Her experience was deeply introspective and primarily kinaesthetic, that is, she experienced neither words nor visual phenomena but rather the depths of her own body. In the interview transcript, which follows, she attempted to put the experience into words, although she felt that it was impossible to do so. The setting for the session was a dance platform out of doors, adjacent to her own studio. The quantity of psilocybin ingested was 30 mg. in capsule form, taken with water.

The second subject also took 30 mg., starting at 1 P.M. She had no wish to sketch or paint, but instead had primarily a visual and extra-verted experience and wanted to use the camera herself to photograph children in the street outside her home, which she was permitted to do. She also photographed flowers, lay for long periods of time in the grass in the garden back of her home, and finally expressed a desire to go to the beach and to wade in the ocean. With some misgivings the experimenters agreed to this, and she was accompanied in her wading by the physician present (an audacious psychoanalyst) and by me. All these sequences were presented in the film, which concluded with the return to her home and her greeting of her young daughter, who had been staying with neighbors during this period of time. The final sequence showed mother and daughter playing together. By this time the effect of the drug had almost completely worn off, though there was some remaining euphoria, causing the little girl to exclaim, "Mommy, why aren't you always this much fun?")

The tape recording of the interview with the first subject was not played. It is transcribed as follows.

The sun was shining. I was facing directly into the sun, and I could sense its radiation very intensely. It was not an undefined sensation. Rather, it was very defined. There was a specific radiation, and I could feel where it came from and I could feel where it went, I could feel the ends of it, and the source of it. And the sun was coming in in this way, and it was the whole thing, all there was. I could feel my breathing as also a kind of motion, always feeling heat in above [pointing to chest]. I could feel my breathing *so deep* that it was as if it were permeating the entire body. I could feel it down into my fingertips. I could sense the heat of the sun and I could feel exactly where the wind was coming from. I could feel what the texture of my skin was, and I would get *thrilled* by things like the distance between my hands and my face. I would get thrilled by making a movement like this [moving hand in dance movement]. It was just thrilling, because I knew where the space was, exactly what the space was, but doing it confirmed it, it was real.

One time I really felt with my cheek, and the funny thing was that all the time I could feel these things in such a vivid way. It was as if I had never felt what my teeth were like before. I could feel the weight of my tongue, how much space it had around it. I noticed that again and again—just where it was sitting in my mouth. It was interesting that when E. did talk to me I would open my eyes and look at him. And when he talked to me—I became aware again of the fact that I was Ann, that I was a specific person, a person-ality, and I found that I was playing a role with him. And that this role had so many pretenses in it, being sort of a hostess, being polite to him, yet not really wanting to be bothered with it. So I knew I was playing this role all the time I was playing it—I played it and knew I was playing it at the same time. And then when I went back into the other world, I was not playing a role and I was not a personality and I was not Ann, and I had no ego. I had no will at all in the usual sense. This was interesting as a comparison, in that every single time I opened my eyes, even when I talked to him, even when I just opened my eyes and just looked at the physical environment, I again was *me* looking. But the moment my eyes closed again, I would go back into this state, and I was a pure state of being, and I didn't feel any differently as a state of being than a tree or a dog or the wind or the sun feels. These things were also states of being but they had a different nature—that was the only difference. I had the nature of a human, of humanness, and that was the difference. But my time and space was shared with them, and that was the source of the harmony of all states of being that I felt. When I would talk to E., that was another matter entirely. I had to give up one thing to get the other, and vice versa. They were completely different. I have still been thinking about the things I have found out about myself through that experience, its by-products and implications.

The most notable part of this subject's experience was precisely a sense of pleasure in being able for a little while to give up "the project of the ego" and to experience her own nature in a more primitive fashion. In an atmosphere of psychological safety, she could permit herself to undergo a loss of ego without feeling vulnerable, and she knew also that she could return to her ordinary social role if necessary, though she found it something of a nuisance.

C   What would happen if the atmosphere were not one of psychological safety, but of threat?

S   In such cases, which we make every effort to guard against, there may occur certain adverse reactions, such as intense anxiety or suspiciousness. If the person is basically distrustful, or if something in the immediate situation should indeed cause distrust, then a temporary paranoid state may ensue. I think that this is what accounts for the earlier interpretations of LSD-25 and psilocybin as psychotomimetic drugs, for they were administered usually in a psychiatric setting and with the expectation, on the part of both subject and psychiatrist, that a model psychosis was about to occur.

C   Did these subjects show any aftereffects?

S   There were no adverse aftereffects; whether or not there were positive aftereffects I cannot be sure. The dancer brought her adolescent daughter and some members of her troupe to see the film a couple of weeks later, and she expressed herself as being delighted with the experience, saying, "It was the most wonderful day of my life." The members of the troupe felt that she had done some unusual and worthwhile movements, but I don't know enough about dance to understand their comments. The other subject described herself as being "charged up and very happy" for the next week or so. Reverberations of the experience seem to fade out completely within two or three weeks, although there is of course still a memory of it.

C Aren't the kinds of things she did in the dance there not very different from behaviors you might expect of her if she were encouraged simply to explore over a period of time? Suppose that the same type of picture were shown and you did not know whether the drug had been administered or not.

S Placebo studies indicate that the subjective experience is distinctive and is not confused with the placebo experience. However, we'll have more evidence on that soon, and in the final version of the film I plan to show behavior sequences both with a placebo and with the actual drug. I am working now with identical twins, and I would like to have a pair of identicals take part in such a session.

C Do you think you could produce some of these relatively wild and imaginative and creative-like experiences in an individual who isn't this kind of person, that is, if you called a fellow out of a ditch where he is digging and asked him to be a subject? What about ditchdiggers and bus drivers and plain Joes?

S Leary perhaps can give us some information relevant to that question, since he has been working with convicts at the Concord Reformatory and his sample is close to the general population average in intelligence. I do know, however, that almost without exception the subjects who have been studied, even those not especially creative, report an increase in creative activities. The increase in the visual beauty of the world which is seen in the drug session does have some carryover in increasing aesthetic sensibility and appreciation. One of our subjects who hadn't read any poetry in the fifteen years since he graduated from college reported that a week later as he was walking by a bookstore he thought, "My, it would be interesting to read some poetry," so he went in and bought an anthology and read it.

C Do you have this same heightened sensitivity to kinaesthetic sensations among nondance people?

S That's a good point. No, usually the experience is predominantly visual, although some subjects ask for music to listen to. In one instance, a modern composer who took part in the research kept his eyes closed for about three hours and reported afterwards that during that time he heard music which he had never heard before. Some of what he heard he used in a composition of his own a few months later. We certainly need research on the relationship between preferred modes of experiencing in the normal state and the spontaneous experience under psilocybin.

C   You mentioned at least one other drug which produces similar effects, LSD-25, and apparently mescaline is also similar. Is it possible that different drugs of this sort may heighten specific features of experience?

S   I have no personal knowledge of either LSD-25 or mescaline, but I am told that they do produce slightly different effects. Comparative studies are certainly needed. If we administered simultaneously to a number of subjects such different drugs as mescaline, LSD-25, psilocybin, alchohol, and perhaps marijuana, masking them in some standard fluid, perhaps cherry syrup, and then filmed the behavior sequences as well as obtaining the subjects' own descriptions of their subjective experiences, we would have valuable data to interpret. As yet no such study has been done, so far as I know.

C   These changes in sensory clarity and brilliance are also reported in people who have been completely curarized, that is, totally paralyzed with curare. They can't move their eyes, but their visual sensations are, as they report, bigger than life. One person reported, "My sensorium was never clearer." Everything seems much more vivid. The guess in this case was that curare had reduced "system noise" by reducing all kinds of body movement. The subject also reported tunnel vision.

S   Eventually I believe that these alterations of consciousness can best be explained in terms of a sort of "field theory of attention." I am attempting to develop such a theory, but it would be premature at this point to present it. I might add that in the course of attempting to understand our observations of the creative process I have had recourse regularly to some of the classical writings of early psychologists, in which formal variables of a sort that might prove finally assimilable to theoretic understanding in physics and biology and a philosophic unification of science are most prominent. I am thinking here of Titchener on attention and methods of introspection, Fechner's valiant efforts at a genuine psychophysics to resolve the mind-body problem, Galton's emphasis on imagery, both in his *Inquiry into Human Faculty* and his "The Visions of Sane Men," James's *Varieties of Religious Experience*, and Peirce's oddly alternating radical empiricism and radical idealism, as expressed, for example, in "Man's Glassy Essence" and in "The Laws of Mind." The relevance of such centrally important concerns to theoretical issues in the psychology of creativity is evidence enough that, in this area of psychological inquiry, the scientific stakes are unusually high.

chapter 8 The Effects of Test Score Feedback on Creative Performance and of Drugs on Creative Experience

Timothy Leary, Harvard University[1]

S   Of all the artificial, dualistic abstractions imposed by language upon the unfolding unity of life, one of the most useful is the distinction between internal and external.   Although our mental processes and our cultures are based upon this differentiation, American behaviorism tends to ignore it and prefers to pretend that only movements "out there" are real and that events registered "in there" are inaccessible to systematic inquiry.

The purpose of this paper is to call attention to the internal, to the neglected issue of consciousness, and to suggest its relevance for the interpretation, measurement, and development of creativity.   The emphasis which we Westerners place upon external behavior and material phenomena is basically a religious decision, betraying our assumptions about the nature of man, the meaning of life, the goals of existence.

As I have listened to the words exchanged around this table during the past two days, I have been impressed by the underlying unanimity as to these basic religious assumptions.   Such a conference could be held only in a materialistic (and in America, Protestant) context.   From what other religious background could come the emphasis upon action,

[1] Now with the International Federation for Internal Freedom.

the external, the material; from what other religious background could come the confident optimism about doing things to nature? Protestantism is of course one of the more recent expressions of monotheism,[2] and from this monotheistic background comes the familiar anthropocentric and manipulative definition of creativity. "In the beginning," says the Bible, "God created the heavens and the earth." "I believe," says the Christian, "in one God, Creator of Heaven and Earth." The basis of Muslim science which kept the intellectual flame going for so many centuries is the similar belief in a single, unified Will, Allah, the "almighty, omnipotent, Lord of the Worlds, the Author of Heaven and Earth, the Creator of life and death in whose hand is dominion and inexhaustible power."

When we assemble here in this magnificently architectured mountain scene to talk about creators and creativity, we might profit by keeping explicit the fundamental tenets upon which our conceptions are based, by being aware of other conceptions, and by keeping alert to the practical as well as spiritual implications of "nonmonotheistic" approaches to man and his nature.[3]

The other conception of man (historically the older, and numerically the greater) places greater emphasis upon consciousness, sees matter and behavior as forms of consciousness, stresses the mystical rather than the mental, and centers divinity and creativity within the realm of human awareness. According to the monotheist, God and heaven and earth are all "out there," and man relying on his spiritual or creative capacity must do something about it. According to the nonmonotheist, what does or does not exist out there is irrelevant; what counts is what is inside. Everything relevant is psychological, is in consciousness. All the universes exist (discovered or undiscovered, created or uncreated) within the human skull. "The psychic self," says Jung (1960), "and the giver of all data are one and the same. The world of gods and spirits is truly nothing but the collective unconscious within me."

Now our basic religious beliefs are of tremendous importance not just morally-theologically, but practically as well, because they determine our philosophy and our psychology. If we are committed to an external,

---

[2] Among other active expressions of a monotheistic approach to life are Catholicism, Islam, Judism, Marxism, and psychoanalysis.

[3] The most influential nonmonotheistic religions include Hinduism, Taoism, and the Southern, Northern, and Zen varieties of Buddhism. Among Western philosophers expressing a mystical, pantheistic point of view we can include most of the early Christians, Gnostics, Plato, Herodotus, Pindar, Pythagorus, Socrates, the later Christian mystics, Blake, Swedenborg, a high percentage of our poets, and, more recently, our own American psychologist William James and the late Swiss psychoanalyst, Carl Jung.

monotheistic belief, our conceptions of what is real, what is true, how things are related, and what to do become defined in external terms. Our psychology similarly takes on a behavioristic and materialistic coloring involving adjustment, normality, socialization, achievement, performance, manipulation of symbols, and deification and reification of words. Creativity is defined as innovation, original production.

For the past two years I have been occupied with research on consciousness—its experimental alteration and expansion. Such research is not new. Even in the West (via introspection and via inferences from so-called dynamic techniques) psychologists have been inquiring into consciousness. What is most eccentric about our studies at Harvard is the combination of methods which are very Western—drugs—with a research philosophy which is currently out of vogue in American administrative psychology. Our data have taught us that the criteria, methods, language, and goals of behavioral psychology do not always apply when we set out to study the internal events of consciousness. We have found ourselves becoming increasingly passive and collaborative, increasingly convinced that the study of consciousness demands an ontology, an epistemology, a logic, and an ethic which is frankly subjective. We have found it increasingly necessary to involve ourselves in the scope of inquiry, to expand our own awareness in order to keep in any sort of touch with our subjects.

We follow here a form of experimentation which is somewhat new and suspect in the West but which is actually the oldest and most traditional form of psychological investigation—the disciplined, systematic expansion of one's own consciousness. The experimental search for inner creativity is, we recall, over three thousand years old and possesses a literature of method and finding which dwarfs our own. Our civilization, our culture, our psychology, and our conception of creativity cannot afford to ignore these achievements and these methods.

But in attempting a productive synthesis, the difference between the two approaches must be respected. Western psychology has never satisfactorily resolved the tension between internal-subjective and external-objective. We have consistently imposed the methods, language, and goals of the external upon the internal. *The two can be related only if their logical separation is kept clear.*

During the past few years I have worked out some philosophical and methodological solutions to this problem. It is my plan today to present a conceptual model for dealing with behavior, on the one hand, and consciousness, on the other, and then to apply the model to problems of diagnosis and change in the two kinds of creativity.

BEHAVIOR—ITS MEASUREMENT, DESCRIPTION, AND CHANGE

Behavior is movement in time/space. The first step in measuring behavior is to locate it reliably in space/time.[4]

A method for diagnosing space/time aspects of behavior has been devised and applied to behavior-change projects (Leary, 1962b). The measurement of movements is more complex. Indeed we can directly measure not movements but only the records of movements—artifacts, recorded sounds, films, records of verbalization. We measure records of movements by reliably determining their extension and duration and then by counting frequency.

Such units of extension-duration provide objective indices of behavior. These molecular indices define the vocabulary of behavioral science. Hundreds of such indices now exist—EEG, GSR, MAT score, the scales of the MMPI, verbal content counts, etc. Until recently such terms were scattered, with no logical relationships. Psychology is in the position of chemistry before Mendeleev. The language of the behavioral sciences will eventually develop, as did that of chemistry, with index terms related systematically into formulae. A crude attempt to develop a systematic grammar and measures for the vocabulary of behavioral indices (with particular reference to verbalizations) has been described in other papers (Leary, 1962b, 1962c) and will be referred to in the section of this article concerned with the training of creative behavior.

Behavior units exist in infinite numbers and endlessly combine and interact, providing a confusing jumble of events. For descriptive purposes it is useful to classify behavior sequences in terms of the cultural games of which they are expressions (Leary, 1962a). A game is behavior sequence characterized by:

Goals	Values
Rules	Space/time locale
Roles	Strategies
Rituals	Language

All learned behavior is considered part of cultural game systems. Instinctual behavior, physical and biological processes, random movements are called play.[5] Many people object to the word "game" because it is seen as derogating the seriousness of life's actions. This, of course, brings us to religious issues—the meaning of life. To avoid this debate

---

[4] Any attempts to "measure" behavior directly via observation, labeling, or naming brings us into the mind of the observer and repeats the old confusion of internal/external.

[5] This definition of natural processes as play follows the Hindu conception of Lila.

one can substitute the term ACTS for game behavior. (ACTS refers to Artificial, Culturally learned, Temporary Sequences.)

For the past several years I have been engaged in the application of these theories and methods to behavior change, for instance, the therapeutic implications of the space/time issue—who goes to whom, when, for how long. Another example is the explicit contract involved in the helping game, the effect of the expert role as opposed to collaborative determination of roles, rules, languages, goals, rituals, and values of the behavior-change sequence. A further illustration is the effect of the coaching model and feedback of results in bringing about and maintaining change (Leary, 1960, 1961b; Leary, Metzner, Presnell, Weil, Schwitzgebel, and Kinne, 1963).

Some extensions of these principles and methods to changing creative performance will be suggested later.

CONSCIOUSNESS—ITS DESCRIPTION AND CHANGE

The description of subjective states of awareness has always presented philosophical problems—ontological (what is real?), epistemological (what is fact?), and logical (how are images related?).

One cause for the problem is that we tend to impose upon the inner world the same terms we use to describe external events, movements, and things. Now the young child, we are told, does not do this. He experiences directly. The process of education and learning is designed to teach the child not to experience directly. He is trained to impose game structure upon his perceptions of the world. He learns to interpret everything around him (and indeed everything inside of him, e.g., the sickness game, the toilet-training game) in terms of its game meaning.

The recent evidence from experimental and developmental psychology suggests that learning is a process of elimination, screening out. We discriminate, select, censor, and distort to fit what we see within the limits of what we expect to see. I refer here to the work of Piaget, Brunswik, and the Gestalt school, the Ames illusions, and the visual experiments of Land.

The well-trained, self-confident adult (and, in particular, the intellectual) finally arrives at that point where he possesses mental machinery to interpret, discriminate, and label everything he perceives and to relate these percepts to others.

I am convinced that the brain, as a body organ, has incredible perfection. It is an absolutely accurate instrument, just like the heart or the liver, perfectly designed to perform its function. Far from being a *tabula rasa*, the human brain in terms of its natural function is capable of an extraordinary range of awareness which has nothing to do with anything that has been learned or anything that is verbal. As a matter of fact, you might argue that the cortex, without external behavioral or verbal impositions upon it, is a perfect organ for survival. Too often, learned sequences, the perceptual, verbal, and sociological, tend to clutter up this magnificent instrument. It is as though our knowledge of hydraulics led us to feel that we could improve cardiac function so that we built springs about the heart to help it contract or imposed our plumbing knowledge upon that magnificent instrument.

While the cultural process greatly simplifies socialization and reduces anxiety (we end up with a name and explanation for everything we perceive), a heavy price is paid for these advantages. Direct experience is lost. We live in a plastic world of labeled abstractions.

Game consciousness is obviously very limited. Nongame awareness of the continuously changing panorama of inner and outer events is infinite. We socialized adults give away about 99% of our available cortical receptivity.

We deal here with the Faustian bargain. For the handful of concepts in Webster's dictionary and for the power of ego control we exchange the timeless infinity of direct game-free awareness.

But not all men make this bargain. There are some to whom we attach such labels as mystic, visionary, artist, esoteric, orientalist—who have warned us for centuries about the Faustian bargain. Such people have stubbornly insisted that it is possible to avoid a complete commitment to the word game, the ego game, and the social game. They tell us that it is possible to transcend (temporarily) the limits of the "I," the limits of the conceptual and the social, and that it is possible to make direct contact with an infinitely expanded universe. Most of us find these warnings disturbing. We have worked so hard to maintain ego control. We'd be lost without *our* egos. And then we have the dread example of those who are unable to (or refuse to) play a consistent ego, word, or social game. Those pariahs we call psychotic.

Even if we were to wish to transcend ego and word—what good would it do? Does a language exist to describe these experiences? How can we apply these ultramundane visions to our on-going ACTS?

But there is, of course, a language. It is the oldest language in the world—the nonverbal language of spontaneous dance, painting, sculpture, weaving, ceramic; the verbal language of religion, poetry, song, myth, esoterica; and the abstract language of mysticism. We are surrounded by clues (manmade and natural) constantly reminding us that there's more—look, there's more. The clues even extend into the academic. The oldest psychological literature in the world is devoted to exactly these issues—the description of ego-transcendent experience and the application of the experience to personal happiness and social harmony. The greatest psychotherapist in world history possibly was the Buddha. "The goal is not to explain the world to those who are thirsty for knowledge. The goal of my teaching is salvation from suffering." Possibly the greatest sociologist and behavior-change coach in world history was Confucius (Jen, Chun Tsu, Li, Te, Wen). Who has expressed the social contract more clearly? Can we afford to leave these concepts out of our behavioral science textbooks?

But even if we accept the psychological and social potentialities of the ego-transcendent state, there come the final questions: How can we attain it? How can awareness be expanded? How can consciousness be changed?

Here again we have a wealth of technical information. Three thousand years before Freud or Wundt, detailed methods were devised for the systematic expansion of consciousness. There are five major forms of Yoga, all designed to provide nongame control of consciousness. One of these, the Raga Yoga, is a disciplined system of psychological experimentation for consciousness expansion. Also threading back to the origins of history, shrouded in myth and deliberate secrecy, are the mystery cults and fraternities—ancient mental health societies, using spontaneity, ritual, and hallucinogenic plants to expand consciousness, to break out of the game for purposes of ecstasy, mental rehabilitation, creative education, and spiritual initiation. These sacred mystic bands were the originators and earliest preservers of every major religion and practically every major philosophic and intellectual movement the world has known. That is where it always starts—in the expanded cortex.

Psychologists and physiologists are currently experimenting with the same methods—limited environment, sensory deprivation, physical shock, prolonged starvation, and sleeplessness. The ego-transcendent state (today in this time of great emphasis upon ego identity) is called by different labels—primary process thinking, psychotomimetic states—but the experience seems to be the same.

The safest and simplest method for consciousness expansion is, of course, the pharmacological. Drugs such as LSD, mescaline, and psilocybin (chemical synthetics of ergot, peyote, and mushrooms, respectively) produce brief and dramatically intense alternations in consciousness.

For the past two years I have been associated with a research project which has studied the effects of psilocybin upon more than 400 volunteer subjects. The therapeutic and theoretical implications of these studies have been reported elsewhere (Leary and Metzner, 1964; Leary, 1962a; Leary, Metzner, Presnell, Weil, Schwitzgebel, and Kinne, 1963; Leary,

Litwin, and Metzner, 1963), and results relating to creativity have been described by Barron (1962b; Chapter 7 herein). Here let it suffice for me to say that the drugs are physically safe, are psychologically harmless (unless in irresponsible hands and even then the residuals are negligible and debatable), bring about extravagant claims of improvement and insight (Ditman, Hayman, and Whittlesey, 1962; Leary, 1962a; Leary, Litwin, and Metzner, 1963; McGlothlin, 1962), usually produce dramatic ego transcendence, and in many cases stimulate creative awareness.

Our project has followed up on these promising leads in two directions: (1) the application of the consciousness-expansion experience to rehabilitation of prisoners, education of graduate students, and inspiration of the clergy; and (2) the development of new linguistic forms for communicating nongame experiences. Just as our studies of molecular units of behavior led to the development of new index vocabularies (Leary and Gill, 1959; Leary, 1962c), so has our study of consciousness led to the development of a new vocabulary for ego-transcendent awareness utilizing charts and crude inner-space cartography (Leary and Metzner, 1964).

This paper began with the statement that different languages, philosophies, and methods of change were required to deal with behavior, on the one hand, and consciousness, on the other. In the preceding two sections of this paper I have discussed, first, behavior—its measurement and change—and then, consciousness—its description and methods for change.

In the sections to follow I propose to apply these notions to the diagnosis and change of creativity, that is, of creative behavior and of creative awareness.

THE MULTIDIMENSIONAL DIAGNOSIS OF CREATIVITY

There is experience and there is performance. *Awareness* can be creative—our experience can be direct, fresh, outside of game connotations; or it can be reproductive, that is, within the interpretative framework of the already learned, in which case we see only what we have been taught to see.

Performance can be creative—we can produce new combinations (whatever the game medium); or it can be reproductive—a repeating of old combinations.

When we oppose these two dichotomous continua of experience and performance in orthogonal axes, a diagnostic circle is obtained. Four "types" of creativity are defined by the four quadrants of the diagnostic circle shown in Figure 1.

Type 1. *The reproductive blocked* (no novel combinations, no direct experience), which I estimate to comprise about 75% of our American population.

Type 2. *The reproductive creator* (no direct experience, but crafty skill in producing new combinations of old symbols), comprising, let us say, the most visible, successful 12% of our population.

Type 3. *The creative creator* (new experience presented in novel performances), of which we can hope for 1% in any Golden Age.

Type 4. *The creative blocked* (new direct experience expressed in conventional modes), a somewhat cryptic 12%.

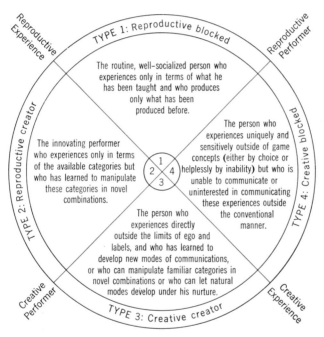

Figure 1 Categories for diagnosing creativity in terms of performance and experience. The diagnostic grid is defined by two axes: experience and performance. Each axis runs a continuum from creative to reproductive.

These four "types" of creativity are obvious by definition and seem to require no elaboration. What does deserve amplification is the social perception of these four types. A person in any of these four quadrants can be seen as effective or as incompetent by his culture—and, for that matter, by cultural subgroups.

If we divide each type into those labeled by their contemporaries as (A) effective and (B) ineffective, we obtain the eight categories presented in Figure 2. These two-dimensional circular grids can be used to plot test scores or content-analysis indices along the two coordinates in order to diagnose the individual. Thus we can work not just in terms of eight

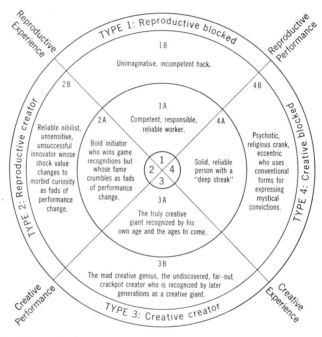

Figure 2 Schematic diagrams of social labels used to describe types of creativity. Inner circle illustrates positive social labels, and outer circle negative labels.

types but in terms of two continua which define a wide expanse of diagnostic space. This system, of course, leads itself to multilevel diagnosis and to the same variety of applications as the interpersonal circle (Leary, 1957). The same mathematical and psychometric methods apply. We can plot the location of scores on check lists of creative experience and creative behavior executed by the subject or by appraisers of this performance. Multilevel discrepancy indices can thus be calculated (Leary, 1956).

THE DEVELOPMENT OF CREATIVE BEHAVIOR

In a previous section I have reviewed some of the methods of behavior change suggested by measurement in space/time theory and the game

model. Now let me illustrate a pilot-study project which tested some
of these methods in a creativity-change program.

The general procedure is as follows. The subject picks out a goal and
practices the game sequences which lead to success. The goal must be
behavioral and capable of measurement. Much confusion is caused
because people engage in games for which there is no way of scorekeeping. Is the game over when the New York Yankees "feel" they
have won? Suppose that the Detroit Tigers "feel" they have won, too.
Suppose that the scoreboard shows that the Tigers won, but they or
their supporters "feel" they lost. The movements in space/time (men
crossing home plate) have to be the criterion.

Thus *feedback* on performance is a key issue. In most of life's crucial
games we stumble in the dark, not knowing how we are doing. The first
step, then, in behavior change is *explicit* definition of the game, learning
the rules, roles, rituals, language, values, and strategies. You need some
way of scorekeeping and you have to study the *space-time locale* and be
at the proper ball park. You aren't going to be a creative artist if you
share your space/time with salesmen. You must be sure that you have
an explicit contract with your colleagues. It is disappointing to come
thundering over the goal line for a touchdown only to be greeted with
yawns because the gang is playing tennis. We tend to do this all the
time. I spend a good part of my professional life doing this. I've done
it at this conference and am probably doing it right now.

You should get a good coach. Behavior, being movement in space/time,
is not changed by words and is not changed by repeating mistakes. And
practice is needed. "Happiness he who seeks may win," says the
Buddha, "if he practices."

In 1961 Frank Barron, William Meyers (at that time a Harvard
graduate student), and I initiated a creativity-change project at the
Rhode Island School of Design which allowed for a preliminary and
crude check on some of these hypotheses (Barron and Leary, 1961). By
matching pairs of students on faculty ratings of creativity forty volunteer subjects of the junior class at the Rhode Island School of Design
were divided into two groups (A and C) whose creativity ratings had
equal means and equal standard deviations. Also, IQ scores were
available on all subjects.

First both groups were tested, under identical conditions, with the
Barron Originality, Independence of Judgment, and Preference for
Complexity Questionnaires, and the Levinson Revision of the Adorno
F Scale, the Bales Balanced F, the Keniston-Couch Agreement Response
Scale, the Meyers College Attitude Test, the Barron-Welsh Art Scale,
and the Guilford Plot Titles Test.

Then, after an intermission, the groups were separated. Group C was asked to "play the role of an extraordinarily original and creative person"; group A, to play the role of a highly intelligent (authoritarian) person. Both groups were then given the Guilford Unusual Uses Test and the Barron Originality, Independence of Judgment, and Preference for Complexity Questionnaires, in that order.

The results indicated that group C (creative set) improved in performance relative to group A, on these tests of ability to think up ideas. This indicates that the creative set increases creative performance, and the authoritarian set decreases creative performance. We may conclude that creativity is not a static quality present in a fixed amount in a given person, but rather that it is susceptible to considerable increase given conditions of high personal motivation and social support. It is also susceptible to considerable decrease, given conditions of interfering motivations and alien social climate. It also suggests that role playing, or set taking, is a specific mechanism for increasing creativity.

The related finding that creativity has a social as well as a personal motivational aspect was shown by the results at the Rhode Island School study on the three Barron questionnaires.

With the creative set, group C increased their scores over their earlier scores with standard instructions. Group A, with the authoritarian set, decreased their scores on the Barron questionnaires. Since these tests are measures of interpersonal and social attitudes, we may conclude that mind sets which affect creative performance also affect interpersonal and social orientation, and vice versa. Creative performance is thus to be viewed in an interpersonal and social context (Meyers, 1963).

Stated in the language of the game model, the results suggest that (1) creative behavior is a game sequence; (2) people have considerable voluntary control over their creative behavior (and, we suspect, other "deep" variables, such as depression, dependence, ego strength, etc.) within stated space/time game lines; and (3) if the game contract is made explicit, behavior will change drastically in the direction that the game role and goal demand. The experiment also suggests that people automatically shift rituals, adjust new rules, and employ the appropriate language once the commitment to goal and role is made—and within explicit space/time limits.

A second test of the game-model approach was then executed. A sample of fifty juniors was selected (at random) for a feedback study. Barron and I met with each subject, opened up the test folder, and explained his creativity test results. We centered on the creativity test scores and attempted to relate them to the student's stated game goals. In every case we found that the student's creativity scores and ratings of originality by faculty members checked closely with his game ambitions.

For instance, one student of commercial design with low scores on originality was rated as solid, responsible, but unimaginative by teachers. She produced a California Personality Inventory profile high in socialization, conformity, stability, and social participation. She consistently checked items which indicated close identification with middle-class family values. We went over this student's creativity questionnaire item by item, indicating where she checked in the "noncreative" direction. Emerging from the subsequent discussion was this message. "I'm a normal, conventional person looking forward to a steady, interesting job in advertising, a good income, and a happy family life. I've no desire to be a tortured genius, sacrificing home and income for the risky Bohemian independence of the artist."

While the student body at the Rhode Island School of Design was significantly above average on indices of aesthetic performance and interpretation, there seemed to be little discrepancy between the level of creativity and the professional goals selected. Painters and sculptors had higher scores on independence of judgment, spontaneous flexibility, and social deviance than did architects or industrial designers.

One conclusion that I draw from these Rhode Island studies is that creativity cannot be judged outside its game context. If we could automatically double the creativity scores (and the personality correlates) of the entire student body, we would probably be causing endless game mixups and conflicts.

Instead of the global term "creativity" it seems more useful to think about (1) the "creativity game" (I want to act like a creative person) and (2) the innovating or original performance in any game sequence. The former is a "personal game" and can be coached à la psychotherapy. The teaching of innovating behavior seems to be a simpler behavior-change proposition. You simply use feedback and coach your subjects.

First the game goal must be defined in objective terms. Let us define creative behavior as the production of new combinations of responses which meet a stated criterion of acceptability.

This sort of behavior can be coached. The production of innovating combinations can be made a systematic routine by employing the game model. The procedure is as follows. List all the known roles, rules, rituals, language terms, and strategies of the game being performed. Then systematically permute these into new combinations. Select the most promising of the new combinations and try them out.

Another method for producing novel intergame combinations is to list as many different games as possible along the two axes of an orthogonal grid. Each box defines an intergame or interdisciplinary matrix. We then simply combine terms (role, ritual, strategies, etc.) from each of the two paired games. Among the many combinations most will be eccentric, some poetic, and some useful enough to label the "originator" as a creative performer.

TABLE 1

The Coaching of Creative Performance: Sample Matrix Used for
Production of Novel Intergame Combinations

Biological-Chemical-Physical Play	Chemical-physical	Physico-dynamics	Sexual-physical	Affective physical	Interpersonal physical	Psyco-physical	Physical-economical
	Bio-chemical	Bio-dynamics	Bio-sexual	Bio-affective	Interpersonal biology	Psycho-somatic	Bio-economic
Cultural Games	Intellectual-scientific	Intellectual dynamics	Sexual intellection	Affective intellection	Intellectual interpersonistics	Intellectual cognitive	Intellectual economics
	Social-political	Socio-dynamics	Sexual politics	Political affective	Political interpersonal	Political intellectual	Political economics
	Aesthetic	Aesthetical dynamics	Sexual aesthetics	Affective aesthetics	Interpersonal aesthetics	Cognitive aesthetics	Economic aesthetics
	Philosophical religious	Religious dynamics	Sexual religious	Affective religious	Interpersonal religious	Cognitive religious	Religious economics
	Recreational	Recreational dynamics	Sexual recreational	Affective recreation	Interpersonal recreation	Cognitive recreation	Television, stage, radio
	Occupational-financial	Economical dynamics	Sexual economics	Affective economics	Interpersonal economics	Cognitive economics	Intragame combinations
	Cognitive	Cognitive dynamics	Sexual cognition	Affective cognitive	Interpersonal cognitive	Intragame combinations	IBM
Ego Games	Interpersonal	Interpersonal dynamics	Sexual interpersonalistics	Interpersonal	Intragame combinations	Competitive thinking	Aggressive marketing
	Affective	Affective dynamics	Sexual affective	Intragame combinations	Dependent anxiety	Anxious thinking	Secure job
	Sexual	Sexual dynamics	Intragame combinations	Sexual bliss	Oral nurturance	Phallic mind	Oldest profession
	Psycho-dynamic	Intragame combinations	Repressed orality	Inhibited anxiety	Acted-out rage	Projected intelligence	Introjected wealth
		Psycho-dynamic	Sexual	Affective	Interpersonal	Cognitive	Occupational
	Ego Games						

Table 1 presents a general illustration of this technique. I have employed the grammatical structure of the behavioral index language mentioned in an earlier section of this paper. Index numbers are omitted and category names employed for the sake of simplicity. Three major categories of games are listed: self games, social games, and chemical-

TABLE 1

The Coaching of Creative Performance: Sample Matrix Used for
Production of Novel Intergame Combinations

Recreational-physical	Chemical religion	Aesthetical physical	Physical politics	Intellectual-physical	Bio-physical	Intragame combinations	Chemical physical
Recreational biology	Religious biology	Aesthetic biology	Biology politics	Intellectual biology	Intragame combinations	Electron microscope	Bio-chemical
Intellectual recreation	Theology	Intellectual aesthetics	Intellectual politics	Intragame combinations	Biological theory, well exploited	Physical theory	Intellectual-scientific
Political recreation	Religious politics	Political art	Intragame combinations	Brain trust	Politics of the nervous system	A.E.C.	Social, political
Aesthetic recreation	Religious art	Intragame combinations	Picasso's Dove	The beautiful theory	Tranart	Electronic music	Aesthetics
Religious recreation	Intragame combinations	Gothic art	Religious crusade	Barron Art Scale	Wallace theory of evolution	Leibnitz	Philosophical-religious
Intragame combinations	Notre Dame football	Home art kits	Olympic games	Crossword puzzles	Zoological hobbies	The chemistry set	Recreational
O'Mally's Dodgers	Church bond drive	The art gallery	Oil politics	Academic politics	Drug inustry	Chemical plants	Occupational-financial
Chess	Talmudič thinking	Cerebral art	Communist art	Cognitive theory	Neurological experiments	Magic mushrooms	Cognitive
Cooperative play	Christian love	Beautiful relationship	Massive rehabilitation	Leary's circle	Sheldon's types	Marital thermodynamics	Interpersonal
Happy games	Buddhist serenity	Serene painting	Spanish anguish	Research on moods	Psychosomatics	The unstable nuclei	Affective
Already exploited	Dionysian rites	Folies Bergeres	Latin lovers	Kinsey	The oldest game	Hormones	Sexual
Repressed play	Projected sin	Introjected beauty	Dulles' foreign policy	Rorschach theory	Libido	Freudian thermodynamics	Psycho-Dynamic
Recreational	Religious-philosophic	Aesthetic	Social-political	Intellectual-scientific	Bio-chemical	Chemical-physical	
Cultural Games				Biological-Chemical Physical Play			

physical measures. Self and cultural categories are subdivided. The double-lined boxes running diagonally from lower left to upper right define intracategory combinations. Within each category there are hundreds of games—for example, under occupational-financial, we would list all jobs, economic processes, etc. These can be combined into new combinations.

Above the intradisciplinary diagonal we have listed sample inter-disciplinary combinations which define new intellectual and scientific games. The terms listed are only a small fraction of those possible. Fame in the behavioral sciences usually comes to the shrewd innovator who places old terms in new combinations and applies these to an observed situation. This sort of fame is, it seems to me, an indication of the primitive philosophic and methodological status of the behavioral sciences. Each box in Table 1 contains the seed for dozens of Ph.D. theses and books, and even for new disciplines.

Below the diagonal we find sample combinations of terms, illustrating intergame combinations. Some are traditional; others, new. The list of such terms is endless, and such combinations are best made by system-atic machine methods.

The most efficient use of this method for creating new performance combinations would involve coding the terms from every cultural game on computer cards. The list of game symbols (usually words) and artifacts (also represented by words) is finite and indeed relatively small. Computers could run through all possible game combinations which would then be evaluated for pilot-study trial. I cannot think of any creative performance which could not be facilitated (and, indeed, most performances entirely produced) by machine. Behavior is movement in time/space, and almost all movements in time/space are better per-formed by machine. Personal game behaviors are, of course, excepted from this generalization.

This statement will be considered a derogation or enhancement of human status, depending on your religious point of view. If your values are material, external, game-oriented, then you will be shocked at the statement that creative performance is best done by machines. If your values are spiritual and if you emphasize consciousness, then you will be delighted. Turn over creative performance and game innovation to machines, by all means, and this will provide more time and energy for man to develop new games from the untapped treasure of his internal life! Remember that a machine can create new combinations of old game units, but only a living organism possesses consciousness from which spring new games.

There are trends in modern literature and art which suggest that this same point is occurring to some "creative experiencers." Certainly after

James Joyce's lexicographical experiments (Huxley, 1959), the function of literature must be seen as conventional or innovating manipulations of a rather impoverished set of verbal symbols. This point of view has been advanced by the work of Burroughs and Gysin (1960), whose cut-up technique makes possible intensely effective communications. Burroughs and Gysin take scissors, cut up their own discursive productions, and put the pieces in a hat along with cut-up phrases from other relevant works. They then pull out phrases one by one, and the fortuitous combinations get the message across in powerful strokes. Examples of the first rough draft of this cut up-and-combine technique are presented below without any polishing whatsoever.

Cut the Word Lines with scissors or switch blade as preferred. The Word Lines keep in Time . . . cut the in lines. . . . Make out lines to Space. Take a page of your own writing or a letter or a newspaper article of a page or less or more of any writer living and or dead. . . . Cut into sections. Down the middle. And cross the sides. . . . Rearrange the sections. . . . Write the results message. Who wrote the original words is still there in any rearrangement of his or her whatever words. . . . Can recognize Rimbaud cut up as Rimbaud. . . . A Melville cut up as Melville. . . . Shakespear moves with Shakespear words. . . . So forth anybody can be Rimbaud if he will cut up Rimbaud's words and learn Rimbaud language talk think Rimbaud. . . . And supply reasonably appropriate meat. All dead poets and writers can be reincarnate in different hosts. (Burroughs and Gysin, 1960)

This cut-up method is, of course, a semiautomatic way of doing what poets have done for centuries—arrange shocking new combinations of phrases from unexpected game contexts. Burroughs and Gysin are telling us that the great poets when "cut up" remain themselves. Baudelaire "cut up" remains Baudelaire. The next step in this logical development of the word game is to develop the poetry-writing machine.

Again, one's emotional reaction to these suggestions betrays his religious basis. If you evaluate words in the values of the monotheistic orthodoxies—Talmudic, scholastic, fundamentalist—then you are disturbed by the poetry machine. If you see the human spirit as far transcending (and indeed shackled by) words, then you are pleased at this spirit-freeing development.

In the past few paragraphs I have attempted to summarize too much—a theory and method of behavior change, the application of this theory and method to creative performance, illustrations from empirical studies and *avant garde* literature, and, finally, some speculations about the future spiritual implications of man's intelligence reliance on machines.

THE EXPANSION OF CREATIVE AWARENESS

The only remaining task is to speak briefly about the final issue: the expansion of creative awareness, the constructive alteration of consciousness. This can be done, simply and directly, by the use of hallucinogenic drugs. The research with which I am associated has administered psilocybin to more than four hundred persons, many of whom are emotionally and financially dependent on being creative. I interpret our findings to confirm those presented by Frank Barron (1962b and Chapter 7 herein) and Aldous Huxley (1954, 1956, 1959). Artistic and literary folks respond ecstatically and wisely to drug experience. They tell us that this is what they have been looking for. They revel in the new and intense and direct confrontation with the world about them. Poets and painters have always tortured themselves to transcend ego-space/time boundaries. They do this by every means possible (including psychosis) and have been doing it with and without chemical stimulation for centuries. They are doing it today. I would estimate that well over half of the nonacademic poets, writers, and composers in America today have experimented profitably with consciousness-altering vegetables or synthetics. I exclude our approved national narcotic—alcohol—from this estimate.

Our work with psilocybin has raised some interesting issues with respect to creative vision and creative performance. We have run more than one hundred psilocybin sessions in a maximum security prison. In addition to bringing about significant test changes in the direction of greater socialization and apparently lowering the crime rate (Leary, Metzner, Presnell, Weil, Schwitzgebel, and Kinne, 1963), these sessions have convinced me that the creative vision, the mystical illumination, is not the prerogative of the intellectual or the theologian. It is a function of the cortex when the cortex is temporarily relieved of word and ego games. More than half of our semiliterate prisoners reported in blunt, nonabstract words what have to be interpreted as mystical experiences (Leary and Clark, 1963). In other words we can take a lower-class, uneducated criminal, whose creativity diagnosis would be type 1-A, reproductive blocked (and socially inefficient) and, via psilocybin, he can experience what Blake saw in his visions. It's all there in the cortex after all.

This is to say, we can help him move from type 1 to type 4—creative blocked. But he does not have the language or the literary skills to communicate his vision. He tells us: "Yeah, doc. I saw all these flames of fire, and, wow, I was scared 'cause I knew it meant the end of me, but then, when I realized it can't really hurt because we're all part of the same thing anyway, so I relaxed and went into it and wham, it was like being in heaven or something, out beyond all those little things we're hung up on and then it was like being reborn and . . . ." Reports like this come from the most verbal of our prisoner group. The majority just look us in the eye, shake their heads in awe, and say simply, "Gee, Doc, those mushrooms are really something out of this world."

In terms of the diagnostic schema, the problem is to help the prisoner move from type 4 (creative blocked) to type 3 (creative creator). Here is where the game model helps. We obviously cannot wait fifteen years while the prisoner finishes graduate work in English Literature, that is, learns the literary game. The status and caste distinctions of the intellectual middle class have successfully shut out the lower-class kid from training in verbal felicity. But what we can do is coach him in the creative production of new combinations. We ask him for the major themes of his vision—fire, death, rebirth, the blind ruthlessness of cops, the ineffectiveness of his mother's religious lectures. Not having an IBM storage system, we go to the next best thing—books and articles which contain phrases about these topics, encyclopedia articles on fire, death, and rebirth, religious education, and criminology. We have passages typed out. We cut them up, and a group of convicts sit around a table pulling phrases out of a hat to construct a mystical poem in blank verse.

Creativity is not a function of lucky heritage or elite training. There are more visions in the cortex of each of us than in all the museums and libraries of the world. There is a limitless possibility of new combinations of the old symbols. A true democracy of creativity—experienced and performed—is possible and is, indeed, close at hand.

C (Barron)   In describing the feedback study with art students, I think you should add what we did exactly. We took the scales that measure originality, and with every student we went over item by item the direction of response which he gave and compared it with the scored direction of response. In other words, what the students learned was how the actual measures indicated creative people behaved, item by item. In a sense, what we were doing was educating them to behave in a way that would enable them to answer those questions or take those tests in the same way as the persons who had demonstrated creativity in what they did. And then we had them take the tests again.

In a sense we were "teaching the tests," after they had taken the tests once. The realistic self-appraisal is extremely impressive because very frequently, when you tell a person how a creative individual answers an item, he will say, "Yes, I know that." I might add, right at this point, that I don't think in terms of the game business, but the same process is involved.

Brown has been doing some very interesting work along the same line. He has his subjects take the Barron-Welsh Art Scale. Then he takes a little child's book in which the two main characters are William Elephant and somebody Owl. They come upon a bunch of clothing lying on the beach. They have never seen human clothes before, and the book tells how William Elephant puts this clothing to some very unusual uses. (It is like an unusual test.) Mr. Owl keeps telling the elephant he can't do that, but he does, anyway. Brown has his subjects read this little story.

Then he says, "Now let that part of you which is William Elephant take over and take this art test again." And people know how to respond. That's the whole point.

C   To what degree is there a spread effect, or is this something specific to this test on which you taught them how to perform?

S   I am convinced that the effect will spread to behavior in general. I think that you can take almost anyone if he is motivated and if he is willing to inquire into the matter carefully enough to make the changes which seem indicated. You can specify the ways in which you can produce greater creativity. You can change your behavior within game limits.

C   I thought that in terms of creativity the subjects did not change, that they said, "No, I don't want to change, that is the way I am."

S   Most of them were doing about what they wanted to do. Suppose that you have a person who says, "Yes, I want to be more creative than I am." I think that you can work with that person in these ways.

C   Maybe we need to form a society like Alcoholics Anonymous just to work with those people who want the treatment, who want to be more creative.

C   Why try to get somebody to do something when he doesn't want to?

C   Can't you develop the desire to be creative by changing goals, establishing goals?

C   Yes, that's what is involved in all this.

S   That is exactly the sort of program we developed in our psilocybin therapy program in the state prison. After the prisoners had psilocybin sessions, presumably they had some distance from their own role situation. We faced the problem of how to help those who wanted to change their life patterns. It's no easy matter. We used the game model which was very successful in the prison. Game language makes a good deal of sense to prisoners. A group of prisoners set up a club, a game which was called "Stay Out." They interviewed other prisoners and said in a blunt way, "If you want to join this club, you have to go along with the game goals. The goal of baseball is to make runs; the goal of football is to score touchdowns. But in this particular situation our goal is to *stay out*. And if anyone plays on our team who doesn't want to make

touchdowns, who doesn't want to stay out, then he should quit."
Positions are set up; strategies are planned. Principles such as cooperation are in effect.

    C   It isn't all quite that simple. You could probably persuade people
to change their responses on personality tests if they really wanted to
appear creative and testified that they did. If you instructed them how
to do this, they would then remember what you said and would turn
around and indeed change their test responses. But if you ask them
then to design a dam which will hold back so much water, or present
another sort of problem with more of an ability-type measure, perhaps
they couldn't solve this.

    S   Right. You have to distinguish between motivation and technical
performance. It's impossible for me to hit 61 home runs in Yankee
Stadium in one year, even though I want to play that game.

    C   I just wanted to make what was an obvious point.

    C   What is the subject's perception of time during the drug state?
Does he feel as if it has taken four to five or more hours or as if he may
have been under for half an hour? Does he have any concept of this?

    S   The time sense is dramatically altered. Several thousand things
can occur in seconds. At other times it may seem like centuries between
two events. Space/time is, of course, a learned, artifactual aspect of
our psychological life.

    C   Could you trace the connection of the drugs to the desire to make
a change?

    S   There are several ways in which psilocybin is useful in bringing
about change in prisoners. The first has to do with getting the prisoner
to give up his own professional role, which is just as important to him
as our role is to us. These roles have been carefully and conscientiously
developed. We want to get the prisoners as well as ourselves to flatten
out the association curves, to use Mednick's phrase.

Now prisoners are notoriously the most difficult members of society
to persuade to do this. A psilocybin experience, if it is run in a supportive nonmanipulatory way, is almost guaranteed to undercut these role
commitments. As the subject in Frank Barron's movie said, "Who
is _____?" This is a classic identity reaction of our subjects.
It's as though the ego is seen as one little dot on a huge expanse of other
possibilities.

Intensely close relationships develop among most people who have
had this experience together. In the past, when these visionary experiences were accidental, the social aspects, the group mystic experience,
was never understood. A Dominican father in southern Spain had this
experience in one century, and a Hindu on the bank of the Ganges in

another century. The possibility of communication did not exist. And because the disciplined mystic experience involves a withdrawal from games and social interaction, your monastic or hermit doesn't have people around. The group drug experience allows this to happen.

C   You speak of social experience. Do you give these drugs to several prisoners simultaneously in the same room?

S   Yes.

C   The fact that they can see other possibilities—does this mean that anything different is going to happen, just because they see other possibilities?

S   Not necessarily.

C   Are these other possibilities other types of games, or are they nongame things?

S   When we began this work we knew very little about the contents of mystic experience. It was difficult to put into words, and we couldn't map these experiences or diagram them in three-dimensional space/time. Currently, our main project has to do with a mapping and diagramming of these experiences. The prisoner, ahead of time, can plot on a map his associative hierarchies. He can decide to stay away from some things, and he can attempt to plan which areas of consciousness he wants to go into. Set and setting account for 99% of what happens. We don't talk about "drug effects." We talk instead about "set-setting-plus-drug effects." In the prison we attempted to arrange the setting in such a way that it would stimulate awareness of the issues the prisoner wanted to study.

Here is an example of "game learning" by means of a nongame experience. In the past three months we have given psilocybin to 33 Christian ministers, priests, and some officials of Eastern religions. Twenty-seven of these 33 subjects (who came with a set which was religious and who took the drug in a setting which was aimed at generating these experiences) reported the most intense religious experiences of their life. I cite this as an example of how a disciplined, collaborative preparation determines the setting, and how a serious preparation of set and expectations can alter consciousness in the direction you want to go. This, we recall, is the goal of Eastern philosophy. I see a natural combination here of Eastern and Western points of view. I think that it is possible to get deep creative insights into whatever behavior sequence or professional occupation you are involved in, as, for example, our ministers.

C   You didn't turn any Protestants into Buddhists, did you?

S   Most of the religious subjects reported the most intensive religious experience of their lives, but there was some question as to whether this experience was Christian. The cortex in its nongame traction contact with the life process moves beyond sectarian ritual. Aldous Huxley tells us that every religious ritual and mythology was originally designed to bring about these experiences. I agree.

We are experimenting with different kinds of religious denominations. Some divinity sent floating down our stream a man who was ideally suited to help us. He was an M.D., taking a Ph.D. in a divinity school. A stubborn, idealistic, Midwestern experimentalist who had nothing to do with the drug himself, he determined to test the hypothesis that the drug experience was religious. He did something that none of us would ever have done, a most reckless, audacious scientific performance.

On Good Friday, in the chapel at one of the universities in the Boston area, he had 20 divinity students and 10 experienced project members participating in a double blind study. There was a very experimental manipulation of setting. The subjects were moved from one room to another according to schedule. This was quite contrary to almost all our principles that you shouldn't impose too much marching up and down on subjects, interfering with their own experience. Half of the subjects, including half of the researchers, ingested psilocybin while the rest of the group had nicotinic acid, a placebo which gives mild somatic affects. There was no question as to who was "control" and who was not. If you ever consider running a double blind study with these drugs, you must not have controls around experimental subjects because no one will be fooled. I knew at once that I had placebo. I knew immediately that two subjects in my group had placebo. I could tell by their red faces and their restless "game" activity that they had nicotinic acid. But they thought that they were on the verge of a mystic experience. They were winking, "We're the lucky ones." They started the "drug game," saying, "Isn't this great. The poor fellows in the other room are being left out of it." Later, after we had been in the chapel and saw other subjects reclining on the floor, obviously completely out of this world, the two called me and said, "Let's go back into the other room." They started playing the drug game again: "How long has it been?" "Gee, I thought I had it." "Now what did you feel exactly?"

C   They were still Christians, in other words.

S   A door banged open, and a man walked in, looked out the window, and said, "Magnificent." And he turned without looking at us as he walked out—it was clear that he was not "playing" social games. We all knew who was placebo and who was mystical.

C   Has anyone ever rejected the experience, or indicated that it was not as euphoric as you have described it?

S   Nine per cent of our subjects have reported unpleasant experience.

C   Anxiety arousing or just unpleasant?

S   Most of these subjects fought the experience. For example, in the Good Friday experience there were ten divinity students who had the real thing. One of them fought it all the way. He kept repeating: "Now when is it going to get over? I'm just not in control of myself. Now, didn't you say it would last four hours? When do I start losing the effects? I'm just not in control of myself."

C   Did this person have to work to fight it?

S   Oh, yes, very hard.

C   He didn't go nongame?

S   No.

C   Are the people who fight it also nonhypnotizable by an appropriate scale? Is there any relationship with this need for control?

S   We have not investigated that. I am confident that there would be a correlation. There is a magnificent selectivity operating here because the cortex is a rather accurate instrument. Some people are committed to control themselves in such a way that the notion of ego transcendence or ego loss is threatening. They sense this ahead of time, and they don't volunteer; if they do volunteer, they don't show up or they postpone it. This was the case of the one resistant divinity student. He didn't show up at the first orientation meeting and came late to the second. If it had not been for the social pressure of the divinity school, which was whipped up to a great fervor, he never would have gone through with it.

C   I got from Barron's report the impression that the subject, even though agreeing beforehand that she would dance or paint when the drug came, didn't want to do it and the effects didn't materialize. However, you give the impression that the prisoners could in a sense set themselves a task for the next session and that at this time they were going to determine what the life goal might be. Is this something that happens often? On this point the two reports seem to be in conflict.

S   It is possible that if I had pressed them that they would. But I didn't feel like asking them to do it.

The first session is a very important one. You can't plan for your first session. No matter how much you talk about transcending the ego, giving up the ego game, surrendering to the greater power, when it happens there are always moments of fright. Of course, courage is the key to creativity or to any relinquishing of the structure of the ego and the ego game. So I would never suggest planning a first session except to keep it free from external stimuli. It is obvious to us now that almost as much courage and discipline is needed to explore and control the fantastically rapid space flights through consciousness as in planetary space voyage. It is only after one, two, or three sessions that a person can move with some foresight or planning to the point where he wants to be.

C   Since food habits are often associated with religion, have any religions started to include some of these mushrooms and such as part of their habits so that they can then have this kind of religious experience—either Eastern or Western religions?

S   These drugs have always been used for religious purposes, not as part of the diet but as part of the ceremony. Now pharmacologists are starting to use tryptomines, which provide a one-hour experience. This gets us down to the Sunday morning church service possibility.

C   Almost all the behavior that you have described has been essentially pleasant, positive, exploratory, a wonderful kind of experience. Hasn't there been any violent destructiveness, or hasn't anyone flown off the handle? You mentioned one prisoner who showed a lot of anger and so forth for the first session, but behavior doesn't seem to go amuck.

S   Some hellish experiences do occur in every session, but in general we have found activity of any sort to be considerably subdued.

C   Has there been any study of autonomic behavior during a session? Are physiological changes correlated with this? Generally physiologically, is the drug a depressant except for the cortical activity?

C   There are some physiological side effects, such as a drop in blood pressure and some muscle tonus changes toward more flaccidity. With LSD physiological results have been very close to nothing, even when the subject was reporting a wave of some kind of feeling. This happened in the only case that I have observed. The polygraph went along as though nothing had happened.

C   It makes a difference when the experimenter is able to establish rapport with the subject in repeated administrations, as Jarvik did, for example. For his sixty cases with LSD, he showed there is no decrement in functions such as arithmetic reasoning and various others. A person can, if he makes the effort while under the influence of the drug, return himself to ordinary ego functioning. In certain motor performances, there was a slight decrement.

chapter 9 Process Versus Product in Creativity:
A Spontaneous Discussion of The Conference Participants[1]

Barron It has been assumed in most of our discussion that we can determine whether a person is creative by observing his behavior or discovering what his products are. I should like to point out that this kind of definition is probably basic to the kinds of prejudices that psychologists have. One could just as well construe creativity as an internal process continually in action but not always observable, or perhaps in some cases fundamentally unobservable.

Fiedler Yes, but creativity surely must be identified eventually by its product—no?

Barron No.

Hyman You mean that a person can go through life being creative and nobody will be able to identify him?

Barron Yes, by this type of definition.

Fiedler But not by mine.

Hyman But how are we going to be able to try to identify creativity, then?

McPherson There are about twenty-six definitions (Repucci, 1960). Take your choice.

Barron But I'm not arguing for one definition in preference to others. I'm simply pointing out an implicit assumption in much of our discussion.

---

[1] The discussion on this topic emerged spontaneously after Drevdahl's report at the conference. In accordance with the group's recommendation, this discussion is highlighted as a separate chapter and each participant is identified.

Westcott   What do you mean by an internal process, as opposed to products or the results of processes?

Barron   I think of it as something that is happening in the central nervous system. My own basic interest in research on creativity stems from the hope it offers that one may find in psychic creation the same formal variables that can be used to describe creative process in all of nature. Psychic creation is simply a special case which gives you entree into the problem.

Hyman   Actually, there are several different gradations between "process" and "product." For one thing there's a lot of work now going on in social psychology dealing with cognitive structure that is quite interesting. A lot of good work has been done toward measuring cognitive structure operationally. Rather than talking about organization or Gestalt form in a way that can't be indexed, people are actually measuring such organization. In this way we can discover that a creative product may or may not be the result of a particular way of looking at the world. The product could be an accidental combination, or it could reflect an actual change or reorganization of the way in which a person views the world. The same product, then, could emerge from different cognitive structures. You could see this if you had effective ways to index changes in the meaning and structure of the individual's experience. I think these changes can be indexed with present techniques. I bet that in the next five years we will be routinely measuring elements and changes in cognitive structure. In this way we may be getting very close, actually, to what Barron is talking about.

Westcott   Wouldn't you think that one place where this might be very "studyable" would be in the development of children who, as they grow up, have to discover for themselves and invent for themselves the millions of things that all adults know anyhow? Here this is going on all around, every day, and you don't have to isolate some person in a special condition to study him creating. It is my feeling that children are doing this constantly. The processes whereby they reach the new views of the world are very much, I would think, like the same processes whereby a scientist reaches a new view of his field.

Parnes   Learning is creating, and creating is learning.

Westcott   I think that it occurs particularly at a cognitive level in children's language learning.

Mullins   You say that no product is necessary for creativity. How do you define product? Is it some useful product, or is there no sign of a product?

Barron   It would of course be unusual to find no evidence of creativity in behavior even though creative process was occurring, but I would argue that this sometimes happens—that is, that no sign of it appears.

McPherson   Even to the person himself?

Barron   He might not be able to compare himself sufficiently with others to see the signs.

McPherson   Do you think that he might be creative but not know that he was creative?

Barron   Yes.

Fiedler   But how do you operationally define this?

Barron   I cannot without considerable further thought offer an operational definition of creative process occurring in the central nervous system without evidence in behavior and without the fact of its occurrence being known subjectively.   Yet from analogy to other internal processes of which we are unaware I shouldn't think this to be impossible in principle.

Parnes   But wouldn't the person know that something is happening, whether he would call it creativity or not?

Leary   I can't understand how there can be any question about what Barron is saying.   I can't understand how anybody would disagree with him.

Guilford   It is not very clear what he means.

Leary   Well, maybe that's why.

Barron   I'm sorry I brought this question up, but I just wanted to point to the prevalence of a prejudice in favor of a narrow operationism in this discussion.

Levine   Sprecher reports that somebody asked an engineer about his creativity, but he didn't consider himself as being creative.   Everybody else said that he was.   His approach was novel.   He was solving problems.   But the engineer didn't think that he was creative—he was just doing his job (see Chapter 19).

Guilford   Maybe what he thought was meant was, "Do you write poetry?"

Sprecher   No, he said, "I'm doing things which are routine to a scientist or a knowledgeable person with my background.   These other people think I'm wonderful in producing novel ideas."   He had a good opinion of himself, but he said, "The things that they praise about me are developed."

Barron   Let me add a couple of reflections to what I have said about internal process.   For example, take the clinical study of epilepsy.   A common way of thinking about epilepsy is to consider only that person to be epileptic who has epileptic seizures.   My view is that the internal epileptic event, which at times erupts in a visible seizure, is occurring constantly. And in the creative person, millions and millions of relevant internal events are occurring although you may see only twenty things that are noticeable over a lifetime. We call these creative acts. But behind those few noticeable events are millions and millions of decisions which are constantly demanded of all of us from childhood on. These decisions form the basis of associational patterns which then become part of the reservoir of thought from which visible creative products are finally drawn. I think that the creative process goes on very often in persons who don't consider themselves to be creative. This may include individuals who get classified in our researches as members of a non-productive and hence noncreative group, simply because for some reason they don't put out, in visible form, actual creative acts.

Westcott I think that the only thing we can say is that if a person does put out productive creative materials, then it seems possible that he's indulging in creativity. But if he doesn't do this, or you don't see any of these products, if he doesn't manifest any of this, then you really don't know what to say about him.

Barron Yes, there are virtually no false positives in identifying "creatives," but there may be a great many false negatives (true creatives not identified).

Hyman But we are arguing on the basis of operational evidence, just as a physicist argues that, given certain kinds of evidence, in order to make a complete picture of the world he has to postulate antimatter and other entities which he will never see, never directly experience. But he does this on the basis of operational evidence.

Holland May I enter another prejudice for this prejudiced point of view? If you'll assume that there is this phenomenon which we cannot identify but which goes on, and if you'll assume that the purpose of science is to help us adapt, and if we cannot communicate what we can't see, hear, or feel, we might as well quit and there's no point to this discussion. I think that most people have accepted a kind of operationalism as the only way to carry on. Now, if you're talking about the severe kinds of operationalism, then I'm with you. But if you leave no room for it, we part company here.

Barron I must admit that I study the clear positive cases and that I do not worry particularly about the cases that I don't know about. Perhaps I should.

Taylor I want to mention that no great progress has been made since the 1961 report, in which the issue of process versus product is just as wide open. I guess the way to express Barron's idea is that we're all sitting on an earthquake which in one sense hasn't happened yet, but which in another sense is really building up beneath the surface right now.

Sprecher   Let me muddy the waters a little bit more by saying, in contrast to Barron's assertion that there are no false positives, people who produce creative acts or novel acts without having creative thinking, that there are such, as one man has urged in the area of chemistry, where by routine combination of many known substances a person can produce a new substance, by doing it on a technician level. Now I would eliminate the false positives by saying, "Look, you can be creative by going about it in a routine, plodding, technician way," and so I would expand my definition of creativity (I've seen lots of shaking of heads around here, but you're all wrong) to say that a person can be creative in the sense that he produces a novel product by a very routine, plodding, technician way, with perhaps little thought. Now that's my contribution.

Levine   Remember the engineers who produced eighteen patents in one month because they were asked to. The patents were assumed to measure novelty or creativity. Some may have come about through work simplification, a definite technique which supposedly produces new ideas.

Mednick   I will bet that many technicians have produced hundreds of miraculous substances only to pour them down the drain without realizing their value. It would not surprise me in the least if most biochemists spend their days tripping over drugs which could cure cancer but simply do not realize it. What I mean to say is that recognizing the usefulness of a product is an important part of the creative act. The question that no one asked me when I discussed my notions relating to creativity was, "How is it that a person who is creative can pick the appropriate combination of associations from the many, many he has presented to him?" It seems to me that this is a crucial question.

Sprecher   Edison's trial and error of many substances produced the filament for the light bulb which would last.

Hyman   If you read Edison's story, you'll see that it's not trial and error.

Sprecher   Yes, it is. It's a very deliberate research of many substances. Well, it's not trial and error in that sense, but it's technician's search.

Hyman   How did he know when to stop?

Sprecher   By a very routine test.

Hyman   Edison's criterion was a complete system of what he needed to find. He had a very clear-cut planned strategy.

Sprecher   No, I've read Josephson's biography of Edison, too, if that's what you're talking about. I'm not referring to the fact that he had a grand conceptual scheme which would encompass more than the light bulb. I'm talking about the fact that in one specific sense he had a problem to solve: "I want this darn filament to last."

Hyman   He had all the specifications of exactly what he wanted in that filament, too.

Sprecher   Then he produced this novel, valuable product in a routine way by just collecting all possible materials in encyclopedic fashion.

Hyman   But first he formulated the complete problem of exactly what he wanted and how he would recognize the product even before he saw it. It is this formulation of a context for searching and for evaluation of his trials that I want to emphasize.

Leary   The formulation could be done by committee. The formulation could be eventually executed by machine. I venture to predict that creative performance or the production of creative expressions will increasingly be seen as a systematic combining of elements which have not been combined before. This again can probably be done best by a machine, and the criterion of when to stop can be worked out by machine, too. Many people who are seen as creative writers, artists, and so forth are technicians who have wanted to be creative, wanted to play the creative game, and fiddled around rearranging symbols. Henry Miller's chapter in Ghiselin's book (1955) is a very nice account of how this author went at the technical problems of being a creative writer. He experimented extensively with imitations of other authors. Finally, he quit imitating, plunged deeply into the "ocean of reality" on his own, and went on to what I would call a creative experience.

Taylor   Can the machines get the illumination that Edison got?

Westcott   Recently some poetry which won a prize was written with the aid of a random number table and a thesaurus.

Fiedler   The computer Illiac has written a symphony.

Parnes   What determines what's fed into the computer?

McPherson   There is an auxiliary computer.

Hyman   Wasn't this the answer to a creative act when the poetry was selected by some group?

Westcott   I don't honestly know, but I would imagine so. Well, it was selected by judges to win a prize. I hear that somebody else is painting by formula.

Barron   Then there's the fellow, the subject of a recent "profile" in the *New Yorker* magazine, who produces modern paintings by machines. He has a machine with paper rolling out of it and brushes, and also something that cuts out the paintings and stacks them up when they're done. He built a tremendous, elaborate machine recently in the courtyard of the Museum of Modern Art. It took him about two months or so. He built it so that it would destroy itself in a noisy and fiery fashion, rather than reproduce itself.

Holland We have a place in Chicago where you buy your own paints and drop them down on a spinning wheel. You can get some very nice pictures.

Hyman Leary, the point that you're making is that, if you can explain the process a man uses and duplicate it with a machine in some way, then that's not creativity. You feel that creativity is some kind of—well, whatever it is I don't know—but something that man can't simulate on a machine, is that it?

Leary I'm distinguishing between the creative experience or the creative process, and the so-called creative product.

Harmon Couldn't you perhaps duplicate these same processes on a machine and, if you did a good simulation, have a creative process— when there's a human being involved?

Barron That's a critical point. If you can get a proper, full description of the creative process, can it be entirely mechanical?

Hyman It's possible that a mechanism already exists but that we don't know it by your criterion. In other words, our machines may already be creative and we don't know it.

Taylor That's the way our computers behave sometimes.

Westcott Isn't it true that a machine that produces some of these kinds of things, or designs something, or writes symphonies, or makes all these associative combinations, does almost infinitely more work than a human being does in accomplishing a comparable end? Well, from what we know about the machines they can whir . . . and in fifteen seconds do five years' work.

Barron But only on what's fed into them. *We* do more work than anything else in the universe—we are the biggest workers.

Westcott As far as explicit combining of a great number of possible associates, the machines can do this. I think that we can't.

Parnes That is, once the associates are determined.

Hyman The new machines with the heuristics built in are better for this purpose.

Parnes May I give you a simple example. Machines are being used for finding new names for drug products, simply by combinations of letters. These machines would never come up with the name "Brand X." You see what I mean?

Westcott Well, if you feed in all the letters and come out with all six-letter combinations, you'll come up with "Brand X" sometime.

Parnes   Only if you predetermine that spaces, as well as letters, are to be used by the machine. But, of course, if you did that, how many combinations are there for the machine to create? I'm not a mathematician, but I'm sure that the number of combinations conceivable before coming to "Brand X" would be phenomenal!

Leary   There is a finite number of combinations because there are only twenty-six letters in the alphabet. There are less than a hundred thousand functional words in Webster's dictionary. Each word has an associative network that can be determined by a very simple empirical study, so that "red," for example, has a cluster of associations to it. All this can be very simply fed in, and then the poetry can be printed out.

Parnes   Did you say there's a finite amount that can be fed in?

Leary   Well, how many symbols are there?

Parnes   But the machine can relate only those elements that are fed into it. If the programmer says only, "Spit out all conceivable six-letter combinations," and the machine does this, it will ultimately spell "Brandx" but not "Brand X." The conglomeration of letters "Brandx" in a list of thousands might look like nothing more to a person reading the list than some of the other weird combinations. But in thinking of single-word names for the product, the human being might get the association "Brand X" in his mind and recognize it as a suitable term even though it did not satisfy the *exact* original requirements as stated ("one word"). The machine could not do this. It would stick rigidly with what it was "told" to do. This is what I meant when I said that the machine would never come up with the name "Brand X." Its associative processes are limited to what is fed into it; the human being's are *infinite.* You never know, in the creative human mind, when what *seems* irrelevant will become relevant. You couldn't exactly duplicate the creative mind in a machine unless you were able to increase its number of associations to an *infinite* number.

Leary   How many games are there that human beings play?

Taylor   You can define X differently every time you use it.

Wight   Doesn't some poetry deal with very remote associations that might not be fed into this machine?

Leary   Actually, remote associates are already being generated mechanically. Mednick mentioned that point in the case of his scientist friend who cut up things and let them recombine. As reported in the previous chapter, we experimented with cut-up recombinations with convicts who've had mystical experiences and who can't report them because they don't have adequate vocabulary. We can sometimes come out with very striking images which reduce this tremendous gap between experience and the expressive communication of it which has bothered all of us for a long time.

Mednick   I think that the role of random behavior in the construction of this "cut-up" poetry is a bit exaggerated. Clearly it does not take much creativity to slice up newspapers; only neatness is important. Thus anybody who is neat can create *original* poetry, and it does not mean a damn thing. The creative act in "cut-up" poetry occurs once after the fiftieth rearrangement of the cut-up words. The constructor has an "ah-ha!" experience and selects this order of words as meeting some requirements. Incidentally this is a way of assessing degree of creativity; that is, the more requirements a product meets, the more creative the product is.

Sprecher   You are saying that this is creativity for Mednick. This is legitimate, so long as you recognize it as yours, but allow other people to define creativity however they wish.

Leary   I think this problem can be resolved because creativity always occurs in terms of some game goal. Now the goal of the game of poetry can be to get the poem accepted by the *Saturday Review*. That's an easy criterion. That's no problem.

Mednick   Let me expand on the question of requirements a bit more. I believe that we can judge how creative a product is by the number of requirements that it meets. This sounds very simple-minded perhaps, but it meets a minimum requirement itself in that it begins to be a researchable definition. Besides it raises some questions which ordinarily might not be considered. For example, is poetry creative? Is painting creative? Except under special circumstances, in terms of this definition the answer to these questions must be no. In terms of the definition, except under special circumstances it is difficult to specify what reliable requirements such products meet.

Biettel   Yes, that's a good point. I was going to mention it. I can see why we perhaps study architects and painters, because painters have set themselves a problem of constant innovation, at present. I want to throw in one more thing. Our culture is heavy in this expressionistic ego-centered feedback with the problem. I like the point that Murray made in the essay in the Michigan symposium about what he called "biotic" creativity. He thought that there was a way to transfer this into the social realm where you don't have the ego-centered relationship to product. I think that type of transfer presents some hope as an image, for the feedback would concern an almost pure process and the product would be a little bit sharable, in a sense.

Westcott   Certainly, in the realm of haikai poetry, a requirement of usefulness is not directly met, so Mednick suggests that it falls outside of this criterion. I wonder whether this criterion does not fit in this case in the sense of the particular task that the artist or the poet is trying to accomplish.

Mednick If you can reliably specify this task, then you have a researchable problem. It seems likely to me that often the aim of a particular artistic work was to communicate a given emotional state to a given group of people. In this case we can ask, Does the painting do this? Yes, it does? It does it beautifully? Then it is wonderful.

McPherson What about time? It might do it at one time and not at another.

Westcott Yes, this is true.

Taylor I'm sure that we can't solve many things here, but there is merit in getting the issues out on the table, as all of you have just done. And I suggest you note our studies wherein we obtained at least crude measures, separately, for processes and for products and found the relationships between each of these (see Chapter 3, Chapter 16, especially score #39, and Taylor, Smith, Ghiselin, and Ellison, 1961).

part III Education and Development of Creativity

chapter 10 The Minnesota Studies of Creative Thinking: 1959–62

E. Paul Torrance, Bureau of Educational Research,
University of Minnesota

S Since the 1959 University of Utah Research Confer-
ence on the Identification of Creative Scientific Talent, our studies of
creative thinking have continued to carry us into devious directions, at
all levels of education, into a variety of disciplines, into many different
kinds of schools both within the United States and in twelve countries
outside the United States, and into the use of a variety of research
techniques. We have continued to give some attention to problems of
measurement, including the creation of new kinds of tasks, experimentation with various types of instructions and administration procedures
and various scoring procedures, and studies of test-retest reliability and
validity. We have continued to study the developmental process in
various types of schools in the United States. In an attempt to understand some of the more puzzling aspects of this process, we have conducted experiments of the course through which children seek consensual
validation from their peers and surrender much of their imaginativeness
and independence of judgment, and we have studied the developmental
process in several cultures outside the United States. A greater portion
of our efforts, however, has gone into studies of the conditions which
will favor creative growth and give creative talent a better chance to
flourish. Our concern has continued to be both with forces in personality, nature, and society and with factors which can be controlled in
the classroom, laboratory, or office. We have also begun creating and
testing instructional materials which we hope will lend themselves to a
variety of creative uses by teachers.

125

In this paper, I had planned to present primarily a summary concerning identification, since this conference series has heretofore stressed the identification problem. However, since some of you are interested in problems of education, I shall omit part of the material that I had planned to give concerning identification and spend more time on some of the education problems, since these have been my own major interest.

PROBLEMS OF MEASUREMENT

Although my primary concern has been to discover what conditions are most desirable for developing and using whatever creative talents individuals possess, the strongest pressures have been toward identification and measurement. During the past year, we have received something over 1,500 inquiries concerning tests of creative thinking. In fact, about 43% of our correspondence has dealt with problems of measuring the creative thinking abilities, rather than doing something with whatever creative talent one has. This has almost forced us to give far more attention to problems of measurement than we had intended. We recognize, however, that we must continue to solve measurement problems in order to make possible progress toward our major objectives and to permit others to study similar problems.

Task development

First, I would like to mention a few of the ideas that we have been dealing with concerning problems of task development since they represent something of a departure from the techniques that we have heard about thus far in the conference.

Since 1959, we have become increasingly aware of the need for enlarging the scope of the tasks used in assessing the creative thinking abilities by including a greater variety of stimuli, involving a larger number of senses, and expanding the limits of the kinds of observations made of task performance. We have tended in the direction of complex tasks having built-in features which make use of what we know about the nature of creative thinking. We have continued to increase our repertoire of nonverbal tasks. To the Circles task, we have added the Squares task, the Parallel Lines task, various versions of the Incomplete Figures Test, the Picture Construction or Shape task (popularly called the Jellybean or the Teardrop Test), a Manipulative Design task, the Science Toy task, and others.

From the very outset, we have used objects which could be manipulated for such tasks as the Product Improvement task and we have used pictures for the Ask-and-Guess Test. We have now adapted the concept of the Consequences task by presenting the improbable situations along with drawings and calling it the "Just Suppose Test," for more appeal and usability with younger children as early as kindergarten. The Sounds and Images Test makes use of tape-recorded sound effects, a progressive series of warm-ups, and other features.

We have also found that we can change the nature of a test task by changing the instructions, the timing, or some other feature. In a three-task nonverbal battery, the first task, Picture Construction, is designed to stimulate originality and elaboration. The ten-minute time limit is more than most children will use. The elaborators, however, do not have enough time, and some of the highly fluent and highly original individuals keep thinking of new ideas, either adding to or completely changing their first idea. The two succeeding tasks increasingly bring out greater variability among the fluents, the flexibles, the originals, and the elaborators. There is not enough time to complete all the possible units and make all of them elaborate, so some compromises have to be made. The Sounds and Images Test was presented with and without cues or examples as a part of the warm-up and with and without invitations to regress. Versions were also produced to appeal to imagination as related to all the senses. No one yet has made any real inroads upon the problem of how many tasks, of what length and variety of stimuli and responses, are necessary to obtain an adequate assessment of creative potential.

Test administration

The issues surrounding individual, oral administration versus group, written administration continue to bother us, especially with tasks requiring multiple verbal responses.

Although the problem is more serious in working with children, we still have tremendous individual differences even among graduate students in ability to write down one's ideas. At the fourth-grade level, scores on group-administered tests of creative thinking correlate more closely with scores on tests of intelligence and achievement than do scores on individually administered tests. At this level it is doubtful, however, that the group test is "really" a test of creative thinking.

Even at the ninth-grade level, there is almost no relationship between scores on tests of intelligence and group measures of creative thinking within the ranges of the upper 25% in intelligence, but there is a relatively high relationship between these two variables within the lower 25% in intelligence. These results may occur because the group test of creative thinking does not give a valid measure of the creative thinking abilities of these children at the lower IQ range because of their test-taking skills, their reading abilities, and their ability to write and to

put their ideas into words. On the Ask-and-Guess Test, test-retest reliabilities range from .46 to .61 in grades four through six when one test
is a written one and the other an oral one, whereas the relationships
range from .75 to .85 when both administrations are written, even with
different stimulus pictures and with a time interval of one year between
testings. As we have begun to explore the possible clinical use of tests
of the creative thinking abilities, it is our opinion that we shall find it
desirable to use both oral and written performances. Individual administration is, of course, quite expensive. Having pupils dictate their
responses in the booths of foreign language laboratories has been tried
and apparently produces improved performance with the various flu-
encies and originality but does not reduce testing expenses greatly.

In the administration of tests of this type, the giving of clues or
examples is an issue. We are just now working out this problem, and
the indications are that giving examples reduces the originality score
and increases the fluency score. A similar issue pertains to emphasis
upon quantity as opposed to some quality like "clever, unusual, and
original." In one study, we obtained indications that instructions to
give "clever, unusual, and original" responses actually freed children
below the fourth grade to give a larger number of responses but that the
tendency was reversed, though not significantly, above the fourth grade.
In another study, when fluency and originality were differentially rewarded, we gave a prize of $2.00 to the one who produced the most
original ideas and $.25 to the one who produced the largest number of
ideas. In the other group the reward was reversed by giving a prize
of $2.00 to the one who produced the largest number of ideas and $.25
to the one who had the largest number of original ideas. We found that
this emphasis on originality in the first group increased the originality
of responses quite decidedly without significantly influencing the fluency,
the sheer quantity of ideas.

We are anxious to do more experimentation with different time limits
for the same tasks. Not only will we be interested in the differences in
scores on such qualities as fluency, flexibility, originality, and elaboration, but also in determining what time limit produces what type of
validity.

A similar issue is involved in determining the most desirable length
of a battery of tasks to be administered at a single setting. In adminis-
tering batteries of about one hour in length, we have noted that many
individuals reduce both the quantity and quality of their production
near the end whereas others maintain about the same pace as at the
outset. Knowing this, we must ask, "Does performance on the first

tasks yield a better index of potentiality than does performance on the last tasks?" or "Does performance on a lengthy battery administered at one sitting yield a better index of potentiality than does performance on the same battery administered at two or three different sittings?" Perhaps a better question would be, "What kinds of potentiality does each condition enable us to identify?" So far as I know, very little inroad has been made on this kind of problem.

Test scoring

We have constantly experimented with different schemes for scoring responses obtained to the tasks which have been developed. At first we were inclined to score the responses to a single task in as many ways as we could think of, including not only such qualities as fluency, flexibility, originality, and elaboration, but also communication, inventivlevel, constructiveness, penetration, resistance to closure, and the like. We knew that such elaborate scoring would be prohibitive in a practical situation but felt that we must go through this phase to determine what kind of scoring would produce the best "pay off." The scoring task became so overwhelming, however, that we had to abandon most of this plan before we obtained our answer. More recent efforts have been in the direction of simplification and systematization. This has increased the speed and interscorer reliability of scoring on most of the tasks, but we must determine how it affects the validity, diagnostic value, and the like of the measures.

Test-retest reliability

In general, test-retest reliabilities after two weeks, three months, eight months, and twelve months have been reasonably satisfactory. Battery totals have in general been quite satisfactory; in the intermediate grades and with college students these have been around 0.88, even with alternate forms of the stimulus materials. In the primary grades reliability coefficients for battery totals have ranged from the upper 0.40's to the upper 0.60's. Test-retest reliabilities for single tasks or for single scores are of course lower. In a sample of college seniors after a lapse of three months, the test-retest reliabilities for single tasks ranged from 0.68 to 0.85 and for single scores from 0.56 to 0.85. In the primary grades, test-retest reliabilities for single tasks and scores in some cases drop into the 0.30's. I am not so concerned about the lack of reliability of the tests in the primary grades as I am about some of the conditions and things which happen to children to cause this low reliability in scores.

Validity

In designing test tasks, working out instructions, and developing scoring systems, we have endeavored to build into them characteristics which make use of the best that we know about the creative processes as they have been revealed in the history of invention, discovery, and other kinds of creative achievement, as well as the results of experiments such as Maltzman's (1960), Gordon's (1961), and others. Most of our attempts to establish some type of validity for our measures have involved one or the other of the following two approaches:

1. Identifying high and low groups on some test measure and then determining whether or not they can be differentiated in terms of behavior which can be regarded as "creative."
2. Identifying criterion groups on some behavior regarded as creative and then determining whether or not they can be differentiated by test scores.

Using the first procedure, we found at the elementary school level that children who achieved high scores on the tests of creative thinking also initiated a larger number of ideas in small-group problems involving creative problem solving than did their less creative peers. When matched for intelligence, sex, race, and teacher, the most creative children proved far more frequently than their controls to have reputations for having wild or fantastic ideas, and to produce drawings and other products judged as "off the beaten track," and work characterized by humor, playfulness, relative lack of rigidity, and relaxation. Weisberg and Springer (1961), using these same tests of creative thinking with gifted (high-IQ) fourth graders, compared the most creative with the least creative. Through psychiatric interviews, the highly creative children were rated significantly higher on strength of self-image, ease of early recall, humor, availability of Oedipal anxiety, and uneven ego development. On the Rorschach they showed a tendency toward unconventional responses, unreal percepts, and fanciful and imaginative treatment of the blots. Their Rorschach responses described them as being both more sensitive and more independent than their less creative peers.

Using this same approach, a group of high-scoring general business teachers were found to behave dramatically different in the classroom from a group of their less creative peers. They asked more questions, asked a greater variety of kinds of questions, gave more illustrations of key concepts, interacted more with their students, and the like.

Through numerous partial replications of the Getzels and Jackson (1962) studies, it has also become clear that tests of creative thinking and tests of intelligence or scholastic aptitude identify different types of individuals. The ways in which they are different describe those high on the measures of creative thinking in ways which might generally be regarded as "creative." They are seen by their teachers as less desirable as pupils, as more difficult to get to know, and as more playful and less ambitious. They choose occupations which are regarded as unconventional or rare and express values which are different from those of their teachers.

Using the Minnesota tests, Fleming and Weintraub (1962) obtained a coefficient of correlation of -0.41 (significant at the .01 level) between six of the verbal tasks and a measure of rigidity, a construct defined in terms of inflexibility, stereotypy, intolerance of ambiguity, and a compulsive need for order.

Using the approach of identifying criterion groups regarded as highly creative or noncreative, we have accumulated several encouraging bits of validity evidence. Children nominated by their teachers on various criteria of creative thinking, curiosity, and the like achieved higher scores on the test of creative thinking than did their peers who were not so nominated or who were nominated as being especially low on the criterion in question. Above the third grade, pupils receiving a large number of peer nominations on various criteria of creative thinking achieved higher scores on the tests of creative thinking than did those who received no nominations. At the high school level, our best validity evidence comes from peer nominations, especially if we use the same criteria in asking for nominations that we use in scoring the tests, that is, ideational fluency (nominating those having a large number of ideas), flexibility (nominating those using a variety of approaches or strategies), originality (nominating those having unusual, surprising, off-the-beaten-track ideas), elaboration, and the like.

At the college level, indications of validity have come from original-idea projects, scores on subject-matter tests requiring creative problem solving, self-initiated learning, and faculty nominations in a technical college where there are numerous opportunities for creative achievements of various kinds.

Highly productive saleswomen in a large department store (Wallace, 1961) scored significantly higher on a battery of creative thinking tasks than did their less productive peers in the same departments. A sample of mental patients, diagnosed as schizophrenic and judged to be on the road to recovery at the time of the testing, exhibited on the tests extreme inflexibility, frequently blocked so that they were unable to produce responses, and produced responses which were obvious, banal, and safe rather than original.

In a pilot study, we differentiated high and low groups of children on a nonverbal Circles task of creative thinking and studied their language behavior as manifested in imaginative stories. The more creative children wrote longer stories, used a greater number of different words, and more frequently used first-person pronouns and other words showing personal involvement, verbs like "said" and "was," conjunctions indicating cause or consequence, and the like.

Nontest ways of identifying creative talent

Although we consider the validity evidence which I have cited as encouraging, I believe that we need to give more careful attention to nontest ways of identifying creative talent. I have already pointed out some of the difficulties some highly creative children have in writing down their ideas. Others, of course, are far more successful in expressing their ideas on paper than they are in communicating them orally or through manipulative kinds of activities. The immediate testing conditions, personality disturbances, unfavorable reactions to time pressures, and the like prevent some highly creative individuals from revealing their creative potential through tests. Holland has reported the use of indicators of creative achievement in high school, and we have done some exploratory work with various kinds of check lists of creative activities, life experience inventories, reading questionnaires, and the like.

In order to identify creative thinkers, most teachers have to redefine some of their concepts and reassess some of their values. Recently I asked two teachers of gifted sixth graders to give me the names of the five most and the five least creative children in their classrooms. To help them in this redefinition process, we used Wallace and Ethel Maw's (1961) criteria of curiosity. Both these teachers commented that they had never before thought of their pupils in this way and admitted that they were forced to place in the low group some of the children whom they valued most as pupils because they were so good in arithmetic computation, spelling, and the like. They felt quite guilty in placing these "prize" pupils in the low group on this curiosity criterion. Quite interestingly, we obtained exellent differentiations on all our measures of creative thinking between the two groups of children nominated as most and least curious. There was almost no overlap between them.

I could give you many examples of how our thinking has taken shape about these nontest ways. I have one that I would like to tell you about, because it was through this example that some of my own feelings about this became clarified.

I first started thinking of this need for redefinition after we had administered our first battery of creative thinking tests in our first school. A third-grade teacher commented that the study had helped the whole school whether our research revealed anything or not. She said, "You have changed the entire way we look at children's behavior. For example, we no longer think of children as being naughty but as creating ideas for being naughty." As I thought about the matter, I began to see what a difference it makes in the way teachers treat children, whether they see them as *being* naughty or as *creating* ideas for being naughty.

The significance of this redefinition became even clearer to me through the experience of a teacher in the industrial arts field in college. He caught one of his students cheating on an examination. The methods he used in cheating, however, were so clever and ingenious that the instructor immediately recognized that he was dealing with an exceptionally talented and creative individual. Suddenly he realized that his assignments had called only for reproductive thinking and that this student had done nothing more than to find more ingenious ways of doing this. As a teacher, he had done nothing to challenge his pupil's unusual talent. Instead of giving this cheater an automatic failing grade or expelling him from the class, the teacher began thinking up more and more difficult problems calling for creative problem solving. The boy began working as he had never worked before. At the end of the course, his achievement was so far ahead of everyone else's in the class that the instructor felt compelled to award him a final grade of A. Here is an example of how the identification of this student's unusual talent required a modification of the teacher's usual definition of the meaning of certain kinds of behavior.

When I use this example with teachers I get into all kinds of arguments. Some say that this is what is happening in higher education and is causing moral depravity of college students, and they heap all kinds of censure on the professors. I can't refrain from asking them, "Which is more immoral, to fail to recognize one's own failure to challenge and develop creative-like talents or to fail to punish this kind of behavior?" I could preach a couple of sermons on this punitive concept in American education, but I will refrain.

It is also well-known that some students lead a double life. They behave quite noncreatively at school and quite creatively in the remainder of their world. In the two or three hundred letters that I have received from parents, there have been some excellent illustrations in which the parents, in fact, have very good insights into this double life which children lead. Such a case is beautifully illustrated in the following excerpts from the letter of a mother whose son apparently falls into this category:

He is now 13 years old and has had a steadily declining academic record that ended in his being retained in the seventh grade this year. . . . He has a burning *main* interest in electronics and rocks and believe me, his knowledge and interest in these two subjects is great.

His teachers, principals, and counselors have told me a confusing variety of things (confusing to me anyway). They all agree he is very bright, very bored (daydreams in class constantly), and very withdrawn though not rebellious. Two teachers have told me the school has destroyed his desire to learn. One teacher told me the school cannot help him because the only "special cases" they are informed enough to help are the "slow" children. Another teacher said to me, "I'll make him work if I have to break his spirit to do it—and ridiculing and shaming him is the only way with children like him. . . ." Last spring the school counselor and principal decided that flunking him was the only way to make him "buckle down and work or else." . . . He can't join the different types of science clubs because he doesn't have a B average—to which the principal urged that he take up football.

Now, I will tell you of the boy *I* know, my son. . . . He is an irresponsible scatterbrain—he just can't harness his brain to such unimportant things as taking out the trash when he's hot on the trail of discovering perpetual motion. He *never* daydreams, *loves* to learn, and is always getting books from the library. He is a hard worker; many times he almost collapsed trying to work an experiment late in the night. He has energy enough for ten people. He has an outgoing, bubbling personality and a terrific sense of humor. All this he is at home and in the rest of the world *until* he gets to school. . . .

A youngster such as this mother describes may or may not rise to the occasion when a test of creative thinking is administered. I am sure that a great deal would depend upon the quality of the relationship established by the examiner, the adequacy of the warm-up process, and the like.

Factor analyses

Thus far, we have run three different factor analyses involving scores on a variety of tasks. Although we have obtained important information from each of them, we have never included a great enough variety of scores to produce a really satisfactory factor analysis.

Availability for general use

Although the pressures have been rather great, we have not yet made available for general use any battery of the tests we have been developing. We have given perhaps a couple of hundred individuals and agencies permission to use them in research and experimental programs. A great deal more of the developmental work which I have just described needs to be done. Certainly we must have more complete norms than we now have. With these we might possibly be justified in making available for general use some kind of an interim battery or research edition. Although the definition of creative thinking which has guided the development of these tasks may not satisfy some individuals, I feel rather confident that high scores derived from them identify individuals who behave in ways which are commonly regarded as creative and that individuals who behave in ways commonly considered as creative achieve higher scores than individuals identified as behaving in relatively uncreative ways.

DEVELOPMENT

I reported some preliminary findings or developmental curves at the 1959 Utah conference. This attempt to establish developmental curves has been expanded and continued. We believe that we can now describe the typical developmental curve in the United States. It is based on data from studies by Andrews of preschool children and research by me and my associates on elementary, secondary, and university students.

Beginning at age 3 there is an increase until a peak is reached at about the age of $4\frac{1}{2}$ years. A drop occurs at age 5, about the time the child enters the kindergarten, and is followed by increases in the first, second, and third grades. At about age 9, near the end of the third grade or at the beginning of the fourth grade, there is a rather severe decrement in almost all the creative thinking abilities. Then comes a period of recovery, especially for girls in the fifth grade. This recovery, however, is largely in fluency and not in originality. The recovery in originality comes mainly in the sixth grade. After this, there is another decrease in the seventh grade with recovery in the eighth and continued growth until a peak is reached in the eleventh grade. After this, there is a leveling off or slight drop near the end of the high school period. As we looked into the literature, we found that these phenomena had been observed by many people.

We have tried to get underneath this problem as to whether or not these are phenomena that we have to accept—that these are developmental things that we just have to put up with and wait until recovery sets in. We thought that we might obtain some useful clues about this problem by studying the developmental process in other cultures. We are now nearing the completion of our data analysis for six cultures outside of our typical American culture. One of our groups is in western Samoa. This group actually divides itself into two subgroups, one from the schools in the larger towns of western Samoa which have been influenced a great deal by the mission schools, and one from the schools out in the remote areas—the government schools—which have been relatively untouched by the mission influences and the New Zealand and American influences. Similarly, in India we have developmental data from several subculture groups, from some of the Moslem schools, from some of the Christian schools, from some of the public schools— one particularly founded on the educational philosophy of Mahatma Gandhi—and the Sikh schools. In Australia we are getting both a rural and an urban sample. In Germany, unfortunately, we are getting only an urban sample. For Norway, where we have not analyzed the data, we have both a rural and an urban sample. We find different developmental phenomena taking place in these cultures. In brief we find that in cultures or subcultures where there are few discontinuities there is no drop in these developmental curves. In cultures which have the cultural discontinuities, as our culture has, at about ages 5, 9, and 13 we find these drops.

C   What determinations go into your plotting this devlopmental curve?

S   In these cross-cultural studies we test children at each grade level from the first through the sixth grade. We use three nonverbal and six verbal tasks. One nonverbal task is the Picture-Completion; another, the Incomplete Figures; and the third, the Circles. The verbal tasks include the Ask-and-Guess Test, the Product Improvement task using the stuffed toy dog, and the Unusual Uses of this same toy. We used the Consequences task but not in the lower grades, so that doesn't really enter in. I think that the result we obtain from the originality scores on the nonverbal tasks, which is one that we have fairly well completed now, gives us perhaps the best picture. Here, as I'm sure that you would guess, it was necessary to develop the originality scoring on the basis of what is original in a particular culture. A response that was very obvious in western Samoa would not be very obvious to American children and vice versa.

Looking particularly at the height of these scores, we find that in some cultures they are disproportionate in how well the children do with nonverbal and verbal tasks. For example, children in western Samoa and Negro children in segregated schools in the United States do disproportionately better on nonverbal than on verbal tasks, whereas in India they do disproportionately better on verbal than on nonverbal tasks. So there are some rather interesting and complex phenomena here.

In addition to the tests of creative thinking (both verbal and nonverbal) administered to about 1,000 pupils from grades one through six in each of these cultures, we have observations by our coinvestigators of the school; detailed questionnaires completed by teachers, including the "Ideal Pupil Check List"; imaginative stories concerning animals and persons with divergent characteristics; and numerous studies in the literature concerning the cultures involved. Thus far, one of the major conclusions suggested by these data is that the discontinuities in the development of the creative thinking abilities are accompanied by cultural discontinuities and personality disorganization. In United States schools where we have evidence that no discontinuity in these abilities resulted at the fourth-grade level, we also have stories of how the teacher has in some way reduced the usual discontinuities of our educational system, frequently by acting outside commonly accepted pedagogical procedures. We believe that if we can establish more firmly that some of our cultural and/or educational discontinuities are associated with personality disorganization and decreased mental (creative) functioning, and that some of these discontinuities are unnecessary, imaginative teachers, curriculum workers, and administrators will be able to devise and evaluate the effects of changes which will reduce these discontinuities.

FACTORS IN PERSONALITY, NATURE, AND SOCIETY

At almost every turn, we run into factors in personality, nature, and society which have a powerful influence on creative thinking. In some of our experiments, these factors have proved to be more powerful than the experimental manipulation being tested. In an experiment designed to produce growth in creative writing among children in the intermediate grades, the experimental conditions failed to produce significant effects. The pupils of teachers with strong creative motivations (as measured by the Personal-Social Motivations Inventory) showed significant gains, whereas those of their less strongly motivated colleagues showed almost no gain in creative writing under similar conditions and during the same three-month period. The creatively motivated teachers also carried out a larger number of creative activities than did their colleagues. Creative activities alone, however, did not produce significant growth.

In an experiment with student teachers, the experimental manipulation produced no more growth in the creative thinking abilities than did control conditions. Needs or motivations, as measured by the Edwards Personal Preference Inventory, however, proved to be quite powerful. Patterns of prepotent needs are rich in their suggestiveness concerning the dynamics of creative growth. The results are too complex to summarize here, but the following elements seem to be rather critical in gains in originality: low needs for order, succorance, abasement, and endurance, and strong needs for change, intraception, autonomy, and heterosexuality. Losses in originality seem to be associated also with low needs for order, endurance, and abasement, but are accompanied by strong needs for affiliation, succorance, nurturance, achievement, and dominance. With these strong needs, the low needs for order and endurance take on different meanings from what they do when accompanied by strong needs for change, intraception, autonomy, and heterosexuality.

Of the factors in nature and society, some of the more powerful in our culture seem to be sex-role expectations, a peer orientation, sanctions against manipulativeness, emphasis upon prevention and intolerance of failure, tyranny of the clock and emphasis upon speed, emphasis upon verbal skills, sanctions against being different (regardless of the social and moral desirability of the difference), emphasis upon the well-rounded or versatile personality, and others. As we examine the data from our cross-cultural studies, as we conduct experiments in which we try to produce some type of creative growth, and as we try to create instructional materials, it is becoming clearer that some of these factors in nature and society are changing and that others are not as inescapable as they have generally appeared to be.

EXPERIMENTALLY MANIPULATED FACTORS

We have also been interested in some of the experimental manipulative factors. We have conducted 20 odd of these experiments, some of them laboratory type and some field type. These experiments have been organized around three problem areas:

1. How can teachers and others create an environment which places a high value on creative thinking and creative achievement?

2. What is the most effective kind of evaluative behavior teachers and others can use to promote creative growth?

3. How can children be helped to develop evaluative behaviors conducive to creative thinking?

On the basis of 22 experiments organized around these three areas, the following conclusions seem to be reasonably supported:

1. After an orientation such as that contained in the manual *Rewarding Creative Thinking*, classroom teachers seem to want to reward creative thinking in their pupils, but many of them are unable to do so effectively because of their own personality characteristics, their perceptions of social expectations, and the like.

2. In projecting plans for discussing with children their creative writing, beginning teachers seem to be preoccupied with the critical and remedial. When encouraged to develop strategies for talking with children which will encourage growth in creative writing, experienced

teachers show a slight predominance of creative strategies over the critical and remedial.

3. Teachers participating in in-service training programs for developing creative thinking tend not to initiate any more creative activities than their colleagues who are working under control conditions.

4. Even though teachers may volunteer to carry out creative thinking activities, they tend to be inhibited in doing so if the principal is not involved in the experiment and does not give his direct approval.

5. Boys and girls in the subcultures studied are rewarded differentially for their creative thinking, and this appears to interfere with the creative development of both boys and girls in certain areas.

6. The type of evaluated practice (criticism and correction, suggestions of other possibilities, and a combination of criticism and constructive possibilities) does not affect performance on similar subsequent tasks requiring creative problem solving. Too frequent use of evaluation during the practice session, regardless of the type, seems to interfere with subsequent performance on similar tasks.

7. Unevaluated ("off the record") practice tends to produce greater originality, elaboration, and sensitivity than evaluated practice in most instances, except at the sixth-grade level.

8. When peer-evaluated practice is used, creative evaluation (constructive possibilities) rather than critical evaluation (defects) tends to be more effective in producing originality, elaboration, sensitivity, and the like, except in the kindergarten, first, second, and third grades.

9. Competition in grades one through six produces greater fluency, flexibility, and originality in creative thinking tasks. Practice and "warm up" does not completely eliminate the advantage achieved by competition. (This does not include an assessment of other side effects of competition.)

10. Individuals tend to achieve along whatever lines they are rewarded. When rewarded for originality, children produced about twice as many original ideas as when they were rewarded for quantity. When rewarded for the originality and interest of their stories, children wrote more interesting and original stories but made more errors in usage, spelling, and mechanics than children rewarded for correctness.

11. If one member of a group is definitely superior to the others in creative thinking abilities, he almost always experiences pressures to reduce his productivity and/or originality and is frequently not given credit for the positive contribution he makes to the group's success. The repertoire of group strategies for controlling creative members and of the counteraction techniques of creative individuals can be identified and used in characterizing the evaluative conditions of a group.

12. Homogeneous grouping for tasks requiring creative problem solving reduces the social stress, enables less creative members to become more productive, and increases the enjoyment of members.

13. More effective teachers in experimental mathematics courses (SMSG) report more trouble-shooting or hypothesis-making evaluative thinking and less criticism and praise than do their less effective colleagues. Effectiveness in this case is determined by pupil learning as measured by pre- and posttests.

14. Students who read and analyze published research reports creatively, in terms of constructive possibilities, rather than critically, in terms of defects, subsequently develop more original ideas in the area of the content under consideration (personality development and mental hygiene), suggesting the importance of the evaluative attitude one has toward the knowledge he possesses.

15. Different evaluative sets (memory, evaluative, and creative) in reading course material (Personality Development and Mental Hygiene) lead to differential performance on different kinds of tests (recognition or multiple-choice, memory or completion, creative applications, and evaluative or decision-making), again suggesting the importance of the evaluative attitude toward knowledge in creative thinking.

16. Students with predominantly creative attitudes tend to do comparatively better on creative tasks than students with predominantly critical attitudes and vice versa.

17. Imaginative stories by children about animals and persons with divergent characteristics provide a promising technique for studying cultural pressures against divergency and consequently against creative thinking. Urban cultures appear to exercise stronger sanctions against divergency than rural cultures within the cultures sampled. Children in special classes for gifted children seem to feel freer of these pressures than children in regular classes. Minority groups (such as Negroes in Georgia) may feel rather strong pressures to conformity.

18. Children in grades three through six can be stimulated to do a great deal of writing on their own if given a reason for doing so. A vehicle such as a magazine containing the ideas produced by pupils seems to increase the valuations of children of their own ideas and of their peers.

19. Allowing credit for self-initiated learning (in a course in Personality Development and Mental Hygiene) seems to increase greatly the variability of what is learned and probably of how much is learned. Most graduate students, though not all, are able to make good use of such opportunities.

INSTRUCTIONAL MATERIALS BEYOND TEXTBOOKS

When we found that our efforts in the area of in-service training were not richly rewarded, we turned our attention to the development of materials and aids which might help teachers in their efforts to develop the creative thinking abilities of their pupils. This first took the form of workbooks. Robert Myers, one of my doctoral students with a creative and experimental bent, devised large numbers of these exercises, tested them on his own fourth-grade pupils, and persuaded some of his friends to try them out. In the winter of 1961, we put some of them together and about 100 teachers tested them. The reports were encouraging, and where we had pre- and posttests the data showed that the use of the materials resulted in significant growth in creative writing and in attitudes relevant to creativity. Since no publisher was willing to take a chance on such materials, Myers and I arranged for their publication from our own resources. With almost no advertising, the workbook has already sold over 2,000 copies, and some rather careful evaluations are being made of its value. A second workbook at the junior high school level, *Invitations to Speaking and Writing Creatively*, has been produced and is now being field tested.

Our attention was turned next to taped materials. We thought such materials might aid teachers in overcoming their own difficulties in becoming "warmed up" and in helping pupils to become "warmed up." We developed a few trial tapes which had very enthusiastic reception. We are now developing a series of experimental tapes for use in the fourth grade. Central to each recording is a dramatized story around which some programmed experience in creative thinking revolves. One-fourth of the tapes will deal with great moments of scientific discovery and invention, one-fourth with historical achievement, one-fourth with the relationship of man to his environment (geography), and one-fourth with fantasy material. In all four areas, the materials are designed to implement the warm-up process and to help the children become more alive, "to stretch their minds." Each category also has some unique secondary objective. The great moments of scientific discovery and invention are designed to acquaint children with the nature and value of the creative process and to communicate the fact that their ideas are of value *now*. An aim of the tapes on historical achievement is to familiarize children with the historical importance of creative achievements; the materials on man and his environment, the importance of creative problem solving in survival; the fantasy material, the enjoyment and value of imaginative activities.

Materials have also been developed for teaching high-achieving elementary children many of the basic concepts and skills of doing creative research, for teaching some of the principles of creative thinking, and the like.

In all this work, we harbor no delusions that creative teaching can be "canned." We believe, however, that research findings in this area are not likely to exercise much influence unless they are translated into tested materials and procedures. We also hope that as teachers use these aids their own creative energies will be galvanized into action, they will develop ideas of their own, and they will value the ideas of their pupils.

FUTURE PLANS

With the backlog of uncompleted projects which I have already described, it seems rather foolhardy to talk about future plans. One comforting factor is that hundreds of graduate students and a few mature research workers scattered throughout the world are conducting related studies, many of them using the same instruments that we are using. All these developments may make possible an accumulation of knowledge that has not been possible heretofore. If I had to predict future emphases in our own program, I believe that I would list the following four areas:

1. Continued test development with extensive experimentation with variations in task instructions, time limits, built-in warm-up devices, and the like.

2. Development of principles for the clinical use of measures of creative thinking with emotionally disturbed children, cases of learning difficulty, delinquents, and the like.

3. Studies of the development of the creative thinking abilities in the blind and possibly in other handicapped groups.

4. Extension of the cross-cultural or comparative studies to include additional cultures and to provide for more complete information about the cultures involved, especially the educational environment.

What we shall actually do in any of these areas will of course depend to a great degree upon what our culture will support.

C I didn't hear you mention anything about prediction on the kind of special artistic and scientific contributions that Holland was talking about—the tests that you use. Have you gone into that at all?

S No. We have not.

C I have a comment concerning the study where you were using a monetary device to reinforce the response set that you were trying to establish via your instructions to your subjects. Lowenfeld reported a study of one of his students at Cincinnati in which some art work was being done. Then they decided to add a financial incentive, a financial reward, and, as I recall, the creativity of the art products was decreased. Is that correct?

C   Yes. The reward was going to be given after the products of the high school class were judged. The creativity of the performance went down in *all* the experimental groups in the study, however. The experimenter was studying extrinsic influences of three types: the art financial award, a peer standard represented by a visual scale to which a student could compare his own work, and what he called an adult (really a professional) art standard. He found that the control groups exceeded all these six-weeks-influenced groups.

S   The one I reported was a brief laboratory kind of experiment where the subject had a 10-minute performance. The monetary reward was used to heighten the difference in instructions to the two groups. We suspected that money was quicker than other kinds of motivation to dramatize the differences in instructions.

We did the same thing with creative writing. We told the subjects that this was a story-writing contest and that a prize would be given for the best story. To one group we described the best story as being the most imaginative, original, unusual, etc., and said, "Of course, you should write legibly and correctly but the thing that *really counts* is originality." In the contrasting condition we reversed this by defining a good story as the one that has the fewest errors in spelling and punctuation, is neat, etc., and we added, "Of course, you want to make your story interesting and exciting and unusual, too, but the thing that *really counts* is the correctness."

When originality is encouraged and is not impeded with "being correct," subjects write longer stories and more imaginative stories but they do make more errors, about twice as many. We frequently find that you get what you reward. This was really just a series of very simple experiments designed to get us into this area. But we have found already from a lot of other educational experiments that people tend to learn and achieve along whatever lines they are rewarded. I have not described the entire series of about 22 experiments in which we get into the whole problem of evaluation and reward. Nor have I dealt with the problems of in-service training programs to help teachers to adopt attitudes more favorable to the rewarded activity, even their paying attention to such things as questions and to helping the child find the answer by creating situations in which he can find the answer.

Probably there is no better reward to the curious child than to get the answer to his question. So I don't think you have to "buy" children into learning what they should respond to, but in a short 10-minute laboratory experiment monetary rewards may heighten the effects of instructions.

C Your findings may make us examine our notions about competition, for a definite feeling in art and in art education exists, and we aren't sure whether it has firm evidence to support it. For instance, in the professional art standard group the production went up in the experimental period over six weeks, but when the children went back to working on their own it went down beyond what it was in the three-week, pre-experimental period. We don't know what to make of that except that the students more or less developed two styles, their own and a professional style, and they had some confusion.

S But we do know that during a very limited period of time introducing competition heightens performance, in either fluency or originality, or both. We don't know how this would work over an extended period or how long it would hold up. We are saying the same thing about homogeneous and heterogeneous grouping, whatever your basic plan. For a short period of time, homogeneous grouping sends production up and decreases the stressfulness within the group, but what the long-period effect would be, we don't know.

chapter 11 Research on Developing Creative Behavior

Sidney J. Parnes, State University of New York at Buffalo

S   First of all, I would like to offer a few definitions, which I think would be very appropriate. Our work is concerned with studying to what extent creative behavior can be developed. To me, creative behavior refers to behavior unique to the individual's conscious self and at the same time effective in solving a problem. I define *problem solving* as recognizing and resolving perplexing situations. Thus we are trying to get people to behave (as far as they themselves are concerned) in a unique and effective manner in recognizing and resolving perplexing situations.

I shall preface my discussion with an old adage that you may have heard in several different contexts: "Give me the courage to change those things that should be changed, the strength to accept those things that should not be changed, and the wisdom to distinguish between the two." This concept is basic in what we are trying to accomplish in our creative problem-solving program—in our attempts to develop creative behavior.

A series of research studies regarding the development of creative behavior has been under way at the University of Buffalo since 1958, supported by the Creative Education Foundation. Arnold Meadow (now at the University of Arizona) and Hayne Reese of our Psychology Department collaborated at various stages of the research.

PHASE I. EVALUATION OF THE CREATIVE PROBLEM-SOLVING COURSE

Phase I was comprised of three studies evaluating the creative problem-solving course offered at the University of Buffalo since 1949, based

145

on the principles and procedures in Alex Osborn's *Applied Imagination*. This course, designed to develop creative behavior, has been completed by over 3,000 students and adults in day and evening classes and in the summer Creative Problem-Solving Institutes. In addition, the program has been offered as an extension course for scientific organizations, industry, the military, and various other professional groups.

About 350 students served as subjects in the studies. Experimental subjects were students in 5 creative problem-solving courses; controls were subjects from 18 other university courses. (A large number of control subjects was needed for matching purposes.) Results of the series of experiments demonstrated that students who completed the creative problem-solving course performed significantly better on six out of eight tests of creative ability than did comparable students who had not taken the course. All but two of the eight tests involved quality scores; the other two were quantity measures. Uniqueness and usefulness of the ideas were the criteria on one of the quality measures.

Persistence of effects

The persistence of these effects was also demonstrated. Matched experimental and control groups were compared on six creative ability tests which had yielded significant or nearly significant differentiation in one of the earlier experiments evaluating the creative problem-solving course. Experimental subjects were ones who had completed the course at least eight months and up to as long as four years before the experiment. Control subjects were students *registered*, but uninstructed, in the creative problem-solving course. No subject had ever before taken the creative thinking tests.

Results indicated that the experimental subjects outperformed two separate groups of control subjects on all six measures. All these measures were statistically significant by comparison with one control group; all but two were significant in the case of the second control group. Results indicate that increased productivity in creative thinking produced by the creative problem-solving course persists for a period of eight months or more after the completion of the course. The duplication of data with two control groups adds to the confidence with which the null hypothesis may be rejected.

The creativity courses are offered in the School of Business, although students from other divisions also elect the courses. Both experimental and control subjects in all three studies were business students, matched for such factors as age, sex, and IQ.

C   But not for motivation to take the creativity course?

S   In the persistence study, yes.   Not in the others.   In the persistence study, we used as control subjects incoming students who had
elected to take the creative problem-solving course.   We tested them
before the classes began.   The experimental subjects were students who
had completed the course one to four years ago.

C   Did you have another control group who were comparable to the
students who were ahead in college, and other things?

S   You mean because of the one to four years' difference in time?

C   Yes.

S   No.   We didn't control for that.

C   Just one other question.   You say that this persistence effect
lasted?   Was there any evidence that it was getting less and less, that
it was declining?

S   Yes.   In other words, there was some evidence of tapering off,
but a very significant amount remained.

More complete details on that particular study are given in the article
"Evaluation of Persistence of Effects Produced by a Creative Problem-
Solving Course" (Parnes and Meadow, 1960).   So much for Phase I
of our research project.   This phase was concerned with studies evaluating the overall creativity course rather than any particular methodologies of the course.

PHASE II.   EVALUATION OF UNDERLYING PRINCIPLES

Phase II of our research involved experiments with two underlying
principles of the course.

Deferred judgment

The first of these is the principle of deferred judgment, deliberately
deferring judgment during the idea-production phase; avoiding critical
analysis of the ideas until after a quantity of alternatives is listed.

C   May I interrupt here?   Have you thought of classifying the different steps you have in the creative process in terms of some other system,
such as Guilford's system, like the idea searching, and so on?   Have
you thought of classifying this way and finding how many cells of this
system you are working in?

S   I think that in a sense we have been doing something informally
along these lines, but that I ought not to take the time to go into it
right now.   I might get way off the research aspect.

C   It would be nice if you do think this through sometime and let us
know.

S   All right.   One comment I would like to make concerns the concept you brought in about evaluation, and how this enters into every

phase. We're in complete agreement with this. In other words, all our work has indicated that you can't put this process of creativity into some mechanically defined 1, 2, 3, 4, order. It's a dynamic kind of process. What we teach an individual to do, in terms of the operational program that we have been evaluating, is, for example, to think of all the possible problems that are implicit in a "perplexing situation" with which he is confronted. We teach him to discover problems in situations in which somebody else might not even see a problem. We are hitting hard at the "problem-sensitivity" factor. Thus we help the student to sense all the possible problems before he tries to decide what *is* the problem. In other words, he is deferring judgment, so to speak, even in the problem-definition stage. Once he has created a long list, we ask him to go back and be very judicial and critical, making his selection of the most *crucial* problem in the situation. Then he begins to break the problem down. Here again, as he subdivides it, he asks himself, "What are all the aspects of this problem?" He thus piles up many, many alternatives, maintaining a noncritical attitude during this proces. After the alternatives are all conceived, he applies his judicial capacities to evaluate and select the most likely areas for exploration in terms of these subproblems. This goes on all the way through idea production, synthesis, criteria listing, evaluation, and development of a plan of action, including final decisions as to what action is going to be taken; who will do it, where, when, how, why, and so on.

C   If you described your technique this way instead of by a name which now has certain limited meanings to most people, it might be accepted differently. For example, if you measured whether your students strengthen their ability to sense problems or strengthen their ability to think (ideational fluency) or perhaps strengthen certain evaluative abilities and certain planning abilities, you could check to see just what is happening. This might be merely a different way of saying the same thing, but it might be much more effective.

S   In other words, I can conceive that we could do further experimentation with other Guilford tests in the evaluative realms and in many of the other classifications besides the specific creative areas that we chose in our first study.

At any rate, regarding the principle of deferred judgment which we use at each stage of the creative problem-solving process, four separate studies were conducted. All four demonstrated that significantly more good-quality ideas (rated for uniqueness and usefulness) were produced when the deferred-judgment principle was followed than when conventional thinking procedures were used. The experiments were reported in greater detail at the 1959 conference.

C   What were the tasks?

S   Items from one part of the AC Test of Creative Ability—the Hanger and the Broom items, which call for the subject to list alternative uses for these objects.

C   In other words, this is not problem solving; it is just generating ideas.

S   But remember that it is generating ideas in terms of usefulness and uniqueness as related to a given task. However, this is a different kind of problem solving from that involved in, let's say, the Automatic Warehousing Problem.

C   In a broad sense all these tests are problem solving because you give the subjects a task that they have to work on.

C   But the task there is to generate a lot of ideas.

C   They solve the problem of generating a lot of ideas.

C   There are not a lot of restraints on the kind of solution.

C   Although, on the one hand, this could be (in a broader sense) problem solving, on the other hand, the criterion Parnes is using, if I am right, is a test.

S   Oh yes, it is a test.

C   I did the same thing with engineers just to check up on this point, and I got his results. But then I had them go on, saying, "Now, which of these ideas, if you had to give me the best single one you generated, would you give me?" In the one set we got a negative correlation between quantity and quality under this consideration.

S   You mean that you had determined the best one yourself as the experimenter?

C   Yes. We tried using the criterion that you wrote in your paper, by having a rating scale on uniqueness and one on usefulness, and then picked the overlap. Under conditions where we had the subjects defer judgment and generate as many ideas as they could, we got more good ones, by that kind of criterion.

S   Well, this indicated, then, more need for the evaluation training in terms of the development of ideas.

C   Yes, that may very well be.

C   We found something very similar to that, but there is a wide variation in tasks. In some tasks the evaluative and the generative scores are correlated positively, and in others they are correlated negatively.

C   We have another task, using Automatic Warehousing and more realistic problems where the subjects have to end up with a final solution and plan. Where we used deferred judgment and had them generate ideas, we obtained curvilinear correlations between quantity and the final quality of the solution. But there is no consistency, except within a problem. In the Automatic Warehousing Problem the people who produced a median number of ideas were the best. The two extremes were not as good. We have other problems, such as when the subjects have to invent something new, where we got the inverse result: the two extremes, those with the most ideas and those with the fewest, were the best in terms of the most inventiveness. Some people generate only good ideas right from the beginning but produce very little quantity.

Extended effort in idea production

S   The second principle we evaluated in Phase II is closely related to the concept of deferred judgment; it is what we call the *principle of extended effort in idea production:* Extended effort in idea production will lead to an increasing proportion of good ideas with increased production. This is very closely related to what Hyman has just been saying in this discussion. We conducted two separate experiments and found the principle to be confirmed in both.

Experiment I was designed to test the hypothesis that more good ideas will appear in the second half of a subject's total idea output regarding a problem than during the first half. Each subject was given a creative thinking problem which involved production of ideas for a five-minute period. The resultant ideas were evaluated by a trained rater. The number of good ideas was tallied for the first half of each subject's total idea list, and for the second half of his list.

The findings demonstrated significantly more good ideas to appear in the second half than in the first half of the idea lists. In addition, a significant relationship existed between total quantity and total quality scores, as was also found in an earlier experiment.

Experiment II was designed to determine whether the type of results found in experiment I with untrained subjects would also occur with subjects trained in the use of the principle of deferred judgment. It was also decided to lengthen the time period to 15 minutes instead of five, in order to see whether a trend could be observed toward *increasingly* greater proportions of good ideas as a subject's total quantity increases. Each subject was given 15 minutes to produce ideas regarding the same creative thinking problem as in experiment I. Resultant ideas were evaluated as in the first experiment. Number of good ideas was tallied for each third of each subject's total idea list—first third, middle third, and last third.

The findings showed significantly more good ideas to appear in the final third of the subject's idea lists. Although there was not a significant difference between first and second thirds, a trend was suggested toward increasingly larger proportions of good ideas with increased quantity.

C Were there controls so that the judges rating the quality of the ideas did not know whether they were first, second, or third?
S Yes. That was always controlled.
C This experiment, I feel, has interesting organizational implications. When someone runs into a problem for which he tries to find a solution, as soon as he finds a first one, he often stops. But this suggests that, if he works at the problem longer, some of his better solutions are still coming up.
S Yes. On that score I'll try to point out something here. Examination of the protocols suggested that the *untrained* subjects of experiment I seemed to start their production with more conventional, unoriginal ideas—high in usefulness but low in uniqueness. Toward the end of a five-minute period, however, these untrained subjects may find themselves exhausted of these ideas and may begin groping for less obvious ones. This may lead to greater production, among the later ideas, of ones high in both usefulness *and* uniqueness, the criteria for the "good" ideas. This finding seems to be consistent with the results of Christensen, Guilford, and Wilson (1957), where uncommonness and remoteness of responses increased with succeeding responses.

In the protocols of the *trained* subjects of experiment II, the data of the first 5 minutes were examined on the same basis as for experiment I. (Subjects had been requested at periodic time intervals during experiment II to draw a line under their last idea.) Analysis of variance indicated no significant difference between first half and second half in that 5-minute period. With these trained subjects, there seem to be many unique and useful ideas among the very first ones; but within a 15-minute period the trained subjects may also tend to exhaust themselves of ready ideas and find that they too have to "stretch" their imaginations more fully. This may explain why their strongest production of good ideas in the 15-minute period does not appear until the last third of their ideas.

In order further to explore the difference in results between trained and untrained subjects, a sign test analysis was made of scored data on hand form 180 *untrained* subjects of a previous experiment (Meadow and Parnes, 1959), for an entirely different type of problem (Guilford's Plot Titles) with a 3-minute test period. These data indicated no significant difference in number of quality ideas produced in first half versus second half of the idea lists.

Thus we have data suggesting: (*a*) for *untrained* subjects, significantly more good ideas among *later* ideas in a 5-minute period, but not significantly more in a 3-minute stint; (*b*) for *trained* subjects, significantly more good ideas among *later* ideas for a *15*-minute period, but not significantly more for a 5-minute stint. Theorizing from the four sets of related data, it might be suggested that subjects will get at least as many good ideas in the second half of their total idea output regarding a creative thinking problem as in the first half, but that with increasing production time the proportion of good ideas in the second half will increase over the first half. It might be further theorized that untrained subjects will show this increasing proportion more rapidly than trained subjects, who have already learned to be more creative in their early ideas. In a sense, both trained and untrained subjects seem to be stimulating their creativity by *extended* effort in idea finding. For the *trained* subjects, a 5-minute period (on the type of problem used) does not seem to be long enough to elicit *extended* effort on their parts. (This might be related analogously to the accomplished musician practicing on a beginner's piece.) However, for *untrained* subjects 5 minutes *did* seem to provide enough time to call for *extended* effort. Much further experimentation is needed with both trained and untrained subjects, given a variety of time limits and types of problems, in order to verify the theory suggested.

The *noncreative* problem solver gets an idea, sees it as a possible solution to his problem, and settles for it without further ado. The *creative* problem solver is not satisfied with his first idea. Like the person who invests money to obtain greater rewards later, the creative person forgoes the immediate reward of applying his first idea, in expectation of a better solution (greater reward) ultimately. A further hypothesis suggested is that the *best* idea will come late in the total production period. We are currently considering experiments to test this particular hypothesis.

C   But how do you determine when an idea is unique in an individual's experience?

S   We don't know whether it is unique in his own experience. We used external criteria.

C   Well, from your definition of creative behavior, isn't it basic to determine whether it is unique?

S   It is. We are very much interested in this point and would hope ultimately to find ways of determining the uniqueness to the *particular* subject. This is an area about which I would certainly like some suggestions if anyone has them.

C   Over how long a period of time does this extend?

S   The longest was 15 minutes.

C   Did you relate this to Guilford's work with Christensen?

C   We got a uniform rate of production in cleverness but an increase in the other two types of scores, uniqueness and remoteness.

S   Yes. In other words, those were the same type of findings as ours.

C   Do the subjects tend to run dry, does anyone know?

S   In 15 minutes they weren't running dry.

C   We had just 12 minutes.

C   I took subjects up to a half hour. They run dry. Mine ran dry in about 16 minutes.

S   Were they trained in creative problem solving?

C   Trained in creative engineering.

S   We ran one trained group on another problem up to a half hour, and they were still running strong.

C   The engineers may have had more restraints on their problems, though.

C   That may be true. We had more complicated problems. Different problems have a flat slope. On some problems, all the ideas seem to come out in the first 5 minutes or so, but on others there is a uniform production of ideas.

S   There are so many variables here. In order to really understand this concept of extended effort, we need to do much experimentation on a variety of problems, a variety of time limits, and so on.

C   One of my favorite anecdotes, which I read in the literature when · I was doing my dissertation on fluency in writing—and found ideational fluency—was the story about a manic. Another person decided that he could produce as many ideas as a manic. He practiced for a while, and then they had a contest (essentially you could call this an ideational fluency test, orally administered). He kept up with the manic for a certain period, but then he ran completely dry while the manic just kept on going.

S   I always tell my students that if they just produce ideas without evaluating them they could easily be outproduced by a manic. And this is the point: that the manic's, of course, are not evaluated, nor are they even necessarily oriented to the problem.

C   I suppose that the ideal creative individual ought to be a manic depressive who originates ideas in his manic phase and is able to evaluate them later.

C   In your instructions, did you clue in subjects who had not taken your class in creativity that uniqueness was one of the criteria as well as usefulness?

S   Nobody was clued to that.

C   The subjects who had had the course in creativity, though, in response to the instruction, "Suggest how you could use a brick," might know that uniqueness was part of the criteria, whereas your controls perhaps didn't.

S What do you think about that?

C I have a comment on this point, too. I conducted an experiment similar to yours here at the university in my creativity classes, in which I gave the Guilford battery before and after. We ran a control group at Brigham Young University. We had significant improvements on the postcourse tests here at the university and also significant differences between our group and the BYU group. But the criticism was brought up afterwards that perhaps all we were doing was teaching them to take the test. I think that this is a valid criticism.

S Well, you used control groups

C Yes. But, as was just pointed out, these people were not instructed that they were supposed to come up with unique ideas, unusual ideas, or with a quantity of ideas, whereas the people in my own course were.

S During the course, you mean?

C During the course, not before the test.

S Well, I think that this gets us back to the question we were discussing before, of what does happen so far as the creative person is concerned. What is preventing anybody from being creative? I say here again that this is the typical person's response in our culture to any question—that is, to be very judicial and very conventional in terms of his response. He has been "programmed" all his life to respond conventionally. Thus he rarely offers a creative idea. In a creativity course, he is reinforced for creative behavior, plus being taught how to evaluate and develop creative ideas to the point that they are acceptable and useful. As a result, he learns how to unleash and *channel* his creative potential, much of which has lain dormant, or perhaps I should say *squelched*, within him. All this is related to Maslow's "self-actualization" theory. He says, "What a man *can* be, he *must* be." (Maslow, 1954)

As a matter of fact I mentioned at the last conference certain interesting data we had. These data showed that, if we said to somebody, "Give me *good* uses for something," as against saying "Give me *other* uses for something," we obtained approximately the same number of ideas under each set of instructions. I would have guessed that, if we asked for *good* uses, this would have inhibited the subjects more than simply requiring *other* uses, and that we would have obtained a lesser number of ideas under the "good" instructions. My whole point here is this: What we think we are doing in terms of our creativity program is getting people to the point where they are willing to explore alternatives—to remove the governor, so to speak, from their minds—and then to test out the ideas they obtain, to see whether they have something better than they otherwise would have had.   And they seem to find that they usually *do*.

C   Let me comment from the point of view of a spread effect.   If you had evidence that these people, when they were outside your course, performed the way they did when they were in your course, then you have some spread effect.

C   There is one peculiar thing about what you say and how you evaluate it, which I think ought to be explored.   The only other evaluations of courses like yours that I know of (I think Guilford may have reported on one in an earlier conference) show something different from what you get.   These other results are consistent in that the subjects give fewer ideas but more high-quality ideas in response to these tests.

S   Are you thinking of the Lackland Air Force Base study and the Nicholson study at Texas?

C   Yes.   Now the suggestion here is that you're just changing the subjects' selecting mechanism; you're not changing their quantity or quality.

S   Excuse me a minute.   In both the Lackland and the Nicholson study, I am reasonably certain that there was not statistical significance on the quantity decrease.   There *was* on the quality increase.   Quality was increased significantly, but quantity was not.   There was actually a reduction in quantity, but it was not significant.

C   I would suggest that what is changed here is the selection mechanism—there is more automatic and quicker recognition of what is a good idea, what is of value—rather than the quantity.   Do you see what I'm getting at?

C   Two different processes: flow and selection.

C   But really, in the test you have to find out whether there is any transfer—whether this applies to other activities.

S   And this is exactly what we are coming to in the next phase.

PHASE III.   EVALUATION OF TRANSFER EFFECTS

Our next efforts, in phase III of our research, were pilot projects to determine possible transfer effects of the creativity course itself to students' work in other subject matter fields.

Physics pilot study

The first study was with physics students.   Physics was chosen not because it was felt that increased creativity would necessarily affect grades in that subject, but because a request was received from the physics department for this type of experimentation with its students. The experiment was designed to evaluate the effects on physics students of a condensed creative problem-solving course. A six-session abbreviation of the University of Buffalo semester course was offered. Sessions were held once a week, for one and three-quarter hours per session. No outside assignments were made, although each student was given a copy of the textbook, *Applied Imagination*, by Alex F. Osborn, upon his "gentleman's agreement" to read it before the end of the semester.

The following threefold hypothesis was tested. A creative problem-solving program taught to volunteer physics students would result in (a) higher scores on creative ability tests as compared with equivalent control students, (b) higher physics grades as compared with equivalent control students, (c) better attitudes toward physics as compared with controls. In addition, attitudes of the experimental students to the creative problem-solving program were studied.

From the students who volunteered for the experiment, 57 were randomly selected as experimental subjects and were matched with a similar group of volunteer students who served as control subjects. Of the 57 experimental students, 55 completed the six-week program.

Creative ability tests were given to both experimental and control students at the end of the experimental program. The tests were those that had yielded significant results in earlier experiments evaluating the University of Buffalo semester creative problem-solving course. An attitude questionnaire was also administered. Physics grades for all students were recorded (examinations and final grades). Experimental subjects also received an additional questionnaire to assess their attitudes toward the experimental program.

The experimental students attained higher scores on five out of six of the creative ability tests than did the control students, significant on most measures. (Preliminary analysis indicates that the experimental students' scores were not as consistently higher—as compared with their controls—as were the scores of experimentals versus controls in research with students who took the entire creative problem-solving course rather than the abbreviated version.)

No significant differences in physics grades appeared between the two groups. When the data were broken down into engineering students versus other students, and into students with first-semester grades of A, B, C, and D, there was observed a marked and consistent tendency for nonengineering C experimental students to improve in grades (whereas this was not true for their C control counterparts). However, the number of students in this category was much too small to be statistically reliable.

No significant differences in attitudes toward physics were observed between the experimental and control students at the end of the course. Factors measured were interest in the subject, feelings of difficulty or anxiety about the subject, desire for involvement with or application of the subject, and value seen in the subject.

On questionnaires given anonymously to the 55 experimental students who completed the course, many interesting findings resulted. For example, (1) 35 saw some relationship, and 20 saw direct relationship, between the creative problem-solving program and physics; (2) 22 saw some relationship, and 30 saw direct relationship, between the creative problem-solving program and engineering; (3) 11 found the training very helpful, 42 somewhat helpful, in other courses; (4) 45 felt the program should be required of all students, or at least of all engineering and science students. Most of the remainder felt that it should not be required, but rather should be offered as an elective; (5) scores of comments indicated specific examples of beneficial effects of the course on the students.

Fifty-two claimed the program had a good effect on their attitudes (none indicated bad effects); 33 indicated that they were a good deal, 22 somewhat, more open-minded to ideas of others; 14 indicated that they were a good deal, 37 somewhat, more self-confident; 22 indicated that they were a good deal, 26 somewhat, less shy in discussions; 27 indicated that they were a good deal, 25 somewhat, more curious; 25 indicated that they were a good deal, 26 somewhat, more sensitive to problems.

The experiment offers some indications that grades in physics might conceivably be affected by the creative problem-solving course. And, of course, the reactions of students definitely suggest other benefits besides better grades. Furthermore, students' reactions provide confidence that a full-scale experimental program for volunteers would be accepted. Therefore, it is planned that a future experiment be conducted with larger numbers of students, of the nonengineering type, for whom the tendency toward positive effects on grades was evident in the present experiment. It is anticipated, however, that the future experiment will be conducted at the very introduction to the subject rather than during the second semester, as the pilot experiment was conducted, and that the creative problem-solving experimental course will be expanded to the full semester. This would allow for the greater effects on creative behavior that were observed in the evaluation of the total-semester creative problem-solving course. The students' grades during both first- and second-semester physics courses might then be followed for possible effects.

Law pilot study

The second study concerning transfer effects of our creativity training was conducted with students attending the University of Buffalo Law School. In this study, 40 volunteer law students were divided into two matched groups, a control sample and an experimental sample. The experimental group received an eight-week training course in creative problem solving, whereas the control group did not receive this training. The course was taught by a practicing attorney who is also a creative problem-solving instructor at our institutes. At the end of the eight-week training course, the control sample and the experimental sample were administered a short form of the AC Test of Creative Ability. On this test the experimental group scored higher (ten-point mean difference) than did the control group, although the difference between the two groups was not statistically significant because of the small number of subjects in each group.

When grades received in law school were compared *between* the two groups, the experimental sample demonstrated more improvement in grades than did the control sample, although this difference was again not statistically significant. However, when comparisons of grades achieved were made *within* each group, it was found that the experimental sample had a statistically significant increase, whereas the control sample did not. Of the 20 experimental subjects, 13 improved in grades, while 7 worsened; whereas among the control subjects, 8 improved, 1 remained the same, and 11 worsened.

We plan to repeat the experimental course next year to check for consistency of the tendency for volunteer experimental students to do better in their law school grades. The course will be strengthened by relating it in more ways to problems of concern to law students. (For example, exploring what possible facts might be relevant in a negligence case; considering how many ways an attorney might have defined a problem, how many criteria he might have considered in evaluating his possible courses of action, and listing alternative courses he might have chosen; considering contingencies an attorney might *anticipate* in drawing a will.)

We expect to repeat the administration of creativity tests, revised from those given last year. These tests will measure creativity in kinds of mental tasks similar to those important to law students. The tests will be administered to the experimental and control subjects (volunteers) both before and after the training period, in order to measure relative gains. (In the previous experiment we had only postscores to evaluate.)

We will continue the analysis of grades of last year's subjects and will also further study their creativity. Last year's volunteers will be offered additional testing, using this year's creativity battery, which includes measures of mental tasks similar to those important to law students.

We also plan to make further statistical analyses of the data, for example, analyses of the relationship between creative ability and law school entrance scores, law grades, etc.

Conclusions drawn from all course-evaluation studies so far suggest that the full-semester course has a greater effect than the short-term versions we have been offering in our pilot experiments with physics and law students. This raises the question as to the effect of an even longer exposure. An advanced course was inaugurated at our university a few years ago, so that it will be possible to conduct further research into this question.

PHASE IV. PROGRAMMING CREATIVE BEHAVIOR

I would now like to discuss briefly with you a project for which we are currently seeking support. This is a project involving the programming of creative behavior—programming the principles and procedures we have evaluated in all the earlier experiments I discussed. Preliminary experimentation in our creativity classes has indicated the feasibility of such programming. I will present the objectives of this research in order to give you an overall picture, and then I will make a few other comments about it.

The ultimate objective is to determine to what extent creativity principles and procedures can be integrated into autoinstructional programs in the physical and social sciences with the result of developing creative behavior while teaching subject matter. The principal hypothesis to be tested is that creative behavior can be significantly increased through programs modified to integrate creativity development, while at the same time the mastery and understanding of content can be held constant or actually increased. A secondary hypothesis is that students' interest in, and attitudes toward, the courses being taught will improve as a result of such modified programs.

The first stages of the research will set out to accomplish the following: (a) reduce all conventionally named aspects of creative behavior, such as originality, sensitivity, flexibility, and fluency to their manifestations in defining and solving problems creatively, that is, to actual behavior which manifests those traits and attitudes; (b) devise means of immediately reinforcing any tendency, however slight, toward such creative behavior; (c) program the principles and procedures of the creative problem-solving course, conduct error analyses, and revise the program, when necessary, for optimum effectiveness; (*d*) ascertain, by using experimental and control groups, to what degree this "optimum" program increases the students' creative behavior as measured by the standardized creative ability tests used in earlier (instructor-taught) course-evaluation experiments.

In later stages, incremental programs that already exist in the physical and social sciences will be modified in such a way as to permit their integration with creative thinking principles and procedures. The existing programs will then be compared experimentally with those to be developed. Comparisons will be made in terms of subject-matter mastery, attitudes toward subject matter, creativity in the academic subject, and creativity development in general.

As a result of the encouragement of research, autoinstructional programs are appearing at a rapid rate in practically every academic field. Inasmuch as the effective programming of a textbook is a costly and time-consuming process, many forward-looking educators are asking themselves whether they should reconsider the entire curriculum before developing programs. This would enable them to incorporate the benefits of such thinking into the new programs from the start. By the same token, it seems opportune and appropriate to seek ways of programming the much-sought creative development of students and ultimately to attempt to incorporate this into the newly emerging autoinstructional materials in all fields. Thus an opportunity may be provided to *plan* for the creative development of students through the new programs.

Conventional, formal education in the past has done but little *deliberately* to develop creative behavior. And currently there is a popular conception that the rigidity of teaching-machine programs may actually tend to stifle creative development. In spite of education's growing concern about the importance of creative thinking, instructors would be hard put to tell what their courses do, *specifically* and *deliberately*, to develop creative behavior.

Encouragement as to the possibility of programming creative behavior is provided by our own experience as well as by many studies reported in the literature. For example, Maltzman, Simon, and Licht (1959) concluded a group of research studies on originality training by asserting that the results support the hypothesis that "originality is a learned form of behavior which does not differ in principle from other forms of operant behavior."

Many psychologists who conduct research in teaching-machine programming think that creative behavior can be programmed. Skinner himself has asserted that teaching machines are by no means confined to imparting explicit repertoires of behavior. Klaus of the American Institute of Research writes:

> The third level of instruction involves the teaching of such capabilities as creative thinking and judgment. This last level of education may be the area in which auto-instruction will yield its greatest fruits. The possibilities of developing a program in this area are derived from two simple observations. First, we have sufficient data to indicate that creativity and judgment are examples of learned behavior. Second, we have evidence to indicate that these behaviors can be taught. What is left is simply a matter of mechanics; that is, identifying exactly those behaviors to be learned and then finding the means to successfully establish these behaviors in the student's repertoire with auto-instructional methods and devices (Klaus and Lumsdaine, 1960).

Other psychologists provide further emphasis. Guilford wrote us that he believes it should be possible to introduce training for creative performance by means of modified programs for the machines. Maltzman, Bogartz, and Breger (1958) have already found that reinforcement can strengthen originality. Cowen (1952) discovered that reinforcement by praise resulted in less rigidity in problem solving. Ways to build this reinforcement into a program are now needed.

C   Are you aware that Stolurow at the University of Illinois has developed some programs?

S   Yes. Has he produced them already?

C   Yes, both a teaching-machine form and a paper-booklet form.

C   There is a technical report out on the Stolurow study.

C   There are three or four little hints here, but by and large my impression is that people who are doing this are creativity researchers more than the usual programmers.

S   Major Decker of Pease Air Force Base is working with me. Day, in Nevada, has done some preliminary work, as well as Barlow at Earlham College. Klaus is working in the area, and Crutchfield at IPAR has just begun his study. It is worth noting here, however, that these research projects are all concerned basically with creative thinking per se rather than with its integration with subject-matter programs. However, the successful programming of creative thinking in itself is a minor part of the overall problem. Actually, the teaching of creative thinking is a remedial educational process in the sense that every course should inculcate creativity and thus eliminate any need for a separate course. This is the long-range goal of the research we are contemplating.

C   May I raise a question? I can see some merit in having a "sensing-problem" kind of activity as a separate package so that a person learns how to sense problems in history, then in music, and so forth. This package wouldn't necessarily have to be combined with his next package on another activity as the one and only thing with which it could be combined, but could be used just for itself or combined with other kinds of packages.

S   You mean just taking the specific aspect and finding ways to program it?

C   Program each of these aspects and then, for a particular kind of creative training, put a series of them together; but they don't have to be all used by others as one single package.

S   This is certainly a very interesting possibility.

As to the feasibility of integrating creativity development with subject-matter mastery, further encouragement is offered by successful experiences with projects based on the integration of creative principles and procedures with conventionally taught courses. Two outstanding examples of courses which have thus been modified are Clark's economics course at the University of Chattanooga and Hansen's marketing course at Harvard. The value of such course modification has been further indicated by the University of Minnesota research regarding the effectiveness of similar integration of creative principles and procedures with conventionally taught courses in language arts (Torrance, 1960). Also, a study by Sommers (1961) reports discovery that subject-matter mastery increased, as did creative ability scores, as a result of an integrated course.

Implications for basic research

Autoinstructional research is usually aimed at ascertaining factors in learning efficiency and determining to what degree each factor or variable can be varied, alone or in combination, in order to develop optimum efficiency in learning. Some variables are functions of the machines, some are functions of the program, some are functions of the students or their environment, and some are functions of all four.

Such learning variables are also creative variables; that is, the more we learn, the more ideas our imaginations have to manipulate. This does not mean, however, that factors which affect learning will necessarily have the same relative effect on creative behavior and vice versa. It seems obvious, however, that while certain aspects are stressed more in creative behavior than in learning and vice versa, the optimum situation would be a happy balance between the two.

It follows that research regarding creative behavior should closely accompany autoinstructional research. Any future research which reveals that a certain procedure has impact upon learning effectiveness should be checked to ascertain whether it is also helpful or detrimental to creative development. This, of course, opens up new fields of basic research in creative behavior. For instance, if reading speed, eye span, speed of association, and other such factors increase retention and comprehension, this does not necessarily mean that they also positively affect creative development. When one considers the part played by incubation in creative thinking, he realizes that the variable "time" may bear so complex a relationship to creative thinking that much research will be needed on this point. Incidentally, research has already indicated that "uncommonness and remoteness of response" increase with time, while "cleverness" has been found to be independent of time (Christensen, Guilford, and Wilson, 1957).

C   Don't you have a hunch that students will enjoy their learning more if they use this other part of their minds?

S   Yes, I do. As a matter of fact, I developed a very brief pilot program, just a sketchy introduction. I gave it to 50 students, and I found that the 25 day students were very much interested in it. They claimed that they enjoyed it. They said that they would like to read a whole book in this way. They felt that it was very effective. In the evening class 2 students out of the 25 said "no"—that this got very dull after it went along for a while. After a little discussion the students helped me work out ways to overcome the dullness for those 2 students. There are certain branching techniques and ideas, and so on, that we have in mind.

Here is one interesting thing that you might like to hear about. I had an item something like this: "If we _____ coated the pencil, it would be very effective for pencil chewers." I'm taking this item entirely out of sequence and out of context, but just picture the item.

C   Licorice.

S   Yes—peppermint or licorice or sugar; 49 out of 50 students said sugar or peppermint or something pleasant tasting. But one said "bitter" coated! Now, in other words, he sensed a completely different problem from the others. This raised the question in our minds as to how we might more realistically program for originality and uniqueness, and we've come up with some ways that we might do this. But time will not permit further discussion on the project of programming creative behavior.

ADDITIONAL RESEARCH EFFORTS AND PLANS

We had a rather interesting opportunity with the National Science Foundation students—the high school seniors who were being selected for this summer's program at our university. To make a long story short, the planning committee of physics, engineering, and medical personnel decided to see whether there was anything we could do in terms of providing them with some originality scores on these science students. So, as a relatively quick, easily scored test, I gave them the short-form AC Test of Creative Ability, using the quantity score only. We gave it to about 500 applicants. The selection committee then asked for the 40 highest scorers on the AC Test, irrespective of whether they would have selected them for interview by their conventional criteria. It turned out that about half of these highest scorers would have been rejected before interview had the creativity score been ignored. The interviewer told me, after his interviews, that he was delighted to get several of these students who were highest on creativity but who otherwise would never have been invited for interviews. Another interesting point is that the high school students went "over the top" on their scores on the AC Test; we couldn't convert the top ones to standard scores because they were above the figures given in the manual for the highest-scoring engineers at AC!

We are interested in undertaking in the future various prediction studies with engineering students and others, as to what creativity-test scores can tell us about future dropout likelihood, grades, etc. We do have some preliminary data on about 500 incoming freshmen who were given a brief creativity test along with our university's general admissions battery, about two years ago. We want to do some follow-up work now, to see what we can learn about any predictive value of those scores. Finally, we have some projects in mind regarding longitudinal studies with these thousands of creative problem-solving students that we've had. We have test scores on several hundred of them, with some of the scores going back as far as 1958. So we may follow up these students not only as to their grades, but also out into industry and graduate school, to see what we can learn of effects on ultimate criteria. We also can study creative problem-solving course grades, which we have for about 1,500, to see what predictive values these may have.

Bloom indicated at the 1955 Utah conference (Bloom, 1963) that the science students who truly become involved in research work and in research roles during graduate training tend to become the productive researchers afterwards. Contrarily, those who do not really get involved in research as they finish their advanced degree requirements, but somehow get by this hurdle without becoming involved, usually manage not to produce research afterwards and also avoid research opportunities, let alone trying to cultivate them. Bloom emphasizes, therefore, that, if the creative are to be found somewhere among the productive, then in science we can reduce our problem by finding the students who truly become involved in research problems during their academic career. Some analogous situations entailing student involvement could also be sought in nonscientific fields.

This may be exactly the kind of thing we can begin to do with the grades we have on students who have completed creative problem-solving courses. The student with a high grade in our creative problem-solving course is the one who has demonstrated the effective ability to sense problems, define them effectively, develop alternative ideas and criteria for evaluating them, and carry through to effective plans of action. It is really a miniature research project that he carries out in the course.

C The same finding, by the way, was obtained in the Veterans Administration study on selection of clinical psychologists. The best predictor for later research creativity was simply whether or not a student had published or prepared for publication a study before he got his Ph.D.

C Bloom said, in effect, in the 1955 report that his kind of separation was whether a person got involved in the role of the researcher, as distinct from seeing the research requirement as merely a nasty hurdle to get over. Torrance, do you have any evidence on your notion that learning by authority may not be as effective as learning by creative thinking?

C I think we have evidence that some individuals certainly learn more effectively when they have an opportunity to learn creatively than when they have to learn by authority, whereas the reverse is true for some others. It is partially a preference for learning in one way or the other.

C How old are these people? Is it partly the academic history that is involved here?

C I think so. It is in the intermediate grades.

C Is there also a problem of identification of the student with the teacher?

C I would suspect so.

C There is very informal evidence of the same kind with college students. Certainly the preferences for the type of teaching which one or another professor utilizes are very varied. Some delight in a vague, independent kind of assignment. Others can't stand these things.

C This is a description of the fluent versus the nonfluent person that appeared in the 1930's in the British journals: Give them the same information and some don't want to start; but for others, that's all they need. The first group complains about needing more information, more instructions as to what to do, and so on.

C I once used the AC Test with engineers. Half of them I had first work on the test under instructions that would satisfy the manager who was looking for practical engineers, and the other half work on it in a way that would satisfy a manager looking for a creative research engineer. Then we switched them around. The most interesting finding here was in terms of their preference—which attitude they preferred to work under. Most of them preferred to work under the "be-practical" attitude, but the ones who preferred to work under this attitude actually did better in terms of the creativity score.

C   They were just maze bright.

C   Maybe that's the answer.

C   We have some results from two different age groups suggesting that there is possibly an age difference in the tolerance for unstructured and structured tests. In our first creativity battery we gave the test which we called the F Test because in preliminary testing it was so frustrating to many people. We gave no instruction whatever except, "Do something with every item." The items were all different. The type of test is sensitivity to problems. If the students could do all these items, they could see a lot of problems. We gave it originally to a ninth-grade group, and they were delighted with it. They had a lot of fun. Why should ninth-grade youngsters take this test better than adults, or at least have a better attitude toward it?

C   I am still reminded of our discussion at another meeting where Suchman, who is teaching students how to ask questions in high school, found out that the second and third grade students already know how. One of Guilford's hunches was that the fourth-grade slump was the place where the students had learned how to ask better questions than the teacher could answer.

C   I think that I have a good idea we could use quickly, regarding the notion of the programmed-learning course. There the answer is down in the slot near the bottom. There could be another little statement that says, "If you have thought up a better answer than this one, put it down here." I think that all of us in taking tests have often wished we had some place to write in answers we consider better than those of the person who made up the test. I can see where I can very easily modify standard psychometrics by adding, "If you can think of a better answer to this, put it in."

C   In our study of Air Force scientists we used that type of score, on how well they cooperated with us on the forms. If they changed the question on the form before they answered it, or otherwise took unexpected liberties in responding to our form, or did not comply with our requests, we scored it. However, this complex "noncompliance" or "alteration of requests" score correlated above .20 with only 4 of our

50 criteria, and these were all negative in the 20's and only with supervisory ratings.

S One of the hardest jobs for the students in our creative problem-solving courses is to sense and select problems in their own lives. They come to me repeatedly and say, "Give me a problem to work on, and then I'll work on it creatively; but don't ask me to pick one out myself." I make them pick the problem out from their own personal lives, their studies, or their work (if they happen to be working), and this "throws" them. Give them a case, and they'll work at it creatively; but asking them to pick a problem out themselves is quite a different matter. We insist on their finding many of their own, in order to help develop in them this sensitivity factor.

C I've tried experiments in my last series of seminars at Aerojet in which I used very nondirective, unstructured types of techniques. A great many of the students found this extremely uncomfortable. They just couldn't live with it. A lot of them withdrew from the class immediately. One fellow went to his division manager and said that I didn't know what I was doing, and asked why they had me teaching this, anyway. Others, though, found this environment very stimulating and much preferred this course to any other type they had taken. Surprisingly, the individual who complained to his division manager had a Ph.D. in mathematics and was teaching an evening course. Toward the end of the series of seminars he said that he had started teaching mathematics in the same way as I was teaching creativity.

C This is why I raised the question earlier about having these programs in small parts, and also of studying individual differences in each of these parts, initially and as they develop. At one stage of this process some one group of people may be best at sensing problems. In the next stage, the thinking up of ideas, another group might emerge as the best (as seen from the dimensional independence, for example, in the structure of intellect). We have a forthcoming report on a theory of education which proposes that we have the students utilize, in turn, each different thinking and learning process in their minds, while they are learning different subject matter. William Hutchinson (1963) has done a doctoral dissertation at the University of Utah which has tested out some of this theory and has yielded positive results that are very provocative.

C I think a lot of what we have been saying here adds up to the fact that some real clues are emerging as to what we can do about individual differences. We have talked about individualizing instruction, without having any idea what can be done about it; but now I think some ideas are beginning to come out.

C   You mean bibliotherapy—improving one's creative ability by reading what is known about creativity?

C   I have a further hunch that we can capitalize more on the group situation—on the talents that are available in a group—and use the motivating forces. One could innovate and another could do the task of judging, using the group as an entity rather than the individual.

C   We decided to feed some of that into our taped program for fourth-grade children.

C   Will there be any plans or thoughts about offering programs in creative problem solving on the second- or even the first-grade level?

S   Let me put it this way. Creative problem solving in college, or with adults, is largely a remedial matter as far as I am concerned. This is why I am very much interested in integrating it with other subject-matter areas. Definitely, I believe that it should be started very early.

C   In the first grade you don't have to teach children the principles of brainstorming. They do it immediately. One thing really woke me up when I did this with a first-grade group. There were five kids, and three of them were very fluent. They could just rattle off ideas for improving a product. There were two very quiet students: one of these would express a new idea, and the three fluent ones would take off on it. Then suddenly one of the quiet ones would come up with a very different idea, which would set the fluent ones off again. These two quiet ones would just change ideas at right angles. I think what happens in adult groups is that the quiet ones are left behind that way—in other words, they keep quiet because they are afraid they'll be laughed at, but quiet kids don't do that. They keep speaking up and sending the group down new avenues.

C   How much does this "spill across" to the ways in which they run their lives?

S   I feel very strongly about this. I like Maslow's concept of self-actualization. We aren't concerned as much about identifying the most creative person (that is a worthy project; don't get me wrong). But what we are primarily interested in is trying to help each person utilize his fullest potential.

My final thought concerns a little experimental design I'd like to carry out some time. I would take the college studies we conducted on deferment of judgment and carry them all the way down, grade by grade, to the first-grade level. My hypothesis is that as you go down the grades, somewhere (I don't know where—second or third grade, perhaps) there wouldn't be any difference between deferred judgment and concurrent judgment instructions; because whether you told the children to defer judgment or didn't tell them to, they would just shout out their ideas regardless. I have tried this on my own six-year-old child, and she will give all kinds of ideas without the slightest concern.

C   Well, we get a little of that when we give test instructions under different conditions: one, to think of many ideas, not caring how good or how poor they are—just as many ideas as possible; and the other, to think of only the most interesting and unusual—try to think of something that no one else will think of. In the first three grades, telling children to think of unusual ideas actually produces significantly more ideas than telling them to think of as many ideas as possible, but at the fourth grade this stops being true.

C   It seems to me that there is a somewhat striking parallel between psychoanalytic techniques and what you're talking about. This is true in most therapy processes, where the beginning is a simple generation of ideas. Some of them are unconnected, and the more unconnected the better, where again the strictures all work against evaluation, against judgment, against being critical. Then later comes the evaluation.

C   Have you given a course to older people, perhaps retired but still very much alive?

S   A few people are teaching courses for retired people or setting up retired groups for creative problem solving, and as a matter of fact I understand that some of them are serving as consultants to companies from which they have retired.

C   They are becoming "un-retired" as a consequence.

S   Yes.

chapter 12 Some Developmental and Environmental Factors in Creativity[1]

John E. Drevdahl, University of Miami

S   The purpose of this study was to provide some possibly pertinent information regarding the environmental circumstances surrounding the creative, as opposed to the noncreative individual, as well as to provide some further information concerning his personal, educational, and social characteristics and experiences. This has been done through the use of recorded interviews analyzed by clinically trained judges as well as by means of objective tests of personality and motivational factors.

Because this study was intended to be a pilot study, the number of subjects was necessarily small; and the results must be interpreted as suggestive only. Despite this limitation, it is encouraging to note that the results of this study are similar in quite a few respects to those reported from other on-going studies in this general area.

PROCEDURE

Possibly one of the most important, and too often ignored, problems in the study of the creative person is the criterion problem. By the time death and history have had their say, it is obviously too late to study the individual. Before some overt display and consequent evaluation of a person's productivity, no adequate means of identification is presently available. Consequently, we must depend upon some sort of contem-

[1] This study was supported in part by a grant from the Cooperative Research Branch of the U. S. Office of Education.

poraneous evaluation of a person in order to categorize him as creative or not creative. The judgments of a small group of experts in the field have been used successfully in the past, but it was felt that a broader base of judgment would be more desirable. This is not to disparage the progress made in the development of multiple criteria as reported in those conferences in the past few years, but simply to emphasize that in the ultimate analysis all evaluation and understanding of human behavior, beyond the reflex level, depends largely upon judgment of one sort or another.

Psychologists were chosen as the potential subjects for this study for several reasons. They were a group with which the principal investigator was thoroughly familiar, a group representative of both the social and natural sciences, and because of the nature of their training a group who might be better able to provide insightful interview information.

In order to select the experimental sample, 10 Ph.D. psychologists were asked to submit a list of persons in the field of psychology whom they felt, on the basis of personal familiarity with their work (not just by reputation), had made decidedly creative contributions to knowledge in psychology. Persons who were independently listed three or more times were then included on a rating list. The final rating list consisted of 228 names of eminent American psychologists plus 12 psychologists who were either highly visible or highly productive but who, in the judgment of the selection committee, were decidedly noncreative. These latter psychologists were included in order to provide a K factor or control, so there would be some evidence that the final ratings were being made on the basis of judgments of creativity rather than of visibility or productivity. The final ratings were obtained by asking each of the subjects to rate others on the list on a three-point scale of creativity:

1. Has shown little evidence of creativity.
2. Has shown significant evidence of creativity.
3. Has made outstandingly creative contributions.

There was no pressure to keep the raters within the limits of the three-point scale; as a matter of fact, more than 50% rated on a decimal basis (e.g., 1.5, 2.7) rather than on a whole-number basis.

In order to minimize rating by guess or by reputation, the subjects were asked to rate only psychologists on the list with whom they were personally familiar. This, of course, excluded a very large number of creative psychologists, because the familiarity of the judges was limited. Despite this inevitability, we felt that those who *were* included would be relatively representative, particularly in view of the fact that the original selection committee had a highly heterogeneous academic origin.

There was an 80% return of the completed rating lists, and only 17 subjects received fewer than 50 ratings, with the average number of ratings being over 100. No one in the final creative group was selected on the basis of fewer than 75 ratings. When the ratings were tabulated, they formed a decidedly bimodal distribution, suggesting that the rating procedure had identified two separate and distinct populations. Despite the anonymity of the raters, their clinical, experimental, or industrial orientation could be determined from the pattern of the ratings (e.g., clinicians tended to rate more clinicians and to rate them higher than they rated other interest groups, and the same with the experimentalists and the industrialists). It was gratifying to find, however, that no such patterning was discernible in the creative group, and that regardless of the rater's apparent interest and identification, the bias did not apply to the creative group. This group was rated high, regardless of the rater's probable bias. All of the 12 control-group members were in the lower 25% of the distribution, although several rated somewhat higher than anticipated. The final experimental sample was selected randomly from the upper 20% of the distribution, omitting every fourth one, so that no subject could be certain whether or not he was ranked in the final creative group.

Letters were then written to the experimental sample, asking further cooperation in undergoing an unstructured, personal interview and in taking several objective psychological tests. Approximately 90% of the prospective subjects replied in the affirmative; but because of scheduling difficulties a little less than 50% were finally contacted. A small sample of productive psychologists from the center of the distribution was used as a control, as well as a small group of psychologists holding responsible academic or professional positions who had shown no tendency whatever toward creative effort, but who, in peer opinion, had the intellectual and educational potential for creativity. This, then, provided an experimental group of 18 subjects and a combined control group of 12 subjects—small samples, but sufficient for the purpose of a pilot study. Additional subjects are still being contacted.

An interview which might best be described as a sample of "autobiographical verbal behavior" was collected from each subject. The length of the interviews ranged from one to three hours. In addition to the interview, the subjects were asked to complete two objective psychological tests, Cattell's Sixteen Personality Factor Questionnaire and Cattell's Motivational Analysis Test. The tests were scored and interpreted by standard methods, but the interviews required a more extensive analysis. For this purpose, a rating questionnaire was devised, and each of five clinically trained judges was asked to rate each subject on each of 89 interview variables.

RESULTS

Comparisons were made between the creative, noncreative productive, and combined control groups on the Motivational Analysis Test, and between the creative, noncreative nonproductive, noncreative productive, and the combined control groups on the Sixteen Personality Factor Questionnaire and the interview variables. Corrected reliabilities on the interview ratings among four out of five judges ranged from .50 to .80. Reliabilities of the fifth judge, compared with the other four, ranged between .21 and .38. Despite this variation, the final score on the interview variables was obtained by averaging the ratings of all five judges. In view of the interpretative nature of a number of the required ratings it was felt that the interjudge reliabilities were satisfactory.

On the interview variables there was a significant difference between the creative, the noncreative nonproductive, and the combined control groups, with the creative group in both instances indicating a decidedly lesser degree of authoritarian relationships with their graduate instructors. There was a difference between the creative and noncreative productive groups, with the latter showing a more competitive than cooperative relationship with fellow graduate students than did the creative group. Skepticism and inquisitiveness were significantly encouraged in the creative group, but not in the noncreative nonproductive or combined control group. There were differences indicating that the creative group had a decidedly less structured graduate training than did the noncreative nonproductive or combined control group. Parental figures provided significantly more educational stimulation for the creative group than for the noncreative productive group, but there was no significant difference between the creative and noncreative nonproductive or combined control groups. The creative group showed a greater degree of independence in college than did the noncreative nonproductive group, but there was no significant difference between the creative and noncreative productive or combined control groups in this regard. The creative group showed a decidedly greater tendency to independence in research than did the noncreative nonproductive or combined control group, although it did not differ significantly from the noncreative productive group. The creative group also showed significantly greater interest than either of the control groups in the dispassionate investigation of behavior rather than in "helping people." Although neither the noncreative productive nor the noncreative nonproductive group was significantly different from the creative group in regard to the influence of its professors, when the control groups were combined they showed a significant tendency to be more influenced by senior professors, especially in the direction of their work, than did the creative group.

The creative group was publishing significantly more independent work while in college than the noncreative nonproductive and combined control groups, but was not significantly different from the noncreative productive group in this respect. It was suggested that the pressure of professional and administrative commitments has interfered less with the current research efforts of the creative group than it has with those of the noncreative nonproductive group. The noncreative productive group was not significantly different from the creative group in this regard. The differences found indicate that neither the creative nor the noncreative productive group had thoroughly outlined and closely supervised training, while the noncreative nonproductive group appears to have experienced much closer supervision and control during graduate training. Those in the creative group show a more positive attitude toward their own graduate training than either the noncreative productive or noncreative nonproductive group, although none of them indicates a thoroughly negative attitude. The creative group shows that it had a significantly greater degree of freedom of choice in regard to both formal courses and research areas than did either the noncreative productive or noncreative nonproductive group. Here the results would suggest that the differences are more in terms of *degree* of freedom than in terms of freedom as opposed to rigidity.

The creative group appears to be very much more industrious and scientifically active than the noncreative nonproductive group. The creative and noncreative productive groups showed fewer signs of neuroticism in early life and at present than the noncreative nonproductive group, although none of them could be considered, according to the ratings, the epitome of adjustment. The noncreative nonproductive group felt considerably greater social inferiority in early life than did either the creative or noncreative productive group, and this feeling has persisted throughout adult life. Results would suggest that authority problems are also more common among the noncreative nonproductive group than among either the creative or noncreative productive group, inasmuch as the attitude toward authority of the noncreative nonproductive group is largely one of active contempt, whereas among the creative and noncreative productive groups it is more nonconcern. These groups appear to be more inclined to ignore than to battle authority. This attitude, however, is less prevalent among the noncreative productive group than among the creative group.

In some regard, the noncreative productive group shows a somewhat striking tendency to have been given fewer home responsibilities at an early age than either the creative or noncreative nonproductive group. It is indicated that the creative group displayed a significantly stronger attachment to and positive feeling toward the mother than the father in early life than did any of the other groups. Reward had been used considerably more frequently than punishment as a training device in the creative group as opposed to the noncreative nonproductive group. There was not a significant difference between the creative and the noncreative productive groups in this regard. The noncreative nonproductive group has a much stronger tendency to avoid criticism than either the creative or noncreative productive group, although once criticism is forthcoming, all three groups are reasonably accepting of it. The creative group showed significant evidence of creativity in early life, as compared with the noncreative nonproductive group, but there was no appreciable difference between the creative and noncreative productive groups in this respect. The creative group shows a significantly greater degree of adherence to the tenets of some orthodox religion than either of the control groups. The ratings, however, suggest that this greater degree of adherence does not indicate any great degree of religious orthodoxy. In addition, the creative group has less need for approval and finds it more often in "in-groups" or "professional groups" than does the noncreative nonproductive group. The noncreative productive group is not different from the creative group in regard to this characteristic. The noncreative nonproductive group shows more concern over relationships with the opposite sex or sexual life in general than the creative group, which is not significantly different from the noncreative productive group in this characteristic.

Early social adjustment was of considerably less importance to the creative group than to the noncreative nonproductive group or to the noncreative productive group, although the latter is not significantly different from the creative group, even though it contributes to a higher degree of significance between the creative and the combined control groups than was found between the creative and the noncreative nonproductive groups. The noncreative nonproductive group indicates a greater fear of authority than the creative, but the creative is not significantly different from the noncreative productive.

The noncreative productive group shows significantly less family pressure for educational achievement than does the creative group; and the addition of the noncreative nonproductive group to the combined control group slightly increases rather than decreases the degree of significance, suggesting that family pressure for educational achievement may well be of considerable importance. The noncreative productive group also shows somewhat more liberal social and political attitudes than does the creative group, but neither group, according to the ratings, could be considered anything but slightly "left of center" politically and socially. It is suggested that periods of greatest creativity came earlier in the career of the creative group than of the noncreative nonproductive group. Again there is no significant difference between the creative and the noncreative productive group. Results indicate that intrinsic motivation is of considerably greater importance for the creative group than for the noncreative nonproductive group. The noncreative productive group is not significantly different from the creative group.

On the Motivational Analysis Test there was only one clear-cut difference between groups. In this instance, the creative group showed a significantly greater attachment to home and family than did the noncreative productive group. On the Sixteen Personality Factor Questionnaire, however, there were a number of differences among groups. On factor E, the noncreative productive group showed a significantly greater degree of dominance, aggressiveness, and competitiveness than did the creative group. There was no difference between the creative and noncreative nonproductive groups on this factor. The noncreative productive group also showed a greater degree of surgency (factor F) and a lesser degree of conscientiousness and persistence (factor G, Superego Strength) than did the creative group. Again, there was no difference between the creative and noncreative nonproductive groups on these factors.

On factor H, the creative group was significantly more adventurous and responsive than the noncreative nonproductive group, but significantly less so than the noncreative productive group. On this characteristic the creative group therefore occupies a middle ground between the noncreative productive and the noncreative nonproductive groups.

On the factor of Bohemian Unconcern (M) the creative group shows a significantly lesser tendency to unconventionality and more concern with practicality than the noncreative nonproductive group but does not differ from the noncreative productive group on this factor. On factor N, the creative group shows a greater degree of sophistication and insight than does the noncreative productive group, but again there is no difference between the creative and the noncreative nonproductive groups. On factors O and Q_4 the noncreative nonproductive group displays a greater degree of insecurity, anxiety, and tenseness than does either the creative or noncreative productive group.

DISCUSSION

No attempt has been made to compare the experimental groups in this study to the normal population. In regard to the Sixteen Personality Factor Questionnaire and the Motivational Analysis Test, such comparisons have been made before. As far as the interview analysis rating sheet is concerned, it is so constructed as to be largely inappropriate for a sample of the general population. However, a considerable amount of further information can be derived by inspecting the relative absolute mean positions of the experimental groups on the rating scale even though they may not differ significantly among themselves. In general, as opposed to the noncreative nonproductive group, those in the creative group appear to have had a considerably more loose-knit, free, and independent type of training. They appear to be decidedly more interested in scientific investigation than in a more socially oriented activity. Their relative nonconcern with other people, authority, rules, regulations, restrictions, and the like indicate a decided degree of independence, unshaken by pressures from the external world. Their personal, social, and emotional adjustment is superior to that of their less eminent colleagues, but it is not by any means (on an absolute scale) close to perfect. They appear to be unusually self-oriented in most respects, paying little attention to such things as social and sexual relationships and public or professional criticism. At the same time, they appear to be able to accept without any overconcern moral and social relationships and activities such as religious affiliation, friendships, politics, and the like. There is, however, in regard to these latter, a tendency to "go through the motions" without any great emotional involvement. This self-orientation and lack of concern with the social environment does not appear to be an attempt to escape, but merely the result of an evaluation of life that places such things toward the bottom of a hierarchy of importance. In general, this group appears to have been given early independence combined with responsibility—much more so than either the noncreative productive or noncreative nonproductive group—and to have received somewhat more family, rather than nonfamily, pressure for achievement, but always within a less emotive and frantic atmosphere than the other groups.

The noncreative productive group differs from the creative group to a lesser degree than does the noncreative nonproductive group. It differs largely in its greater concern with people and social relationships and its lesser independence and responsibility, in its greater competitiveness and rebelliousness, and in a smaller degree of family pressure for educational achievement. The noncreative nonproductive group, on the other hand, appears to have had a much more stormy childhood and maintains a much more contemptuous, emotionally tinged, and rebellious attitude toward society in general and authority in particular. These persons have undergone a more rigid, well-outlined professional training than the creative group and appear to have been more concerned with, and diverted by, interpersonal and social relationships. This group also shows more signs of neuroticism and feelings of insecurity and inferiority, both in early life and at present, than does the creative group. The noncreative nonproductive group also appears to be considerably more fearful, dependent, and concerned with both peer and public approval.

The implications of these findings must, because of the pilot nature of the study, be considered cautiously; but within that limitation, some interesting speculations may be made. The first is that early childhood training may be of somewhat less importance in the development of creativity than is sometimes suggested. There is no indication, for example, that sibling or Oedipal rivalry has much to do with differences in creativity. The most important factors in the early home environment appear to be the delegation of definite responsibility at an early age, and the valuation within the family group of education and/or knowledge for its own sake. These items appear to be considerably more important than whether or not the family is of professional, middle-class origin.

In addition, it would appear that a nondirective, relatively unstructured, advanced training is of significant benefit. The outstanding feature, educationally, is that the creative group and to some extent the noncreative productive group, as opposed to the noncreative nonproductive group, received what might be described as a "laissez-faire" type of graduate training. They had few, if any, required courses, an encouragement of research activity to the exclusion of formal courses, and significant freedom of choice as to both courses and research. The experiences of the members of the creative group might better be described in their own words:

We had tremendous freedom at _____ University. This period was a very interesting one. We were taught practically nothing. We developed a colloquium and generally taught ourselves. Now I think we tend to keep our students in class too much.

Or:

I very often read a Ph.D. thesis done under me, and I don't know what is in it until I open it. _____ made an appointment with me to discuss his thesis. I assumed it was about the plans for it. Well, he brought the completed thesis in; and, you know, that's the way it ought to be.

Or:

Frankly, I think things now are going to the dogs. I approve of the apprenticeship program of training. Here we have no required courses. Students do research. When I was a graduate student the same situation existed. Why, when it came time to get my Ph.D., I took my publications, bound them, and retitled them, and it was accepted.

This would seem to speak poorly for the increasingly structured, rigidly outlined educational programs now so prevalent. The American Psychological Association is an outstanding offender in this respect with its multiplicity of evaluative and inspecting committees. It might behoove the APA, as well as other educational and professional agencies, to place more faith in institutional faculties and less upon roving bands of "inspectors general." There can be little doubt that conformity, enforced to the point of producing emotional reaction, is detrimental to creativity.

Also of interest is the possibility, in view of the apparently greater feminine identification of the creative as opposed to the noncreative productive and noncreative nonproductive groups, that such identification might not be as personally and professionally destructive as is suggested by some analytically oriented psychologists. The problem of feminine identification would appear to be more a problem of the individual's acceptance of it than its mere existence.

Still another factor that might well be considered in both child training and in educative procedures is the extent to which responsibility for behavior is placed upon the individual. The creative group appears to be more responsible, self-accepting, and tolerant than either of the control groups. It seems apparent that this is derived from a family and educational experience where responsibility and self-acceptance are coupled, and where dependency and its consequences, anxiety and rebelliousness, are diminished.

Several other characteristics of the experimental groups, even though their statistical significance might be questionable, were discernible from an examination of the interview protocols. In general, the creative group came from a background where the "right" sort of behavior was expected but where there was little overt coercion in regard to this behavior. The individual was given a good deal of freedom and personal responsibility at an early age with the largely *unenforced* expectation that he would behave in a creditable manner.

There was also an apparent element of emotional coolness in the family relationships. It appeared that respect was a more important factor in these relationships than a strong emotional attachment; and although emotional attachments most certainly were not lacking, they appeared to be secondary. This is in marked contrast to the noncreative productive group, where emotional relationships were decidedly emphasized, but where conflict—emotional and/or social—was outstanding, and to the noncreative nonproductive group, where partial rejection and/or suppression were added to the emotionality and conflict.

One might speculate at this point that the outstandingly creative individual is one who, at an early age, effectively intellectualizes his emotionality, whereas one who is decidedly productive and somewhat creative tends to displace his emotionality. Those who are creatively unproductive tend to suppress or repress their emotionality and consequently feel inhibited and bound.

There are several other factors which may be of interest, the first being the receptiveness of the subjects to the interviewing procedure. All but one of the creative group were most receptive and socially responsive; and their reaction to the interview situation would lead one to suspect that, for the most part, they were as cooperative and responsive as they were capable of being. One bit of evidence for this is found in the manner of expression and its change, which is apparent in most of the interviews. In the first ten to twenty minutes, the subject's language was polite, objective, and scientific to a large degree. After that period, more often than not, "father" had become "the old man" and "my sibling" had become "that stupid brother of mine."

Two other factors regarding the general characteristics of the experimental group might deserve some comment. Although almost half of the persons included in the original list of prospective subjects were applied psychologists (those sanctioned by the American Board of Examiners in Professional Psychology), only three applied psychologists were in the creative group; and those particular three were equally noted for their contributions to other areas of psychology. (The others in the creative group were in experimental and theoretical psychology.) This appears to be a rather sad commentary on the effectiveness and meaningfulness, for research at least, of the American Board Examinations. The other factor involves geographic location. If you draw a line from Washington, D.C., through the Menninger Clinic to Los Angeles, you will have isolated, in the upper portion, the entire creative population. Five institutions—Stanford, California, Minnesota, Harvard, and Yale—contributed by far the majority of the creative subjects.

I think that these results also tend to emphasize the possibility that, lacking an extremely pathological childhood situation, adolescent and adult experiences have more effect upon basic patterns of behavior than many of us have been willing to admit. They also suggest that there may be more hope of *producing* rather than merely identifying creative talents.

We are now beginning a more intensive longitudinal study of developmental factors (provided that support is forthcoming), using as a source of information not just the potential subject, but also objective measures of his environmental circumstances and his unique response to those circumstances as he develops. Information will also be collected from a variety of informants (e.g., parents, siblings, companions, instructors, wives, husbands, etc.) who see the subject from a unique point of view.

In several instances in the study just reported, information of an unusually illuminating nature was obtained from close relatives or friends of the subject and aided considerably in the interpretation of the subject's own expressed attitudes, feelings, etc.

Now let me spend just a few moments on possible implications of this study. I hesitate to apply these results, because of their very tentative nature, to a specific situation; but let us consider a problem with which most of us are familiar—that of education in psychology. This has become increasingly structured and solidified in recent years, until it is just the opposite of the sort of educational experiences reported by the creative subjects of this study. It seems to me that psychology, and particularly clinical psychology, has developed a pathological concern for regulation, re-regulation, and more regulation. The ever-increasing emphasis on examinations, certifications, licensure, diplomacies, fellowships, superdiplomacies, and super-supercertifications is leading psychologists into creative and intellectual sterility. The fact that our present procedures are not producing the type of persons we theoretically claim to train (psychologists first and clinicians second) is evidenced by the Miami Beach conference report, which pointed out that the median number of publications for clinical psychologists is zero. I can't say that I am surprised at this information because, when we train students to be so completely dependent upon rigid rules, regulations, and the approval of thirty different boards and committees before they make a step, it would be ridiculous to expect them to suddenly change their character and involve themselves in a research project where there are no guides and no one to tell them what to do.

C   Isn't it true that zero publications is also the median for the total profession?

S   That I don't know. I hope not.

C   It's approximately true for practically all sciences.

S   Picture the newborn clinician who, out in his first responsible position, comes up with the idea, "Here is a good project for investigation." What happens? He has to decide how to go about it. So he consults the recommended procedures of APA Committee A—no help; then the stipulated practices of APA Committee B—still no help; then the recommended research suggestions of the Society of Experimental Psychologists—not applicable; then the research restrictions of the Code of Ethics—lots of restrictions but no positive suggestions; then the proceedings of the APA Committee on the Relationship between X and Z—nothing there; then the recommendations of the APA Committee on the Committee on the Relationship between X and Z—still nothing. Finally he realizes, for the first time in his embryonic career, "My God, there are no rules!" and he beats a hasty retreat from this foreign and foreboding area, vowing never to go near it again.

The safest thing for a clinician to do in our present professional and intellectual climate is to avoid all possibility of criticism by avoiding anything new. My own research on the creative personality, as well as the research of others, has convinced me that the sort of person who advocates, accepts, and is happy with multifarious rules, regulations, acceptable procedures, etc., is not ever going to be creative and productive. The creative person (the researcher) is one who disdains such rigidity, conformity, and consequent sterility.

C   You're going to make it difficult for our graduate students to finish their work.

C   At least they'll have one professor to sympathize with them.

S   Even though the results of perhaps most studies of creativity are tentative, as a body of knowledge there is, as Calvin Taylor points out, much consistency, and we now have the problem of putting it to use.

C   The picture you draw here of the clinician so bound by rules and regulations and referring to committees and so on . . . it seems to me that it is drawn for emphasis with an exceedingly broad brush.

S   My point was not in terms of any specific regulations of *research* activity, but of regulation of activity, mostly professional or training activity, so that one gets into the habit of responding only to regulations.

C   Do you think that a great deal of the restriction of productivity in terms of research is a function of the fact that the principal job description is a service description? The clinician is to perform specific services, and from ninth to tenth on the list he is to do research, where applicable. Research is, I presume, a minor part of what he wants to do and is expected to do. The identification of a creative clinician is almost impossible because his most creative, most significant work is done in private. Although I bet that a particular clinician is a hot shot, he may be a mess when the office door is closed. Or another one who doesn't seem to be able to do anything may be absolutely first class in a clinical situation.

C   Your evidence shows the creative group adhering to a significantly greater degree to the tenets of some orthodox religion than either of the control groups.   Yet you also say that the ratings suggest that this greater degree of adherence does not indicate any marked degree of religious orthodoxy.

S   I meant on an absolute scale from complete religious orthodoxy to no religion whatsoever.

C   I vaguely remember reading some opposite findings, and I wonder whether there is any other evidence on this.

C   MacKinnon found that his subjects were low on religious values, not directly on orthodoxy.

C   Some studies show very large differences between eminent scientists of one religious group and those of another.   How do you define this designation of orthodoxy?

S   By membership in any religion.   I agree with the comment that the findings in my study and in MacKinnon's study of architects are very similar—and it's not collusion, since we have not had any contact with each other before.

C   In our study, the creative architects grew up in families where there was much less emphasis upon formal religious practices.   There was a good deal of emphasis upon ethical values and considerations, with expectations that the children would incorporate in themselves some values, but there was a great deal of freedom in the way that they would do this.   In early life history factors, there is again remarkable congruence between our findings and those that you have reported— sort of an emotional distance rather than close emotional ties within the family; early expectations that the child would do what is right, giving him a great deal of freedom to act in his own way, with the child very seldom infringing the kind of implicit standards of the family, roaming, being quite independent, and so forth.   So there is the remarkable congruence not only with respect to personality but also with respect to the early kinds of life history circumstances that seem to foster creativity.

C   Many of the sciences in turn have had somewhat of a struggle with religion.   Psychology seems to be one that has been more involved in this struggle in the recent era than some of the physical sciences, which had their main conflicts earlier.   I wonder whether there would consequently be differences across scientific groups at any one period of time.

C   There is a very large difference between scientists who are practicing Catholics and those who are practicing Protestants. The differences between proportions are quite substantial from some studies.

C   But apparently this varies with countries in time, for among the scientists voted in a recent poll to be the ten outstanding Louis Pasteur and Newton were obviously devoutly religious and highly orthodox. Some others in that top ten were completely the reverse.

C   In the IPAR study of women mathematicians, without knowledge of who was in a creative group and who was in a control group, the life history interviewers rated each subject on certain psychoanalytical mechanisms, including sublimation of emotional reactions and reaction formation. Sublimation was clearly associated with creativity, and when Drevdahl used the term "intellectualizing emotion," it seemed to be quite equivalent to sublimation.

C   Do you have any information on birth order of these various groups?

S   No.

C   Did they know anything about what you were doing, that it was something about creativity? And did the lows know that they were lows and the highs sense that they were high?

S   Yes, unfortunately, the lows knew that they were lows.

C   You say that "the creative group shows a significantly greater degree of adherence to the tenets." Can we change the word "tenets" to "values"?

S   No, it was specifically dogma. But none of them would be considered strongly orthodox in any way, if they were compared with the general population.

C   I happen to know several people who I think are quite creative researchers who started out in clinical training at least in their first year or so in graduate school or maybe went all the way through as clinicians. I'm wondering about how much the lack of productivity of the practicing clinician or counselor is due to the kind of person he is, the kinds of—I would say—skills and talents he has, his orientation toward life, rather than to any particular educational experience that he had. I wonder what you think about that.

S   I think that the other things you mention are probably of equal or perhaps greater importance. I have to make the assumption that educational experiences do have some effect on people. This effect may be minor, but if it is leading them to, or putting them in, a situation that is restrictive, then they learn to behave in a restrictive situation and find that more natural than a free-floating, unstructured situation.

C   I want to speak about a criticism of the selection of criterion groups and criteria by all of us. In order to be creative, you have to be an artist or a scientist, or in psychology you have to publish research. I think that in the case of the clinician this approach is irrelevant. He goes into this area because he initially wants to become a practitioner of some kind, and he may do this very creatively. We ought to be determining how one can be creative as a clinician, as an administrator, or as a leader, so that we do not, in any sense, lose the potential creatives for good. In the same way, we say that if a person does not achieve in arts, science, leadership, or grades, he must be no good. This is ridiculous, and people are beginning to realize it. For example, from a very literal interpretation of the evidence on the Strong Interest Inventory, an accountant cannot be creative, nor can a bricklayer.

C   We have a controller who may be the most creative member of our university administration.

C   Part of this reflects our biases as psychologists. For example, you are not a good psychologist unless you hate administrators, it seems. At least you dislike them, or do not have any friends among them or have just distant relationships, which I think is unfortunate, as is to hate or dislike or be uncomfortable with religious people. It is unfortunate that we don't recognize any of these biases, although we all know them as soon as somebody mentions them.

C   I think the comment has come up repeatedly that a person can be creative in any endeavor. Any endeavor that a person can do can be done more or less creatively. But I think we often ignore that by going back to these usual two or three criteria.

C   Are you suggesting that, when we release some of these data about creativity, we may have a counterpart to the "organizational" man, a new model which everybody will then pattern himself after in order to be creative?

C   No. What I am saying is that we ought to try devoting some effort to some other areas. That is all I am saying.

C   When you select or apply a criterion like this across the board with heterogeneous groups, what you come out with as distinctions between high creatives and low creatives very often correlates with the interests or the motivation of the people involved rather than what it really takes to be creative. I would think that a better way to get at what it takes to be creative would be to select only people who are attempting to achieve in a particular area. Then whatever differentiates between high and low achievers only within this area presumably would reflect what it takes to be creative.

C   I disagree with you. In the 1959 conference someone mentioned that there is an important difference between the student who is creative or productive on his own, and one who is told to be so by his teacher. The latter person says, "All right, sir, if you want me to, then I will be." The spontaneous interest of the former student in producing or being creative may be one of the most important things we are looking for, the difference between someone who has to be told to do something, and one who does it naturally.

C   I think it is important that you choose criteria that are appropriate for the particular people whom you are studying.

C   I would accept that, but I would argue that for the people under study by Drevdahl the opportunity to publish was there. Perhaps the clinician does not naturally have publishing ability, so that he would be hampered on this publication criterion if his creativity is devoted to the individual. But I don't think that this is a criticism of the basis of selecting the people for minimum publication.

C   I don't see why self-induced creativity should be of a higher order than externally induced creativity. Those in universities are either subtly or less subtly reminded every so often that creativity is highly encouraged. I don't know that it is less significant to make a great discovery in chemistry because the chairman of the department said, "Isn't it about time you did something?", than to make a comparable discovery on one's own.

C   Another important consideration is the inhibiting factor in someone who is not creative because he is smart enough to know not to be creative in his setting. Changing the situation to remove that inhibition and allow his creativity to emerge is just as important as the identification of his creativity.

C   There are some other ambiguities here. In defining creativity, some people are referring to those who know when to be creative and when not to be. Others are referring to a desire to be creative even when this is unnecessary or uncalled for, that is, an overall attitude to go after the unusual. The other ambiguity I see is that some are thinking of creativity as an end in itself, whereas others obviously regard it as something desirable because it will produce results that in some sense are good for science or for humanity.

chapter 13 Progress and Potentiality:

Career Determiners of High-Level Personnel

Lindsey R. Harmon, National Academy of Sciences–National Research Council

        S My research has not been too directly on the subject of "creativity" but rather on high-level personnel, the selection of people who may be productive as scientists, and manpower problems generally at the doctorate level. Many of the people with whom our research deals are creative in the sense that their work results, every now and then, in a more or less extensive restructuring of concept structures in the science areas. They make important new discoveries, devise new techniques which open up diverse avenues of scientific development, or construct new theoretical formulations—all these kinds of activities no doubt can be classified as creative. But such activities or achievements are relatively rare, and persons who characteristically operate in these ways are also rather rare. A few creative people can spark the work of many lesser men. Most of the work of most scientists is likely to be somewhat more mundane. The careful teasing out of the fine structure of fact along lines which some earlier creative act has suggested; the testing of hypotheses derived from an accepted theoretical framework; the accumulation of data which, most of the time, will reveal no important divergencies from the customary ways of thinking about our world—this is the workaday world of most of the research people with whom our studies deal. Others are teachers, or combine research with teaching, or are administrators of scientific laboratories, along with more or less research of their own, or do consulting work in science, or they may engage in various combinations of these activities.

187

In our follow-up validation studies of the selection techniques used in the National Science Foundation fellowship program, the contributions of the people studied are evaluated on a broad basis. This basis includes creativity as one of many components, often not clearly distinguished, which make a man more or less valuable as a scientist. Thomas Kuhn, one of the more creative of the individuals who attended the last Utah conference, spoke of the "essential tension" between the creative activity and that of building carefully and well within an accepted theoretical structure. This is a tension which exists within individual investigators, as well as one which describes the relationships between the more and the less creative individuals. For the optimum growth of science, we need to consider this relationship between the "movers and shakers," on the one hand, and the more prosaic builders on the other. The latter are, and need to be, the more numerous. It is therefore the latter, and primarily the more prosaic activity of most people, which constitutes the bulk of our research on scientific manpower problems. It is for this reason that I speak of "high-level manpower" rather than "creative individuals" although, as you will see, we do not ignore creativity and its genesis.

What I will do here is to try to pull together several rather scattered strands of evidence regarding the factors affecting decision making, and try to weave them into a meaningful fabric. I am not sure that this can be done with any great assurance at this point, particularly inasmuch as the evidence is primarily correlational, rather than experimental, and we therefore cannot be very sure whether phenomenon A causes B, or B causes A, or both result from some other set of conditions which we have not observed. My approach to this subject may at first be more cautious than dramatic, but I will proceed in the reverse of the developmental order, considering first those observations that relate to people who have already attained the doctorate, then go to the graduate school and to evidence relating the secondary school and graduate school levels, then to some elementary school developments, and finally to some experimentation at the preschool level. Having described these somewhat scattered findings, I will make a wild attempt to show that they may be part of a consistent schema. I appreciate the opportunity to discuss these matters with you and believe that I will profit more from your comment and discussion than you are likely to gain from my evidence or attempts at systematization. If all of this adds anything to what we know or believe about creativity, I shall be thankful.

Our follow-up validation studies present some evidence regarding the employment of people with postdoctoral training: they are predominantly in jobs in the academic setting rather than in government or industry. Because there is an interaction between field of specialization and subsequent employer category, with bioscientists in greater proportion going into academic jobs, and because a higher proportion of bioscientists have postdoctoral training, we are in a poor position to say what are the chains of causality here. However, we partially controlled this situation, by splitting out the various fields. Again it became apparent that in every field with numbers high enough for reliability, except for biology, the postdoctorals go more frequently into academic jobs. The only generalization which I care to venture at this point from these results is that there seems to be an element of intellectuality or affinity for situations affecting learning, or for the acquisition and diffusion of knowledge, that runs through these data, whether such concern is exercised primarily by the employers or the seekers of employment, or both.

Going back one step to graduate school, I can report now what I could not at the last Utah conference, because the data became available a few months after the conference. Some of you have seen these data in my *Technical Report* #15, on research on fellowship selection techniques, supported by the NSF. Table 1 presents the data of the validity of five predictor instruments against a rating criterion of scientific accomplishment. The ratings were rendered by supervisors for the most part, partially by colleagues—in all cases by persons nominated by the ratee himself as those knowing most about his scientific accomplishments. You will note that among those who held NSF awards we obtained positive validities for quantitative test scores and advanced achievement test scores of the Graduate Record Examination, but little validity for the verbal score. The grade-point average in undergraduate work had modest validity, except in engineering, and ratings at the time of application for fellowship, a decade before the follow-up, had considerable validity. Finally, a weighted composite score, with weights predetermined on the basis of quite other evidence than these validities (the summary score) was pretty good. You will also note an interesting and puzzling phenomenon, for which we have as yet no adequate explanation—the validity is almost entirely within the awardee group; these same predictors did not work for the nonawardees.[1]

What can we make of this evidence? There is a suggestion in the poor showing of the verbal test that our academic world overweights verbal

---

[1] Subsequent research by Dr. John A. Creager, with larger numbers of cases, showed validity coefficients similar to those reported here for the awardees. But, in his results, both nonawardees and awardees had similar validity patterns. See *Technical Report* #22, Office of Scientific Personnel, National Academy of Sciences–National Research Council.

TABLE 1

Validity Coefficients of Five Predictor Instruments
Against a Rating of Scientific Accomplishment

		Math.	Physics	Chem.	Eng.	Biol.	Weighted Mean of Five Fields
Verbal	Awardees	.49*	.13	−.23	−.08	.24	.11
ability		(19)	(78)	(48)	(09)	(61)	(219)
	Nonawardees	.04	.00	.09	−.41	−.20	−.09
		(07)	(44)	(29)	(13)	(47)	(136)
	Total	.51**	.15	−.07	−.29	.09	.08
		(26)	(122)	(77)	(22)	(108)	(355)
Quantitative	Awardees	.62**	.17	.09	−.30	.31*	.22**
ability	Nonawardees	−.02	.23	−.17	.21	.07	.08
	Total	.64**	.28**	−.01	−.06	.22*	.21**
Advanced	Awardees	.21	.34**	.08	.79*	.26*	.28**
achievement	Nonawardees	−.28	.06	.20	−.35	.02	.02
test	Total	.25	.32**	.13	.12	.16	.21**
Grade-point	Awardees	.51*	.21	.21	.04	.08	.19**
average	Nonawardees	−.42	−.25	.16	−.06	.13	−.03
	Total	.49*	.04	.20	.00	.12	.13**
Descriptive	Awardees	.24	.19	.40**	.44	.34**	.30**
report	Nonawardees	−.09	.05	−.05	.47	.02	.05
score	Total	.43*	.19*	.22	.32	.17	.22*
Summary	Awardees	.49*	.42**	.28*	.66*	.49**	.43**
score	Nonawardees	−.16	−.03	.02	−.05	−.02	−.02
	Total	.55**	.33**	.18	.24	.24*	.28**

* Coefficients significant at the 5% level.
** Coefficients significant at the 1% level.
Numbers of cases are shown in parentheses in the first three lines.
The final column in Table 1 gives the mean (through the z transformation) of the five coefficients, weighted according to the number of cases in each field. It must be noted that many of the coefficients in this table are based on very small N's. For this reason some of the largest coefficients are not significant.

ability, as compared with the job requirements of most scientists, and has tended to promote differentially to the graduate level persons whose verbal capacities outstrip their functional performance, so that when we follow them up, the verbal test has lost its validity leverage. There is also the strong hint, in the better showing of the ratings as compared with the objective tests, and also as compared with the grade-point averages, that professors in evaluating their graduate students are able to sense something important, probably in the general area of personality, that goes beyond what our more objective measures can show. The rating called "descriptive report score" was a global one of overall

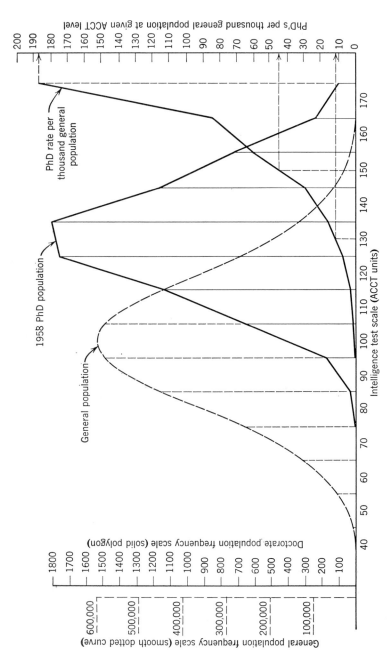

Figure 1 Distribution of general intelligence test scores from high school records of 1958 doctorate population compared with general population score distribution (both expressed in terms of Army General Classification Test scores).

promise as a Ph.D. candidate; the raters were frequently concerned with imagination, curiosity, persistence, emotional stability, etc. These personality traits, which relate to a person's ability to release his energy effectively in the attack on a problem, constitute the second scrap or thread of evidence which I wish to pick up today.

We have made other studies, in which we have gone back to the high schools from which came all the Ph.D.'s of 1958 of United States origin. We obtained data on the test scores in their cumulative records, their grades in mathematics and science courses, and their class rank on graduation. A fairly extensive report on this research was published in March 1961 in *Science*. I wish today to pick out three or four items from these studies which give some evidence regarding career determiners. The first concerns the ability levels of these people. Although they are superior to the general population, as shown in Figure 1, they are not as much superior as many of us would have supposed. A few actually obtain intelligence test scores below the general population mean. Some of these low scores are undoubtedly measurement errors. But from a careful examination of the transcripts, at least a few seem to be accurate measurements: they were consistent through several tests, the high school grades were consistent with the tests, and the doctorates, when finally attained at the age of 40 or later, were in fields not noted for their intellectual rigor.

A second item of evidence concerns the size of the high schools from which these people came. The proportions of the high school graduates from each size of high school who later attained the doctorate are shown in Figure 2. Size alone is not important, as is indicated by the discontinuity at the highest level. At the top end of the scale we move into a group of high schools, chiefly in New York City, where there is selection on the basis of academic ability, as well as great size of school. At the other end of the scale, in the smallest schools where the intellectual life is likely to be impoverished for a number of reasons, the probability of an eventual doctorate declines catastrophically. We have at present only a minor amount of evidence regarding the intellectual climate in these smaller schools, but in general I am sure you know what it is— a rural school, most likely, where most of the parents had a high school education at best, and frequently not more than a grade school education. The chief function of the high school is seen by many of the smaller communities—in the Midwest at least—as that of winning basketball games for the glory of the local hamlet. Science is taught by the athletic coach, and only an occasional intellectual has the stamina, the devotion, or other irrational motivation to remain and teach in such an inadequate school. So only a few students from these schools go to college, and of those that do, a disproportionately small number continue on to graduate school.

A third item of evidence emerged when Dr. Jessie Bernard, a sociologist from Pennsylvania State University, came down to look over our data. She was interested in women doctorate-holders, primarily. She had us run off the distributions of ability measures for the women and found that in every field the women doctorate-holders attained higher

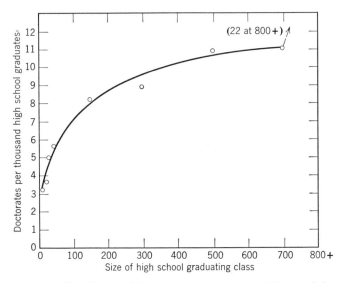

Figure 2   The relation of doctorate productivity to high school size.

scores on the high school intelligence tests than did the men, the differences ranging from 2.2 points on the Army General Classification Test scale for education to 8.3 points in the social sciences. In the physical sciences, where very few women attain doctorates, the difference was 6.3 points in favor of the fair sex. My conclusion at this point is limited to the simple observation that if an assortment of people is required to jump a miscellaneous set of hurdles, those who have had to leap the highest hurdles will on the average have the most ability. There is no question in my mind that women have a tougher time than men in the graduate schools.

C   And not just there: differential selection and retention enter at every level beyond the high school.

S   Quite true. I should have included these other steps too.

A fourth item of evidence, and one which is more directly on the topic of career choice, is the finding that there exist distinctive patterns of high school achievement for people whose doctorates are in different fields. It would be no surprise, I presume, to note that more bioscientists had biology courses in high school. But it was a distinct surprise to us to find that even mathematicians and physicists could be distinguished on the basis of their grades in math and science in high school courses. The mathematicians did slightly better in their math courses; the physicists did distinctly better in the laboratory sciences and took more lab courses than did the mathematicians. We have not now available the details of these data for the various fields, but we expect in the coming weeks to try out a multiple-discriminant analysis technique on the 7090 computer to try to measure quantitatively the extent to which the pattern of high school grades and course choices distinguishes the various fields of doctorate specialization 12 to 16 years later. The evidence, as we have seen it in looking over a number of tables too cumbersome to include here, is that there is a surprising number of good data. Apparently experience with high school courses is very important in heading people in the direction of one field of specialization rather than another. This experience is of course a compound of many things, including native ability, opportunity, the personality of the teacher, the circumstances of competition in the high school and in the particular course, preclusive concerns at this level with nonacademic activities, and the advice and encouragement of teachers, friends, parents, etc. I hope that we will have more of a definitive nature to report in the months to come.

Below the high school level, I cannot report evidence from our own researches but wish to suggest the pertinence of a number of developments since the last Utah conference. One of these concerns the teaching of math courses at younger and younger levels—introducing students to advanced mathematical concepts in the grades, teaching calculus as a regular thing in high school, etc. I am not at present close enough to these developments to report on them with any degree of comprehensiveness or authority. Suffice it to say at this point that the evidence seems unambiguous that children of very tender ages can learn mathematical ways of thinking that we used to believe had to be reserved for college or even graduate school levels. For perspective here it is worthy of note that 100 years ago in this country one had to go to college to get a course in plane geometry, and a course in the calculus was hardly available anywhere. So we *do* see a mass movement over time, and very recently a quickening of this movement, together with some perception of how much farther it may go in the not-too-distant future.

Another experiment which some of you may know about—and perhaps may know much more about than I do—concerns the teaching of reading at the age of two and one-half to four years of age. This has now progressed to the stage where a rather complex electronic teaching machine—a "responsive environment"—is replacing the "Model T" operations of the first experimental phase, where the only mechanization was a portable electric typewriter that the child played with while the teacher held the control switch in her hand to prevent injury and, at a later stage, to provide or withhold reinforcement of the child's spontaneous operant behavior. The significance of the findings here relates not merely (and perhaps not primarily) to the early age at which children can learn to read, but rather to the nature of the environment in which they thus learn. It has been described as entirely "autotelic," that is, a self-motivated play environment, in which the child explores and learns what happens in response to his exploration. What he finds is that, when he hits the keys of the typewriter, he obtains different responses from his environment, depending on which keys he hits. The "teacher" (now the loudspeaker) says "a" or "9" or "semicolon" or "per cent" or whatever, and a symbol which the child sees on the key also appears on the paper in the machine. In a surprisingly short time he associates the key-pushing behavior on his part with these patterns of sounds and knows the alphabet. By a progressive phonetic approach, he learns the sound of syllables and then is able to take on whole words, even very long ones. We saw a movie in which a child was reading one-syllable words projected on the screen from a filmstrip which he himself controlled. The word "infinitesimal" appeared suddenly. The child sounded it out correctly, and the teacher simply said, "It means very tiny." The child took it in stride and went right on with the rest of the words. The general finding of this work is that children can learn to read rather well in 12 to 14 weeks, and, as the principal researcher (Omar K. Moore, a sociologist) told me, "Of course the brighter ones learn faster. The average ones perform merely at the prodigy level." The work is being done in a private school near New Haven; a number of Yale University staff members are concerned with it—psychologists, sociologists, mathematicians, philosophers, engineers, linguists, etc.

One more item, and I will quit this woolgathering and start to spin my web. In California a few years ago some teachers of the dance filmed the progress of a group of seven or eight children from a rural community in the mountains in learning expressive movement in dance form. About two weeks, or three at the most as I recall it, were used, on an hour-a-day basis, in the teaching. The learning progressed, as did O. K. Moore's research, on a systematic basis from the simplest activities to the more complex, but always in a play environment. The children were not taught *how to dance*—they were encouraged to *feel music* and to express, each in his own way, what they felt. It proceeded from simple hand-clapping to more extensive bodily movements, and at the end of this brief period two of the girls, one about five and the other about ten, were dancing superbly, in an entirely improvised and spontaneous fashion, to music which was new to them, at least in the context of dancing. Each child developed an individual style, a gangling adolescent boy leaping like a gazelle, the girls whirling and swaying and tapping in fantastically beautiful and coordinated movements of body, arms, legs, head, and hands, in perfect time to the music—each interpreting through the dance just how this music made him feel.

Well, where does this take us? Tying these diverse strands together and weaving a fabric of consistent thought may be a bit presumptuous. Yet I'll try it and will appreciate your comments, or your own attempts to make something quite different out of this evidence, together with whatever other data you may feel are relevant.

In summing up and characterizing these rather heterogeneous scraps of evidence, the first point concerns human learning potential. There is excellent evidence of far more learning ability—mathematical, verbal, aesthetic (and, I would add, social-emotional)—than our psychometric philosophy has characteristically assumed. Second, we have some strong hints as to how all these potentialities may be better developed. In some areas, indeed, soundly based technologies are already in operation, as in programmed learning and the use of teaching machines. These techniques of drawing out and developing latent talents have a strong family resemblance to the conditions discussed frequently in these conferences and elsewhere as fostering creativity.

Third, the grade and course-choice patterns at the high school level which characterize fields of doctorate specialization can be assimilated as readily to the reinforcement principle as to a doctrine of constitutional differences. When regional and school-size differentials are also brought into the picture, the reinforcement interpretation is greatly strengthened, and a genetic interpretation encounters severe embarrassments. (As an aside, the somewhat contentious tone of *this* assessment is probably a reflection of the difficulties I have had in giving up a deeply rooted hereditarian bias, derived from my Patersonian training at Minnesota during the early 1930's.)

Fourth, we have a negative kind of evidence—evidence of the inhibiting effects of our cultural norms on the development of learning capacity in our standard educational procedures. This is shown by the differential production of doctorates in different sections of the country, by schools of varying size, and by sex, even though the ability potentials of these several groups are assumed to be approximately equal. Indeed, the evidence is that the women, and the people from smaller high schools, who eventually attain the doctorate are somewhat superior to their competitors from more favored environments. We have interpreted this as indicating that they have had to hurdle higher barriers.

Fifth, we have strong evidence from our follow-up studies of the importance of personality traits in on-the-job achievement, and suggestive evidence that our "academic ladders" overemphasize verbal abilities to the neglect, perhaps, of some social-emotional qualities that are significant for actual working performance. And, finally, we have evidence from the examination of the vocational destinations of those who have undertaken postdoctoral training of a continuation of the sorting-out process along academic versus nonacademic lines—a tendency which may or may not be associated with the verbal-ability emphasis just mentioned. Further research on this point is needed, and is under way, because there are at least two widely varying interpretations of this finding. These two formulations work in quite opposite directions from the standpoint of creativity. The extremes of these two points of view may be stated as follows: (a) this postdoctoral training represents a continuation of the ivory-tower existence and a prolongation of infancy into what should be adult years, and (b) it represents a sharpening, focusing, and refinement of intellectual tools, and social-emotional maturation as well, which may be vastly significant for the improvement of higher education and advanced training.

Having made these rather sweeping characterizations of the evidence which I have chosen for emphasis today, let me now give very briefly what I consider the significance of this evidence for the educational process and, finally, for the development of creative talent. The data from these psychometric studies bear out anthropological evidence of the profound importance of the cultural forces impinging on individuals in directing their growth in talents, character formation, and general attitude toward the world and toward themselves. Whatever the ultimate limits of genetic capacity, we have evidence that the range of human talent has scarcely been fully explored under conditions which optimize growth possibilities, and we have evidence of significantly different subcultures in American life. This gives us good reason to believe that the learning processes in childhood could be vastly accelerated and that the learning process can be made an interesting, exciting, and self-rewarding activity. This activity, if it feeds on itself as we have seen that it can, may well incline children so strongly to the full development and exercise of their capabilities that the learning times we have heretofore assumed for the whole educational process may be cut by a factor of 2 or perhaps even more.

The implications of this conclusion need to be spelled out to fully appreciate its significance. It means that instead of spending, on the average, 24 years in the attainment of the doctorate, the student need spend only 12 for the same degree of learning. If we add 12 to the usual school-entering age of 6, we have Ph.D.'s granted at the time of life when now we graduate "children" from high school. School entering need not wait until 6, as we have seen, but this age is good enough to illustrate the point. We have the potentiality of equipping young men and women with the typical intellectual tools of the doctorate holder at the age of 18 instead of 30. These people may well have attained such satisfaction from this process that they will not consider their education completed by this time, but they should be vocationally prepared at a very high level. They will, if our social-emotional education has proceeded apace with the intellectual, as it should, be prepared for marriage and family life as well at this age as we usually find them at 30. The long and frequently traumatic years of deferred gratification between the time of physical maturity and the undertaking of adult activities and responsibilities can be vastly reduced. The years of greatest creative development, as shown by many studies and summarized periodically by Harvey Lehman, will be available for intellectually prepared and emotionally healthy adults, with a very real expectation that the creative activity of the scientific community, and of society as a whole, will greatly prosper.

From the standpoint of career choices, this possible outcome has a further significance, and one with additional creative possibilities. We have seen the progressive development of more and more specialization in our scientific training and elsewhere. We have the "two cultures" of C. P. Snow, and probably more than two, if our culture were looked at even more broadly. We have at the same time a great churning development in the scientific disciplines themselves, with crossing-over of techniques and ways of characterizing data, with the proliferation of interdisciplinary fields. We cannot see where this may end, but we can perceive quite clearly that it expresses a need for more broadly based education in the sciences, so that people do not become overspecialized too early, with the increasing threat of early obsolescence as new science and new technologies develop with ever greater rapidity. Meanwhile, the extension of the life span at the upper end and the increasing realization of the advantages to the individual as well as to society as a whole of keeping older persons active in constructive and productive (and even creative) enterprises mean that we must look forward in the future to more and more "retooling" of our scholars, scientists, and technicians in their middle and later years. The earlier and more vigorous and more healthy development of interest, skill, and satisfaction in learning should equip our 18-year-old Ph.D.'s with a set of attitudes which may be far more adaptive to the conditions of life of the twenty-first century than are those which characterize the doctorate holders of the mid-twentieth century. We may look forward to a far more harmonious balance of Kuhn's factors of tradition and innovation *within the individual*, to the end that one's career choices remain flexible and adaptive, and his outlook and behavior both more creative and more constructive than we find in the great majority of scientists today.

C   I was fascinated by the notion of jumping hurdles. How high should they be?

In regard to teaching machines, for instance, Parnes mentioned that the more creative people like bigger steps. How can we set them at the right level and in a progression, making them larger and larger? I also remember the story of a famous violinist who said that it was dangerous for a good violinist to teach beginners because the hurdle was too great— the differential between pupil and teacher. This is as bad as having too little difference between pupil and teacher.

C   I think the critical factor here is that the great violinist doesn't really know why he is great. He can't pass this quality on to his students. He can't analyze the movements he makes, the things he does that differentiate him from the ordinary violinist.

C   That wasn't the point, though, although it may also be involved. The point was that the model the learner may aspire to may present so great a gap from the learner's ability that it may discourage any movement in the desired direction. Also, if the gap is too small it may not encourage effort. Presumably the optimal-sized hurdles are challenges to people and get them going.

S   I wouldn't write off the great violinist per se. His ability as a teacher needs to be distinguished from his ability as a violinist. An example from another area is Paul Rosenbloom, one of the country's leading mathematicians. He goes into the elementary grades and teaches there, doing a wonderful job. He finds it possible to communicate with these children in ways their regular teachers can't. But not every mathematician could do that. Rosenbloom can because of the sort of person he is. You simply have to recognize two different abilities: ability to *do* and ability to *teach*. They aren't necessarily correlated.

C   The same has been found with linguists. By using good linguistic methods and a native speaker of a foreign language, a good linguist can teach people a language he himself does not speak. It is a question of the understanding of content versus the understanding of how to teach this content to others.

C   Would you think that, in this possibility of cutting the time of schooling of a Ph.D. by a factor of 2, some important incidental learning would be lost? You might call it familiarity, or "soaking in" a certain area of learning. You could conceivably turn out a very good specialist in 12 years. The question is whether you could turn out any kind of a generalist—and I think that most people who are creative are much more generalists than specialists.

S   The person with a Ph.D. at 18 doesn't have to stop his learning, and by 30 he ought to be a lot further along with both incidental and explicit learning than we typically are now by that age. This is the way I look at the question. If he gets the kind of start we have been postulating and obtains the kinds of satisfactions out of learning that are possible, he isn't going to quit simply because he's got his degree.

C   This suggests two things. First, the notion of general education beyond the Ph.D., which is a little bit foreign now, would have to come into play. Second, this might not then lower the age at which principal productivity begins to occur, certainly not as much as would be suggested if the person were, so to speak, complete at age 18.

S   I'm afraid that I don't go along with this idea of a person being complete. Thinking is a continuing process; it is never complete. To look at the matter a different way, what chance has a person *now* of making any important contribution at the age of 18? Some people do, but only rare geniuses. On the other hand, you could expect that people who are essentially vocationally prepared at age 18 (assuming that society accepts them as such) can "get into the swim" and be producing as much (or as little) as our typical Ph.D.'s do now. (Somebody has mentioned that the modal publication rate is still zero.) Getting the doctorate at 18 doesn't guarantee anything, but it does suggest advantages from a number of sociological aspects.

C   Let's consider definitely specialized additional training. For instance, Richard Solomon in 1957 took a Guggenheim fellowship in which he did a clinical internship. He had a career both behind him and before him in experimental psychology, but he took a *clinical* internship. Now this would be a kind of continuing education, learning in new areas. I think that this sort of thing is relatively uncommon but would be a necessary part of what you were speaking about.

S   I go along completely. Several times I said something about the importance of retooling. I think that we have to look forward to much more of this than we have in the past. People may go back to school on a full-time basis for a period of years, or they may find various other ways of retooling. This is why the idea of being complete at 18 is not acceptable to me.

C   You are aware of the postdoctoral fellowships—senior research participation programs? It seems to me that people of 30 to 35 are doing this more than people of 40 to 45. What are the facts?

S   I don't know the typical ages, but the NSF senior postdoctoral minimum is five years beyond the doctorate. The point of your comment, as I see it, is still valid whatever the present situation is: we need more social invention in exactly this area.

C   There has been some talk to the effect that people who switch fields later in life are more creative. Is there any substantiating evidence?

S   There are good reasons to suppose that this may be true, but I don't know of any evidence. This area needs more research.

C   I think that Donald Pelz of the University of Michigan has some evidence—happily in that direction. But I don't know much more about it. In various research groups he has been studying, where a man is switched into a research group, he brings the more original ideas out of the group. This occurs independently of his age.

C   Getting a degree at age 18 makes it more probable that someone could, at age 35, close one nice career and then start all over again. If this were in the culture as an approved and supported thing, it could happen.

C   If he changed his name, and maybe his country too!

C   And had plastic surgery!

C   We became interested in this problem about changing major fields because we heard both this and the opposite story. We found opposite evidence, and it replicates: the achiever stays in the same general area. We use a special definition of "change," and this is another problem. We speak of a change in terms of moving from one major area to another major area. This would not include the change of moving from chemistry to physics.

C   What of the criterion, though? Do people who change their major field really turn out later in their careers to be much more creative than those who stayed in the same field? Do you have later information?

C   No. All I have is some longitudinal studies where the people who did not change (by our definition) achieved more than those who did. This agrees better with certain other data and is inconsistent with the change notion. For instance, the more creative people become involved in a subject earlier and persist with it.

C   How successful were the field switchers before they changed? Also, what was their reason for switching? These questions are both important. For example, some of our famous chemists are switching to biology, after very successful careers, because of strong motivations to see whether they can find something in a new area. Another point worth mentioning is the comparison of science and invention. In looking over the histories of these two fields, it seems to be true that switching fields is more productive in invention, in the technological areas, than in science areas. This may be because one must assimilate so much more background before he can do much in science—we just don't know.

C   At one point you suggested that for the optimal growth of science there needed to be more "prosaic builders" than "movers and shakers." Why do you feel that there needs to be this relationship?

S   Because one person with a creative idea can restructure a whole field. It will take a great many people a long time to rebuild the field on the basis of the new conceptualization—to rebuild the detail of the structure and to tease out all the facts that are necessary to get to the point where the need for another restructuring would be evident.

C   Can't these builders be classified as creative people too?

S   This is an important point. It *could* be so, through the building into one person of two attitudes, of the converging and the diverging ways of looking at subject matter—of looking at the world. The two functions don't *have to be* separated so that one person is creative and another is more methodically constructive. They could exist in the same person, but that is rare. I am struck here by an analogy with the operation of the big synchrotrons. You know that they are being built now with alternating gradients whereby they alternately focus and defocus an electron beam. This principle has made possible great results that could not be achieved by trying to keep the beam focused. It's a divergent and convergent process that occurs *successively.*

C   If someone said to you, "We don't want too many creative people," what would you say?

S   I'd say that I don't detect any shred of danger from that direction in the foreseeable future. We never have had enough so far.

C   The creative people are here now. They just haven't emerged.

C   It is a common statement in business administration today, "Well, we've got too many ideas already."

S   I'm aware of that. One person here told of saving a company $320,000 through new ideas and of having scared the administration by doing it.

C   By the year 2010, after we have all extended our best efforts, we may have to face the issue of too many creative people.

S   Then there ought to be enough creative people around to find the solution. (*Laughter*)

chapter 14 Developing Creative Research Performance in Public School Children

John R. Jablonski, University of Pittsburgh[1]

S   In attending this conference I, perhaps like a few others, come as a misfit; but I come with the idea that even the misfits may be effective in stimulating some creative thought.   I am director of a cooperative research participation program for high school students, which is sponsored by the Addison H. Gibson Laboratory, University of Pittsburgh, School of Medicine, and the boards of education of high schools where we are working.   The program is supported primarily by the National Science Foundation; however, approximately one-third of the overall cost is met by the local school boards.   We find that local high schools will usually cooperate if they can understand what they are trying to do.

Although most of the NSF-supported programs are for high-ability students, we have chosen to create an environment wherein any student who wishes to do research is given the opportunity to do so.   He can work on a project already begun by a university staff member, or he can come up with his own idea of a research problem, for which we are able to get some kind of supportive assistance from key university

[1] *Editor's note:* Now with the National Science Foundation, working in Special Projects in Science Education to stimulate science education on a national level. Knowing firsthand the value of his unequalled pioneering work described briefly in this chapter, I join with key persons in the Pittsburgh public schools in hoping that he will find a suitable setting for continuing (without too long a period of interruption) his own unusual efforts in incorporating research participation into both secondary and elementary schools.   His new address for academic year 1964-5 is Boston University, Boston, Mass.

people. In selecting students, we do not ask for their IQ's or for their academic grades, but we have collected this information incidentally. Some day, when we have a few graduate students, we are going to analyze their productivity in research in relation to their IQ's and their scholastic standings. We already have some indications that these two are not good selection criteria for a research worker. I think that the motivational aspect and the creating of a mood are more important, so we have tried to stress these in our program.

The students are first put into a program in which they are taught the rudiments of what research is and how to conduct it. Then they are given faculty privileges to go to the library to do background reading on the various projects that they have evolved in their own thinking. Many times we have had to alter some of the proposed projects because they were rather detrimental experiments that should be done only in a well-controlled environment.

Next, each student presents a protocol of his experiment for review. The protocol is examined very carefully for clarity of presentation to ensure that the student is saying what he wants to and that he is showing evidence of some library work. If he does not show the latter, he is not permitted to continue in the program. After the protocol has been accepted, the student will conduct his research. The students present progress reports at various times, during which their protocols may be torn to bits by their peers so that they are faced with many suggestions consisting of new ideas and new avenues of research to follow.

We are working in the high school itself, *not* in the university laboratories which are often heavily equipped and well staffed with individuals. However, equipment is not a major problem because these young people build most of what they need.

We give the most intensive effort to the program in the summer, but now we are also continuing with these students into the academic year. In their regular school science classes the students tended to create an uncomfortable environment for the high school teachers. Consequently, we established a program to show teachers how to work with a student who is doing research in a given area so that the teacher is not uncomfortable when the student knows more than he about that area. This program for teachers is working out very well. The teachers like it because now they feel free to say to the student, "I don't know, but let's either go to the literature or call the advisor involved."

If what the student needs to know is something that he should find in the library, all our advisors have agreed not to tell him the answer; we think that part of the research process is knowing how to find out where information is. We have even gone to the extreme; for example, one boy wanted to do amino acid separation. This is a very simple biochemical procedure if one knows where to find it. This procedure is available in a book on the shelf behind me in my office. Although this student had full access to my library, I would not tell him what book it was in. I stressed this point strongly. He worked from three to four weeks trying to find the information. He was so stunned when he finally realized that the answer was in a book right behind me that his experience carried over to his college career and he has never forgotten it. He now knows how to use the library, too. This is just one instance of what the high school program has been doing.

The kind of research that we insist upon is not the cookbook variety of biology and chemistry. This summer we are also working in an area of physics, although we are limited in terms of equipment. When these young researchers come up with an original problem—and their problems are original—then the advisor is put to the very hard task of evaluating it; therefore, the advisor's work is doubled because a greater number of questions arise. The advisors like this very much, but they don't have time to answer all the questions. This tends to result in an expansion of the research program.

This summer, with both the student and teacher programs, we will have 120 high school students and 22 teachers who will work with the students in the areas of biology, chemistry, and physics. Although the courses are to some extent basic, we like to think that they are elite courses in biochemistry and microtechniques. This year we are adding microbiology and nutrition courses. We ask the staff members who give the courses to direct the course content to what a high school teacher might be able to use in his or her own teaching and supervision of student research. The school of education has been very happy, because in the past no one has made much effort to give teachers content that they can apply in their high school courses. We think that this is going to be beneficial for the teachers and for long-range development of high school science course content.

During the summer program, we allowed both students and teachers to sit in on these courses. The comment has been made to me, "Doesn't it make the teachers feel uneasy to be in the same audience with the students?" We dealt with this problem by means of a very short introductory session with the teachers, in which we said, "The students are going to be here too, and they are going to ask many questions. You may feel that the students know more about some specific problem than you do!" And they often do! But as science includes the process of continuous learning, we stress that saying, "I don't know," does not imply loss of face. This has eased the problems, and so far we have had many teachers work on a research problem too during the summer in order to get first-hand research experience themselves.

I was asked by the county school superintendent to conduct an in-service institute for elementary teachers so that they could apply more science and scientific procedures in the elementary grades. Their response has been encouraging. One teacher who vowed she would never have animals in her classroom took two rats to allow her students to learn about growth. She was given the simple research problem for her students of how to measure the growth of an animal. Even though most children know that they grow, they really don't get the "feeling" for growth until they play with these classroom animals and become involved with them in addition to learning how much food they eat. In the university laboratory school the students began to learn that many conditions are involved in an animal's growth, which is not just a matter of getting heavy or increasing in length. Other observations were made. We put the animals into a small confining cage and then after a two-week interval transferred them into a larger cage. Without telling the students what to look for, we asked them, "What did you see?" These fourth, fifth, and sixth graders had a wonderful time. They said that when the animals were in the small cages they were not growing. "Well, how do you know they were not growing?" They answered this question by referring to the data they had collected. Their rats' weights did not increase as much when they were kept in the small cage as when they were moved to the large cage. From this they evolved the idea that an animal must have a certain amount of area in which to expand and therefore that growth is partly affected by the animal's environment. The children had never thought about space around an individual as being necessary for growth until they made their own observations.

So I have been "playing around" with education in the elementary grades. I said "play" because this is the atmosphere we have tried to create for both the elementary and the high school program, that is, that it is fun to learn and fun to work hard. To give you the idea of how well these young people respond, a number of high school students relinquish vacations with their parents because they are having too much fun working hard during the summer! Their enthusiasm is an attitude which is created. The younger fourth, fifth, and sixth graders are fantastic in the way they are able to synthesize a research problem when given a general area. This is essentially what we have encouraged the high school students to do, but the fourth, fifth, and sixth graders respond very well too. They can't wait until the time to do this work comes around, since we are working with them only one day a week.

This kind of program takes a lot of time because we work with individuals and small groups as much as possible. The students are doing something which is different to them but which can often be made part of regular class activity. Our experience in the elementary schools has brought into focus the problem of the need to evaluate what is happening in this kind of educational experience. Fortunately, or unfortunately, up to this time we have been involved only with the individual and with the individual's response to this form of learning experience. But I shall say more about evaluation later.

Referring to individuals, I want to mention the unusual example of one of our high school students. We had a boy apply to our first program who had an IQ of 86. One of his former teachers came to us and said, "You don't want him in your research program. He can't read." We indicated to his teacher that his reading difficulty wasn't our problem; it was his problem. She insisted that he was only in the sixth percentile of reading ability for sophomore students in high school. And we said again, "Well, that is still his problem. The point is that the student researchers must read, and they must synthesize a protocol of an experiment based upon what they have read; if he can do this, he can be in the program."

Not only did this boy get into the program but also his IQ has been re-evaluated, and, even though I don't like IQ's, he is now rated as 110. He has graduated and gone to a junior college where he is maintaining a C+ average; he made an A in chemistry and A in biology. His problem remains, of course, reading, and so he had a C− in English. But remember that this boy was considered not to be college material because of his grades and IQ, so that, through this motivating experience, we think we have salvaged a potential college graduate.

This young man's project has opened up so many other questions that we are still working on answering some of the basic ones resulting from his research problem. His project was to observe the effect of three different commercially available diets upon the growth of an animal. Everyone knows from scientific literature and the companies' advertising that these particular commercial diets are "good." Each manufacturer says that his feed is the best for everybody's animals in any laboratory. So this boy asked a simple question: "Do laboratory rats grow at the same rate on all three diets?" In our laboratory we had been using these diets regularly, but we didn't know the answer so we said, "Go ahead." We knew that this project might give us information that we could use, but we had not asked the question in just this fashion.

After the first experiment the boy asked, "Since the animals show a distinct preference for one of the diets, what effect does the preference for this diet have on other processes in the rat? Will the diet affect the animal's ability to maintain a tumor transplant?" This again was his own question; it was not suggested to him. To answer this question, after an additional year and summer's research, we initiated a three-school cooperative program to evaluate the effect of diet preference on tumor growth. Following the observations made there, we have gone into a study of immunological aspects of the diet upon the animal's ability to produce antibodies. We even had a college student work on this research project for her college tutorial thesis. Thus, we are now engaged in a rather large research project based upon some of the findings that this boy, with an IQ of 86, made and the questions that he asked as a result of his high school experimentation.

This is a cooperative program, which links together the university personnel, high school and elementary teachers, students, their parents, and school boards. It would probably fail if any one of the links between these groups were broken. We don't go out and ask people to join our program. It is not to satisfy our egotistical needs that we want them to approach us. However, we are of the opinion that, if either the students or the teachers do not put forth this effort, the whole idea of this motivational aspect is lost and the training experiment will fall apart. We are letting the idea incubate—the idea of having people ask us to come to the program. I'm not worried that we'll have enough people. The Mellon Institute in Pittsburgh has been contacted in order to obtain more advisors for the program, so whenever we find we haven't enough university people, the Mellon Institute is available to tap. At least ten people have called me up and said, "If you need me, let me know. I'll be very glad to work with you and your students."

When evaluating a program of this nature, where there is nothing tangible other than research or progress reports, we have found that it is necessary to determine first what we can evaluate and how to obtain these data. This is something we are going to concentrate on this summer. At present evaluation of this program is in the hands of Calvin Taylor, Gary Cooley, and others from the University of Utah. One observation can be made (I'll say intuitively and don't correct me): the students who become well versed and oriented in research procedure tend to be less creative unless the stimulus of excitement and wonder is maintained. Most of the high school sophomores who come in rarin' to go are now beginning to produce better, more rapidly than many of the seniors in our program. The outstanding seniors, of course, who have a feel for research are still doing much better all the way round.

The Junior Academy of Science and the Westinghouse Science Talent Search judges have indicated some reactions to our students' scholastic ability. Some of the students were invited to submit applications to these organizations after all the other local schools had sent in theirs. We were asked, "Won't you send some of the students from your program?" This question was directed to a high school teacher who has worked very closely with me with the result that some of our students entered 5 different categories of some 15 different sections. These students were awarded first and second prizes in the particular areas in which they were enrolled and from there went on to the state finals. At the state finals they competed with another group of our students who came from a cooperating school 40 miles away. Those students had also taken all the honors in their local contest. One of the comments of the college instructor judges was that the students talked in such an informed way that the judges could not even ask an intelligent question. These two groups of students took first prizes in biology and the physical sciences in the Pennsylvania state finals. Seven students from our program took one-third of the total awards in the whole state of Pennsylvania. These students also won three Westinghouse Awards in 1961.

From the reports brought back to me, the judges found these students so well trained in their areas and so much at ease with their subject matter that they just couldn't believe high school students were so capable. I think that this indicates what has been a problem all the way along. When people say students cannot do a thing, I say that the main reason they cannot do it is because no one wants to work with them to see whether they can do it.

We plan to continue this type of program for the coming year. We are keeping our minds and operations flexible so that we can change or add as demonstrable evidence is obtained. It is a lot of fun to see these youngsters develop in a favorable atmosphere. We keep trying to ensure that high stimulation of the students will be maintained and that their productivity will be carried over in later work. After this summer, we hope to obtain a follow-up history of all the students who have been in our program. It is going to be very interesting to see what they have done after they have been in a project of research participation; if possible, we also want to see how they are evaluated by the colleges they have entered or the high schools they are still attending.

C   Are these students going to grow bigger because they have more mental space around them?

S   The student has no restrictions placed upon him, you see, even in dealing with a different idea or a simple experiment based on the question, "Does an animal prefer one of three different diets?" Almost any researcher in biology would tend to call that a stupid experiment. But from this idea so much other meaningful research has been proposed that my summer is going to be very busy.

C   A striking feature about the case of your student with poor reading ability and consequently a low IQ is that we may too often assume in education that if a person can't read, he therefore can't think.

C   I am very pleased to hear this paper, because I have spent a little time discussing with Harmon the ideas in his paper about cutting educational time in half.   I was trying to convince him that the changes in the educational system necessary to accomplish this could be made quite rapidly.   However, Harmon feels that it is much easier to describe the changes than to actually make them.

C   Is the decline in involvement and activity on the part of the seniors due to the preclusive effect of other things they have to do in their senior year—things they are expected to do?   Do you have any evidence on this?

S   I haven't evaluated this factor yet.   Do you want my opinion? I think part of it is hormonal because they are seniors and not because of the number of their activities.   They get a superior feeling as seniors, but whenever we challenge this during a little skull session with them they go back to being highly productive.   In such an intimate person-to-person relationship between advisor and student, the advisor can watch for this, because it does come out in various insidious ways, and then can deal with it.   Some seniors can become truly cocky because they are head and shoulders above their high school teachers in certain areas. Yet does the teacher who is working with them realize this and accept it? I think that there is a psychological effect whenever one feels he is really accomplishing something.   These young people generate a lot of excitement about doing something worth while; maybe this is the first time they have ever been allowed to do something worth while.   I think that this is part of it.

The other thing is that, as new students come into the program, they always look to the seniors because they are "the experienced pros" in research; they "know all the answers now" and the others have to find out what the seniors have done.   However, what we call the "king and queen" activity is very quickly broken down by the "peasants" who are learning the technique.   We have watched it happen, without getting involved with the students at the time.   For the seniors it is better when their peers, even though they may be sophomores or juniors, can pull them down a peg and let them realign their own sights.

Another aspect of the decline in the seniors' involvement is the fact that we sometimes tend not to pay as much attention to them because they already know some of the techniques of research and so we expect more of them. And, like all young people, they're undergoing tremendous physical changes; I think that we have to be aware that they alter their approaches to this research activity as well.

C Another question concerns laboratories. You are in a biochemical research laboratory in the School of Medicine. Are there other departments? How extensively are other people involved? You are only one person, and this program grows just so much with your spending merely one-third of your time on it. I'm concerned that a lot more people should be helping it grow.

S The powers above told me to tell the students at the first school that we would set up a program at their high school during the summer if their school system would permit it. When I first talked with these students, I had no idea of setting up a summer program; I had no idea of getting into education or creativity or anything like this. I was just out there to talk to the students to stimulate their interest and thinking in science. The first year we had 23 high school students in the program. When it grew to 65 last summer, we had six teachers from the School of Medicine in the university handling the courses in biochemistry and microtechnique. But we realized, when the director was dead tired and didn't want to see a high school student at the end of summer, that more people had to be involved.

This year more university teachers have taken part in the seminar activities. They have commented enthusiastically, "Aren't these young students a delightful group to work with! They ask the most interesting questions—questions that I'm writing down." We taped all the seminars. The questions these students asked without information or previous knowledge were tremendously stimulating for the researchers, because the students did not worry about whether the problems could be studied or not. They just asked logical questions, and off they went!

I asked those who had been our seminar speakers, "If I can find some sort of support for you, will you work with our students?" After they agreed, I had 11 other university people who said, "We will act as advisors if you need us in the areas in which we are competent." So this summer we are going to use these people, 8 of them being from the Department of Physics, which has been opened completely to us by the head of the department. There we are going to work on the idea of original research in physics on a feasible scale, depending upon our facilities.

One of the students is going to measure the mass of an electron with equipment that he will build himself. We will lend him a vacuum pump, and we are going to try to borrow a diffusion pump. In our work we can find ways to use such devices in several different experiments. Again, why let a piece of equipment sit in the university laboratory? Let's take it out to the high school whenever it can be used!

We are happy that there are people in the Natural Sciences Division in the School of Medicine, and in other laboratories, who will be working with us as advisors. They are going to meet with the students once a week for progress reports and follow them through the school year. They will meet as a group in each particular area. We have students from about 32 different high schools who are coming in to us once a week during the school year, but we work in only 5 high school buildings during the summer. Students from these schools will come in initially as a group to have their "skull sessions." This makes the conservation of the university scientific personnel a problem, too.

We don't want the scientific personnel to be involved in our program unless they get as excited about it as we do. We know that they will become very much interested, but we want to start them slowly with small doses and then let them take over areas of instruction gradually. Interest is spreading through the university. In fact, I envision a program of this kind in social sciences, English, and several other disciplines because the main tool we are using is just getting the youngster excited about education, teaching him how to think or maybe how to think logically.

C   Your program has approximately doubled each year?

S   We are in our fourth summer. We started out with 23 students the first year. The second summer we had 38 instead of the 25 for whom we had budgeted, and I started to seek support from the local high schools because we needed money for teachers. We asked the school districts to supply a portion of the teacher's salary for the summer. The next year we planned for 50 students but took on 65 students and 10 teachers. This year we will have 120 students and 20 teachers, which are a few more teachers than we had planned.

One other point about the number of students applying: we found that some of the students who had attended our seminars religiously did not apply. Luckily, when Calvin Taylor stopped in Pittsburgh to work with me on the research evaluation forms on our students, he suggested that we might be losing some creative young people because they could not write in a literate form what they were thinking. So we sent letters to the students who didn't apply but who had regularly attended these seminars. We are now setting up an additional program for the student who did not write a protocol but who had an idea and would like to follow it. We are going to help these students learn how to write a protocol, and we will work very closely with them in giving them experience in research participation.

C   Are you bringing the English departments in on this?

S   Only indirectly; they have not gotten into it as English depart ments.

C   I had a very interesting nonmushroom (i.e., nondrug) experience at Harvard my year there. A couple of years earlier they had set up seminars for freshmen. So I announced a research seminar in the psychological problems in disarmament. Ten freshmen eventually were in it, although there were many more applicants. Each of them did a research project. First, like your high school teachers, I found after about two meetings that everyone in the seminar knew more than I did about the problems. And, second, each of the students went out, started a research problem of his own, and developed it thoroughly. They did some extremely clever, interesting things on a Ph.D. level (I'm still thinking of Harmon's report). These projects showed great ingenuity and tremendous energy.

S   The problem is that our educational environment has not progressed to the stage where this is well accepted. Those who have worked with young students and have seen their research will accept them and their level of productivity, but the rest of the education family just cannot as yet. This constitutes a threat to their survival because these young people are coming up with very fresh and exciting ideas. Our biggest problem really is the one with their teachers, but once we get the teachers over the hurdle they have as much fun as the students.

C   In relation to my work, two things you said are of interest. One is that the uninformed students asked questions about an area which stimulated and actually seemed to be helpful to people who had been working in that field a long time. And, second, you said that newer students are more apt to be more creative and productive than the ones who have been around a while. Do you have some hypothesis?

S   The older students asked the better questions of the younger students when they gave the progress reports, but the younger students were often the more imaginative and creative and were working harder with a tremendous energy output.

C   Could it also be that these older students have spent a couple of years in reading the literature, which may have so oriented them that they no longer appear creative?

S   This might be a factor, too. But we force them to think by asking them questions and making comments somewhat like the one mentioned earlier: "Let's put out some patents." I think creativity is a basic psychological need, but my opinion is that people sometimes need to be reminded, realigned, or refocused on what they are doing.

C   Obviously you can't take all high school students into your program. I get the impression that you are now selecting them on the basis of the protocols that they write. How are these protocols evaluated? What determines which students you take, and which ones you don't?

S   When we get these protocols, we find two things almost uniformly present: there is a spread of content, and the student is able to synthesize "a" problem. Sometimes a student selects a tremendously big problem, but that is all right.

Initially the students are not asked to limit their problems. However, when we review their protocols with them in detail, we help them to shrink their problems so that they can focus on an experiment which is feasible with the facilities available and which can be completed in a given time.

We have had many failures, by the way, but we think that failure is part of the educational experience of the student. Not every experiment has to work. I don't believe that the student will necessarily feel depressed if he has an unsuccessful experiment; what we do is show him that his experiment, while logically planned, did not work out and the question is to find out why.

We have one girl in the program who has been trying to breed Chinese hamsters, an extremely difficult task. There is only one man in the United States that we know of who is breeding Chinese hamsters. This girl even involved her father in building a cage designed by this one successful breeder. This is fantastic! She has stayed with her project, and this summer she wants to continue further because she feels that there is an answer which she can find if she stays with the problem. We have not asked her to do this. She asked us, "May I continue with this experiment?" I said, "Why don't you take another variable?" And she said, "No, I want to get these Chinese hamsters to breed." I was thinking that it might be better if she had a little success, so I said, "In addition, let's do some parameters of the biochemistry of the animal." She liked my suggestion because it concerned part of her problem. But she really cannot be diverted from her problem; she still has to be involved with breeding Chinese hamsters. If I were to have her work with yellow hamsters, I know that she would have success, but she would not get the excitement of discovery because everybody can succeed. Just put yellow hamsters of the two sexes together and they breed. I think that this girl has accumulated a degree of knowledge about her subject that we consider the good student should possess.

You can tell good students very quickly by the degree of knowledge they have acquired and the amount of literature they have read. The poorer student doesn't read as much and also doesn't synthesize as elaborate an experiment. We have students who, for very simple experiments, have turned in 45 to 50 references within a month. When we ask them about their projects, they know what they are talking about. They will bring up obscure things, unheard of for high school students. We have given all of them faculty privileges to the library. The librarians shook their heads when they heard 120 students were coming this summer, because even the first summer the 23 high school students checked out more books (in my name) than the whole School of Medicine did. This is no joke; they signed my name (which is a task in itself). They identify themselves with their problems and the literature on them. They bring in obscure journals of 1887, or they ask me what my feeling is about such and such a person's research. I don't even know who the person was. I tell them to bring me the article and let me read it, and we can then discuss it with each other.

C Have you discovered a new method of retrieving information?

S Old information is brought to light by the students in their library search.

C How many are selected from the applicants? How many protocols do you get from which you select your people?

S Last year we had protocols only in certain areas which we defined. In competition for the 65 student openings, 120 protocols were turned in. This year we had a seminar before the summer program. We felt that we had lost a lot of time last summer just working on the protocols, so we decided to get this job out of the way during the spring months, because we wanted the youngsters to have more time in the summer both for research work in the laboratory and for library work.

In the seminars we presented the whole idea of writing a protocol. Then we had several university people talk about their own research, showing how they attacked their problems, to give the students a better idea of how various scientists work. In fact, we had people from three different areas in the university talk about electron microscopy, since each person had a different approach to the use of the electron microscope. Their discussions brought out the idea that one can use an instrument in many different avenues and ways, that he need not keep his mind on only one little area.

Approximately 175 protocols were submitted. We eliminated a number of them, not because they were bad, but because they were submitted by graduating seniors, and we were trying to keep this program in the high school. However, these graduating seniors were chosen as alternates. The students who can't write protocols will be placed in a program apart from the others. They will be in the laboratories more and will be worked with separately. We are doing this so that the person who made the effort to write a protocol will not feel that the other person is being put on an equal level. This would not be good psychologically, because many put a lot of effort into writing their protocols.

C Are protocols rejected primarily because you feel when reading them that the students weren't really serious about them?

S No. This has been something rather interesting, which I don't understand. Whenever a student has set about to write a protocol he has usually come up with an original idea, based upon his reading. When we did not have any written protocols, the ideas were poorly expressed, making it most difficult to select students. A group of students from one school system had well-written protocols, but they did not have the ideas or concepts of science. Their protocols had to be rejected on this basis. This year, with the preliminary seminar, students had the same information to start with, such as how the protocol should be written and what science is. We had eight Saturday sessions from 9:00 A.M. to 3:00 P.M., with a huge turnout. We began with 380 students in an auditorium with a capacity of 280, so students were sitting on the stairs and on extra chairs. They kept coming back, but the number dropped to 250 because some finally found out that this was not what they wanted to do. The students were able to come to a decision so that when they did submit a protocol, it was usually fairly sophisticated. My idea is not to reject any persons who have an idea, but to nurture them and let them blossom out as the boy with the IQ of 86 did.

C I get the impression that you turn down about half the protocols you get.

S We had 170 protocols this year and are going to take 120 of these students.

C Why don't you take the other 50?

S Mainly because of space. But we want to try Taylor's idea that the students who couldn't write still have something to contribute if we can get them to write. So we're going to make more space available. We have taken over wings of high schools for this program and have used their chemistry and biology labs, even though they had their own summer programs going on. The schools tried to allot us as much space as possible, because they were very happy to work with our program.

C You try to take all who submit protocols, but you simply can't?

S That's right.

C There is another aspect to my idea about those who don't write protocols. It seems possible to me that some persons who cannot initially write protocols may be nonverbal thinkers and learners. Perhaps some of them can initiate and conduct successful research without having written a protocol beforehand. And perhaps they will be much more ready and capable of giving verbal expression to their work at the end of their project, after they have gained insight into their problem during the process of completing it. Maybe the only way we will have much of a chance to get anything written from a few of these nonwriters is by having them give a final oral report which we tape-record and then transcribe and edit for them.

C   If one makes certain assumptions about what is going on here and forgets that scientists are needed, what you describe is simply *good education of the right kind.* I'd like to volunteer a suggestion based on something I've seen work in the arts. When any educational facility in-the-depth is offered with a small student-teacher ratio, all that the applicants really need is motivation. For instance, if I offer a studio-in-depth to last for five weeks in one studio, and 100 people apply for only 30 openings, I don't need prior screening by means of protocols or anything else. The motivation of the accepted 30 is sufficient in itself.

C   May I insert a letter that I received regarding another case with a *recorded* IQ score well below average? This case illustrates the *extreme* misuse of considering an IQ score to be far too important, even more important than actual performance. It indicates that the thinking of certain people is badly reversed as to which is the predictor test and which is the criterion (not even considering the other secondary error about the language problem in this testing).

I have just finished reading "Let's Look Again at Those IQ Tests" in the December *Readers' Digest.* Your name is mentioned and I am taking the liberty of writing to you for advice in regard to placing a child who is now in my class.
One of my students is 12 yr. 4 mo. old and is in my 5th year slow normal class of thirty children. She entered our school in 1st year when she came from Puerto Rico. The family still speaks nothing but Spanish at home. She did poorly in 1st and 2nd years. She was left back in 2nd year but the second time around was marked satisfactory in everything. Now I have her in the 5th year. She has had 100% every week in spelling and arithmetic. In Social Studies she is very good. In a reading test for speed and comprehension given by the Reading Counselor she came out 2nd from the top. Yet her IQ tests are very poor. First she had 63 IQ, then 71 IQ, and last week back to 63 IQ. Yet in performance in the class she is *by far the best I have.* I have never seen any signs of her being ungraded. I have taught over thirty years and in that time have had many ungraded children, but in my opinion she is not one of them.
In talking with the school psychologist and several teachers they feel I am doing her an injustice by keeping her in a normal class. They claim that with a 63 IQ she should be in a special, ungraded program. One even said, "Performance doesn't count." She is 12 years old and working to capacity. There are others in the class who get very low marks and these low ones, the teachers claim, are just not working up to capacity. I know many are not working to capacity, but in life what we do is what counts and not what we *could* do. But the student in question is doing it. She had a 63 IQ only last week but she is

performing daily at 100% or very near it. She wants to be a nurse and from what I can judge would make a good one. Shall I put her in an ungraded class and kill her chances of being a nurse? Shall I keep her and let her go along with the slow normal class? Her 3rd and 4th year teachers agree with me that she is not ungraded, yet her IQ is 63.

"My questions are: What would you do? Keep her? Put her in Ungraded? I'd greatly appreciate your opinion. I want to do what is best for her.

Gratefully yours,
(*Signed*) (Maria's teacher)

Do you want to know the sequel to this case? The teacher (who is near retirement) had great courage to fight hard for her student. But in the course of events the teacher became ill and was absent for two or three days. She told me that when she returned she found that the school system had quietly but quickly plucked her top student out of the regular class and put her back into an ungraded class.[2]

C Oh, my gosh!

[2] Two further letters were received on Maria's case.

Latest letter: Almost two years ago I wrote to you about Maria who was in my class. I inquired about putting her in a mentally retarded class because her IQ was 63 but her class work was excellent except for reading. She was a 3rd year reader because of language difficulty. She spoke only Spanish at home and with all her intimate friends.

Later after you and I had corresponded about Maria you spoke to me on the phone and I remember you said it would take courage on my part to fight it—to fight having her railroaded into a retarded class.

She was taken out of my class and placed in a retarded class against my better judgment. A college professor spoke to Dr. _____, our school superintendent. That led to further complications. After I had thought things were quieted down I was sent for by the district superintendent. The day after my interview with her I was so full of my subject that I sat down and wrote you about the interview. I didn't send it because Dr. _____ [the above college professor], who read it, said it was written in a state of emotionalism—which was true—I just came across the letter and I am going to send it to you for it clearly shows what a district superintendent can do to a mere teacher. I am now retired so what she thinks or doesn't think no longer concerns me.

* * * * * * * * *

Enclosed letter: When I wrote to you asking for advice on the Maria case I said that I would keep you posted on the outcome. When we spoke together on the phone I told you Maria was put in the retarded class. I thought the case was closed but last week I was called, along with my principal, to the office of the district superintendent. She had gotten a request for more information on the case from the superintendent's office.

My principal and I went to the district office yesterday and for one full hour I was, figuratively speaking, "knocked down and stepped on." When I tried to rise I was knocked down again and again. The district superintendent was not at all interested in hearing my side of the story. I was ridiculed and scorned for writing to the authorities mentioned in the *Readers' Digest.* "Don't you know the *Readers' Digest* is only for the layman? No professional person would pay any attention to it. Your so-called authorities! Who are they? Just college professors and what do they know about testing in our city? What right did you have to question our Testing and Guidance Bureau and our Board of Education? They have paid your living all these years. It shows how stupid and ungrateful you are. You wrote for one reason and one reason only—notoriety. You weren't interested in anything else, you wanted publicity. If I had known you were that sort of teacher I would have settled you long ago."

I tried to get over to her that Maria was at the very top of my slow normal class. That caused a real explosion! "What do you know about testing? Of course the kind of tests you would give she could get 100% (my tests were taken directly from tests in our books). They mean absolutely nothing. That shows how stupid you are to even think your tests and opinions amount to anything. I never dreamed I had anyone in my district as stupid and ignorant as you!"

I had made the cardinal sin of writing next to Maria's two IQ marks the word "language." I had not changed any marks. At the request of my principal several weeks ago, I crossed out the word "language" in red ink and initialed them. Now that was the particular string on the harp that the district superintendent played on over and over. I still believe that the low IQ's are a result of language difficulty but who am I to have an opinion? I am only the child's teacher! Over and over the district superintendent called me dishonest and a cheat.

I suggested to her that she read the letters as soon as my brother returned them to me. "Don't you dare mention your brother to me! No doubt he is as dishonest as you. I wouldn't think of reading the letters from such people." I mentioned the vice president of the Princeton Testing Bureau. He was sneared at. "And this college professor! Imagine a man who teaches at that college answering such a letter as you wrote. What kind of an authority is he?" I said, "Why not read his letter?" "I wouldn't read any of the letters." My principal spoke up then and said he'd like to re-read them and send some rebuttals. The district superintendent said, "They are not worth wasting your time on!" However, the real fly in the ointment was Dr. Guilford of Southern California. It was stupid of me to write to the other men but imagine anyone being so stupid as to write to someone way out in California! "California no less!" That was a big ha-ha to them both. What would he know about IQ's in our city? How stupid could I be!

During the entire hour I was berated in a high-handed and sneering way and repeatedly told how stupid and dishonest I am. Over and over I was told I wrote the letters just for notoriety. As the harangue went on and on it became more and more ludicrous to me. I came away not angry or upset but in my heart sorry that a woman in the position of district superintendent (with a large salary) could be so lacking in understanding and so rude and discourteous. Over the eighteen or so years that she has been our district superintendent I have often heard of her high-handed and tyrannical ways with teachers, principals, and even parents but I had never witnessed it. If this were the 14th century I am certain I would have heard, "Off with her head!"

When the three o'clock bell rang I, without being dismissed, just got up and walked out. The district superintendent and my principal sat licking their chops like the cat who had swallowed the canary. They thought they had completely swallowed and digested me. I wonder if they will get indigestion later? Perhaps—who knows?

Sincerely,

(*Signed*)   (Maria's teacher)

chapter 15 Readiness for Creative Explorations in a Public School Setting

Norman Brust, Fairmount Elementary School Principal,
Downers Grove, Illinois

S My purpose in being present at this conference is to hear what has been found about creativity and to report some of the research activities that are being carried out in the Downers Grove Public Schools.

Lorraine Loy from the University of Utah has been conducting a study about creativity with some of our teachers and pupils in grades one through six. She is using three verbal and three nonverbal creativity instruments developed by Torrance.

These instruments have been administered to teachers and to their students. We hope to find whether there is any correlation between the highest scores of creativity obtained by teachers and the aspects of greatest growth in creativity by the teachers' students.

Furthermore, we hope to see whether this study bears out the report of a fourth-grade slump as found by Torrance. To obtain further validity of the creativity instruments, correlations will be computed between student biographical information, teacher ratings, and the results of the creativity instruments.

Lorraine Loy has some indications from her master's thesis (Loy, 1961) that, when a person verbalizes a concept under certain conditions, this concept is less well retained. I cannot give you all the thought behind this, but she believes that there might be a high correlation between creativity and unverbalized concepts that are intuitively understood. Therefore, she has developed a series of tests made up of abstract symbols from which concepts can be developed. She plans to correlate the

220

results of these tests with the creativity instruments, biographical information, and teachers' ratings.

In our high school, we have several projects under way that have some relevance to creativity. One project deals with identifying creative industrial-arts students, and another one is predicting grades that high school students will obtain during high school and college. Mullins (Chapter 19) has done his research along a similar line. He used aptitudes, school grades, and creativity criteria, and we are planning to use one other, that is, the student's perception of himself.

Our future plans will revolve around developing methods of helping our students and teachers respond creatively to situations. It is my hope to be able to take some of these basic findings about creativity back to the teachers in Downers Grove and to see whether we can apply them. To me one of the striking things in education is this tremendous gap between basic research and the practical application of it. Taylor, Ghiselin, and Wolfer (1962) have written about the importance of bridging this gap.

I think that we are starting to do more about this, but we have a long way to go. Great efforts are being made to close the gap in the areas of mathematics and science. This national effort, pushed by federal funds, is being felt on the local level. In the educational profession there is an appalling lack of initiative at the local, state, and national levels. I believe that the most important thing to be done is to provide opportunities for teachers to develop a research orientation and to help them carry on classroom studies that are related to an overall local-school research project.

I think that those working in basic research probably have a responsibility, too. I realize that many of you have a feeling of the importance of doing your research just for the idea of doing it; this is vital in itself. However, I think that you, as a group, can bring more to us. During a conversation this morning, Barron said that he has been talking with elementary school principals about some of the things he has done. I know that Torrance has been working with elementary teachers, too. I feel that we are going in the right direction. I think that teachers are ready to accept this and want to—and they can get excited. I have seen our teachers become highly involved in the small research activities that we are now doing. I believe that the development of well-founded applications can expand much faster than most people realize.

C   You need some mechanism for getting teachers to accept this sort of thing. Is anything being done through the subdivisions of the National Educational Association (NEA), the educational associations of the state, or local educational associations?

S   Very little has been done, and there is little emphasis on such a mechanism.   If these associations believed that it was important, the funds and efforts would have been provided, I feel.

C   I have noticed a tremendous development along this line over the past five years since I have been back in educational research.   As I reflect upon my correspondence, there has been a tremendous upsurge of requests about research from school systems, many of them signed by directors or coordinators of research in a public school system.

C   I had in mind mainly a diffusion of information through the teachers' organizations about things like Jablonski is doing.

C   The 1963 Yearbook of the Association for Supervision and Curriculum Development (ASCD) will be devoted entirely to this transmission of information.   And that volume goes out to about half a million teachers, I imagine.

C   The ASCD has been holding institutes east and west this year dealing with this same problem, acquainting people in various school systems with the need for these research and development activities.

S   There have been activities on a very high organizational level, but little of it has affected the local school situation and, most important, the teacher.

C   May I briefly restate the points that Ghiselin, Wolfer, and I made in our 1962 article?   As we studied this problem of *Research* and *Development* (R and D), we sensed that the thing that is missing in education is D.   There is some R (especially in the basic behavioral sciences) and there are great numbers of educational practitioners, but there is no bridge between them.   In the national R and D program, the D program is usually from 3 to 5 or even up to 10 times the size of the R program both in funds and in human effort.   But in education there is no real developmental bridge that is systematically functioning between the R and the practitioner.   The practitioner can rightly say, "Your research stuff isn't manageable, suitable, usable, retooled, and so on."   So we argue that there needs to be a vast systematic bridging effort by specialists whom we have called "educational engineers" in order that the needed work across the bridge be accomplished, but in general such specialists do not yet exist to do this retooling effort, to shape it up, etc.   And this human effort in D activities will have to be 3 to 5 or more times the R effort.   A few and maybe many of us here are now being asked for numerous things by educators.   Torrance has been deluged even more than we have.

C   I was wondering how many states you have covered.

C   We get requests from practically all states (plus some foreign nations).   They are asking us to do eveything in addition to our basic research, aren't they, Torrance? They merely want us not only to do all the necessary research but also to give them all the products in a suitable form so that they can just plug them into their system. We are nowhere nearly adequately staffed or financed to answer their requests properly, nor do we yet have the know-how concerning all things required to put basic research findings across the bridge and to retool them into suitable shape for educational practice. I feel that the soundest approach is to admit that not very much is yet known by anyone about the missing bridging activities, so that without delay we should set out to determine what is needed.

S   This is why I suggested that it would be good to start out, as Jablonski had described, by having teachers engage in some classroom research projects, in opening-school workshops, or in middle-of-the-year workshops and summer programs where teachers can come together, as we have come together here, to catch the spirit of the types of activities that are going on in their school, in other schools, and in basic research.

C   Who is the better seller of your program, you or your teachers who have gone through your research activity? In other words, if you can get your teachers excited, I think that you can make this program move ahead.

S   This is, of course, the big hurdle. Once you break this barrier of getting teachers involved, it may go like wildfire.

C   Our experience in one brief attempt to bridge the gap was that the teachers were much more ready for such an attempt than were the administrators, especially the higher-level ones. The latter were conservative and cautious and had their "defenses up" very high. They acted as if they had never heard of a precedent of researchers talking directly to a school district. But the two teachers whom they invited as a last-minute gesture were lively and interested, more outwardly interested throughout the discussion than were any of the administrators. If we could have dealt directly and solely with these teachers, I think that we would have been off and running. As it was, we were under other pressures and decided—to use a common educational expression— that there was not enough "readiness" among the administrators. A bigger selling job would have been required *by us* than we had time to attempt, even though we were invited to their school district in the first place to make this presentation.[1]

---

[1] The sequel to this story is that when our meeting was finished I gave one of the top administrators in this district a copy of our final research report and a set of our approximately sixty new communication and creative ability tests. At that time he seemed quite puzzled as to what he should do with these materials, but later he wisely decided to pass them on to the supervisor of the two teachers who had been

S   I hope that as an administrator I am never accused of lacking readiness for this sort of venture. I think that you have made a proper step by inviting one of us to this conference. It has been most enlightening, and I am enthusiastic to the tips of my toes.

---

so responsive in this session. Shortly thereafter, one of these two teachers inquired widely in her school district where she could get copies of our materials. Her supervisor finally located them in the files (where she had disposed of them) and gave them to the inquiring teacher. This enterprising teacher promptly turned them into training exercises which she installed as part of her regular classroom work. The students responded very favorably and asked for more of these "thinking" exercises. Later she was asked to tell all the new school teachers in the district about the many new things she was doing in her English classes, practically all of which had emerged from our basic research project. So three or four years later we were delighted to discover that this bridging attempt did prove to be successful once the materials had been placed in the hands of the classroom teacher. (Contrarily, this bridging attempt would have died completely after our session if we had had to depend solely on all the other minds, except hers, that we encountered in that school district.)

part IV Criterion and Prediction Studies

chapter 16 Predicting Creative Performances from Multiple Measures

Calvin W. Taylor and Robert L. Ellison, University of Utah

S   We think that in Toynbee's challenging chapter he is warning America to examine its values. We need to ask ourselves how much we value creativity. In judging men's works and products, what value do we place on their creativeness as compared to their other qualities? We know that in the days when America was founded, creativity was a highly precious commodity. Are we now lethargic in our attitude toward this attribute, even to turning our backs on it, and if so, will we awaken before it is too late? The realization of the basic value of our people's creative thinking and products is vital to our progress.

To us as creativity researchers the criterion problem is highly important. We must ask ourselves whether some of the criteria that now exist are truly measuring creativeness and are the only criteria we want, or whether there are other creative criteria which Toynbee, for example, might consider important but on which researchers are also turning their backs. In our own work we are almost stunned by the complexity that we have found in our large, wide-sweeping efforts on the criterion problem. We are getting many creative and noncreative criterion dimensions. These results make us keenly aware that, as *each* new criterion dimension is isolated, a new and important psychological phenomenon is revealed for exploration.

Let us begin by giving you a brief preview of our work. We have set for ourselves one of the hardest of tasks in terms of both work and the likelihood of obtaining highly positive results. We are doing intensive criterion studies of creativity and then holding up multiple criteria of creativity (that are dimensionally independent) as external targets

227

against which to validate our psychological scores. The task would be much, much simpler if we were to restrict our target for prediction to only one single creative dimension (or if we were to restrict our definition of creativity to a simple, single-dimensional one). On our 166 Air Force scientists (Taylor, Smith, Ghiselin, and Ellison, 1961), we obtained over 50 criterion measures. These were intercorrelated and factored into 14 dimensions of creative and other kinds of contributions of scientists. On our several samples of National Aeronautical and Space Administration (NASA) scientists (now totaling about 2,000 persons) we have dealt with anywhere from 5 to 9 creative and other external criteria of the contributions of each scientist. We used official NASA records on contributions when available and profited as much as possible from our earlier Air Force criterion study in constructing new criterion measures.

We have thousands of intercorrelations among tests which we will hardly mention because we want to give greater attention to our validity coefficients against the external and difficult-to-obtain criteria, such as ratings by experts of each scientist's research reports and publications on originality, elegance, significance, etc. In the Air Force study, 130 psychological scores, drawn from the most promising ones reported in this conference series, were validated against each of 14 external criterion factors. In our later NASA studies we have completed the rigorous check of determining the cross validities of several biographical scores against each of 5 to 9 external criteria on several samples. Some of these are cross validities obtained on different samples of scientists at different NASA research centers using somewhat different criteria. We have focused our NASA work on a single type of predictor, a lengthy Biographical Inventory, which we have learned is possibly the best single creativity measure, perhaps because it is the most complex.

The two most promising definitions of creativity to emerge in this conference series, namely, Ghiselin's and Lacklen's ideas on the creativity criterion problem (Ghiselin, 1963; Lacklen and Harmon, 1958), have been successfully employed. These two definitions, reported at the 1957 conference, had been independently formulated a decade or more earlier. We constructed our creative criterion measure for our Air Force sample upon Ghiselin's formulation, which is applicable across disciplines, that is, the more creative the contribution, the more it restructures man's universe of understanding. Ghiselin's formulation for creativity as we have used it on scientists reads as follows:

You are to rate a man's ability to initiate and regulate activities of his mind, in scientific work, outside the already achieved patterns of understanding. Judging by any indications, consider his power to carry this process through all three stages: first, by forefeeling in the stir of uncrystallized awareness, some needed order unspecifiable because no expression of it exists as yet; secondly, by yielding attention and energy to that inward dynamic condition, developing it indirectly through whatever action, such as observation, study, or meditation, it may prompt; and thirdly, by registering its character in shaping some mental or physical substance into a new configuration. Consider, in short, his power to create a new scientific insight.

In our studies of NASA scientists, we have based our creativity criteria upon Lacklen's formulation that the more creative the contribution, the greater the area of science that the contribution underlies and therefore the greater its breadth of applicability.[1] Lacklen's formulation has been adapted into a 15-point rating scale with 7 written steps along the scale. The definition of creativity which precedes the scale is as follows:

Rate the product of the man's work as to its creativity. Consider the implications of his work, its impact, the originality of the approaches used by the scientist, the comprehensiveness and novelty of the solutions, the degree to which his work has opened the way and stimulated further research and has raised new, unforeseen problems. In short, evaluate the importance of his work in terms of its *breadth of applicability. DO NOT* consider other aspects of his performance—*ONLY* the creativity of his work.

The first descriptive statement on the NASA scale, defining the lowest degree of creativity, is as follows:

His work has demonstrated very little creativity or originality. It usually has provided no more than a rather simple solution to the immediate problem.

The last descriptive statement on the scale, describing the highest degree of creativity, is:

The impact of his work has been quite exceptional. His creative solutions to complex problems have broad generality and have even opened up important new areas of investigation with wide implications.

Other Air Force and NASA criterion rating scales were adapted from those presented by Donald Taylor at the 1957 Utah conference (Taylor, 1958).

Other Utah studies completed or in process will also be mentioned. These will include our attempts to retool our measuring devices to make them suitable at earlier ages, such as at the beginning of graduate work and at the high school level for use in connection with the National

---

[1] Lacklen presented his creativity criterion formulation at the 1957 Utah creativity conference (Lacklen and Harmon, 1958), and Gamble elaborated on it at the 1959 conference, telling how NASA and its predecessor, NACA, have developed and used this standard since 1947 for evaluating the past accomplishments of applicants (Sprecher, 1959).

Science Foundation's interesting summer science program for high school students.

BIOGRAPHICAL STUDIES OF NASA SCIENTISTS AND OF SCIENCE STUDENTS

In our studies of the relationship of biographical information to success in science, approximately 1,600 scientists have filled out one of our 300-item multiple-choice questionnaires. The vast majority of this work has been conducted in conjunction with NASA.[2] In a discussion of the biographical items in the Biographical Inventory, the term "biographical information" is in one sense a misnomer. The Biographical Inventory contains a wide variety of questions about childhood activities, experiences, sources of derived satisfactions and dissatisfactions, descriptions of the subject's parents, academic experiences, attitudes and interests, descriptions of leisure activities, value preferences, self-descriptions and evaluations, etc. The items thus encompass a wide variety of information because they are not limited to a narrow definition of what constitutes biographical experiences. By using such a broad biographical approach, potentially we can attempt to measure not only previous life history experiences, including past environmental effects on a person, but also to assess the outcome or manifestation of the hereditary-environment combination as it is personified in the individuals studied.

Before the NASA project, two studies had been conducted to explore the relationship of biographical information to scientific accomplishment, one by Ellison (1960) and one on Air Force scientists, noted earlier. The validities found between biographical scores from the empirically derived keys (scoring keys built on the data at hand) for each criterion and the scores on the corresponding criterion were extremely high on the initial sample in both studies. No (double checking) cross validation was attempted in either of these two preliminary studies because of the relatively small sample size, but the best items from both studies were identified and retained for future use in the NASA project. However, a priori scoring keys (keys built on our best hunches at that time) for the biographical responses also worked well on the sample of Air Force scientists, yielding better validities than any of the other 100 nonbiographical psychological test scores.

---

[2] Robert Lacklen and Allen Gamble of NASA are the monitors of the contract which was initiated in July 1959. I first met Lacklen in 1956 through Jim Burke's liaison work. Quite independently at that first meeting, Lacklen and I both stated that we felt the best single prospect for measuring creative potential was a lengthy, well-developed and well-analyzed and scored biographical inventory. These judgments were made long before 1960, when our Air Force validation results became available.

We have not been completely orthodox in our Biographical Inventory research. In both these studies, the items that were keyed and retained for use in future research were somewhat arbitrarily selected. In other words, they were not identified strictly in terms of the usual level-of-significance requirements. These requirements were waived with the conviction that a consistent relationship, even in the lower levels of validity across studies and samples, was more important in the long run than a single statistically significant correlation in any one study. Our approach has admittedly been actuarial in nature, being built upon "experience-table" information for each item, so that the total information accumulated is utilized in order to maximize the results obtained. The items so identified across a series of studies would probably meet the requirements of statistical significance as the sample size increased. The typical alternative-criterion correlations obtained and scored tended to be rather low, ranging from about .20 to .40, with at least a certain minimal percentage of the sample choosing each alternative to the item. The items so selected to form a longer combined test resulted in the high initial validities even though each item-alternative accounted for only a small percentage of the valid variance. We have sometimes described the Biographical Inventory with its many items and alternatives as an instrument consisting of a great many little oars, with each oar pulling only slightly in the right direction, but with all the oars in concert exerting a powerful pull. We also caution people not to lean too heavily on any single oar.

The first study of the Biographical Inventory

Based on the two previously mentioned Utah studies, a new form (Form A) of the Biographical Inventory was constructed and administered to 354 NASA scientists. The form consisted of 300 items which were subjectively classified into four sections: developmental history (up to age 21), parents and family life, academic background, and adult life and interests. The criteria used in the study of NASA scientists can be classified into three types: criteria available as official records at each of the NASA research centers, two criteria on the number of publications and the number of patents collected from the scientist, and criteria constructed by the investigators for research purposes only. For the first administration an overall evaluation measure, which we have termed an official rating, was already available at the research center. Three criteria were administered for research purposes only, a productivity check list, a creativity check list, and, three months later, a seven-step creativity rating scale. Both the creativity check list and the creativity rating scale were constructed on the basis of Lacklen's formulation as previously described. The correlation between the creativity check list and the creativity rating administered three months later was .69. Considering the time interval and the radically different nature of the criterion forms, this reliability estimate was considered satisfactory.

In the data analysis, the sample of 354 scientists was arbitrarily divided (on an approximately random basis) into two subsamples of 178 and 176. A separate item-alternative analysis was performed on each sample against each of three criteria. In the item-alternative analysis, biserial correlations were computed for each alternative in each item against each of the criteria. Large computers have been utilized for all statistical work. Following the item-alternative analysis, we tried a variety of scoring keys and weighting of alternatives and have retained from 125 to 150 items per scoring key, with one or more alternatives entering into the scoring of each item. Empirically derived keys were constructed on each of the two samples and applied to the opposite sample, so that a double cross-validation study was carried out. The average cross-validity coefficient on the two samples was .55 on the official overall-rating criterion and .52 on the creativity criterion. In one of the two subsamples, complete data were available on the two creativity criteria. The cross-validity coefficient of the best biographical score against a combination of the two creativity criteria was .59, a remarkably high cross validity for only a single test and for such an early period in the history of creativity research and measurement.

If the above validity coefficient of .59 was corrected for attenuation (unreliability) *in the criterion only* (a justifiable correction), the corrected validity coefficient increased so that it reached approximately .70. Thus, with a perfectly reliable criterion measure, approximately half of the variation in creative performance could be accounted for with only one total biographical score—an extremely high degree of prediction. Further leverage on predicting this criterion could be obtained by multiple correlation techniques, that is, by a best-weighted combination of biographical subscores.

The four subscores of the Biographical Inventory, ordered in terms of their validity, were, first, adult life and interests; second, academic background; third, developmental history; and last, parents and family life.

The second study of the Biographical Inventory

Before the second study, a new form (Form B) of the Biographical Inventory was constructed; this form was based on the best items of the previous administration. The "deadwood" items were eliminated to make room for new items to be evaluated in this form, with the hope that in the new set of 300 items the percentage of "livewood" would be increased. The best items from Form A (i.e., those which worked consistently across both subsamples) were subjectively reclassified into the following four substantive categories: (1) independence, (2) professional self-confidence, (3) general intellectuality, and (4) miscellaneous. These four keys were applied to the biographical responses of the scientists at the second research center to obtain four subscores and a total score.

At this center a revised form of the creativity rating scale was administered as the sole criterion score collected for research purposes only. A number of official evaluations were available, and data were collected on the most appropriate ones. These ratings were the following: knowledge of work, initiative, judgment, industry, reliability, and cooperation. In addition, the number of publications and the number of patents were obtained for each scientist.

Although these scientists had different work specialties, were at different geographical locations, and were measured on a slightly different creativity criterion than was used at the first administration, the average cross-validity coefficient for the total creativity biographical score based on the previous study was .47 against the creativity criterion on scientists at the new research center. With the use of multiple correlation techniques on the four subscores of the inventory, correlations in the low 50's were obtained, with "professional self-confidence" being the most valid subscore.

Again the same procedure was followed in analyzing the data. Briefly, the total sample of 300 scientists was split into two subsamples of 148 and 152, and an item-alternative analysis was carried out for each sample in a double cross-validation design. The cross-validation results from the item analysis at the second center were generally not as high as those obtained from the analysis at the first center, although a cross-validity coefficient of .60 was obtained in predicting publications. The average cross-validity coefficient for predicting creativity across the two subsamples at the second research center was .48. A comparison of this correlation of .48 with the correlation of .47 obtained by using the keys from the previous study indicates a high degree of stability in the biographical keys; it also indicates that it probably will not be necessary to build separate keys for each NASA research installation. The extent to which these keys would hold up in an industrial situation remains to be determined. The official rating scores which were available at the research center were without exception not very predictable, evidently because of the manner in which the official ratings were obtained.

The third study of the Biographical Inventory

Another form of the inventory was constructed in which the best items from all the previous studies were used. This form (Form C) has recently been administered to over 800 scientists at a third NASA research center, where 97% of the biographical inventories distributed were completed or otherwise accounted for.

At the third NASA research center, in contrast to the other two research centers visited, there is no existing rating procedure for the evaluation of the scientific personnel. Promotions are handled by means of letters of recommendation and by meetings of those concerned. Thus, the criterion measures collected at this center may have been influenced by this comparative lack of rating experience. The only criteria collected were ratings on scales constructed by the investigators, consisting of the following: quantity of work, skill in getting along with people, creativity, and an overall evaluation.

The procedures followed in this third study were again the same as in the previous administrations. After the total sample was divided into various organizational subsamples, cross-validation coefficients were obtained which ranged from .41 to .48 for the creativity criterion. For the prediction of the number of publications the average cross-validity coefficient on the total sample was .62. We have not yet obtained the results from applying the keys from the previous studies of the inventory to this sample.

Examples of item content of the Biographical Inventory

In this section a few examples of some of the better biographical items will be presented with a brief discussion of the types of items which have generally failed to contribute to the identification of scientific talent.[3] A factor analysis of the discriminating items in the Biographical Inventory, presently under way, will contribute additional information about both the interpretation of the items and their interrelationships. It should be remembered that the following relationships are characteristic only of the majority; there would be some individuals whose responses to each item would be exceptions to the general finding. All the items cited related to the creativity criterion and on occasions to other criteria as well. Since there may have been some distortion in the responses of

---

[3] Among the items which did not discriminate were those dealing with such characteristics as birth order, the majority of family-child items, demographic variables, and items dealing with specific segments of childhood experiences, such as Boy Scout achievement and childhood play experiences.

the subjects, the extent to which these responses correspond to the actual situation remains to be determined.

A number of items demonstrated that characteristics of self-determination and individualistic orientation (or inner directedness) are positively related to the criteria. A facet of this is concerned with how the individual scientist elects to expend his energies and to what area of his life he devotes himself. For example, a definite task orientation appears to be involved in the following question. If an individual responds that, to a great extent, he is the kind of person who becomes so absorbed in his work and interests that he does not mind a lack of friends, this response was positively related to the criteria, whereas another person's response that this does not describe him at all was negatively related to the criteria. Another example of an item in this area is as follows:

> Assume that you are in a situation in which the following two alternative courses of action arise. Which one of the two would you be more likely to do? (A) Be a good team man so that others like to work with me, or (B) gain a reputation through controversy, if necessary, as one whose scientific word can be trusted.

Response A was correlated negatively with the criteria, and response B was positively related. Wherever this attitude of independence originated, it evidently tended to have been present during the student's academic career. For example, if the scientist reported that he questioned his professors on subject matter considerably more often than average, his response was positively related to the criteria.

The relationship of undergraduate college grade-point average to success as a scientist has been shown by many investigations to be at best low; however, occasionally a few items in the academic section of the Biographical Inventory which are concerned with self-reported academic performance emerge with a low but consistent relationship to supervisor ratings. For example, a B.A. or B.S. degree or less has a negative relationship to the criteria, whereas the Ph.D. degree has a positive relationship. If a student describes his college undergraduate work as being well above average and himself as being satisfied with his progress, this response is positively related to the criteria. If the student succeeded exceptionally well in his *engineering* or *biological* science courses, this has a positive relationship to the criteria, while a response of succeeding fairly well has a negative relationship. Other items, such as those concerned with success in *mathematics*, *physics*, and *chemistry*, have *not* consistently shown a relationship with the creativity criterion.

One of the more consistently surprising items which has demonstrated a positive relationship to creativity is concerned with attitudes toward making repairs around the house before the age of eighteen. If the subject responds that he had a *strong dislike* of making such repairs, this response is positively related to creative performance. It is suspected that this item is related to the personality factor of femininity. Previous research has shown that this dimension has some relationship to creativity. It may also reflect certain sensitivities and an orientation toward ideas as opposed to more mechanical interests.

This discussion would not be complete without a brief statement of the types of items that have failed to discriminate. Generally speaking, items that measure a small specific segment of previous experience or a specific fact in a life history have not been fruitful. For example, items such as the extent of participation in childhood job enterprises (cutting lawns, washing cars, etc.) or the number of times that the subject had changed residence by the time he entered college, or the age at which he held his first paying job, or the highest level of achievement he obtained in the Boy Scouts, have not survived the validation process. Another area which has so far proved barren for identifying scientific talent concerns descriptions of various parental characteristics, such as a mother's or father's dominance, affection, encouragement, strictness, or permissiveness. Although it is expected that this is an area of definite importance, it has proved to be extremely difficult to cultivate successfully. One of the reasons is probably the complex network of interactions that exists between the subject's parents, so that when any one facet of their behavior has been measured it does not provide enough information about how the other parental characteristics interact; thus, by itself the characteristic being measured appears unimportant.

It would be difficult to estimate the number of items which either have been tried out in one form of our inventory or have been carefully examined for their potential discriminating power. Certainly the number exceeds 1,000. Undoubtedly it would be possible to construct additional valid items to add to the Biographical Inventory, but according to our current understanding and measurement skills most of the fertile ground has already been plowed. Consequently, gains in the near future through item construction will probably be small, although not necessarily unimportant.

Heterogeneity of the Biographical Inventory

Recently we completed a small piece of exploratory research which highlights the complexity and the stability of the Biographical Inventory. In Form C, 12 landmark personality items were selected from French (1953) in order to relate the biographical items to previous research findings on typical personality instruments. These landmark factor items were as follows: dominance, interest in philosophy, mas-culinity-femininity, persistence, self-confidence, sensitive attitude, so-ciability, gregariousness, emotionality, autistic thought, and intelligence. In an exploratory attempt to see how the biographical items related to these dimensions of personality, 6 of the landmark personality items were held up as criterion scores in an item analysis. Although the land-mark items themselves had a very low correlation with the regular criterion measures of creativity, productivity, etc., scores from the bio-graphical keys which were built to predict these personality landmark items correlated substantially higher with the regular criterion measures. For example, the item measuring dominance correlated .12 with cre-ativity; yet the dominance score from the biographical key of approxi-mately 74 items correlated .37 with the creativity criterion. Thus, even though the dominance criterion item had a very low relationship with the creativity criterion, the key built to predict the dominance item also succeeded in predicting the creativity criterion. This was to be ex-pected, at least to some extent, because of the much greater length (74 items versus 1 item) and thus the consequent greater reliability. An-other probable reason is that many of the items which went into the lengthened key were complex factorially and thus measured other as-pects of the creativity criterion. This explanation is supported by the fact that scores from the dominance key correlated .83 with the bio-graphical scores that were specially keyed for the creativity criterion. The cross-validity coefficient of this same empirically keyed dominance score against the dominance criterion item was .50. Of the other 5 landmark items which were held up as criteria in an item analysis, all were predicted with cross validities ranging from .38 to .62, the majority being in the .50's. These findings again illustrate the complexity of the inventory as it predicted these different areas of personality. This pro-cedure of keying biographical items against a landmark personality item provides an efficient way of building a longer biographical test for that personality characteristic.

Biographical scores for identifying scientific talent in younger age groups

The question has been raised whether the items in the Biographical Inventory are not primarily concerned with topics which are pertinent only to adults and to actual on-going research activities. This question implies that these biographical items would not be very appropriate or valid if administered to younger age groups, such as high school students or college seniors, because the items are oriented too much toward the activities of mature research scientists.

A study on this problem supported by the National Science Foundation (Taylor, Cooley, and Nielsen, 1963) highlights some of the complexities involved in early identification of scientific talent, since it implies that our present educational program is not geared to give the most appropriate kind of training as far as creative scientific achievement is concerned. In the NSF-supported summer science program for high school students, some of the students have the unusual opportunity to participate full time in research activities. Others participate in advanced classroom-only work. The main interest of our study, in which Gary Cooley and Elwin Nielsen have been the research assistants, was to determine whether the creative and productive characteristics found for scientists on the job, as discovered in recent studies of Air Force, NASA, and other scientists, were measurable on high school students in these programs and whether these same characteristics were more closely related to the performance of the students in these research activities than to classroom-only performances.

The data analysis has revealed that two distinct groups can be identified, a research achievement group and an academic achievement group. In general, the predictors with validity for the academic program tended to have low, zero, or negative validities in the research programs, and vice versa. In this study the Biographical Inventory was modified to be appropriate for younger age groups. It was found that the vast majority of the items could be used without modification; a few were revised, and a few dropped. Because some items had to be rewritten, because scoring keys were constructed on mature scientists, and because predictive (follow-up) validities rather than concurrent validities were to be determined, we expected the revised Biographical Inventory not to work very well, if at all, in such short-range predictions. However, the results indicated that, of all instruments used in this study, the Biographical Inventory was the best overall predictor of creative performance. In one of the research participation groups in which we felt we obtained the most valid criteria, the Biographical Inventory scores correlated .47 with supervisory ratings on creativity. Needless to say, this is a remarkably satisfactory test of cross validation. Certain biographical keys that worked well in the research programs did not work well for the academic programs and vice versa. The two extreme examples are that the scores from the "professional self-confidence" key were valid for two-thirds of the criteria in the research programs but had no significant validities whatsoever in the academic sample, whereas scores from the "miscellaneous" biographical key were as good as any biographical scores in the academic programs but had no significant validities in the research programs.

We thought that the initial Biographical Inventory would probably be more appropriate for college seniors than for high school students, since college seniors more closely resemble the adult samples upon which the Biographical Inventory was developed. Some data have been obtained on this latter issue, although the criteria were not as directly pertinent as those used in the study of high school students. Victor Bunderson has been working on an evaluation of present and potential fellowship-selection information at the University of Utah, where the research committee awards approximately forty graduate fellowships per year. Selection has been based largely on grade-point average and open-ended letters of recommendation. This study seeks to evaluate these sources of information for fellowship evaluations in the light of various criteria of graduate student performance. As a part of this research, a modified Biographical Inventory was administered for research purposes only to a number of seniors and graduate students who applied for a fellowship. Ratings were obtained a year later on their graduate student performances, including their research potential. Again the Biographical Inventory scores proved to be the most valid predictor of these multiple criteria; in fact, early indications are that the Biographical Inventory, by itself, overshadows the validity of the official, collective judgment of the fellowship committee, who had used the entire folder of materials for each applicant in making its decisions.

Future biographical research activities

An examination of the different types of items included in the various biographical inventories shows that, in the number of characteristics measured, they are very heterogeneous and complex. One of the activities under way is an intercorrelation and factor analysis of the biographical items, along with appropriate criterion scores. Such an analysis will yield a great deal of information about this type of inventory. Of special interest is the possibility that factor analysis will contribute to the development of more independent and efficient subscores within the inventory than our existing subjective classification of developmental history, parents and family life, etc., has yielded. This in turn should contribute to higher validity coefficients from combined subscores, thus increasing the predictive potential of the Biographical Inventory. Another type of useful information from a factor analysis of the items will be the identification of the most promising areas in the inventories. From these leads, it should be possible to construct new items and thereby further improve the instrument.

An additional future research activity concerns the problem of determining the long-range follow-up (predictive) validity of the Biographical

Inventory. That is, what will the validity of the inventory be when it is administered to a group of new college graduates or other NASA applicants who are then followed up to determine their degree of success on the job? For this purpose, a short form of the inventory can be developed in order to decrease the time necessary for an applicant to complete it. Another problem which may arise in the administration of the inventory to potential employees is the possibility of distortion or deliberate falsification. Some work has already been completed on this problem. Various types of correction scores (such as an exaggeration score and a false modesty score) have been developed, so that the distortions or falsifications that do occur can hopefully be identified and used to improve the instrument's efficiency.

The Biographical Inventory has usually been found to measure somewhat different criterion variance from other traditional types of selection tests. It therefore seems advisable to consider studies on some of these other kinds of measures found to have promise in research on creative scientific talent to see how well they supplement the Biographical Inventory scores. Such additional validation work could take full advantage of the criterion data as well as the biographical data already available on NASA scientists.

In summary, all our research results obtained to date indicate that biographical information is a very promising, if not the most promising, single means of identifying creative and other types of science talent.

The cross-validity coefficients obtained are considerably higher than those typically reported for the prediction and identification of creative or of other types of scientific talent by means of other kinds of predictors, such as high-level aptitude tests, intelligence measures, college-grade-point average, and personality test measures. It is our conviction that continued research should be carried out to exploit thoroughly the potential in the biographical approach so that the identification of creative scientific talent can be accomplished with as much accuracy as possible.

CRITERION AND VALIDATION STUDIES ON AIR FORCE SCIENTISTS

The results on the criterion phase of our research on Air Force scientists, presented at the 1959 Utah conference, are available in Chapter 5 of *Scientific Creativity: Its Recognition and Development* (Taylor and Barron, 1963). In this section of the paper a review of a few general findings from the final project report on criteria and predictors will be presented, as well as later analyses and thinking on this study.[4] The

---

[4] For a complete presentation of the validation phase of the study as well as a review of the criterion findings see the final project report by Calvin W. Taylor,

56 criterion measures and control scores obtained for each scientist from 8 different sources were boiled down to 14 criterion factors plus 1 control factor of age, work years, and length of service at the organization studied. A striking finding in this criterion study was that no single criterion measured more than 4 of our 14 criterion dimensions, and most criteria spanned from 1 to 3 of the total criterion dimensions. We therefore conclude that, when merely a single criterion measure from only one source of information is used, there is a good chance that many performances and contributions on the job are being missed. In other words, overall success in science is not a unitary phenomenon but has many dimensions in which creative and other kinds of contributions are made.

Further analysis of our multiple criteria

At the 1959 conference, several persons asked about a second-order factor analysis of our correlated first-order factors. Undoubtedly, some of these persons hoped that simplicity would thus finally emerge. However, even though some simplification was found in a second-order analysis, the general picture was still one of great complexity in the criterion area.

Our correlations among the 14 first-order factors were factored and 7— not merely 1 or 2—second-order factors were obtained. Under my supervision, Roger Rompel has recently refactored these correlations and obtained an orthogonal rotational solution for the 7 second-order factors (see Chapter 3 by Ghiselin, Rompel, and Taylor for some details of this factor solution). Five of the 14 first-order factors had some creative features in their composition. All 5 of these (but no other first-order factors) emerged with loadings above .25 in a second-order factor which we labeled "general creativity." We were quite pleased with this clean-cut linkage among these 5 creative first-order factors.

We will not focus further on the other second-order factors except to note that two independent recognition factors emerged, namely, "non-material recognition" and "material recognition and success." Both these kinds of recognition were independent of (unrelated to) the creativeness of the scientist's work. In other words, both kinds of contributions that were recognized and rewarded either materially or not materially were independent of the general creativity dimension. This finding may be related back to Toynbee's warning that we in America

William R. Smith, Brewster Ghiselin, and Robert Ellison, "Explorations in the Measurement and Prediction of Contributions of One Sample of Scientists," *Technical Report ASD-TR-61-96*, Aeronautical Systems Division, Personnel Laboratory, Lackland Air Force Base, Texas: April 1961. vi + 62 pages.

are not placing importance or value on creativity. There is also a hint in a weak second-order factor called "submissive conformity" that a small part of originality in written work may function to give a person a below-average rating by his supervisor on overall performance. At the 1959 conference we reported several other troublesome but intriguing results like this that were found in our earlier first-order factor-analysis study of criterion measures.

Predictability of creative and other criteria

In this study we were frustrated when it became necessary to select only a few from the large number of intellectual and nonintellectual tests that appeared to be promising, primarily as seen from the reports at the 1955, 1957, and 1959 Utah creativity research conferences (Taylor, 1956, 1958, 1959). For example, Match Problems, Consequences, Word Association, Pertinent Questions, Apparatus Test, Visual Imagery, and Revision II were the only intellectual tests used; these sampled less than one-fourth of the intellectual characteristics which we felt at this early stage to be potential components of creative performance. Consequently, even though 130 scores from 14 tests were collected and each of these scores was validated against each of the multiple-factored criteria found in the initial phase of this project, we felt some dissatisfaction with having omitted a number of other promising measures. We tested the scientists five different times, over a two-year period, to obtain the entire battery of 130 test scores. Across the successive waves of data collection, our sample on whom we had sufficiently complete data shrunk from the 166 scientists in the criterion study to 107 in the later validation study. William R. Smith, the field psychologist, was responsible for the large and difficult data-collection activities in this project.

We ended with 42 scores from a biographical information inventory, 17 scores from self-ratings, 1 score on grade-point average, 12 scores on minimum satisfactory level of aspirations, 10 scores from Cattell's Motivational Analysis Test, 26 scores from Saunders' Personality Research Inventory, 2 scores from the Creative Process Check List, and 16 scores from the seven aptitude tests.

Three of the initial criteria ("peer rankings on productivity," "supervisory ratings of creativity," and "supervisory ratings of drive-resourcefulness") were retained with the 14 factored criteria to make a total of 17 criteria used in the validation study. Frankly, these 3 initial criteria were retained mainly to communicate some findings to any readers who were hesitant about accepting findings based upon the factor results.

A list of the 17 criteria, arranged in order according to the percentage of the 130 psychological scores that were valid for each criterion, is as follows:

Likableness as a research team member (44%)	Supervisory rating of creativity (29%)
Scientific and professional society membership (43%)	*Supervisory rating of drive-resourcefulness (25%)
Current organizational status (38%)	*Originality of written work (20%)
*Judged work output (35%)	Visibility (20%)
*Supervisory ratings of overall performance (35%)	Recognition for organizational contributions (17%)
Peer rankings on productivity (35%)	Recent publications (14%)
*Productivity in written work (32%)	Contract monitoring load (11%)
Creativity rating by laboratory chiefs (29%)	*Status-seeking, "organizational-man" tendencies (08%)
	Quality (without originality) of research reports (02%)

The 6 criteria that are marked with an asterisk were selected for the purpose of developing empirically keyed biographical scores, with 5 keys (for 4 subscores and 1 total score) being determined for each of these 6 criteria. If all of these 30 empirically keyed scores on the Biographical Information Inventory included in the above ranking of the criteria were omitted from consideration, the criteria would rearrange themselves only slightly in terms of their percentage of significant validity coefficients for the remaining 100 test scores.

The initial "supervisory rating of creativity" (Ghiselin's definition) and the three factored criteria entitled "supervisory ratings of overall performance," "creativity rating by laboratory chiefs," and "originality of written work" were the 4 that we considered to be the most creative of the 17 criteria. Two other factored criteria, "productivity in written work" and "judged work output," also contained some creative features in their composition.

Characteristics associated with creative contributions[5]

We are in an early state of research knowledge regarding characteristics of creative persons. All our experience and all the research results to date indicate that no single characteristic by itself accounts for much

---

[5] See the final project report cited in footnote 4 for an even longer list of characteristics generally associated with *all types of contributions* of scientists. The self-ratings on creativity and on inner directedness also topped this more general list.

of the total phenomenon of creativity; in other words, many human characteristics are usually involved in making creative contributions. This generalization can be illustrated by examining our findings about creative characteristics in this study.

The four criteria named above as having the most creative features in them were singled out for particular analysis. We found 40 of the 96 predictor scores considered for this analysis to be valid against one or more of the four creative criteria.

The following list contains the descriptions of the psychological characteristics of the creative scientist, as found in our sample of Air Force scientists. The first two characteristics were valid for all four of the most creative criteria, the next five in the list were valid for three of the four criteria, the next set—through "intellectual thoroughness"—was valid for two creative criteria, and the rest were valid for only one of the four most creative criteria. The scores which identified the more creative persons were as follows: creativity, inner directedness, drive, cognition, quantity of reports, theoretical contributions, nonmodal biographical response, desire for principles, discrimination of value, aggressiveness, being well-liked, professional self-confidence, low sociability, high self-sufficiency, dedication to work, self-reported academic level, intellectual thoroughness, mathematics ability, resourcefulness, flexibility, independence, intuition, impulsiveness (low score), self-sufficiency, attitude to work, belief in rights of groups, masculine vigor (low score), progressive (versus conservative), reading skills, listening skills, administrative advancements, being well-known, level of original work, assertion (low score), sadism-narcissism (comfort), grade-point average, liking to think, and social desirability (low score).

These results clearly indicate the complexity of the prediction problem in terms of the number of variables functioning in creative performances. At least at our present state of knowledge, no single-variable panacea and no single-variable theory will serve in this area. Our present theory of creativity would definitely be described as a multivariable one along these lines: creative performance is dependent upon a large number of relatively separate variables, each one of which accounts generally for only a small, unique, and frequently almost statistically insignificant part of the total variation in creative performance. The validities of the best single scores for each criterion ranged in the .40's, .30's, and .20's with a sizable number of scores being valid for most of the criteria.

It is noteworthy that the *self-rating on creativity* (as defined again by Ghiselin's approach) was valid for each and every criterion possessing some creative features, including two additional criteria with such features. Certain other characteristics, such as a high score on self-sufficiency and independence and a low score on sociability, have emerged with indications of validity in nearly all creativity studies in which they have been tried. This early consistency is quite striking.

Validities of different types of predictor tests

The nine main types of predictor measures used in this study and the number of scores for each type of test are listed in Table 1. This table shows the percentage of scores valid for each type of test against the 4 most creative criteria and against all 17 criteria. One will quickly notice that the biographical scores were more frequently valid than any other type, especially against the creative criteria, and that the self-ratings ranked second in validity. A predictor score was considered valid each time it correlated .19 or greater (above the .05 level of significance) with a criterion.

TABLE 1

Percentage of Scores Valid for Each Type of Test against
Creative Criteria and against All Criteria

Number of Scores per Type of Test	Type of Test	4 Most Creative Criteria	All 17 Criteria
30	Biographical Inventory (empirically keyed)	63%	47%
12	Biographical Inventory (a priori keyed)	46	34
17	Self-ratings	26	33
1	Grade-point average	25	22
12	Minimum satisfactory level	25	22
10	Cattell's Motivational Analysis Test	7	8
26	Saunders' Personality Research Inventory	7	8
2	Creative Process Check List (a priori)	0	6
16	Intellectual aptitude tests	0	4

The percentages presented for the empirically keyed biographical scores were spuriously high because empirical keys had been built for 2 of the 4 most creative criteria and for 6 of the 17 criteria.

A few additional comments are warranted. The overall undergraduate grade-point average was valid for only 4 of the 17 criteria and barely valid for 3 of these 4, including one creative criterion. Stated conversely.

the grade-point average was unrelated to 13 of the 17 criteria. While there may be some restriction of range in grades, we should all remember that the odds are that more validities which are approximately zero in a restricted range will remain essentially zero than will become nonzero in an unrestricted range of talent.[6] At least in one of these studies where the correlation was .06, a wide range of grade-point averages was present in the sizable sample studied, with some grade-point averages being below C.

A general illustration of this point was given to us by Don Anderson of Australia, during his recent visit to our campus. The Appointment Board of the University of Melbourne reported that the Shell Company of Australia came to them and said, "Have you any more of those fouled-up science students you sent us last year? The last lot of them was pretty good."

We have previously reported that the number of years of education was unrelated to 12 of our 14 criterion factors, being related only to productivity (not quality) in paper work (i.e., effectiveness in completing paper work) and to membership in professional societies (for which it is often a prerequisite).

In the motivation area our straightforward minimum satisfactory level scores had a considerably higher percentage of significant validities than the more elaborate Motivational Analysis Test with its 10 scores. The Personality Research Inventory was generally functioning not much above the chance level, although a few of its scores displayed some promising and meaningful validities. The results for both theoretically derived and empirically derived scores for the Creative Process Check List constructed by Ghiselin are reported in Chapter 3.

The 16 scores from the 7 intellectual (high-level) aptitude tests did not yield very promising results. In certain cases (such as Revision II and Visual Imagery) some restriction of range was present. However, no restriction of range was evident for the other aptitude tests. For example, four scores were derived from the Word Association Test: the total number of associated words written, the total number of close synonym-type words, the total number of remotely associated words, and the number of different sets. When the 4 word association scores

---

[6] The reader is also referred to the subsection entitled "The Inadequacy of Undergraduate Grades as Substitute Criteria for on-the-Job Research Performance" in Chapter 5, pp. 72–75, of *Scientific Creativity: Its Recognition and Development* (Taylor and Barron, 1963), and to the article "Good Scholars not Always Best," in *Business Week*, February 24, 1962, pp. 77–78, for three studies where undergraduate grade-point averages were unrelated to research performance in scientific work. Similar results are cited in an article entitled "NASA Tries New Recruiting Tests," in *Missiles and Rockets*, May 7, 1962, p. 17.

were validated against the 17 criteria, only one of the 68 validity coefficients was significant at the .05 level. I personally am puzzled and troubled by this low batting average for the 7 high-level aptitude tests which we so carefully selected from a much longer list of more than 30, all of which we felt were promising candidates for this validation study.

C Why didn't you use an instrument that had been studied for validity for those things?

S Perhaps you mean that we probably should have used Cattell's Sixteen Personality Factor Questionnaire. We used a Personality Research Inventory that Saunders, one of Cattell's students, had produced since the 16 PF was developed.[7] The names of the scores from this newer inventory sound more relevant for creativity, since the inventory is claimed to measure self-acceptance, tolerance of frustration, tolerance of ambiguity or complexity, self-sufficiency, aggressiveness, social conscience, social status, aspiration, masculine vigor, liking to think, aggressive versus conservative, etc.

C I am still concerned about your choice of instrument. There are a number of well-studied instruments with some indication of validity that might be better.

S We were willing to try what Saunders recommended to us as the latest and the most promising new personality instrument, but maybe we missed the boat on it. We did encounter a similar reaction to yours after we had committed ourselves to using that inventory. This reaction led us to request additional testing with Cattell's Motivational Analysis Test, which was strongly recommended to us.[8]

C I really can't understand this impoverishment on the prediction side when you have done so much work on the criterion end. Why didn't you use things like the Strong Inventory, which has been thoroughly studied and has demonstrated high validities, and the MMPI and the CPI? It seems to me that they are natural choices.

S I don't think 130 predictor scores from 14 different measuring devices administered to busy scientists can rightfully be called impoverishment on the prediction side. We did consider the CPI, as I recall, but never seriously considered the Strong or the MMPI. With hindsight knowledge about our results for the Saunders Personality Research Inventory, we recognize that we may have made a mistake in using it, though we are not very confident that much better results would be obtained for other personality inventories of this general type. The results which you feel are move favorable for other instruments were

---

[7] Test obtained through personal communication with D. Saunders, 1959.

[8] Test obtained through personal communication with R. B. Cattell, 1959.

not known by us and were not available to us at the time when we made our decisions, during the period from 1957 to 1959.

C   The Strong Inventory is the granddaddy of them all and probably the best.

S   Maybe our willingness to try fresh things is at fault, but you must realize that the Strong Inventory yielded anything but promising validities in Donald Taylor's studies reported at the 1957 Utah conference (Taylor, 1958); the average for 10 validity coefficients for its most relevant scores was .02.

C   The Strong Inventory has never before produced sizable validities in this area.

C   It certainly has, as you will see later in MacKinnon's report (Chapter 22).

S   It may be healthy to be trying a variety of instruments across the whole creativity research movement. In fact, the most convincing evidence in science is obtained when different investigators use different approaches and techniques in different laboratories but find essentially the same results on a given problem.

C   You can always go back to the same subjects with other predictors.

S   Of course, we would also like to double check, against creative criteria on other samples of scientists, some of the results for individual tests and combinations of tests that were valid for our Air Force scientists.

Multiple correlations for a battery of 52 predictor scores in the Air Force data

After pondering the cross-validation results on the complex Biographical Inventory and believing that the true spirit of exploratory science is to try something to see what comes of it, we decided to compute multiple correlations for a large battery of test scores from our Air Force study. In other words, we wondered whether a long set of *tests* would yield the same results as a long set of biographical *items* had yielded. The Fisher-Doolittle technique was utilized for computing several multiple correlations simultaneously, using a standard set of 52 scores, in turn, against each of the 17 criteria. We selected the 52 scores with all of the 17 criteria in mind so that the scores which proved to be best for each criterion were included. We also included an occasional score with the hope of getting a suppressor effect. We wanted to know what the magnitude of the multiple correlation would be when we used a large number of test scores, most of which correlated significantly but none of which correlated very highly with the criterion in question.

We felt that this situation paralleled the situation for items in the Biographical Inventory. We wanted not only to determine the percentage overlap that could be obtained for each criterion but also to subdivide the overlap into the portions that could be attributed to each of the test scores (expressed in the form of beta $\times$ r products, that is, the beta weight times the validity coefficient for that test, where beta is the best weight) to see what we would get out of this analysis.

Table 2 shows the result of this analysis for the four most-creative criteria and for the other two criteria with some creative features. At the bottom of the last page of the table one can notice that the battery of test scores overlaps approximately half or more (50.0%, 46.8%, 70.7%, 71.0%, 66.0%, and 65.4%) of what the particular criterion measures (the criterion variance) on this same sample on which these best weights were computed. (Note that four of these six multiple correlations are in the .80's.) One will also notice that this overlapping of each criterion, shown as the column total, is accumulated mainly from a large number of small contributions. In fact, for a single score the contribution of 6% is quite infrequent, and a contribution of 10% is definitely rare for any criterion. Other observations are that all multiple correlations are quite high on the initial sample, just as they have been for our total biographical score, but no single test score usually makes much of the total contribution. In other words, the large total overlap is obtained through many small, separate, low contributions, the same as found for our Biographical Inventory. Through this analysis, we have also learned to have considerable respect for low validities, even in the .20's, especially if we have enough of them.[9] In other words, if high validities are not being found and if low validities are all that are available, then we would like to have as many of these low validities as we can get; that is, we need as many different kinds of scores with validities in the .20's, .30's, and .40's as possible so we can use the best combinations of these scores for each criterion studied.

The question of shrinkage of multiple correlations is, in our opinion, best handled by cross validation. We are now asking ourselves this question: If we checked these results in a cross-validation study, would we get about the same amount of shrinkage as we have had in the results for our Biographical Inventory, which still holds up at a reasonable level in the .40's and .50's or maybe even approaching or reaching the .60's?

By cross validation on a new sample we always mean that we are using the scoring keys that we developed from the previous sample. In our

[9] This relates back to Guilford's article (1948) in the *American Psychologist* about psychological programs during World War II, wherein Air Force researchers learned to have respect for low validities against external criteria.

TABLE 2

Percentage of Creative Criteria Variance Accounted for by Each Predictor (Beta $\times$ r Products) and by All Predictors ($100R^2$)

					Criteria		
Predictor Scores		Originality of Written Work	Creativity Rating by Laboratory Monitor	Supervisor's Overall Evaluation	Creativity Rating by Supervisor	Productivity of Written Work	Judged Work Output
Number	Name	4	7	8	17	1	6
1	Drive	.2	4.4	10.8	3.0	5.4	-1.4
2	Math ability	-.8	-.3	-1.0	-2.4	-3.4	-2.9
3	Resourcefulness	-.4	.7	2.6	.0	-.4	5.7
4	Cognition	11.0	2.8	3.6	4.6	.8	5.8
5	Integrity	2.2	-.4	1.2	4.7	.6	-2.4
6	Desire for principles	.4	4.7	3.4	2.4	-1.8	5.5
7	Desire for discovery	.4	-.0	1.0	.4	7.5	1.1
8	Informative ability	1.0	.1	-1.8	.2	-.9	-5.2
9	Flexibility	-.1	-.6	.7	-1.6	-.5	3.8
10	Independence	-.2	-.9	-2.3	-1.0	.6	12.0
11	Discrimination of value	2.9	-1.8	8.2	2.8	3.8	5.7
12	Intuition	.0	-.2	-7.0	-4.8	-1.8	-1.2
13	Creation	4.1	-.3	1.4	2.4	2.3	.6
14	Compulsiveness	-.1	.7	.6	.6	1.2	.6
15	Talkativeness	.0	.2	-1.0	1.3	-.1	.0
16	Self-sufficiency	.3	1.7	.7	-2.1	-2.1	1.1
17	Gregariousness	.6	-1.9	-1.0	-.3	-1.0	-.5
18	Aggressiveness	-.8	.6	3.9	7.0	1.3	-1.4
19	Belief in rights of individuals	-2.2	-.4	-.8	1.8	.3	1.3
20	Social consciousness	.2	4.2	2.0	-.9	.9	4.8

21	Status aspiration	.0	1.6	1.2	.3	.4	.8
22	Masculine vigor	-.2	-1.6	1.4	-.2	-.0	2.0
23	Progressive vs. conservative	5.2	-.1	.0	1.1	-.0	.6
24	Total no. of ideas retained	.2	.0	-.2	.1	-.2	-.0
25	Per cent correct of marked	1.6	4.4	.1	.2	1.0	-.6
26	Reading skills	.6	.9	1.3	1.2	.0	-.2
27	Writing skills	.9	.7	.4	-.4	.0	2.3
28	Quantity of work output	.0	.0	-.7	-.0	-.0	-.2
29	Being well liked	.2	—	7.2	9.9	6.0	4.0
30	Being well known	.5	—	3.1	2.4	-1.6	.0
31	Quantity of reports	4.8	-.1	-.5	-2.6	4.1	1.0
32	Theoretical contributions	-.1	.4	2.0	7.4	6.1	-2.7
33	Level of original work	-1.0	.1	-1.0	.6	.8	3.6
34	Total acceptable modifications	.5	-1.1	-.1	1.8	-.0	-1.2
35	Assertion	.7	4.9	2.1	1.8	.6	8.9
36	Self-sentiment	.4	1.6	.8	-.4	.7	-1.7
37	Career	.0	-.1	.6	.3	3.2	.1
38	Super-ego	.0	-.1	-.1	-.0	2.2	1.4
39	States of feeling	1.1	.2	.6	-.1	.2	.9
40	Grade-point average	.1	4.4	1.3	1.2	.0	.3
41	Professional self-confidence	3.2	.6	-1.3	-.0	9.4	4.8
42	Emotional restraint	-.1	4.8	.4	-.0	-.6	4.1
43	Low sociability	.7	.5	11.2	12.5	-2.0	-.9
44	High self-sufficiency	1.0	3.5	-.2	5.5	1.4	.2
45	Inner directedness	-.2	.5	4.9	1.7	7.1	.6
46	Dedication to work	.4	-3.0	-1.8	-.6	4.7	-2.7
47	Liking to think	1.7	6.9	.3	-.4	10.3	-.3
48	Intellectual thoroughness	-.8	-1.2	-.2	-1.1	-3.5	-2.9
49	Social desirability	.3	1.5	2.9	.9	2.0	2.6
50	Self-reported academic level	.6	.4	5.5	7.2	-1.3	3.6
51	Model response	2.7	1.8	3.9	3.8	4.7	-.2
52	Superv. vs. scientists rating of job—scatter and shape	10.8	.8	1.2	-.1	-.0	4.7
	Total per cent of criterion variance overlapped $100R^2 =$	50.0	46.8	70.7	71.0	66.0	65.4
	Multiple correlation coefficient $R =$	.707	.684	.841	.843	.812	.809

biographical studies, if we would rekey our inventory on each new sample, we would practically always have validities at least in the .70's and .80's. We now report only our cross validities, never our initial validities. We have cross-validated the Biographical Inventory on subsamples within a research center as well as cross-validating it at different research centers.

C   When you compute your optimum data for each sample separately, do you ever see whether there is the same rank order of validity coefficients across samples?

S   We have not done this exactly; but we have sought for a consistency of results across samples for items we have retained—and hopefully we would find some consistency across samples in the best weights found for tests in a battery.

C   I was wondering about an unweighted combination, just adding equal weighted (i.e., unit-weighted) scores.

S   We have done this type of thing with our Biographical Inventory. By and large, a simple scoring system across a large number of items has worked about as well as a more complicated one, although we haven't exhausted the possibilities. Another kind of cross validation which is not strictly replication but which yields another type of validity is to double-check our results through follow-up predictive validity techniques.

The multiple correlational analyses of the 52 test scores suggest, then, that, on the initial sample studied, about half or more of the variance in any of 17 criteria of creative and other scientific contributions may be overlapped by a best-weighted sum—a linear regression combination of 15 or more valid test predictors, although the shrinkage of overlap on cross-validation is as yet unknown.

In this analysis we have used only biographical scores derived from a priori keys (numbered 41 to 50 in Table 2), not scores from empirical keys. Our best single hope now for initially high validities would be to use empirically keyed scores from our latest, well-developed, and thoroughly analyzed Biographical Inventory. The same general picture was found for each of the remaining 11 criteria, using the standard battery of 52 scores. We have not yet had a chance to reduce this standard battery of 52 to a shorter one of 40 or 30 or 20 scores, wherein we might try to eliminate some of the negative values that emerged from these analyses, as illustrated in Table 2. Nor have we yet had the opportunity to attempt to select a best set of tests with one criterion in mind at a time. Nonetheless, we would predict that sizable cross validities for the battery of test scores would emerge, as have already been found for our total biographical score.

These analyses also argue that creative performances are very complex and that no single-variable test, no single-variable training program, no single-variable change in working conditions, or no single-variable theory of creativity will account for much of the total phenomenon unless the single variable happens to be a mighty complex one in itself. In other words, our evidence from multiple studies argues strongly that creative performance is a very complex multivariable phenomenon and that the early measurement of creative potential should also involve a complex battery of scores if we hope to account for a very high percentage of all that is involved. In other words, we may need to measure 10, 15, 20, or more dimensions of human performance if we want to account for very much of creative behavior.

We then raise the question about the price of measuring creative potential. If creative performance is highly desirable and highly valuable, perhaps at our present stage of knowledge and state of measurement we must be willing to pay a price of considerable testing time and expense in order to function at a very high percentage of efficiency in identifying creative potential. These requirements may not really be as great as they seem if we realize that this nation has spent a great deal of time and money for education per se, even though we are now discovering that the costly grades which evaluate student performances may have very limited validities in terms of later creative and other important performances. In fact, it could be said that our educational program is the longest and most expensive test ever built, so that we have good reason to hope in the future for greater validities from school grades.

In these lengthy school programs, it may be wise to make time available for creative and other kinds of performances and assessments which might predict future performances with greater validity than grades now do. We should probably also give students creative and other kinds of experience during their educational programs which will enable them to complete self-ratings and other self-report forms after having had more full personal experiences with the nature of these types of performances. These last recommendations we make strongly and with confidence because self-ratings and other self-reports, including the biographical reports, appear to us to be the most single promising approach at present to the identification of creative potential.

HIGHLIGHTS OF OTHER RESEARCH ACTIVITIES

Analysis and validation of the Myers-Briggs Type Indicator[10]

We have recently received the results from our analysis of the Myers-Briggs Type Indicator, an instrument which attempts to assess the major dimensions of personality according to Jung's theory (Myers, 1962). It is an instrument which, according to other investigators, is supposed to be quite useful also for the identification of scientific talent. However, this was the first time the instrument had been applied to the full range of talent found in an ongoing research organization. In this instrument (and according to Jung's theory), either *extroversion* or *introversion* (E–I) describes the direction of a person's interest. Extroversion involves an interest in the external world, and introversion an interest in the interior world. *Sensation* and *intuition* (S–N) are two distinct ways of perceiving. Sensation is a direct form of perception; intuition is indirect, holistic, and typically enriched by information which the perceiver adds to what is given by the stimulus. *Thinking* and *feeling* (T–F) are two distinct and contrasting means of evaluating phenomena. Thinking is a logical process, capable of being formalized, that results in impersonal judgments of right or wrong; feeling is a more subjective process which results in the acceptance or rejection of phenomena and judgments. The authors of the Myers-Briggs Type Indicator have added another dimension of *judging* and *perceiving* (J–P), which was only suggested by Jung. This fourth scale is designed to indicate whether the person relies primarily upon a judging process or a perceiving process in his dealings with the outer world.

Persons taking the instrument can be scored either in terms of continuous scores (e.g., ranging from the extreme degree of extroversion to the extreme degree of introversion) or simply in terms of a type classification (e.g., either the extroversion or the introversion type).

On the basis of the theory underlying this instrument, a person may reasonably be expected to develop most skills with the processes he prefers to use and in the areas where he prefers to use them. If he prefers extroversion (E), he should be more mature and effective in dealing with the environment than with ideas. If he prefers sensation (S), he should be more effective in perceiving facts than possibilities. If he prefers thinking (T), he should be more mature in his thinking judgments than in his feeling judgments. If he prefers judging (J), he should be

[10] The cooperation of C. D. Ferraro in the administration of the Myers-Briggs Type Indicator is gratefully acknowledged.

more skillful at organizing his environment than in adapting to it. The converse is also true for each scale.

The three different kinds of data analysis carried out and the results on each were as follows:

1. The four Myers-Briggs continuous scores obtained on scientists at the first NASA research center were intercorrelated with the available criteria and with the biographical keys. The only scale which had any significant correlation with the criteria was the sensation-intuition scale, which correlated .21 with the official rating criterion and .24 with the creativity criterion. Since this scale correlated .31 with the biographical creativity key, it measured very little of the criteria which was not already measured by the Biographical Inventory. When the best of the above results for the Myers-Briggs were incorporated in a multiple correlation, less than .01 was added to the prediction of creativity than was possible with scores from the Biographical Inventory alone.

2. According to the Jungian theory, the independent scales themselves are not as important as the unique combination of traits. Thus, an SN combination is qualitatively different from an ST. Each combination of the traits produces a different kind of personality configuration or personality type. There are 80 possible combinations of the types. In order to assess the contribution of information about types, every possible combination of types was correlated with the criteria and with the biographical scores. Briefly summarized, the results for type scoring did not indicate any degree of prediction which would compare with or significantly supplement the Biographical Inventory. When all possible combinations of the type scores were used, the highest cross-validity coefficient obtained was .26 with the official rating criterion.

3. The 166 individual items within the Myers-Briggs Type Indicator were subjected to the typical item-alternative analysis procedure utilized for analyzing the Biographical Inventory. Even though this technique has been very powerful in the analysis of biographical information, the results obtained for the empirically keyed scores for the Myers-Briggs had about the same order of magnitude as those above for the traditional scores. The highest cross-validity coefficient obtained was .29 out of seven empirically constructed keys.

The conclusions appear self-evident. The Myers-Briggs Type Indicator was found to be very limited for predicting any kind of measured success in science; in comparison, the well-constructed Biographical Inventory has substantially more promise.

Other relevant studies

Maida R. Withers (1960) completed a master's thesis in which she reported some significant relationships between creative paper-and-pencil aptitude tests and rankings on creative dance performance. Tony Jacobsen, who is now working in our research laboratory, reported in a study completed at San Jose State College (Jacobsen and Asher, 1963) that a test he developed to measure Aschner's concept-constancy construct correlated significantly with performance on four creativity criterion problems. Lorraine Loy, another graduate student, is working at Downers Grove Ill., on the problem of the interrelationships of creative characteristics in teachers and in their students. Frank Williams has attempted to develop creativity in United Air Lines personnel and to follow up the employees after their training.

William Hutchinson (1963) has completed an interesting dissertation at the University of Utah on creative and productive thinking in the classroom. His study has successfully tested our educational theory in which students are considered as thinkers, not merely learners, and in which the teacher attempts to have students use a wider variety of thinking and learning processes while simultaneously growing in subject matter knowledge (C.W. Taylor *et al.*, 1964).

Elwin Nielsen (1963) has just reported in his dissertation that a biographical inventory of approximately 125 items will probably be of at least 30-dimensional complexity as found in the factor analysis of two subsets of 60 and 70 different sets of items. This finding supports our statement that the Biographical Inventory measures a great hodgepodge of things about one's life history and can cut across the entire gamut of past experience.

C   Maybe biographical inventories are new personality ratings that are better than the traditional types of personality inventories.

S   This is quite possible. A biographical inventory is probably better than most if not all of the personality tests that are traditionally used. I also doubt that any personality test has ever been so thoroughly constructed, item-analyzed, and revised. Across our five successive biographical forms we have completed eight alternative-item analyses against several different criteria each time.

We also built five empirically keyed biographical scores for the motivational criterion of supervisory ratings on drive-resourcefulness. These biographical scores proved to be quite successful in being valid for an average of half of our multiple criteria, not counting the motivational criterion on which the scores were keyed. These results contrast sharply with those for motivational tests recommended to us by others, which have "washed out" almost completely in our validation studies on creativity and on communication abilities (Taylor, Smith, Ghiselin, Sheets, and Cochran, 1958). Consequently, we would also bet that the biographical inventory approach would prove to be the best one now available for measuring motivation.

C   Do you have intercorrelations between your criterion factor scores?

S   The intercorrelations for the criterion factor scores of the Air Force data can be found in the Air Force final report (Taylor, Smith, Ghiselin, and Ellison, 1961), and in the 1959 Utah creativity conference report (Taylor, 1959). The second-order factors were obtained by factoring intercorrelations of our best estimated scores of first-order factors. The intercorrelations between the NASA criterion scores have not yet been published but will be presented in the final report for that project.

C   I have a question about your second-order factor study. What was your reason for choosing rotation? Was it a theoretical reason?

S   To fit the data. The rotations didn't ever move much away from orthogonality. Rompel worked under my supervision. We decided to keep the solution orthogonal and then finally see whether we wanted to move away from orthogonality. The final orthogonal solution fit the data so well that we decided we did not need to rotate further to an oblique solution.

C   Do you plan to substitute the second-order factor scores for first-order criteria?

S   Each time one factors, first order, second order, and so on, he loses the unique variance in the things factored. So one factor-analyzes only the portions that the scores have in common. However, although one loses something with each factor analysis, he may simultaneously be gaining in insights.

C   Although your factors on the second order are orthogonal, wouldn't the first-order factor scores be correlated?

S   Yes. Rompel found that these intercorrelations are not very high, even between best estimated scores for each of the first-order factors. Most of the intercorrelations are close to zero, but a few of them range from the .20's to the .30's.

C   I think that there are some possible ambiguities in your conclusion about the multidimensionality of the criteria of creativity. If I understand correctly, what you are doing is based on always ordering individuals one at a time on various indices and then correlating these indices to get your factors. It is pretty clear to me that you can get at least three or more different factor structures if you do other things, such as taking individuals across occasions. And within an individual you may get just the ipsative factors, for example. I don't know, but I suspect that it is impossible to go backwards from where you are to what happens within an individual. I am wondering whether you are implying that you would consider creativity to be complex and multidimensional within an individual.

S   The descriptions of personality characteristics associated with creativity in an individual probably are complex if we consider this long list of characteristics to be valid. However, if we consider these characteristics to be peripheral correlates to creativity, rather than central and essential to the creative process, then the question emerges as to whether the cental, internal creative processes are simple or complex. But in all our results complexity shows up strongly every time we look at creativity, either on the predictor side or on the criterion side. I therefore believe that great complexity would also be found within a creative individual.

C   What kind of model are you using? Is there somehow or other a summation within an individual? Does a happy combination of variables happen to determine the fact that he is creative, or is it an integrated pattern of some kind with a person that is formed under certain conditions?

S   We are using a linear multiple-regression equation with a best weight for each score in the equation according to the criterion under consideration. Let me describe it from the psychometric side. We would say that probably an individual would have a particular combination of these characteristics, but whether they would vary much from time to time, I don't know. Across creative people there might be somewhat different combinations, but for creative people as a group some kind of average combination or combinations is crucial. And the more things that go into this average combination that a person possesses, the more likely he will be to make a particular kind of creative contribution. We, of course, recognize the possibility that more than one pattern of characteristics may lead to the same type of creative contribution. The multiple-regression equation will not display more than the one average pattern of characteristics, however.

C   I would not go along on the previous comment, though. I would say that what you have is not necessarily evidence that creativity is a very, very multivariable type of thing. You may have a situation where there are just two or three variables (maybe even only one) that are crucial and underlie all these things you are measuring. I am thinking of a dissertation by Bolk at the University of Minnesota in which he reported that underlying many of the scores on the Strong Vocational Interest Blank were certain performances on the Kent-Rosanoff Word Association Test. There are some keys on the Strong Vocational Interest Blank which are less common in society, so people who tend to show uncommon verbal habits will score very highly on these keys, only because of these uncommon verbal habits. And yet behind what is apparently a multivariable type of thing, there is actually a single underlying variable that can be isolated. For example, in many of the measures you have here, two things that are involved are the individual's verbal behavior and his thinking behavior. That is, what kind of verbal habits does he have? And in filling out any self-report inventory, these kinds of things will be very important in determining what the person says. Certainly I wouldn't say that there is any real evidence of only one variable, but I would not cast aside the possibility that there are just a few.

C Could one say that giving unusual responses on an inventory is itself a unitary thing? A person can vary from the norm in a great many different ways.

C If it is a single kind of variable as seen from one approach, it might be a very complex one when viewed from another perspective. It could be a complex one in terms of its causal factors. There are many reasons why people can be tall, but this does not remove the fact that a person is tall. But when you say he is tall, it does not mean that he has eaten Wheaties all his life.

S Yes, I would raise two questions about your single underlying variable: first, what percentage of the total creative phenomenon does it account for, and is it in fact quite a complex variable itself? I see the total issue as something like this. I am saying that there may be relatively a large number of necessary characteristics and conditions in a person which in combination can approach being sufficient to account for creative performances. The alternative view is that there may be only one or two characteristics or conditions in a person that would be sufficient in and of themselves for creative performance; all other things would be quite auxiliary. I, too, can hope for great simplicity, but from the evidence to date I feel that we are fooling ourselves if we believe that creative performance is really simple rather than complex. In other words, my conclusion from both our predictor and criterion findings (including the findings in our second-order criterion study) is that creative ability is highly complex in nature rather than simple and that many important variables—15 or 20 at least—rather than only two or three are important. Even our underlying second-order criterion factor called "general creativity" is in reality a single, fixed, composite, complex dimension which probably fails to account for more of our total set of initial ratings and other criteria of creativity than it accounts for; it is a single dimension, whereas all of our initial creative criteria, as a set, span a six-dimensional region. So I interpret all our evidence as pointing toward complexity in creativity, toward a multiplicity of variables that are important, both on the criterion and on the predictor side. Then, by inference, I believe there is great complexity in the educational and other environmental conditions that are optimal for creativity. Therefore, I am interested in trying to locate and identify each of the important variables in creativity so that their specific roles and effects can be determined and can be more fully understood.

chapter 17 Progress in the Discovery of Intellectual Factors

J. P. Guilford, University of Southern California

S   The Aptitudes Project at the University of Southern California, now near the end of its thirteenth year of operations, is continuing along the lines indicated in reports of the first three University of Utah conferences. Very early in our research efforts, we were reinforced in our belief that our approach to basic studies of the composition of human intellect had struck pay-dirt; consequently we have continued to work along the same vein. Although the social benefits have not been immediately obvious, it has been our hope that we are laying a broad and firm foundation upon which future outcomes will be based.

Our basis of support from the beginning has been the Office of Naval Research, Personnel and Training Branch. Currently we have additional support from the U.S. Office of Education, Cooperative Research Division, and from the National Science Foundation, Social Sciences Division and Biological Sciences Division.

I noticed, after reaching here and after hearing some of the papers, that I had not included in my survey anything particularly on the results of my further thinking on the implications of the "structure-of-intellect" concepts, and the model, for general psychological theory. Since the 1959 Utah conference I have had published three papers dealing especially with this matter (Guilford, 1960a, 1960b, 1961).

In these articles I have attempted to apply some of the new structure-of-intellect concepts toward accounting for some traditional concepts in psychological theory. This step has the advantage of effecting some continuity in psychological theory, but, more important, it gives some time-honored concepts empirical bases that have been largely lacking before. Factor concepts and the concepts based upon them are in the category of empirical concepts; we can point to empirical bases in terms of classes of tasks involved in tests that measure the factors. Thus, by allocating such concepts as "induction," "deduction," "reasoning," "problem solving," "learning," and "creativity" to certain factors in certain segments of the structure of intellect, we give to those abstract terms some concrete ties. We also integrate them into a single theoretical framework—the structure of intellect.

A number of things said at this conference suggest various theoretical connections with the structure-of-intellect model. Much is said about the worrisome criterion problem, for example. I might say, incidentally, that our way of using factor analysis has one great advantage in that we do not have to worry about the criterion problem. Factor analysis provides its own criteria. You may not agree with me on this, but I am quite ready to defend the idea that the best kind of construct validity is found through a factor-analytic approach.

C   I would join you in that view, though time will not permit a full explanation of my reasoning on it.

C   To show that there is not unanimity, I will mention that I hold a different point of view.

S   I am just expressing my own view on this, without wishing to take time out to argue the point now. Along this line, I have a great hesitation in doing any predictive validation studies until I know the factorial nature of the predictors, and even of the criteria. I think that Calvin Taylor has done a wonderful job in the study of criteria of creative performance in research science, approaching the problem in terms of analysis to determine the basic, underlying variables involved. He has found out that some of the numerous possible indices of scientific performance can be related to creativity and some are irrelevant with respect to creativity. Without this information, any or all of the criteria might have been adopted on an a priori basis in trying to predict creative scientific performance. We now know which ones we have to predict in order to take care of the creative aspects of scientists' work. Incidentally, the creative aspects did not represent a single factor.

Another echo from earlier reports that comes to mind is Mednick's announcement that he is an avowed associationist. I wish to go on record as saying that I am a reformed associationist. The association concept certainly cannot be sneezed at because it has been with us for over 2,000 years and under it we have made tremendous progress in psychology. Mednick shows with ingenuity what can be done with the concept in the way of developing tests for creative qualities. But I insist that we must go beyond the associative idea. I propose that the six product categories or concepts in the structure of intellect—units, classes, relations, systems, transformations, and implications—provide the way to do it; that they be substituted for the one concept of association.

I would challenge Mednick, or anybody else, to show how units can be accounted for under the associative principle. Wundt tried it and failed. Titchener tried it and failed. Nor can the product of transformations be conceived in any way that I can see in the form of associations. As a matter of fact, I would be willing to say that none of the products can be fully accounted for in terms of association, with the possible exception of the product of implication, where contiguity of experiences probably is the main basis for development of implications. The use of six product concepts in place of the one concept of association gives a much wider scope with which to tackle theoretical problems.

A progress report is easily organized in a temporal sequence. I shall begin with recently completed studies, describe briefly research now in progress, and then give our view of future plans, immediate and less immediate.

RECENTLY COMPLETED STUDIES[1]

For the past four or five years, our major theoretical orientation has been the structure-of-intellect model. Our strategy has been to determine whether factors predicted by the model could be demonstrated as differentiated by factor analysis. Tests designed for a factor analysis have been constructed according to the unique specifications that characterize each vacant cell of the model. A new direction has been designed to determine whether the factors found for adult, young males can also be demonstrated at younger age levels and for both sexes. The younger age levels have been the sixth and ninth grades. Concentration has been upon the operation category of divergent-production (DP) abilities.

Completed studies have verified at the lower age levels practically all of the previously known DP factors, insofar as they have been investigated. The studies have also demonstrated five new DP factors at the ninth-grade level and six at the adult level. Because it is believed that the DP abilities have unique contributions to make to successful creative thinking, these results should be pertinent to the subject of this conference.

Before these studies were initiated, it was believed that five of the

---

[1] Guilford's three-dimensional model of his "structure-of-intellect," together with the 61 factors found to date in this model, are presented in the appendix at the end of this chapter.

hypothesized six semantic factors in the DP category had been demonstrated, but only two in the symbolic category and two in the figural categories. One of the latter, divergent production of figural classes, or figural spontaneous flexibility, had not been securely placed, for it had been identified only logically with Thurstone's factor of fluctuation of ambiguous figures (Thurstone, 1944), without empirical evidence that this factor satisfies the specifications called for by the structure-of-intellect theory. The best empirical evidence would be in the form of substantial correlations between tests of rate of fluctuation of ambiguous figures and tests that are parallel in form but not in content with those which demonstrate other (symbolic and semantic) spontaneous-flexibility factors.

Variations in factor structure with age and sex

In our largest factor analysis to date, the results from which have been published in our *Report* No. 26 (Guilford, Merrifield, and Cox, 1961), the subjects were the ninth-grade students in Los Angeles' Louis Pasteur Junior High School (omitting students with IQs below 95) and in the Claremont, Calif., high school.[2] The subjects were subdivided into four groups: (1) a total group of mixed sex from the Claremont High School; (2) a group of boys with IQs from 95 through 119; (3) a group of girls of like IQ range; and (4) a group of students with high IQs of 120 and above. The last-mentioned group was drawn from both the junior high and senior high school and hence overlapped the first group to some extent. By these groupings we were able to compare factor structures for boys and girls of similar age, IQ, and education and also the factor structures for two IQ levels, and for restricted ranges as well as the full range at the ninth-grade level. Each group numbered more than 200.

In this study, eight DP factors that had been recognized previously with adult males were under investigation: DSU, DMC, DMU, DMR, DSS, DFT, DMT, and DMI, to use structure-of-intellect symbols (see Table 1). In each case, the first letter, D, stands for divergent production; the second letters, F, S, and M, stand for figural, symbolic, and semantic content, respectively; and the final letters, U, C, R, S, T, and I, stand for the products: units, classes, relations, systems, transformations, and implications, respectively.

A special comment must be made in connection with the factor DSS— divergent production of symbolic systems. This factor was previously thought to have been demonstrated by use of the tests on Expressional Fluency and Simile Interpretations, tasks involving the organization

[2] This study was the direct responsibility of Philip R. Merrifield, Assistant Director of the project, and Anna Cox, Research Associate.

TABLE 1

Matrix of the Divergent-Production Factors in Three Content Categories,
Showing the Factors That Have Been Demonstrated
and in What Kinds of Samples

Content Categories

	Figural	Symbolic	Semantic
Units	DFU 9th grade Adults	DSU Word fluency* 9th grade Adults	DMU Ideational fluency 6th grade 9th grade Adults
Classes	DFC 9th grade Adults?	DSC Adults?†	DMC Spontaneous flexibility 6th grade 9th grade Adults
Relations	DFR‡	DSR 9th grade? Adults	DMR Associational fluency 6th grade 9th grade Adults
Systems	DFS 9th grade? Adults	DSS 9th-grade boys 9th-grade mixed	DMS Expressional fluency 6th grade 9th grade Adults
Transformations	DFT Adaptive flexibility 9th grade Adults	DST‡	DMT Originality 6th grade 9th grade Adults
Implications	DFI 9th grade	DSI 9th grade Adults?	DMI Elaboration 6th grade 9th grade Adults

* Name formerly assigned to the factor is given.
† A question mark means that only one test hypothesized for the factor actually came out significantly on the factor.
‡ Hypothesized factors DFR and DST have not yet been investigated.

of words into sentences and phrases, respectively. Since we hesitated to recognize sentence-building tests as indicators of ability to construct varieties of semantic systems in general, we had settled upon the idea that, because sentence structure is also a symbolic system, the factor has been recognized as DSS. There have been doubts about this conclusion, however, so we constructed two new tests that call for producing systems having more clearly symbolic properties.

The new tests for factor DSS were Make a Code (using letters and numbers) and Number Combinations, which requires the construction of a number of equations, given a few digits and the four numerical-operation signs. There were only two such tests in the battery, for it was expected that if the formerly recognized DSS factor were, in fact, DSS, these two tests would simply help to define it in this analysis. If the old DSS factor were, in fact, DMS, the two groups of tests would separate.

The two groups of tests did, indeed, clearly separate, with a new DSS factor, weakly defined by one or two of the new tests, in three of the four analyses (missing in the case of the girls' sample, only). This result called for the moving of the factor demonstrated by sentence-building or phrase-building tests to the cell DMS.

I should like to digress a bit to discuss the importance of the DMS factor, in fact, all the factors of divergent production of systems. All of them should be very important, in connection with the work of artists, mathematicians, and scientists. Many writers on the subject of inspiration, intuition, or insight in creative production report that a kind of system, call it a theme or a motif or a scheme, emerges full blown. The problem of intuition or insight goes beyond the product of systems, of course. It includes questions of how any product is generated where it is needed in creative thinking. It is important that we find out how systems and other psychological products develop and the conditions that affect their development. The fact that most of the development is unconscious should not stop us.

While I am on the subject of systems, I should like to suggest that Barron's trait of preference for complexity is probably related to systems abilities. It is particularly in connection with systems that we are concerned with the variable of complexity. The more creative people may prefer complex designs because they are able to cope with complexity. They find simple designs unchallenging and uninteresting.

All four of the analyses at the ninth-grade level verified the eight previously known DP factors. Comparisons of factor loadings in the same test can be made between the results for the four groups and results for typical male adults by reference to Table 2. There is con-

TABLE 2

Factor Loadings in Leading Divergent-Production Tests in Three Populations of Different Ages

Factor and Tests	6th-Grade Students	9th-Grade Students				Adults
		Total	Boys	Girls	High-IQ	
DFU						
Make a Figure		.72				.48
Make a Mark		.54				.45
DSU—Word fluency						
Word Fluency		.49	.51	.51	.39	.62
Suffixes		.51	46	.40	.54	.71
DMU—Ideational fluency						
Ideational Fluency		.46	.50	.47	.43	.44*
Plot Titles (low quality)	.45*	.30	.47	.34	.46	.49*
Consequences (obvious)	.51*	.53	.52	.52	.46	.54*
Utility (fluency)		.50	.58	.57	.28	.54*
DFC						
Varied Figural Classes		.35				.42
DSC						
Number Grouping		. . .†				.33
DMC—Spontaneous flexibility						
Alternate Uses	.35	.45	.32	.33	.38	.44*
Utility (shifts)	.10	.40	.45	.49	.57	.56*
DSR						
Letter Group Relations		.41				.35
Number Rules		.15				.35
DMR—Associational fluency						
Associational Fluency	.33	.45	.38	.42	.38	.55*
Simile Insertion	.34	.50	.03	.32	.39	.44
DFS						
Making Objects		.36				.35
Designs		.31				.35
Monograms		.07				.57
Sketches		.10				.57
DSS						
Make a Code		.48	.37	. . .†	.40	
Number Combinations		.09	.35	. . .	.05	
DMS—Expressional fluency						
Expressional Fluency	.35*	.47	.48	.41	.44	.59
Simile Interpretations		.36	.32	.36	.30	.52
DFT—Adaptive flexibility						
Match Problems II		.54	.51	.44	.53	.42
Planning Air Maneuvers		.58	.49	.47	.43	.42
Match Problems III		.56				.44
Match Problems IV		.47				.32
Match Problems V		.56	.41	.48	.48	
DMT—Originality						
Plot Titles (high quality)	.38*	.44	.47	.40	.35	.47
Consequences (remote)	.36*	.18	.36	.22	−.02	.40
Alternate Signs		.37	.15	.31	.31	.42
DFI						
Decorations		.51	.58	.44	.58	
Figure Production		.47	.40	.39	.46	
Production of Figural Effects		.32	.57	.34	.39	
DSI						
Symbol Elaboration		.46				.47
Limited Words		.35				−.03
DMI—Elaboration ability						
Planning Elaboration	.31	.43	.41	.42	.49	.44
Possible Jobs		.14	.35	.46	.59	

* The loading is a mean of from two to five replicated estimates. A blank means that the test was not administered to such a sample.

† The test was administered, but the factor did not emerge.

siderable consistency among the groups, with two notable exceptions. One is for the Consequences Test, remote score, indicating that Consequences is not a good test of factor DMT for the ninth-grade students. The other is for the Number Combinations Test, which is not a very good test for the new factor DSS. Factor DSS did not emerge for the results from the sample of girls. There is nothing in the comparisons of means and standard deviations for the two tests from the boys' and girls' samples to account for this result. Apparently, both of the new DSS tests fail to reflect to any substantial extent individual differences in this ability.

A marker test, Seeing Problems, was inserted in the test battery in this study, just in case some of the new tests might have some variance in factor EMI (evaluation of semantic implications) or "sensitivity to problems." That factor came out in all four analyses as an incidental result, showing that it is differentiable for the adolescent age group.

We happened to have available two new tests for the hypothetical factor DFI (divergent production of figural implications), parallel to factor DMI (elaboration ability). There was room in the battery for these two tests, and they offered an opportunity to clear up a puzzling question, so they were included. The perseverating question pertained to the previously known factor DMI. Two tests had carried the burden of segregating it, Planning Elaboration II and Figure Production. Planning Elaboration II is clearly a semantic test, but Figure Production appears to involve both a figural and a semantic content. This test asks the examinee, starting with a minimal line or two, to construct upon this basis a meaningful object. The latter specification suggests a semantic aspect to the test.

In the new study, the question was whether Figure Production would remain with the semantic tests (a new test, Possible Jobs, had been included to help determine factor DMI), or whether it would go with the new group of tests on DFI. The results bearing on this question were quite decisive. Figure Production went with factor DFI, with loadings of only .10, .24, .25, and .14 on DMI. The previously significant loading of Figure Production on DMI might be attributed to some degree of positive correlation between the two factors DMI and DFI. A new test, Production of Figural Effects, was similar to Figure Production, the main difference being the instruction not to make a meaningful object. One might suspect these two tests of being alternative forms of essentially the same test and therefore conclude that the obtained DFI factor is a specific. A third test, Decorations, designed for DFI and having leading loadings on DFI, however, helped materially to establish the generality of that factor. The nature of Decorations is somewhat different from that of the other two tests.

Two kinds of incidental results coming out of the study involving these four analyses are of some interest. One pertains to sex differences of means in certain test categories. The differences are small and not always statistically significant, but they are rather consistent in direction. Boys tend to obtain higher means of scores for tests of semantic flexibility, whether for factor DMC or DMT. On the other hand, girls tend to obtain higher means for tests of the three fluency factors, DMU, DMR, and DMS. There is no ready explanation to offer for these systematic sex differences except to say that tests of DMT have been found slightly correlated positively with measures of such traits as confidence, and negatively with such traits as need for discipline and orderliness. We might expect sex differences in these three traits to be consistent with the sex differences in flexibility.

The other incidental finding concerns the relations of IQ tests to tests of DP abilities. The scores from IQ tests that we used in correlations represented mental age. The tests were the vocabulary and reading-comprehension parts of the California Test of Mental Maturity and the Stanford Achievement Test, and the Guilford-Zimmerman Verbal Comprehension test. Each of three groups had 2 scores and the fourth had only the verbal comprehension score, making 7 essentially CMU scores that could be correlated with each of the 14 verbal DP tests. The 98 coefficients range from $-.20$ to $+.52$, with a mean of $+.18$. These estimates of correlation between IQ tests and DP tests are essentially in line with those usually found.

On examination of the scatter plots for correlations involved between IQ, in the range 62 to 144, and scores from the DP tests, we find that the regression of IQ on DP score is nonlinear, with negative acceleration. Students with high IQs can have quite a range of DP score, extending below average. Students with low DP scores can also have quite a range of IQs. There is an unusual deficiency of students with both high IQ and low DP scores. There is some deficiency, but not so great, of students with both high IQ and low DP scores. The sizes of the curvilinear correlations are now being checked. With most DP tests, a kind of break comes at an IQ level of 120. Above that level, there is not much relationship at all between IQ and DP scores; below that level, perhaps even substantial linear correlation.

C A triangular-shaped plot?
S Yes, essentially.

C   Oral DP tests differ a little bit, don't they? Some lower IQs go up on DP.

S   We have not used oral tests, but the fact that at the lower levels the correlations are much higher calls for explanation. There may be a more general phenomenon to the effect that at lower IQ levels most intellectual tests are more strongly intercorrelated. This might suggest a more oblique factor structure at low-IQ levels. The phenomenon might be limited to correlations of verbal tests with IQ tests, however, which would mean that for low-IQ subjects words cannot be made simple enough to avoid introducing verbal comprehension variance, in other words, IQ variance. Another hypothesis would be that we need different tests to find differentiation of factors at lower-IQ levels. Torrance's suggestion that oral tests would give more DP variance supports this hypothesis.

The negative correlations between some DP tests and IQ tests are of special interest. In our experience, they are most likely to occur between verbal comprehension (CMU) scores and ideational fluency (DMU) scores. This result suggests that the greater our stored supply of items of semantic information the more slowly we can retrieve sets of them for indirect uses as in transfer, that is, for indirect use. It is likely that if the vocabulary test sampled only the stored information in the categories called for in the DMU test, for example, all the objects that are white and soft and will float on water, the correlation should be even higher in the negative direction. This principle is in line with that found by D. M. Johnson and his co-workers (Johnson, Johnson, and Mark, 1951). A ready hypothesis is that with more available items of information there is more mutual interference in recalling them. In this connection one also thinks of the phenomenon of proactive inhibition. The more we learn of any kind of information, the more difficult is recall of any of the information in the set.

Calvin Taylor has touched on this point of retrieval of information. It is an important matter in connection with fluency and flexibility. Experiments on the conditions for good retrieval should be initiated. He further suggested that ease of recall may depend greatly upon the way in which information is put into storage, and I agree. Determining whether this is the whole story will depend on future experiments.

DP factors at the sixth-grade level

The study of DP factors at the sixth-grade level was restricted because the testing time was limited to four hours. We could not cover as many factors as usual or use as many tests for each factor. Nevertheless, it was possible to demonstrate five of the DP factors: DMU, DMC, DMS,

DMT, and DMI, as well as the evaluation factor EMI (sensitivity to problems). The factor loadings seen in Table 2 are generally smaller than in the case of older populations. In part, this result is due to the use of the ϕ coefficient as the index of intercorrelation. It is due also to the fact that some tests were cut in two, the halves being used as separate tests. The starred coefficients in this particular case mean that the average loadings came from the two forms of the same test. Usually more than two loadings were significant (.30 or higher) where part scores were used, indicating that the factor is probably not just specific to the two parts.

A study of nonverbal DP factors

A study was designed to investigate the eight remaining unknown DP factors in the figural and symbolic content categories.[3] Now tests were constructed to meet the known specifications for the vacant cells, without achieving any satisfactory tests for hypothesized factor DFR (divergent production of figural relations) or factor DST (divergent production of symbolic transformations). Customary marker tests for other factors were included in the battery of 29 tests adopted for analysis.

The six-hour battery was administered to two samples, both in excess of 200. One group of subjects was composed of Naval Air Students at Pensacola, Fla., and the other of ninth-grade students at the Claremont, Calif., high school. Two parallel analyses were carried out.

Five of the six investigated factors were more or less well demonstrated in results from the ninth-grade sample, and all six in results from the adult sample. Factor DSC was not found for the ninth-grade group. The new DP factors demonstrated in both were DFU, DFC, DFS, DSR, and DSI. No light was thrown on whether the new DFC factor is identical with Thurstone's factor of fluctuation of ambiguous figures. A perceptual fluctuation test is best administered individually, with special apparatus, whereas our testing has been confined to printed tests given in groups.

At any rate, we now have information that 16 out of the 18 DP factors in the three content categories can be differentiated. Table 2 reports some factor loadings in common to the two groups of subjects, and Table 1 indicates which factors are now known and in what populations. In the appendix to this report is provided a list of the intellectual factors that have been demonstrated and located in the structure of intellect, and of some of the better tests for each factor and their sources.

---

[3] Most direct responsibility for this study was assigned to Arthur Gershon, Research Associate.

STUDIES UNDER WAY

Our next studies designed to explore unknown factors in the structure of intellect are concentrated upon two categories. One is the category of evaluation, the operation category in which fewest factors have been demonstrated up to the present time. The other is the content category of behavioral information, in which there has been practically no exploration by factor-analytic methods.

New basic factor-analytic studies

In the search for significant psychological resources involved in creative production, we should not discount the evaluative abilities. In ordinary divergent thinking, where quality is of any concern, we have a continual interplay of idea-test, idea-test, and so on. I have been impressed by the book by Miller, Galanter, and Pribram (1960), *Plans and the Structure of Behavior*. In it, they insist that the very first thing that happens in an organism upon stimulation is evaluation, a testing of the situation. The typical paradigm of behavior is test-operate-test-operate-test, beginning and ending with evaluation. The fact that a test comes first is in line with the fact that a creative person must first be aware of the existence of a problem, one of the kinds of evaluative abilities.

The evaluation area is being investigated in three studies, along the lines of semantic, symbolic, and figural contents, in that temporal order. A battery of tests in the semantic category has been administered to the tenth-grade students at the two La Puente, Calif., high schools.[4] It happens that the program in these high schools includes some special experimental instruction on how to think critically, which dovetails well with our testing needs. In October 1961 about 1,100 students took our six-hour semantic-evaluation battery.

The same students were administered later an inventory that emphasizes interests in different kinds of thinking, including critical thinking. The inventory will be factor-analyzed or item-analyzed, or both, to achieve psychologically homogeneous sets of items for scoring. The relations between inventory scores and factor scores will be of secondary but not minor interest. The scoring of the tests for this study is essentially complete.

Tests are being developed and tried out in preliminary testing preparatory to setting up a battery of symbolic-evaluation tests for a second-factor analysis in the evaluation area. Some of these tests are being used in a validation study in connection with high school mathematics, as will be described later.

[4] Kazuo Nihira, Research Assistant, is in direct charge of this study.

Test development is also under way, looking toward an analysis of abilities in the area of behavioral cognition.[5] This is our first venture into the entirely uncharted theoretical area of behavioral abilities. Behavioral cognition may be roughly equated to social perception or to empathy. It involves awareness of the mental states of other individuals: an awareness derived from perception of outward signs in the commonly recognized category of expressive behavior. One ability is expected for each kind of product, from units to implications.

Thus far, the behavioral test material is in printed form, being composed mostly of line drawings. We expect to consider sound stimuli and motion-picture material later. In order to avoid semantic content we have used verbal material sparingly. Preliminary testing shows that there is not as much danger of this kind of contamination as we had expected. On the other hand, we have found that, if figural tests have much fine detail, there is danger of bringing in some figural variance. Preliminary results show that it is possible to develop tests of this nature with reliability sufficiently high for factor-analytical purposes and that some new kinds of variance are involved.

The tests of behavioral cognition that we have prepared cover the six kinds of products, from units to implications. I might tell you about one implication test that does not seem to work; it will also give you an idea of the kind of test we have produced. Perhaps you have seen a little book showing facial expressions of the actor, Fernandel. We have used many of these expressions, each with alternative statements as to what might have been said to him just before he made a certain face. This test has not correlated well with other tests of cognition of behavioral implications, but it does correlate with tests of cognition of behavioral units, so we are revising it slightly as a units test.

C　Are you going to use motion pictures?

S　We are staying away from them as long as we can, not only because of the technical difficulties involved and the expense, but because thus far we don't feel the need for them. We are also afraid that if we show any amount of continued action we will become involved in factorially complex items. This is not what we want for factor-analysis purposes. Motion as a stimulus is definitely very important as a cue to behavioral information to be cognized, and it should be used some time.

C　Film would be very interesting to use in studies of intuition—to run it both backwards and forwards.

[5] This study is in direct charge of Richard deMille, Research Associate, assisted by Maureen O'Sullivan, Research Assistant.

S   After the factor analysis which we hope to do on behavioral cognition, we plan to go immediately into the study of DP abilities involving behavioral information.   Abilities in this area should be very important for dealing creatively with people.

A comprehensive analysis of DP factors

Two six-hour batteries, one mainly of semantic tests and the other mainly of figural and symbolic tests, have been given to the same ninth-grade subjects at Claremont High School, in connection with the two completed studies mentioned earlier, one battery in October 1959 and the other in January 1960.   A single-factor analysis is planned, in which 16 of the DP factors could possibly be demonstrated.   The chief value of this analysis should be in determining how well the parallel factors in different content categories can be differentiated from one another. We have had instances before in which certain figural and semantic factors pertaining to the same kind of product have appeared to be confounded in analysis.   One of these was the possible confounding of DFI and DMI, a case mentioned earlier, and the other was the possible confounding of factors DFT, DST, and DMT in an unpublished study (with the Institute of Personality Assessment and Research, University of California at Berkeley).

A validation study for predicting achievement in mathematics

A very comprehensive study is under way in which numerous factors will be related to achievement in mathematics at the ninth-grade level— beginning algebra and general mathematics.[6]   Most of the factors believed to be pertinent have been selected from the content category of symbolic abilities, in relation to algebra, plus a smaller number of factors in the semantic category, in relation to both algebra and general mathematics but probably more to the latter.

An eight-hour battery of tests, usually two tests for each factor, was administered in October 1961 to the ninth-grade students in the Lynwood, Calif., high school.   A general mathematics achievement test constructed by our project was given to all students at the end of the first semester and again at the end of the second semester.   An algebra achievement test was administered to algebra students only, at the same times.   We shall also have available for criterion information the evaluations made by teachers.   A two-hour battery of new experimental tests in the symbolic-evaluation category was administered during the second

[6] Hugh M. Petersen, Research Assistant, has the major responsibility for this study, in which he is assisted by Ralph Hoepfner, Research Assistant.

semester. A factor analysis of tests and criteria will be carried out, as well as multiple-regression analyses.

Relations between aptitude and nonaptitude traits

A study is almost completed on relations between all six of the DP factors in the semantic category, teachers' rating of aptitudes and other traits, and inventory scores of nonaptitude traits for children at the seventh-grade level.[7] Among these nonaptitude traits, interests in different kinds of thinking were emphasized. The inventory items were factor-analyzed to form homogeneous groups for scoring. The thinking-interest factors are very much in line with those previously found for adult males. The subjects were in general the same as those tested with a larger battery of DP tests a year earlier in the sixth grade, for whom some results are reported in Table 2.

Studies of rotation methods in factor analysis

Affiliated with the Aptitudes Project is a new project, Investigation and Comparison of Analytical and Graphical Methods of Rotation in Factor Analysis.[8] Both contrived and empirical factor matrices (principal component or centroid) are being rotated, using a variety of analytical methods and also graphical techniques.

Results thus far indicate that the analytical methods are more or less alike in distortion of the factor structure away from meaningful solutions obtained by the graphical methods. The general tendency is to shift variances of tests toward a few strong factors and away from weaker ones, leaving a number of factors with only one significant loading (.30 or higher). Some of the usual requirements of simple structure are thus violated.

C   We have had one problem in using Thurstone's analytical rotational solution, where we found the rotation generally didn't move much away from the trial vector locations.

S   We are trying to see whether we can get a better mathematical statement of the Thurstone principles of simple structure. As yet, nobody has been able to do this very well. For one thing, Thurstone's specifications are actually pretty loose and cannot be fully expressed mathematically. This is one of the troubles with the analytical methods of rotation now in existence; they are based on only a segment of those specifications.

We are also trying to find out how one can combine the computer and

---

[7] This study is the primary responsibility of Sheldon Gardner, Research Associate.

[8] Wayne S. Zimmerman, Principal Investigator, Philip R. Merrifield, Director, and Charles D. Hamburger, Research Assistant, are the investigators in this project.

the psychologist operator so that the operator can watch what is going on and exert his judgment occasionally where it is necessary. I think that no ordinary test battery will give you an optimal situation for a purely analytical rotation. If you knew enough to build such a battery, you wouldn't have to do the analysis in the first place. Most of our research factor analyses aim to find something new, in untried territory, where we cannot produce ideal batteries. We shall therefore have to seek rotational methods that will work with imperfect sampling of test variables.

C   Incidentally, I used the rotator at the U.S. Army Personnel Research Office. This was fascinating and quite efficient, I thought. It is an oscilloscope device that will give you one at a time and in rapid fashion all the two-dimensional plots. It was a fascinating device on which to obtain solutions, a real gadget to play with.

FUTURE PLANS

Very similar to the validation study in connection with beginning algebra and general mathematics is a study planned in connection with plane geometry. In this investigation, figural abilities from the various operation categories will play important roles. Parallel with this study will be a basic one, a factor-analytic exploration of the six hypothesized figural-evaluation factors. New tests designed for such factors will also be selected for validation in the prediction of achievement in geometry, in view of the obvious logical aspects of that subject.

Not so imminent are other basic explorations of uncharted locations in the structure of intellect. The operation category of memory has much unknown territory, which has received no attention thus far from our project. Most of our past and present analyses have selected for study the factors of one operation category at a time, exploring vertical slabs of the model. For a change, we are contemplating studies in two horizontal layers. One is the layer for classification abilities. This set of abilities should be of general psychological importance because of the well-known processes of concept formation and the use of classes in thinking. Another layer to receive special inspection is that for transformation abilities. This set of abilities should be important to investigate because of their probable unique relation to creative thinking.

SUMMARY

In general, the theoretical model of the structure of intellect has served very well as a heuristic device for generating hypothesized factors and for suggesting tests for them. In several basic analyses in which experimental hypotheses were derived from the model, we have rarely been disappointed. In the few instances in which factors are not demonstrated as anticipated, we have a basis for possible revisions of our conceptions in connection with the model. The concepts of the major factor categories should have general psychological significance and should be useful in investigations by other than factor-analytic methods.

In the validation studies that we are just starting, there is a pattern that we believe will be worth adopting in connection with each school subject. It should be a way of reaching an understanding regarding the basic intellectual abilities that serve as resources in mastering the content and the skills of the course. A single criterion of achievement may not be even moderately predictable from scores for any one primary intellectual ability, where so many different abilities may be involved in a complex criterial performance. It should be feasible and fruitful to analyze criteria as well as predictor tests, or to break criteria down into components, as Calvin Taylor and his associates have done for the criterion of creative, scientific achievement (Guilford, 1960b). Knowing something about the intellectual resources needed for mastering certain aspects of a course, we can anticipate student weaknesses and diagnose them when they occur. We may also gain insights as to needed improvement in teaching a subject so as to make use of available intellectual resources and to provide more desirable intellectual exercises.

I should like to stess this point about exercises. It seems to me that they could often be planned along the lines of the factors. It would be quite a simple thing to do because we know the nature of the tasks involved. In this connection, we can pretty much forget about heredity. There is plenty of evidence, in the work of Parnes and others, that tailored training in thinking pays off. The learning of thinking skills should be an important educational goal.

C In our stocktaking book, *Creativity: Progress and Potential* (Taylor, 1964), we stress quite strongly the need for basic research on fundamental characteristics, intellectual and nonintellectual, on which the researchers in creativity can draw. It has been interesting to watch your work unfold (or maybe appropriately fold into three dimensions) across the period of the conference series. I do sense that the verbal slabs are more filled in than the nonverbal. In your reports on selected factors in creativity (and I don't know what portion of a creative criterion that is), you would have a kind of complex factor somewhat centrally located in what might be twenty or thirty dimensions of your more pure factors, after you had singled out the ones that seem to be potentially important in creativity.

S That's possible. You are evidently thinking about such a factor found among criterion variables. This might or might not coincide with a higher-order factor found from correlations among primary axes representing structure-of-intellect factors recognized as more directly contributory to creative performance.

C   With the large number of intellectual dimensions possibly involved in creativity, isn't it likely that no single one of them by itself will account for a very large part of the variance in a creativity criterion?

S   That is very true. Where a great many factors are involved in a complex criterion performance, such as scientific research, no one structure-of-intellect factor is likely to show much validity; it cannot, because you have to divide up the predictable variance in the criterion in many ways. A combination of tests of *all* the relevant intellectual factors, however, should give substantial prediction. Adding nonaptitude and aptitude predictors in a composite should do even better.

C   When you go to your drafting board and do your rotations, do you do them blind or are they labeled in some way?

S   We do them blind up to the last part of the rotation job.

C   This means that the points are numbered but you don't know what tests they are.

S   Yes. We always do a lot of brushing up after we know what the tests are. In doing this we often achieve simpler structure as well as better psychological meaning.

C   I have a question about the educational implications here. I don't see the logic, from the mathematics of factor analysis and from the fact that these factors are derived from individual differences, for extending this to the educational sphere. It's possible that a certain educational approach could affect all factors simultaneously without changing factor structure at all.

S   If you gave all children equal training in all respects, you would probably have one big G factor. We probably find some differentiation of factors because children are trained unequally in different skills. This comes more from outside the school.

C   Then it is possible that you could train children all on creativity factors and come out with just one factor called "creativity"?

S   If each child were equally developed on every creativity factor. If you mean that all the children were brought to the same level, there would be no variance and no factor found in individual differences.

C   There is some possibility that after training the variance might increase.

S   Except for the fact that ceilings limit development.

C   Why did you say to forget about heredity?

S   Well, we know too little about the contributions of heredity to the development of intellectual skills, whereas we can point to success in differential learnings and can control such learning.

C Yes, but the ease of shaping the material may very well be different, depending upon inherited constitutional factors.

S There is a heredity problem, I grant you. It may be that there is an innately determined relation-seeing mechanism of some kind, for example, and that this mechanism may be exercised to different degrees in connection with different kinds of information to produce differentiation of the relation-cognition factors. If this possibility were generally valid, the product factors would be differentiated by heredity and the content factors by training, and each factor would be a joint product of the two sources of determination. These are questions that we shall have to face some day. In the meantime, we know that training promotes development in performance.

C I should be very much surprised if such a factor as fluency is not strongly determined by heredity.

C This reminds me of the discussion with Cattell in the 1959 conference in which he said that some personality factors are quite susceptible to change and variation whereas others are rather stable and dominant (more determined by heredity). We may have the same kind of thing across these intellectual characteristics. Some would be quite susceptible to variation, and others not so.

C There is a further thing here, which goes back to some of the remarks about association theory, too. It seems to me that after the matter of information storage there must be some rules you could specify or characteristics you could list of the system which has the greatest flexibility of storage in it. I think that it has to do with how complex you can permit a connotative meaning structure to become, so that new items of information get assimilated in some such fashion that in the brain they can fit this way or that.

S Probably. Also there is the matter of degree of hardness of systems or hardening of classes, to the extent that you can't pull things out of the class or out of the system.

C One other point. The more unusual a person's classes are, the more he must go at a rapid speed farther and farther away from everybody else's way of thinking so that persons who are a little bit different at the age of six in terms of unusualness of associations should be very, very widely apart by the time they are thirty, as a function of the fact that they are continually building up these complexes.

S I think that looseness of classes is the secret of spontaneous flexibility, a factor we have placed in the classes category. A person who is flexible in this respect keeps himself thinking within larger, more comprehensive classes, so that his scope of hunting for stored ideas is broadened; he is not restricted to narrow categories.

C   I would like to say something that I think is extremely important about the relationship of factors to processes. I hope you did not mean that by not using movies you are avoiding a dynamic approach. But you do mention the model of where divergent and convergent thinking alternate. I was wondering whether you are going to do much in the way of how, over time within an individual, these different factors or processes, or whatever they are, alternate or intermingle with one another to produce a rather complex behavior.

S   During the process of creating products?

C   That's right.

S   In answering this question, we might go back to the crude steps of the creative process handed down to us from Wallas, in which the preparation phase is primarily concerned with information search and information gathering. Here cognition is the operation mainly involved, although the operations of convergent and divergent production may help to derive information. Thus, stored information is involved, and hence the operation of memory. Then, in the stage of incubation, we are told that nothing much happens, although from the looks of things something *is* happening because of the sudden emergence of ready-built themes or systems. Thus, during incubation and the moment of inspiration, there is a production of systems or of other psychological products that may be involved. Then, later, there is said to be evaluation, although you cannot rule evaluation out of earlier stages. In information gathering, for example, there is selection between relevant and irrelevant information. So all along the way occurs much interplay of all kinds of operations, some relatively more prominent than others at each stage.

C   Is one of your products or operations an integration ability to put together all these different abilities so as to be able to verify a particular problem?

S   You mean how to integrate properly the use of these abilities? This might be a special problem. I hadn't thought of it. Do you mean that some other ability or trait might be involved in the integration of these activities?

C   Yes. Do the systems or transformations somehow include that so that you have a hierarchy here?

S   There is also the similar problem of translations of information from one content category to another (e.g., figural to semantic or semantic to figural) and the question of whether new abilities are involved in effecting these translations.

C   I was just thinking of the case of Willie Mays.   If you factored him properly, in the end you would still have to add something called Willie Mays.

C   There is a study (I can't cite in detail), which had high-level aptitude tests in it to give a cross-section kind of measure of a person. These tests predicted a criterion fairly well.   The researcher readministered these tests several times and got a learning curve on each person on each test.   He found out how much they gained on each test—some had reached a leveling-off region of their curve and others continued to improve with each retesting.   This increment of gain for each person on each test added additional valid variance that the cross-sectional testing didn't do.   So the nature of my question is, Are there in the processes across time—you might call them the learning processes, or the learning strategies or thinking strategies (according to Bruner)— do you think that these are additional dimensions of intellect that you have or have not yet sampled?

S   When you say "strategies," I think you're putting this issue in the right category.   Strategies, I think, may be a form of behavioral systems to a large extent.   How one organizes his own resources and his own information in order to achieve some result is a matter of behavioral systems.   Another important, and simple, explanatory source of what determines that factor functions will operate together is the environment or the task.   Most tasks are of a nature that calls for a number of abilities brought into play together.

C   I think that this question was asked at the 1959 conference, but I don't remember the answer, so let me ask it again.   As I understand it, each one of the cubes in the structure of intellect represents a factor, and you have ordered these factors along what looks like three dimensions.   Are these dimensions continuous, or are they discrete?

S   The limits of the dimensions are as you see them here.

C   Do you move from figural to symbolic to semantic without any discrete steps?

S   These are discrete steps.   There is no necessary linkage between them.   I did try to make the order logical, but I haven't found any empirical basis for supporting the order.

C   You also said, as I recall, that the two adjacent cells sometimes end up as one and sometimes are quite different, and that you haven't been able to arrange it so that the closer the cells are together the higher the relationship is.

S   No, we haven't determined actual factor intercorrelations, but the factors that sometimes come out together are in the same layer, same row, same product.

APPENDIX. PROGRESS IN THE DISCOVERY OF
INTELLECTUAL FACTORS

THE KNOWN FACTORS AND SOME OF THEIR TESTS[9]

This appendix has been prepared for the benefit of those who would like concrete referents for the factor concepts and those who may want to utilize factor tests in their research.

The factors are listed in systematic order, following categories in the structure-of-intellect model. The major sequence is in terms of the operation categories—cognition, memory, divergent production, convergent production, and evaluation. Within each operation category, the products are taken in turn: unit, class, relation, system, transformation, and implication. Within each product category, the content categories are taken in turn—figural, symbolic, and semantic.

A three-letter code designation is given for each factor, as well as the traditional name for the factor, usually assigned before the model was completed or before the model nomenclature was taken seriously. The code letters are as follows, describing in turn each of the three dimensions in Figure 1, a model of the structure of intellect.

First Letter (operation)		Second Letter (content)		Third Letter (product)	
C:	cognition	F:	figural	U:	unit
M:	memory	S:	symbolic	C:	class
D:	divergent production	M:	semantic	R:	relation
N:	convergent production	B:	behavioral	S:	system
E:	evaluation			T:	transformation
				I:	implication

[9] The sources from which various tests may be obtained are also given in terms of a code system:

A: used in a study by Adkins and Lyerly (1951).

Ca: used in a study by Carroll (1941).

Cr: used in a study by Christal (1958).

ETS: Educational Testing Service, Princeton, N.J., in the standard factor-analytic battery edited by John W. French.

Kn: used in a study by Karlin (1942).

Ky: used in a study by Kelley (1954).

LLT: used in various studies by L. L. Thurstone.

SS: Sheridan Supply Co., Box 837, Beverly Hills, Calif.

USAF: United States Air Force, Personnel Research Laboratory, Lackland Air Force Base, Texas. Forms modified in aptitudes research at the University of Southern California are designated as USAF-M.

Other forms, without symbols, were designed as experimental tests by the Aptitudes Project, University of Southern California. Permission to reproduce certain ones is usually granted to recognized investigators. Exceptions are tests subsequently published or tests that have not yet been factor-analyzed.

If the order of the three parameters is kept in mind, the few duplications of letters in different lists should not be confusing.

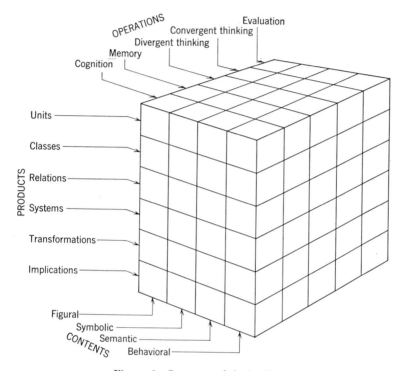

Figure 1   Structure of the intellect.

1. COGNITION

CFU(V)—VISUAL COGNITION (sometimes called "speed of closure")

Street Gestalt Completion. Write the names of objects presented in silhouette figures with enough parts blotted out to make the task of cognition sufficiently difficult for testing purposes. (LLT)

Parts, 1. Items, 24. Working time, 3 minutes.

Mutilated Words. Recognize words in which part of each letter has been erased. (LLT)

Parts, 1. Items, 26. Working time, 4 minutes.

Peripheral Span. Recognize letter flashed $\frac{1}{25}$ second in peripheral vision. Individually administered. (LLT)

Dark Adaptation. Recognize letters in dim illumination. Individually administered. (LLT)

CFU(A)—AUDITORY COGNITION[10]

Haphazard Speech. Recognize short phrases spoken with unusual inflection and pitch changes. (Kn)

Illogical Groupings. Recognize short phrases spoken with grouping contrary to sense of the passage. (Kn)

Singing. Recognize words in a short selection sung with piano accompaniment. (Kn)

CSU—SYMBOL COGNITION

Anagrams. Make shorter words using only the letters of a long word, e.g., "generations." (LLT)

Word Combinations. Make a new word using the last letters of one word and the initial letters of the next; e.g., the combination "beam pledge" gives the word "ample."
Parts, 2. Items per part, 15. Working time, 8 minutes.

Omelet Test. Recognize a word whose letters have been scrambled; e.g., "ricah" is to be seen as "chair."
Parts, 2. Items per part, 15. Working time, 4 minutes.

Disemvoweled Words. Recognize a word whose vowels have been removed; e.g., "f ct r" is to be seen as "factor."

CMU—VERBAL COMPREHENSION

Guilford-Zimmerman Verbal Comprehension. A multiple-choice vocabulary test. (SS)
Parts, 1. Items, 40. Working time, 12 minutes.

Wide-Range Vocabulary Test V-3. A multiple-choice test. (ETS)
Parts, 1. Items, 50. Working time, 10 minutes.

Reading Comprehension. Answer multiple-choice questions concerning meanings in a paragraph. (USAF)

Information Test. Part of the Wechsler Adult Intelligence Scale.

CFC—FIGURAL CLASSIFICATION

Figure Classification. Recognize classes of three sets of figures each and then assign given figures to the classes.
Parts, 1. Items, 15. Working time, 6.5 minutes.

CSC—COGNITION OF SYMBOLIC CLASSES

Number-Group Naming. State what it is that three given numbers have in common, e.g., 35, 110, 75. Answer: divisible by 5.
Parts, 1. Items, 15. Working time, 3 minutes.

Number Relations. In a set of four pairs recognize a pair of numbers that does not belong for lack of a common relation that determines the class, e.g., A, 2-6; B, 3-9; C, 4-12; D, 6-15. Answer: D (since 6 × 3 does not equal 15).
Parts, 2. Items per part, 15. Working time, 10 minutes.

---

[10] It is quite possible that this factor will have to be reclassified as CFS(A), since the test material would seem to involve systems rather than units.

CMC—CONCEPTUAL CLASSIFICATION

Word Classification. Select the one word in a set of four that does not belong to the class, e.g.,

ship engine canoe log

Answer: engine.

Verbal Classification. Assign each word to one of two classes, or to neither, each class being represented by a set of four words.

Parts, 2. Items per part, 40. Working time, 8 minutes.

Sentence Evaluation. Decide whether each given sentence conveys fact, possibility, or a name.

Parts, 2. Items per part, 15. Working time, 9 minutes.

CFR—FIGURAL RELATIONS

Figure Analogies. From multiple choices, select a figure that completes an analogy.

Parts, 2. Items per part, 15. Working time, 10 minutes.

Figure Matrix. From multiple choices, select a figure to fill a matrix cell, in a 3 × 3 matrix with a different relation in columns and rows.

Parts, 1. Items, 15. Working time, 7 minutes.

CSR—SYMBOLIC RELATIONS

Seeing Trends II. Find a repeated relationship between successive pairs of words in a series, the relations being in the form of spelling or alphabetical properties, e.g.,

three other either brother smooth

Answer: "th" moves one letter to the right.

Parts, 2. Items per part, 12. Working time, 16 minutes.

Word Relations. A kind of analogies test in which the items of information related are words, the relations being in the form of spelling or alphabetical properties, e.g.,

calm call self sell help _____

1. helm 2. hell 3. heal 4. held 5. shell Answer: 2.

Parts, 2. Items per part, 15. Working time, 15 minutes.

CMR—SEMANTIC RELATIONS

Verbal Analogies. From multiple choices select a word to complete a meaningful relationship.

Parts, 2. Items per part, 15. Working time, 12 minutes.

Word Matrix Test. Discover relations in rows and columns and then supply missing word, e.g.,

stocking shoes galoshes
yolk _____ shell

1. wagon 2. eat 3. hen 4. white 5. egg Answer: 4.

Parts, 1. Items, 15. Working time, 12 minutes.

Cards S-1. From a group of six drawings of a card shown rotated and/or turned over, indicate which ones show card not turned over. (ETS)

Parts, 1. Items, 20. Working time, 6 minutes.

Cubes S-2. Indicate which items present two drawings that can be of the same cube and which cannot, judging from markings on the faces of the cubes. (ETS)

Parts, 1. Items, 44. Working time, 5 minutes.

Guilford-Zimmerman Spatial Orientation. Indicate the position of a boat with respect to the landscape after a pictured change in the boat's position. (SS)

Parts, 1. Items, 60. Working time, 10 minutes.

Circle Reasoning. Discover the rule for marking one circle in sequence with other circles and dashes.

Parts, 1. Items, 15. Working time, 8 minutes.

Letter Triangle. Find the system by which letters of the alphabet are arranged in a triangular pattern, with some vacant position, and then select one of five alternative answers (letters) to fill a designated position.

Parts, 2. Items per part, 8. Working time, 12 minutes.

Guilford-Zimmerman General Reasoning. A multiple-choice arithmetic-reasoning test in which numerical computation is minimized. (SS)

Parts, 1. Items, 27. Working time, 20 minutes.

Ship Destination. Find the distance of a ship to a port, taking into account the influences of an increasing number of variables. (SS)

Parts, 1. Items, 48. Working time, 15 minutes.

Mathematics Aptitude R-1. Solve five-choice verbally stated problems, using arithmetic. (ETS)

Parts, 1. Items, 20. Working time, 10 minutes.

Necessary Arithmetical Operations. Given the facts of a problem, select from multiple choices the pair of number operations needed to solve the problem.

Parts 2. Items per part, 15. Working time, 15 minutes.

Necessary Facts. Given all necessary facts but one, state the one that is missing to make the arithmetical problem structure complete, and then select from among alternatives.

Parts, 2. Items per part, 10. Working time, 10 minutes.

Paper Form Board Vz-1. Draw lines in an outline figure to show how a few separated and scrambled black pieces would fit together to form a complete figure. (ETS)

Parts, 1. Items, 42. Working time, 7 minutes.

Punched Holes VS-2. Indicate the pattern of holes in an unfolded paper that has been shown folded and a hole punched in a certain location. (ETS)

Parts, 1. Items, 10. Working time, 3 minutes.

Surface Development Vz-3. Indicate which lettered edges in a drawing of a solid figure correspond to numbered edges, or dotted fold lines, in a plane diagram of the unfolded sides of the solid. (ETS)
Parts, 1. Items, 6. Working time, 6 minutes.
Guilford-Zimmerman Spatial Visualization. Indicate among alternatives the position of an alarm clock after illustrated maneuvers. (SS)
Parts, 1. Items, 40. Working time, 10 minutes.

CMT—PENETRATION

Similarities. Give as many as six ways in which two given objects are alike.
Parts, 2. Items per part, 6. Working time, 10 minutes.
Social Institutions. List things wrong with institutions, such as taxes, divorce, etc. The score is the number of farsighted, needed improvements given.
Parts, 2. Items per part, 6. Working time, 10 minutes.

CFI—PERCEPTUAL FORESIGHT

Competitive Planning. Starting with four incomplete, adjacent squares, add one line at a time, playing for two opponents, in such a way as to maximize the numbers of squares completed by both. (USAF-M)
Parts, 2. Items per part, 20. Working time, 20 minutes.
Route Planning. A maze-tracing test, in which the examinee indicates through which lettered points he *must* pass in order to reach the goal. (USAF-M)
Parts, 5. Items per part, 8. Working time, 20 minutes.
Planning a Circuit. Trace visually an electrical circuit diagram with overlapping wires and indicate which pair of terminals should be attached to a battery to make the circuit work. (USAF-M)
Parts, 3. Items per part, 12. Working time, 12 minutes.

CSI—COGNITION OF SYMBOLIC IMPLICATIONS

Word Patterns. Arrange a given set of words efficiently in a kind of crossword-puzzle pattern; e.g., arrange the words "bats," "easy," "hot," "tea," and "the" in a matrix of empty squares so as to use as few squares as possible.
Parts, 2. Items per part, 5. Working time, 20 minutes.
Symbol Grouping. Rearrange scrambled symbols of three kinds to achieve a specified systematic order in as few moves as possible; e.g., given the sequence — O X X X —, achieve the sequence X X X — — O by moving one symbol at a time according to rules.
Parts, 2. Items per part, 8. Working time, 10 minutes.

CMI—CONCEPTUAL FORESIGHT

Pertinent Questions. Write as many as four questions, the answers to which should help to reach a decision in a conflict situation. (SS)
Parts, 2. Items per part, 4. Working time, 12 minutes.
Alternative Methods. List as many as six different ways of accomplishing a certain task.
Parts, 4. Items per part, 1. Working time, 14 minutes.

2. MEMORY

MFU—VISUAL MEMORY

Reproduction of Designs. Reproduce geometric-type designs after having had a brief exposure. (Ky)

Map Memory. Select from multiple choices the segment of a map previously studied. (USAF)

MSU—MEMORY SPAN

Memory Span—Digits. Repeat series of digits immediately. (Ky)

Memory Span—Letters. Repeat series of letters immediately. (Ky)

MMU—MEMORY FOR IDEAS

Picture Recall. Report information or answer questions regarding items of information remembered from a picture previously studied. (Ky)

Memory for Ideas. Reproduce a brief, one-paragraph story after hearing it once, not verbatim. (Ky)

MSR—ROTE MEMORY

Picture-Number Ma-1. Paired-associates recall of numbers paired with pictures. (ETS)

Word-Number Ma-2. Paired-associates recall of numbers paired with words. (ETS)

First Names Ma-3. Paired-associates recall of first names of individuals, last name being given. (ETS)

Color-Word. Paired-associates recall of words associated with colors. (Ky)

MMR—MEANINGFUL MEMORY

Sentence Completion. Supply missing words in sentences previously perceived in full. (Ky)

Related Words. Paired-associates recall of words associated with other words. (Ky)

MFS(V)—MEMORY FOR VISUAL SPATIAL ORDER

Space Memory. Identify the form that was previously exposed in each of five sections within five squares. (Cr)

Position Memory. Recall the position of a number-word pair approximately 4 hours after the initial administration of the Number-Word Test. (Ky)

MFS(A)—AUDITORY MEMORY (formerly classed as MFU(A))

Musical Memory. Recognize musical compositions heard earlier. (Kn)

Rhythm. Recognize rhythmic patterns of taps. (Kn)

MMS—MEMORY FOR TEMPORAL ORDER

Position Recall II. Recall on which of four study pages of a previously administered test each of 48 drawings appeared. (Cr)

Sequence Memory. For each pair of test titles, indicate which one was administered earlier in a battery given 3 days before. (Cr)

MSI—NUMERICAL FACILITY (formerly classed as NSI)

Addition Test N-1. Add sets of one- and two-digit numbers. (ETS)
Parts, 1. Items, 90. Working time, 3 minutes.

Division Test N-2. Divide two- and three-digit numbers by single digits. (ETS)
Parts, 1. Items, 90. Working time, 3 minutes.

Subtraction and Multiplication N-3. Subtract two-digit numbers; multiply two-digit numbers by single digits. (ETS)
Parts, 1. Items, 90. Working time, 3 minutes.

Guilford-Zimmerman Numerical Operations. Add, subtract, multiply, and divide numbers; a multiple-choice test. (SS)
Parts, 1. Items, 132. Working time, 8 minutes.

3. DIVERGENT PRODUCTION

DFU—FIGURAL FLUENCY

Sketches. Given a simple figure, such as a circle, repeated 12 times, make different objects.

Make a Figure. Given three lines, e.g., two short, straight lines and a curved line, make different combinations in limited time.
Parts, 2. Items per part, 1. Working time, 6 minutes.

Make a Mark. Make simple figures of a specified kind, e.g., open figures composed of curved lines.
Parts, 2. Items per part, 1. Working time, 4 minutes.

DSU—WORD FLUENCY

Word Fluency. Write words containing a specified letter, e.g., the letter "s." (SS)
Parts, 2. Items per part, 1. Working time, 4 minutes.

Suffixes W-1. Write words ending with a specified suffix, e.g., "-sion." (ETS)
Parts, 1. Items, 1. Working time, 4 minutes.

Prefixes W-2. Write words beginning with a specified prefix, e.g., "sub-." (ETS)
Parts, 1. Items, 1. Working time, 4 minutes.

First and Last Letters W-3. Write words with specified first and last letters. (ETS)
Parts, 2. Items per part, 1. Working time, 5 minutes.

DMU—IDEATIONAL FLUENCY

Ideational Fluency. Write names of things fitting relatively broad classes, e.g., things that are white and edible. (SS)
Parts, 4. Items per part, 1. Working time, 12 minutes.

Topics If-1. Write ideas about a given topic, e.g., working on the railroad. (ETS)
Parts, 1. Items, 1. Working time, 5 minutes.

Theme If-2. Write as many words as possible about a given topic. (ETS)
Parts, 1. Items, 1. Working time, 6 minutes.

Thing Categories If-3. List things that are round or that could be called round. (ETS)
Parts, 1. Items, 1. Working time, 2.5 minutes.

Plot Titles (Nonclever). List appropriate titles for a given short short story.
Parts, 2. Items per part, 1. Working time, 6 minutes.

Consequences (Obvious). List consequences of a proposed unusual event, e.g., no babies born for one year. (SS)
Parts, 10. Items per part, 1. Working time, 20 minutes.

Utility Test (Fluency). (Based upon the former Brick Uses). List uses for a common brick and a common wooden pencil, total number of responses being the score. (SS)
Parts, 2. Items per part, 1. Working time, 10 minutes.

DFC—FIGURAL SPONTANEOUS FLEXIBILITY

Varied Figural Classes. Given a collection of three figural objects that can be conceived as representing different classes, which ones of five single figures can be classified with the three?
Parts, 2. Items per part, 5. Working time, 4 minutes.

DSC—SYMBOLIC SPONTANEOUS FLEXIBILITY

Number Grouping. Given a set of several numbers, group at least three of them to a class, the same numbers being needed to form different classes, e.g., this list: 2   3   4   6   17   23   36.
Parts, 2. Items per part, 3. Working time, 6 minutes.

DMC—SEMANTIC SPONTANEOUS FLEXIBILITY

Utility Test (Flexibility). List uses for a common brick and a common wooden lead pencil. Score is the number of shifts of classes in consecutive responses. (SS)
Parts, 2. Items per part, 1. Working time, 10 minutes.

Alternate Uses (a Revision of Unusual Uses). List as many as six uses for an object, such as a newspaper, other than the common use, which is stated. (SS)
Parts, 3. Items per part, 3. Working time, 12 minutes.

DSR—DIVERGENT PRODUCTION OF SYMBOLIC RELATIONS

Letter Group Relations. Given a set of four letters that are related in several possible ways, select other sets of four that have the same relations; e.g., given the set C   A   E   F, do other groups exhibit any of the same relations?
Parts, 4. Items per part, 8. Working time, 12 minutes.

Number Rules. Given a starting number, relate one or more numbers to it in various ways to achieve a given result; e.g., starting with 2, arrive at 6 (answers: $2 + 4$; 2×3; $2 \times 2 + 2$).
Parts, 2. Items per part, 5. Working time, 10 minutes.

DMR—ASSOCIATIONAL FLUENCY

Associational Fluency. Write synonyms for each of several given words, e.g., for the word "hard." Possible answers: difficult, heartless, solid, brittle, etc. (SS)

Parts, 2. Items per part, 2. Working time, 4 minutes.

Simile Insertions. Supply a variety of appropriate words to fill each blank in a given simile, e.g.,

The fog is as _____ as a sponge.

Possible answers: soft, dense, opaque, full of holes, etc.

Parts, 2. Items per part, 2. Working time, 4 minutes.

Controlled Associations. Write a number of synonyms for each given word.

Parts, 2. Items per part, 4. Working time, 14 minutes.

DFS—DIVERGENT PRODUCTION OF FIGURAL SYSTEMS

Making Objects. Given a few figures and lines, construct from them, with nothing added, specified, meaningful objects, e.g., lamp, clown, etc.

Parts, 2. Items per part, 9. Working time, 6 minutes.

DSS—DIVERGENT PRODUCTION OF SYMBOLIC SYSTEMS

Make a Code. Invent a variety of code systems, using numbers and letters.

Parts, 1. Items, 1. Working time, 5 minutes.

Number Combinations. Given a few simple numbers, e.g., 2   3   4   5   6, construct a number of different equations.

Parts, 2. Items per part, 3. Working time, 8 minutes.

DMS—EXPRESSIONAL FLUENCY

Expressional Fluency. Construct a variety of four-word sentences, given four initial letters, no word to be used more than once, e.g.,

"W_____ f_____ r_____ d_____."

Possible answer: "Who found Rover dead?"   (SS)

Parts, 4. Items per part, 1. Working time, 8 minutes.

Simile Interpretation. Complete in a number of ways a statement involving a simile, with explanatory remarks, e.g.,

"Woman's dress is like the autumn; it _____."

Possible answer: "— shows many changes of color."

Parts, 2. Items per part, 2. Working time, 4 minutes.

Word Arrangement. Write a number of sentences, each containing four specified words.

Parts, 2. Items per part, 1. Working time, 8 minutes.

DFT—FIGURAL ADAPTIVE FLEXIBILITY

Match Problems II. Given a set of adjacent squares or triangles of the same size, each line being composed of a match, take away a specified number of matches to leave a specified number of squares (triangles) with no matches left over, solving each item in as many as four ways.   (SS)

Parts, 2. Items per part, 5. Working time, 14 minutes.

Match Problems III. Similar to Match Problems II, with some more difficult items requiring more insight.

Parts, 2. Items per part, 5. Working time, 12 minutes.

Match Problems IV. Similar to Match Problems II, except that the number of matches to be removed is not specified.

Match Problems V. Similar to Match Problems II, except that the number of remaining squares is not specified.

Planning Air Maneuvers. Select the most direct path in "skywriting" letter combinations (two capital letters) with an airplane. (USAF-M)

Parts, 2. Items per part, 20. Working time, 16 minutes.

DMT—ORIGINALITY (semantic adaptive flexibility)

Plot Titles (Clever). Write titles for a short story, only clever titles being accepted.

Parts, 2. Items per part, 1. Working time, 6 minutes.

Consequences (Remote). Give remote (distant in time or in space or in sequence of events) consequences for a specified event. (SS)

Symbol Production. Produce simple symbols to represent given activities and objects.

Parts, 2. Items per part, 60. Working time, 10 minutes.

Riddles (Clever). Give clever solutions to riddles, e.g., "What city is liked best by actors?" Possible answer: "Publicity."

Parts, 2. Items per part, 10. Working time, 12 minutes.

DFI—FIGURAL ELABORATION

Decorations. Given articles of furniture in outline form, add decorative lines and markings. (SS)

Parts, 4. Items per part, 6. Working time, 12 minutes.

Production of Figural Effects. Given a very simple line or two, build upon the given to produce a (nonmeaningful) figure of some degree of complexity. Scoring is in terms of amount added.

Parts, 2. Items per part, 6. Working time, 6 minutes.

Figure Production. Same as the previous test, except that a meaningful object is to be produced.

Parts, 3. Items per part, 4. Working time, 9 minutes.

DSI—SYMBOLIC ELABORATION

Limited Words. Given two common words, make a number of new word pairs from the letters included, using all the letters given; e.g., given shirt bean, possible answers could be: "hairs bent" or "bears thin."

Parts, 2. Items per part, 4. Working time, 10 minutes.

Symbol Elaboration. Given two simple equations involving letters, deduce a variety of other equations that follow from them, e.g., $V = R + K$ and $T = K \times C$.

Parts, 3. Items per part, 2. Working time, 9 minutes.

DMI—SEMANTIC ELABORATION

Planning Elaboration. Add detailed operations needed to make a briefly outlined plan succeed. Scored in terms of number of details added.

Parts, 2. Items per part, 1. Working time, 16 minutes.

Possible Jobs. For a given symbol, suggest a number of different occupations or jobs for which it might stand. For example, a glowing electric light bulb might symbolize an electrical engineer, a missionary, or a night worker of some kind.
Parts, 2. Items per part, 3. Working time, 10 minutes.

4. CONVERGENT PRODUCTION

NMU—CONCEPT NAMING
Picture Group Naming. Provide the class name for a group of five pictured objects.
Parts, 1. Items, 24. Working time, 6 minutes.
Word Group Naming. Provide the class name for a group of five words, e.g.,

volcano   sun   fire   Africa   oven

Parts, 2. Items per part, 15. Working time, 10 minutes.
Seeing Trends I. Name the meaningful trend in a group of words, e.g.,

century   year   decade   day   week   second   minute

where the order is not fully correct but there is a trend.
Parts, 2. Items per part, 15. Working time, 10 minutes.

NMC—CONVERGENT PRODUCTION OF SEMANTIC CLASSES
Word Grouping. Given 12 common words, put them into four, and only four, classes, leaving no extra words.
Parts, 2. Items per part, 10. Working time, 10 minutes.
Figure Concepts (Uncommon). Given a collection of pictured objects, combine them in classes, the score being the number of uncommon classes.

NSR—SYMBOLIC CORRELATES
Correlate Completion II. Discover the rule by which two pairs of words are related, and then apply it to a third pair, completing it, e.g.,

calm   call   self   sell   help _____

Parts, 2. Items per part, 15. Working time, 12 minutes.
Letter Series. State which letters properly continue the sequence of a series of letters, e.g., A   R   B   R   C   R _____   _____ .
Parts, 2. Items per part, 15. Working time, 8 minutes.

NMR—SEMANTIC CORRELATES
Inventive Opposites. Write two antonyms for a given word, the first letters of the responses being given, e.g., the opposite of "dry" may be either w_____ or m_____. (LLT)
Parts, 2. Items per part, 15. Working time, 6 minutes.
Vocabulary Completion. Produce a word that fits a given definition and begins with a certain letter, e.g., The husband of a queen is a k_____. (LLT)
Associations III. Produce a word that is similar in meaning to two other given words, e.g., true _____ front. Answer: false.
Parts, 2. Items per part, 15. Working time, 12 minutes.

NSS—CONVERGENT PRODUCTION OF SYMBOLIC SYSTEMS

Operations Sequence. State the order in which a sequence of numerical operations should be performed in going from one number to another, e.g., starting with 5 to reach 1 by applying the three operations: $\times$ 2, $\div$ 7, $-$ 3.

Parts, 3. Items per part, 10. Working time, 12 minutes.

Word Changes. State the order in which to place words in order to go from a given starting word to a given goal word, e.g., starting with the word "set" change one letter at a time, ending with the word "cry." The words to be used are: day sat dry and say.

Parts, 2. Items per part, 6. Working time, 8 minutes.

NMS—SEMANTIC ORDERING

Picture Arrangement. Given the four pictures of a comic strip, indicate the temporal order needed to make sense. (A)

Parts, 2. Items per part, 8 and 12. Working time, 7 minutes.

Sentence Order. Indicate the temporal order in which three stated events should be placed to make sense.

Parts, 2. Items per part, 10. Working time, 6 minutes.

Temporal Ordering. List steps in appropriate order to complete a project, e.g., planting a new lawn.

Parts, 4. Items per part, 8. Working time, 16 minutes.

NFT—FIGURAL REDEFINITION

Concealed Figures CF-1. Indicate which of four complex geometrical figures contain a given simpler figure. (ETS)

Parts, 1. Items, 49. Working time, 10 minutes.

Penetration of Camouflage. Locate faces hidden in complex pictorial scenes. (USAF)

Parts, 2. Items per part, 10. Working time, 10 minutes.

Hidden Figures. Indicate which of five simple figures is concealed in more complex figures of the Gottschaldt type.

Parts, 2. Items per part, 15. Working time, 12 minutes.

Hidden Pictures. Find human or animal pictures hidden in a complex scene. (LLT)

NST—SYMBOLIC REDEFINITION

Camouflaged Words. Find the name of a sport or game concealed in a sentence, e.g., "I did not know that he was ailing." Answer: sailing.

Parts, 2. Items per part, 10. Working time, 8 minutes.

Word Transformation. Indicate new divisions between letters in words of a phrase, e.g., "there do live" to become "the red olive."

Parts, 1. Items, 20. Working time, 5 minutes.

NMT—SEMANTIC REDEFINITION

Gestalt Transformation. Select one of five alternative objects, or parts of objects, to be used to serve a stated purpose.

A sample item reads: To Light a Fire
                                1. cabbage
                                2. fish
                                3. pocket watch
                                4. string
                                5. pipe stem
Answer: Pocket watch (use cover as condensing lens).
Parts, 2. Items per part, 10. Working time, 10 minutes.
Object Synthesis. Name an object that could readily be made by combining
two given objects, e.g., a coil spring and a basketball. Answer: punching bag.
Parts, 2. Items per part, 12. Working time, 10 minutes.
Picture Gestalt. Indicate which objects in a photograph will serve stated
purposes.
Parts, 1. Items, 24. Working time, 10 minutes.

NSI—SYMBOL SUBSTITUTION

Form Reasoning. Solve simple equations that are given in terms of combina-
tions of familiar geometric figures.
Parts, 1. Items, 20. Working time, 12 minutes.
Sign Changes. Given the condition that certain numerical-operation symbols
are interchanged, solve simple equations.
Parts, 2. Items per part, 32. Working time, $1\frac{1}{3}$ minutes.

NMI—DEDUCTION

Sequential Association. Indicate the best order for four words to produce a
chain of associations, e.g., the words:

                        pen   pig   read   write

Answer: pig   pen   write   read.
Parts, 2. Items per part, 5. Working time, 3 minutes.
Attribute Listing II. State the essential attributes of an object that is to serve
a certain purpose, e.g., to drive a long nail into a hard post, no hammer being
available.
Parts, 1. Items, 1. Working time, 2 minutes.

5. EVALUATION

EFU—PERCEPTUAL SPEED

Guilford-Zimmerman Perceptual Speed. Identify among five similar ones the
drawing of a common object that is identical with the given object.
Parts, 1. Items, 72. Working time, 5 minutes.
Identical Forms. Mark all the forms in a row that are identical with the one
at the left of the row. (LLT)
Parts, 1. Items, 60. Working time, 5 minutes.

ESU—SYMBOLIC IDENTIFICATION

Letter A Sd-1. Check the four words having the letter "a" in columns of 40
words each. (ETS)

Parts, 1. Items, 50 columns. Working time, 2.5 minutes.

First-Digit Cancellation Sd-2. In a row of 30 digits, indicate each digit that is like the first one in the row. (ETS)

Parts, 1. Items, 75 rows. Working time, 3 minutes.

Scattered X's Sd-3. Circle the seven X's among letters scattered over a page. (ETS)

Parts, 1. Items, 7 pages. Working time, 5 minutes.

ESR—SYMBOL MANIPULATION

Symbol Manipulation. Mark symbolically stated relations "true" or "false" according as they are consistent or not consistent with other statements.

Examples: Given: $x\,S\,y$ (x is smaller than y)

Then: $x\,E\,y$ (x is equal to y)

$y\,G\,x$ (y is greater than x)

$y\,NE\,x$ (y is not equal to x)

Parts, 1. Items, 25. Working time, 7 minutes.

Sign Changes II. Indicate which interchange of algebraic signs will make an equation correct; e.g., which two of the operation signs should be interchanged to make this equation correct?

$$(5 \times 4) + 2 = 8 \div 2$$

A. − and ÷   B. + and −   C. + and ×   D. × and −   E. + and ÷

Answer: E.

Parts, 2. Items per part, 10. Working time, 14 minutes.

EMR—LOGICAL EVALUATION

Logical Reasoning. Decide which of four alternative, verbally stated conclusions follows logically from two premises. (SS)

Parts, 2. Items per part, 20. Working time, 20 minutes.

False Premises D-1. Indicate which conclusions logically follow from stated premises (nonsensical statements). (ETS)

Parts, 1. Items, 25. Working time, 8 minutes.

Inference Test. State the most justified conclusion that can be drawn from a given statement.

Parts, 2. Items per part, 8. Working time, 10 minutes.

EMS—EXPERIENTIAL EVALUATION

Unusual Details. Point out incongruities in each sketch of a common situation, e.g., contradictions, missing parts, etc.

Parts, 2. Items per part, 16. Working time, 8 minutes.

Social Situations. For a verbally stated social situation, e.g., "A man taking his 'date' to a movie finds he is without funds," select from alternatives the wisest course of action.

Parts, 2. Items per part, 15. Working time, 10 minutes.

EMT—JUDGMENT

Practical Judgment. Select the best alternative solution among those given for a practical predicament. (USAF)

Parts, 1. Items, 30. Working time, 30 minutes.

Practical Estimations. Make quantitative estimates regarding common objects, e.g., matchboxes, windshields, etc.

Parts, 2. Items per part, 15. Working time, 12 minutes.

EMI—SENSITIVITY TO PROBLEMS

Apparatus Test. Suggest one or two needed improvements in common appliances, such as a telephone, toaster, etc.

Parts, 2. Items per part, 10. Working time, 14 minutes.

Seeing Problems. List problems that might arise in connection with common objects, such as a candle.

Parts, 2. Items per part, 10. Working time, 12 minutes.

Seeing Deficiencies. Point out the way in which a described plan of action is faulty, e.g., in paving a street and then laying a sewer.

Parts, 2. Items per part, 10. Working time, 20 minutes.

chapter 18 The Assessment and Prediction of the Creative Performance of High-Aptitude Youth

John L. Holland, National Merit Scholarship Corporation[1]

S I would like to tell you about some of our research. What I have done in this report is to skim and summarize the things which I feel are the most important. We have a tremendous number of negative results and many findings of little significance. But I would like to give you a quick view of what we are up to, what we seem to be finding, and what I think it means.

The annual scholarship programs of the National Merit Scholarship Corporation provide an unusual opportunity for studying talent. In our research, we capitalize on this opportunity in several ways. We try to obtain information which will not only be of practical value in the administration of scholarship and financial aid programs, but which will also further our understanding of the nature of talent and its development. Our goals are exemplified by the major areas of our research:

1. The identification of talented students.
2. The influences of colleges.
3. The conservation of talent.
4. The vocational behavior of talented students.
5. The personal development and mental health of talented students.

Although the identification of talent is the area most pertinent to our conference topic, research in the other areas makes it clear that every-

[1] Now at The American College Testing Program, 330 East Washington Avenue, Iowa City, Iowa.

thing is related to everything else. I will indicate some of these relationships as I review our research.

THE IDENTIFICATION OF TALENT

In our study of talented students, we are trying to devise effective ways of finding those high school students who will perform creatively in college and in their vocations. At the same time, we hope to develop a theory of achievement and creative performance which will serve to integrate our knowledge of achievement and to stimulate research.

In our studies of identification we are concerned also with the prediction of academic achievement (grades) and of social achievement (leadership). Not only are these kinds of achievement socially relevant, but also they provide useful contrasts with creative behavior.

Our criteria of creativity are obtained from lists of achievement assumed to be creative in nature. Generally, these achievements occur infrequently, demand long-term effort, and are accorded public recognition through prizes, awards, or publication. At the present time, these criteria are limited to unusual accomplishments in science and the arts during the high school and the undergraduate and graduate years in college. However, we plan to develop more comprehensive criteria of creativity and other socially relevant behaviors in the college years and to extend these criteria to achievements which occur during the post-college years. Such criteria will help to define our goals more explicitly and to integrate our efforts. Table 1 summarizes our present criteria and gives some typical items for each criterion.

Performance of any of these criterion tasks means that you have acquired certain basic skills. You have done more, however; you have won public recognition for a task in which there is considerable competition. You do not get awards of this type frequently; they occur rarely. They require long-term effort, and we think that they require imagination and some ability to innovate and create.

Our chief method for studying creative achievement has been to assess large samples of National Merit Finalists, using psychological devices which predict performance in college and career. The finalists in each yearly competition are assessed in high school and polled for their subsequent achievement during each college year and for several years after college. At present, we have followed six student samples for periods of one to six years (Holland, 1959b, 1960, 1961; Holland and Astin, 1962). These successive longitudinal studies differ from one another in that the assessment devices, inventories, and scales and the background information for each student group have varied from year to year. Each year, we use the most promising variables from previous

TABLE 1

Some Examples of Criteria of Creativity at the High School,
College, and Postcollege Levels

High School

Science
Won a prize or an award of any kind for scientific work or study. How many?
Had scientific paper published in a scientific journal.
Gave an original paper at a scientific meeting sponsored by a professional society.
Placed first, second, or third in a regional or state science contest. How many times?
Art
Received a rating of "Good" or "Excellent" in a state music contest.
Exhibited or performed (not at school) a work of art (painting, musical composition, sculpture).
Won a prize or an award in an art competition (sculpture. ceramics, painting, etc.). How many?
Had poems, stories, or articles published in a public newspaper or magazine (not school paper) or in a state or national high school anthology. How many?

College

Science
Received a prize or an award for scientific paper or project.
Gave an original paper at a scientific or professional meeting sponsored by a professional society or association. Name of society or association.
Had scientific or scholarly paper published (or in press) in a scientific or professional journal. Give reference here if published.
Invented a patentable device. If yes, indicate briefly its nature.
Art
Won one or more speech or debate contests.
Had minor roles or leads in plays produced by college or university.
Received an award for acting, playwrighting, or other phase of drama.
Had poems, stories, essays, or articles published in a public newspaper, magazine, anthology, etc. (not college publication).

Postcollege

Science
Received a research grant. If yes, indicate nature.
Received a prize or an award for scientific paper or project.
Had scientific or scholarly paper published (or in press) in a scientific or professional journal. Give complete reference here if published.
Invented a patentable device. If yes, indicate briefly its nature.
Art
Had poems, stories, essays, or articles published in a public newspaper, magazine, anthology, etc. (not college publication).
Won literary award or prize for creative writing. How many?
Composed music which has been given at least one public performance.
Won a prize or award in an art competition (painting, sculpture, ceramics, etc.).

assessments to make a new assessment. Thus we have been able to sift through a great range of inventories, scales, and background information, so that we now have a smaller set of assessment materials which predict student achievement.

The principal results of these longitudinal studies can be briefly summarized: in high school and college, the student who performs creatively in science and art tends to resemble the stereotype of the scientist and artist. Tables 2 and 3 show some of the attributes and background variables which are related to scientific and artistic creative performance. The summary for the student who performs creatively in science is as follows.

The scientific achiever has high scholastic aptitudes, especially in mathematics. His history is characterized by past scientific achievement and, to a lesser degree, academic achievement. His artistic achievement tends to be low.

The scientific achiever conceives of himself as scholarly, hard-working, original, and self-confident. Teachers see him as an original person but a poor leader.

He prefers vocations of a scientific or mechanical nature and dislikes social or artistic callings. Relative to other achievers, he is less concerned with status.

He is introverted, he defers gratification without difficulty, and he is inclined to be somewhat depressive in mood. He has a wide range of interests and activities, including creative hobbies.

Although not characterized as "original" by originality scales, he regards himself as original, as do his teachers. These judgments are supported by his interest in creative hobbies.

This empirical characterization formed the basis for the following theoretical formulations. Scientific achievement, like other kinds of achievement, appears to be a product of a special life history and of inherited aptitudes, especially mathematical aptitudes.[2]

Social and family background

The scientific achiever tends to come from a somewhat lower socio-economic group than the artistic or social achiever. Since this group does not emphasize sociability and social graces, students from such a background are more likely to have a penchant for things and ideas than for interpersonal relations. This hypothesis is exemplified by the values of the scientific achiever's father, who is more concerned with his son's being curious than with his being dependable. The relative

---

[2] Similar summaries have been prepared for the student who does well at academic, social, or artistic tasks; they are presented in another paper. (Holland, 1962c).

TABLE 2

Correlations between Three Criteria of Academic and Creative Performance
and 72 Aptitude, Personality, and Background
Variables for Boys†
($N = 649$)

| Variable | Creative Performance | | High School Grades |
	Scientific	Artistic	
1. HSR	00	08§	– –
2. Scientific performance	– –	15	00
3. Artistic performance	15**	– –	08
4. SAT-V	02	−09*	−04
5. SAT-M	04	−19**	09*
6. Humanities comprehension	−01	03	02
7. Scientific comprehension	06	02	04
8. Creative activities (NMSS)	36**	37**	−03
Gough DRS			
9. Intellectual competence	−03	02	−01
10. Inquiringness	00	02	02
11. Cognitive flexibility	02	01	−09*
12. Aesthetic sensitivity	01	12**	01
13. Sense of destiny	03	23**	−04
14. Total score (above 5)	03	15**	−03
15. Potential success (PIV)	01	04	01
Originality-personality			
16. Complexity-simplicity	07	07	−14**
17. Independence of judgment	10*	03	−11**
18. Barron originality	07	08*	−12**
19. Mastery	11**	10*	13**
20. Deferred gratification	11**	06	11**
21. Breadth of interest	09*	23**	00
22. Self-evaluation	01	23**	24**
Ghiselli			
23. Initiative	11**	07	−02
24. Self-assurance	09*	12**	11**
25. Occupational level	01	11**	−07
VPI			
26. Response Bias	−02	13**	05
27. Infrequency	−07	−01	03
28. Physical activity	18**	−04	02
29. Intellectuality	23**	03	07
30. Responsibility	−17**	20**	05
31. Conformity	−07	01	06
32. Verbal activity	−10*	11**	00
33. Emotionality	−05	31**	02
34. Control	−02	12**	15**
35. Masculinity-femininity	10*	−05	03
36. Status	−18**	18**	12**
Self-ratings			
37. Originality	15**	27**	−01
38. Popularity	−05	10*	12**

TABLE 2 (continued)

| Variable | Creative Performance | | High School Grades |
	Scientific	Artistic	
39. Drive to achieve	08*	22**	28**
40. Independence	15**	20**	06
41. Self-confidence	10*	23**	13**
42. Perseverance	11**	15**	27**
Teacher ratings			
43. Citizenship	00	09*	26**
44. Popularity	01	05	17**
45. Social leadership	00	10*	19**
Father's values and goals			
46. Defend self	−01	00	−02
47. Ambitious	06	00	05
48. Curious	11**	−08*	−09*
49. Dependable	−10*	−02	02
50. Good student	−02	06	16**
51. Happy, well-adjusted	−02	01	−06
52. Independent, self-reliant	−02	04	−12**
53. Popular	−01	01	09*
54. Self-controlled	−01	00	−06
PARI			
55. Fostering dependency	−01	−06	05
56. Seclusion of mother	01	−02	10*
57. Martyrdom	03	−03	09*
58. Strictness	−07	03	03
59. Irritability	−11**	−05	−02
60. Excluding outside influences	03	−06	06
61. Suppression of aggression	07	−04	08*
62. Rejection of homemaking role	−02	−11**	02
63. Equalitarianism	−05	03	02
64. Approval of activity	00	−07	06
65. Avoidance of communication	05	03	12**
66. Suppression of sex	03	−04	05
67. Ascendancy of mother	−05	−09*	05
68. Intrusiveness	10*	03	05
69. Comradeship and sharing	−07	−02	06
70. Acceleration of development	07	−03	10*
Miscellaneous			
71. Degree (level) sought	15**	13**	04
72. Father's educational level	05	05	−08*
73. Mother's educational level	−02	03	−10*
74. Birth order (first born)	09*	−04	01
75. School size	−02	−04	03

* Significant at the .05 level.
** Significant at the .01 level.
† From *Journal of Educational Psychology*, 1961, 52, 136–147.
§ Decimal points have been omitted.

TABLE 3

Prediction of Scientific Achievement over 1-, 2-, 3-, and 4-Year Periods*

Variable	Source	Time Interval							
		1 Year		2 Years		3 Years		4 Years	
		Boys	Girls	Boys	Girls	Boys	Girls	Boys	Girls
1. Scientific achievement (HS)	VPI	30†	35	21		20	25	16	24
2. Physical activity	NMSS			16				22	18
3. Play	VPI			-15					
4. Status	VPI			-14					
5. Artistic achievement (HS)				-10					
6. Social leadership	Teacher rating			-13				13	
7. SAT-Math					12				
8. F Cheerful	16 PF			-11					
9. College grades (HPR)						13			
10. Psychological mindedness	CPI					13			
11. Creative activities (A)		14						24	
12. Creative activities (B)								23	
13. Scholarship	Self-rating							22	
14. Physicist	SVIB							18	
15. Drive to achieve	Self-rating							18	19
16. Social Science teacher	SVIB							-17	
17. Aviator	SVIB							16	
18. Breadth of interest (HS)								14	
19. Verbal activity	VPI		18					-13	
20. Originality	Self-rating							12	
21. Emotionality	VPI							-11	
22. Self-confidence	Self-rating							10	
23. Accountant	SVIB								
24. Originality	Teacher rating	12							
25. Curious	Father's values	12							21
26. Dependable	Father's values	-16							

* From *Journal of Educational Psychology*, 1962, 53, 132–143.
† Decimal points have been omitted.

TABLE 4

The Prediction of Achievement over a 1-Year Period
by a Scientific and by an Artistic Index

Rube Goldberg Index	Type of Measure of College Achievement	
Scientific*	Total scientific achievement .43	Rare scientific achievement .37
Artistic*	Total artistic achievement .31	Rare literary achievement .18
		Rare music .61 Rare graphic .33 Rare dramatic .09

* Each of these two Rube Goldberg indices consisted of seven items.

lack of family social activity at this economic level may be conducive to introversion (psychological-mindedness), curiosity, and creative or individualistic activity, since it forces the person to rely on his own resources for amusement. Consequently, the child is likely to develop his intellectual rather than his interpersonal skills.

School experience

Such a background produces a child who is studious, although his lack of social leadership and enthusiasm and his unsociability may make him somewhat less desirable to teachers. His introversion leads to his isolation from the group and the community.

Personality

These family and school experiences combine to produce a person who uses intellectual and scientific activities both as a source of gratification and as a way of isolating himself from dissatisfying social relationships. He has developed superior self-control and the ability to postpone immediate pleasure. He dislikes and avoids situations requiring social skills. His alienation from conventional values results, in part, from his isolation from others and his rejection of social relationships as goals. Because of his self-direction and imagination, the scientific achiever gradually comes to feel that the drive for good grades conflicts with the pursuit of his own interests. Consequently we find that at the college level—as opposed to the high school level—scientific achievement has negligible and sometimes negative relationships with grades.

If we compare the predictive efficiency of different types of variables in our yearly assessments, we find that, next to similar *past* achievement, the best predictors of achievement are self- and teacher ratings, interest inventories, and simple check lists of creative activities and interests. With a few exceptions, true-false personality and originality scales are next in order. Parental attitudes scales and scholastic aptitude tests are the least efficient predictors of later achievement.

This crude ordering suggests that for purposes of prediction we can abandon our efforts to construct sophisticated inventories, and concentrate instead on securing more elaborate records of past achievement and more systematic reports of the student's self-conceptions, interests, and daily activities.

These findings led Dr. Nichols and me to construct some simple indexes of achievement and creative performance for the 1960 assessment (Holland and Nichols, 1962). These predictive scales, which we call the "Rube Goldberg" indices, consisted of four to eight items, such as the choice of major field, number of creative hobbies, number of past achievements in the relevant area, and self-ratings of originality and drive to achieve. It is important to note that none of these indices contained ability measures. Table 4 shows the results of the Rube Goldberg indices for the prediction of achievement in the first year of college. Although there is considerable variation in efficiency, the correlation of .61 between the index for artistic achievement and musical achievement, a predictive correlation over a one-year period, suggests that this approach has merit. We plan now to extend it by constructing indices which entail other domains of influence in addition to the student's attributes—parental attributes, the student-college interaction, and the nature of the college environment.

In our assessment of National Merit Finalists in 1961 we developed a new inventory for the prediction of achievement. It included about 1,000 objective items relating to the student's self-estimates, achievements, aspirations, daily activities, experiences, vocational goals, and interests. Although we have not yet polled this group again for its undergraduate achievement, we have performed some preliminary analyses. We are in the process of building scales to assess *potential* for achievement and creative performance in scientific, oral, persuasive, artistic, literary, and musical fields at the high school level. The item analyses of some 273 activities and interests of a sample of 500 boys produced a scientific scale whose concurrent validity with scientific achievements is about .47 for a cross validation of 200 boys. A review of the 38 items in this scale suggests that the boy who achieves in science likes scientific subjects in school, prefers to read scientific books and articles, spends his spare time building scientific equipment or engaging in related activities, etc. In short, the science achiever spends a large portion of his time and effort on what we consider scientific activities and hobbies. Of special interest, the items checked by the scientific achiever suggest that he is also a competent musician.

When this new scale is put to a predictive test, the correlation between the scale and scientific achievement will probably be smaller than the tentative concurrent correlation. In the meantime, since an informal review of the data suggests that predictive errors are due in part to our failure to give differential weights to the criterion items, we are developing a weighting scheme for high school achievement. We will then recorrelate the scientific scale against the weighted criterion to see whether we can obtain a higher correlation.

Because of the earlier success of our brief check lists of unusual accomplishments and creative behavior (Holland and Astin, 1962), in 1961 we added additional items to these check lists to see whether we could obtain more reliable criteria. (The original check lists for artistic and scientific accomplishment have reliabilities as low as .36.) In addition, we divided the global artistic scale into specific scales and developed a scale for leadership. These check lists of accomplishment in scientific, oral, persuasive, artistic, literary, and musical fields prove to have reliabilities which range from .48 to .86. And despite their heterogeneous content, total scores (all six scores added together) for boys and girls have reliabilities of .82 and .75. The success of these revised check lists suggests that we can use scales consisting of real-life, socially significant achievements to predict undergraduate and adult accomplishment with unusual efficiency, even when we limit such attempts to highly selected groups of students. We have labeled the more unusual accomplishments —winning an award in a national contest, publishing a story, and the like—as "creative" or imaginative achievement. These achievements are being ordered so as to discover if students identified as "creative" by this standard differ from students who have high performance scores but are not necessarily distinguished by such unusual accomplishments.

COLLEGE ASSESSMENT STUDIES

Concurrent with these longitudinal identification studies, we have been developing assessment devices for characterizing college environments. Our goal is to learn how colleges affect the student's achievement, level of aspiration, and choice of major field and vocation. A secondary, but important, goal is to find valid and practical ways to characterize colleges and universities. Unless we can describe the college, it is impossible to study what happens when a certain kind of student goes to a particular college or to specify those institutional attributes which influence the creative performance of students.

Our first studies in this field were college population or student input studies. We guessed that many of the effects that colleges and universities were assumed to have could be explained by the kinds of students they attracted in the first place. Accordingly, we polled college freshmen and their parents to learn the expectations, attitudes, and other personal attributes of students entering different kinds of colleges. These early studies revealed that different colleges do attract different kinds of students.

In one early study, it looked as if a college's production of students who later went on to attain the Ph.D. was due in large part to the ability of the students the college attracted. In a second study, colleges were compared for their production of Ph.D.s after they had been equated for the scholastic aptitude of their student bodies. Groups of over- and underproductive colleges were identified and compared for their gross characteristics—type of control, size, and the like—and for their atmospheres or environments as reported by the students. The results of this second study suggested that certain faculty behaviors were important in stimulating or inhibiting intellectual achievement.

At this point, several ideas occurred to us. The college atmospheres which were thought to be conducive to Ph.D. production appeared to be those created by large groups of students interested in science and the arts. In addition, we learned in a study of vocational choice that the percentages of persons seeking the Ph.D. varied greatly from one major field to the next. These speculations led us to re-examine our earlier results. We discovered that, when we controlled for the percentage of students seeking the Ph.D. as freshmen and for the percentage in natural science, the correlation between Ph.D. productivity and college environment was greatly reduced. For example, the correlation between the total Ph.D. productivity of a college and the percentage of entering students seeking the Ph.D. was .81.

This third study was not without defects in sampling and design. A fourth and more crucial kind of study was planned, using a sample of 265 institutions. In this study, it was found that a college's actual Ph.D. output can be accurately predicted from three student input characteristics: the percentage of boys, the percentage of students in the different major fields, and the intellectual level of the students (Astin, 1962b). For different groups of colleges—technological institutions, men's universities, coeducational colleges, etc.—the correlations between the actual Ph.D. output and the predicted output ranged from .62 to .98. Of equal importance, we found that these predictions approximate the reliability of the phenomenon we were trying to predict. For example, the correlation between the predicted and the actual Ph.D. outputs for coeducational colleges was .62, but the reliability of the actual output for these institutions was only .73. Similarly, the correlation between expected and actual Ph.D. outputs for technological institutions was .98, and the reliability of their actual output rates was .97. Even though these results demonstrated that an institution's output of Ph.D.s is primarily dependent upon its input of students, it was also possible to show (*a*) that public institutions were "overproductive," that is, produced more than their expected proportions of Ph.D.s significantly more often than private institutions; and (*b*) that men's colleges located in the northeastern states were significantly "underproductive."

These findings are grossly misinterpreted. People interpret them to mean that Astin and Holland, and particularly Astin (*laughter*), is "anti-college" and opposed to the idea that colleges do anything wonderful or useful. This article does not say that. It says that they have little to do with the relative production of Ph.D.s. That is a different matter. (Of course, we have suspicions about other things they may or may not do.)

In a more recent longitudinal study of college effects, we have found that the talented student's motivation to seek the Ph.D. is positively affected by the smallness of the institution, by a low "conventional" orientation in the college environment, and by a high percentage of females in the student body. Attending a small coeducational liberal arts college appears to enhance the student's motivation to seek the Ph.D., whereas attendance at one of the northeastern men's colleges, once again, appears to reduce Ph.D. aspiration.

During the same period that we have been studying Ph.D. productivity, we have also been trying to find ways to characterize college environments. As a preliminary step, we used the College Characteristics Index (CCI). Later we revised this instrument to obtain separate scales for faculty and students. These preliminary analyses led to several important results and ideas.

First it was clear that the CCI has many redundant scales, as do our revisions of it. Second, the division into faculty and student scales seems to add little. Third, it was difficult to interpret the a priori CCI scales, since the items called for considerable subjectivity on the part of the student. Finally, it seemed to us that the CCI was largely an account of the characteristics of the student bodies at an institution, that is, the number of students, their ability level, and their fields.

To test this hypothesis, we obtained information about the size of the college, the average ability of its student body, and the division of the college population into six major areas of concentration, using this profile of major fields as an index of the college environment. We discovered that this new technique, the Environmental Assessment Technique (EAT), was correlated with various CCI scales according to our predictions (Astin and Holland, 1961).

In short, we can tell what students will say about their college environment (in CCI terms, at least), merely by knowing the size and ability level of the student body and by counting the number of majors in each of the six broad areas at a particular college.

The EAT was validated again for a new group of colleges by polling students and predicting what they would say about their colleges. But both the CCI and the EAT are limited instruments for learning about colleges, since one requires subjective interpretations by the students, and the other is concerned with a restricted set of student attributes.

In an effort to extend our understanding of colleges, we obtained information about 33 institutional characteristics of a group of 335 colleges and universities. These characteristics included type of control, physical and financial variables, faculty variables, and student variables. Six factor analyses were performed to see whether we could develop a smaller set of variables to substitute for the 33. These factor analyses suggested that we could characterize an institution by using from six to eight variables and that the EAT variables made psychological sense (Astin, 1962c).

Currently, we are trying to develop an inventory of college experiences which will not depend on the subjective judgments of the students. In the meantime, we have performed two studies of vocational choice and achievement in which we were able to characterize colleges with the EAT and to study the effects that they have on students.

An important by-product of our college studies is Astin's report on the relationship between high school grades and selected creative accomplishments. The group studied was an unselected sample of 127,000 college freshmen, so a wide range of talent is represented. The analyses make it clear that academic performance in high school has small or negligible relationships to creative achievement.

STUDIES OF VOCATIONAL CHOICE AND MAJOR FIELD

Concurrently with the identification and college studies, we have done a series of studies of vocational choice and major field. Such studies, although they may appear to be peripheral to the study of creativity, have produced a number of useful insights. The empirical results of these studies are summarized in two monographs (Holland, 1962a, 1962b). The results which seem especially significant with respect to creative performance are summarized as follows:

1. A student's choice of major field or vocation is a powerful index of his potential for creative performance and his personality, values, aptitudes, educational and vocational aspirations, daydreams, etc.

2. Scientific and artistic "interests" are predictive of creative performance in these same areas. So-called "interest" measures are among our more efficient predictors. Scientific and artistic interests are also related to a great variety of originality and personality variables which are predictive of creativity. These results provide substantial replication of the earlier work of Barron, Gough, and MacKinnon.

3. In a simple study of the interaction of students and their colleges over a four-year period, we found that artistic achievement (by our check list definition) occurred more frequently when the student attended a college whose environment was congenial with his personality type. For this analysis, the student was characterized as being one of six personality types, and colleges were categorized in the same way, using the EAT. I hate to expose you to my delusional system, but what it boils down to is that there are six kinds of people in the world and there are six kinds of environments, and you can code them 1 to 6, put them together, and make predictions. A lot of people think that there are seven or eight, but . . . (*laughter*). The resulting 6 × 6 table shows that the congruency of student-college code is conducive to achievement. Congruency of student and college is also related to becoming a leader and to stability in major field. In general, student achievement, stability of major field, and vocational choice, are more closely related to student than to college attributes.

4. If we assume that vocational preferences are a measure of personality, our results suggest that creative parents have creative children. Specifically, we found that the scores of the student and both his parents on a brief tolerance of ambiguity scale by Budner have low but significant correlations.

SUMMARY

Figure 1 gives an overall picture of our research studies. First, we have defined creative performance as an unusual accomplishment which requires the solution of an ambiguous problem, which is socially adaptive, and which is given public recognition. This tentative definition resembles an earlier definition by Barron and others. It led to the study

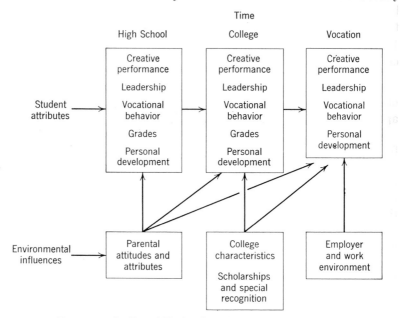

Figure 1   Outline of National Merit Scholarship Studies.

of six kinds of accomplishment—academic, persuasive, scientific, artistic, literary, and musical. Specific criteria have been enumerated for the high school and college levels; others will be developed for the post-college years. Second, we have found several ways to characterize the college (the EAT, for example), in order to study creative performance in terms of the interaction between the person and his environment. Our assessments of parents and employers provide similar environmental information. Third, from our use of a comprehensive set of assessment devices for determining creative potential, we have developed a more economical set of predictors. The arrows in Figure 1 indicate the concurrent and predictive relationships that we have studied or plan to study. Finally, some future reports will be concerned with the development of a more explicit conceptual scheme for comprehending our empirical results.

C   There is something here that I cannot understand. In your report you concluded that "seeking the Ph.D. comes from the nature of the students a college gets in the first place and that different faculties have little or no differential influence on such an outcome." And later, "Congruency of student and college is also related to becoming a leader and to stability in major field. In general, student achievement, stability of major field, and vocational choice are more closely related to student than to college attributes." You have it, and you don't have it.

S   No. You are misinterpreting us. The first statement is about the Ph. D. In the second one, we are *not* talking about the Ph.D.; we are talking about staying in the same major field and are saying that college does have an influence, from what we can tell. The college has something to do with becoming a leader.

C   What do you mean by becoming a leader?

S   Elected to one or more student offices. If you initiated a business enterprise, you get a point. If you initiated a new student group, you get a point. If you won a prize for leadership, you get a point. These are real live things, not scores.

C   But Ph.D. attainment is also student achievement, of a sort.

S   Yes, of a sort. But student achievement, as we are using it, really should be called artistic achievement. We mean a rather general term. Artistic achievement, student stability, field, and leadership are the kinds of student achievements about which we are speaking. Stability and field are not exactly achievement, but the others are.

C   This works, then, only for the artistic people and for leadership?

S   Yes. It did not work for science in this particular study. Science was not related to achievement in science. I would not put much weight on this because our scientific scale at the time we did this study was one of our very worst scales. It was very short.

The possibility for doing something outstanding in science is much more limited, as far as we can tell from the distributions of achievements of science as opposed to art, leadership, and almost anything else. It is much more difficult to achieve, or there are fewer of these scientific achievements.

C   Do I interpret from what you say that if the student and the college match, so to speak, the faculty has little or nothing, from your studies, to do with the degree of success of the student in this college? Is that a correct interpretation?

S   Well, you are not quite right. You have to go through all the prohibitions. We controlled on 38 different input variables for these three kinds of effects: stability in major field, artistic achievement, becoming a leader. We took all those things which would indicate the student has some potential for achievement or change and discovered that they are not different for students entering different colleges.

The evidence we got would not support college having any effect. It is possible that it may, but again our measure of college environment may be quite inadequate. I should add a caution here: in assessing colleges, we are now in the stage we used to be with personality. That is, we know little about it. We think that we have some useful measures, but there has been little exploration of this area, so that it is difficult to know in some of these instances what the controls ought to be. For example, we do not know what the controls should be for stability in field. Initial degree of certainty about a major field or choice is unrelated to change in choice, whereas the high peak on the Strong Interest Inventory is related to choice.

The total number of major fields in a college is not related to instability, whereas the commonsense finding is that the more major fields there are, the more change you ought to have because you are putting out a big menu. But it doesn't work that way. While we got positive results, we think, we really shouldn't believe them too much.

C   I keep thinking of the old idea that a student will learn in spite of anything we do to him, if he is a good student, and I wonder if this is any support for that kind of notion.

S   Well, it is because all the relationships that we do find are much more closely tied to student attributes. There is no doubt about this. Whatever college effects we find, when you can estimate through a contingency coefficient, are in the order of about .10 to .15, .20 at the most. On the other hand, the student contingency coefficients related to Strong attributes or vocational interests will be as high as .45. Again, these findings are still tenuous. Schools are being categorized in a very crude, simple-minded way. However, we think that this has promise because Astin's factor analysis replicated many of the factors we found for the EAT; that is, this census of colleges, in the form in which we had it, made sense. For example, Astin found a masculinity factor which corresponded very closely to what we call realistic, and femininity went with the aesthetic atribute, and so on.

C   May the student go to any college of his choice and enter any field he chooses? Are the scholarships in any way selective?

S   There are several kinds of scholarships in the National Merit program: unrestricted scholarships provided by the National Merit Scholarship Corporation, and sponsored scholarships which may be unrestricted or may require that a student's parents work for a certain business, belong to a particular union, or attend a specific college. All students must, however, first qualify as Finalists in the National Merit program.

C I would like to hear you expand on what the students say about the colleges themselves.

S I will let my colleague, Astin, expand on that for you. What do you mean by what they say?

C A year ago, I had a couple of students to my home from Reed. And I just wondered whether these were typical Reed students or whether they were unusual. How can you tell the validity of what any particular student says about his college in relation to his larger group?

Astin You can't. You can only guess at it. This is one of the difficulties with the College Characteristics Index, where you find an accidental sample of students and ask them to tell you what their college is like. But if you can accept their reports as valid observations, using just our finalists, we can predict how they will evaluate their college quite accurately in many different dimensions by knowing merely what the distribution of major fields is, what the size of the institution is, and how bright the students are. With these facts we can predict quite accurately what the students will say. Whether their reports are valid, I don't know.

C These are based on what your scholarship students said about the college?

Astin Yes. We take a modal report about the college on a particular item. What we usually get is a scale. We take the median report on that scale for the students at each college and correlate it with the EAT characteristics. They correlate quite definitely in predicted ways. The students will make observations about whether the faculty gives much attention to individual students, whether there is a competition for grades, whether there is an emphasis on sports—a great variety of things.

chapter 19 Current Studies of the Personnel Research Laboratory in Creativity

Cecil J. Mullins, 6570th Personnel Research Laboratory,
Aerospace Medical Division (AFSC)

S   This presentation will be an amalgam of four separate studies.   There is very little organization naturally present among these studies, so I shall impose one, that of chronology.   I shall begin with one study recently finished and published, continue with two which are finished but not yet published, and end with one which will be finished soon.

STUDY 1.   PREDICTION OF SCHOOL SUCCESS AT SQUADRON OFFICER SCHOOL

Last year we were given the task of identifying young officers with scientific and engineering talent to be trained and subsequently assigned to research and development work.   What was wanted seemed to be a battery or batteries which would be immediately available and which would do two things.

First, the battery was to predict school success in scientific and engineering studies, since completion of school work in these areas was a prerequisite to being assigned to research and development work.   This phase of our problem posed no unusual difficulties.   We felt that the usual aptitude variables would do about as good a job as we could do.

It would have been desirable to have some success criterion obtained in engineering and scientific studies, but we did not have any such criterion immediately available, and immediate results were wanted.

We did have access to course grades in Squadron Officer School (SOS), which is a 14-week course for young lieutenants and captains. The emphasis of this course is primarily on communications arts and leadership. It was decided, for a number of reasons, to go ahead and use SOS as a situation in which to get some quick results.

Second, a battery was needed which would predict on-the-job success of young research and development officers some years from now, after they have completed the prerequisite training and have had time to function on the job long enough to provide us with success criteria in the field. The final validation of this battery is still some time off, but we did have some intermediate criteria at SOS which might provide us with useful information.

Squadron Officer School routinely collects a set of instructor ratings on all its students, including "originality and creativeness," "logical reasoning," and a global evaluation called "officership." We decided to use these three ratings in our study as early criteria.

Also, as a matter of routine, SOS collects a quantity of educational background and aptitude information on its students. We decided to use 11 of the educational background variables and 5 of the aptitude variables in our study.

We also decided to administer three types of ratings or tests designed by Calvin Taylor, from which we obtained nine scores. All in all, we had 29 variables, which are listed in the right-hand column in Table 1.

Analysis

Taking each of the four criteria in turn, we asked these two questions:

1. How well does a best-weighted combination of variables currently collected at SOS on entering students predict their success on this criterion?

2. Do the experimental tests designed by Calvin Taylor and his team (Taylor, Smith, Ghiselin, and Ellison, 1961) add anything of value to predicting this criterion?

A multiple linear regression model was decided upon as offering the most definitive answers to our questions. A multiple R^2 was computed between each criterion, and a set of predictors composed of the information routinely collected at SOS (the background variables and the aptitude measures). Then another R^2 was computed between each criterion and all 29 predictors. The difference between these R^2's can be tested for statistical significance, indicating whether or not the Taylor tests are able to add anything to the standard variables already being collected. The reason we used this approach is a purely practical one. The other information is already collected routinely, and consequently,

TABLE 1

Validity Coefficients for 25 Variables against 4 Criteria
(Including Criterion Intercorrelations)*
($N = 845$)

Variable Number	Criteria				Definitions
	1	2	3	4	
					Criterion Variables
1.	...	68	68	67	Cumulative course grade
2.	68	...	72	77	Officership rating on Form 82
3.	68	72	...	75	Originality and creativeness rating on Form 82
4.	67	77	75	...	Logical reasoning rating on Form 82
					Educational Background Variables
5.	25	21	26	25	Civilian educational level (quantified in 13 intervals from 1 = not high school graduate to 13 = doctor's degree)
6.	20	14	22	18	Mathematics level (quantified in 7 intervals from 0 = no college math through 6 = differential equations)
7.	17	13	24	20	Six semester hours of physics (1 if yes, 0 if no)
8.	13	11	16	12	Six semester hours of chemistry (1 if yes, 0 if no)
9.	08	05	06	05	Six semester hours of accounting (1 if yes, 0 if no)
10.	03	01	03	06	Eighteen semester hours of accounting (1 if yes, 0 if no)
11.	10	08	15	11	Two years of engineering college training (1 if yes, 0 if no)
12.	10	08	08	10	Two years of college training in physical science (1 if yes, 0 if no)
13.	10	08	09	09	Two years of other college training (1 if yes, 0 if no)
14.	12	10	16	15	Three years of college training in engineering (1 if yes, 0 if no)
15.	15	11	13	13	Three years of nonengineering college training (1 if yes, 0 if no)
					Aptitude Variables
16.	34	30	36	27	ACE Psychological Examination (Q-score)
17.	46	34	49	36	ACE Psychological Examination (total score)
18.	50	34	48	38	ACE Cooperative English Test (total score)
19.	41	23	39	28	ETS Pre-engineering Ability Test (Part I)
20.	33	24	34	27	ETS Pre-engineering Ability Test (Part II)
					Experimental Test Variables
21.	17	15	13	12	Satisfactory achievement scale (quantity of work)
22.	07	09	08	04	Satisfactory achievement scale (level of original work)
23.	14	13	13	09	Satisfactory achievement scale (total score)
24.	23	22	24	16	Self-description (drive)
25.	06	05	07	06	Self-description (curiosity)
26.	11	09	13	10	Self-description (flexibility)
27.	13	11	19	11	Self-description (creativity)
28.	23	19	26	18	Self-description (total score)
29.	34	22	32	23	Biographical Information Inventory (on-the-job creativity key)

* Decimal points have been omitted.

if these new variables are going to do anything for us, they have to add predictive value on top of what has been collected.

Results

The complete intercorrelation matrix among the 29 variables listed in Table 1 was computed, and the validity coefficients against the four criteria have been extracted from that matrix and presented in Table 1.[1] Incidentally, one small point of interest should be noted at the top of the criterion columns in Table 1 where the criterion intercorrelations are presented. It is evident that the four criteria are quite highly related. Apparently, the ratings on criteria 2, 3, and 4 were made after the raters had taken a long, penetrating look at the school grades.

Eight multiple correlations were then computed, two for each of the four criterion variables (1–4). For each criterion a multiple correlation was found first for an entire battery of 25 variables (5–29) and secondly for only the 16 official variables (5–20), excluding the 9 experimental test variables. For the accumulative course grade the multiple R^2 was .350 for the full battery and .303 for the shorter battery. For the second criterion, officership ratings on Form 82, the multiple R^2's were .200 and .163, respectively; for the originality and creativeness ratings the multiple R^2's were .341 and .311; and for the logical reasoning rating they were .213 and .200. On comparing results of these two batteries, it was found that the experimental variables added significantly to prediction of the first three of our four criteria (at the .01 level), although the increase was very slight. The increase in predicting the rated logical reasoning criterion is the only one that did not achieve significance at even the .05 level.

If our interest in these tests were confined to the SOS situation, we would consider these results rather disappointing. However, in view of the fact that the tests could add a significant prediction in such adverse circumstances, we were encouraged enough to administer them to one more class ($N = 1,000$). All these data have been stored for use against better criteria as they mature. Are there any questions on this study before we go on?

C   It could be argued from Table 1 that your last three criteria are not moving far away from course grades. But if they do move farther away into new dimensions of performance, you might get better results for the experimental tests, or at least you would expect different results, would you not?

S   Yes, but we simply can't know.

C   In this first study you saw the rating forms and objective information as not adding anything much to what you already had. But there is another way that you can look at this: "Could you use these perhaps instead of those you already have?" If you consider the unequal lengths

---

[1] The interested reader can write to the author of this chapter for further information about the complete intercorrelation matrix, the means, and standard deviations for all variables, plus the regression weights for the multiple correlational computations (including the sequence of adding each variable into the battery).

of the tests, the short, brief self-ratings were the best predictors. In other words, if you were to equate the (time) length of these and the length of your ACE tests, then the corrected validities for the self-ratings would have been the higher.

S   Once again we were somewhat constrained by the situation. In the SOS certain kinds of information are collected routinely, and we are not likely to change this procedure, though we might add to it.

STUDY 2. PREDICTION OF HIGH SCHOOL GRADES BY CREATIVITY TESTS

The results of work done by Getzels and Jackson (1963) suggest that both aptitude batteries and creativity batteries contain independent validity against high school grades, and that one set of tests added to the other set might increase prediction of school performance beyond what can be done with either set alone.

This study is concerned primarily with answering the following questions:

1. How well do creativity tests predict school performance, compared with the usual kind of aptitude predictors?

2. How much is gained, in predicting school performance, by adding aptitude tests to a battery of creativity tests?

3. How much is gained, in predicting school performance, by adding creativity tests to a standard aptitude battery?

It is conceivable that there are important sex or grade differences connected with these three questions. Therefore, a fourth question was asked, namely:

4. Are there important grade or sex interactions in our prediction system?

In April 1960 we had the opportunity of testing the entire student body ($N = 225$) of Hondo High School, Hondo, Texas. These students had already taken the Project Talent battery of tests. We administered 20 more tests, among which were 5 which we expected to be related to originality or creativity. These 6 tests, which constituted our creativity battery (see the appendix to this chapter for more complete descriptions) were as follows:

1. Color-Form C. A test of flexibility.
2. Word Meanings C. Complexity.
3. Brick Uses. Originality.
4. Omnibus Opinion Survey—Complexity Scale.
5. Imagery Clearness. Ego strength.

6. The Flanagan Creativity (Ingenuity) Test, which had been administered as part of the Project Talent battery.

For the aptitude battery, we selected from the many Project Talent scores available the following variables, which pretty well blanketed the aptitude area:

7. Vocabulary (Project Talent #102).
8. Visualization 2 (Project Talent #281).
9. Arithmetic Reasoning (Project Talent #311).
10. Clerical Checking (Project Talent #430).

Hereafter in this chapter, the numbers 1–10 will be used for this battery of aptitude and creativity tests. Our criterion of school performance was school-grade average for the school year 1959–60.

We decided that a multiple linear regression analysis would best answer our questions. The first step was to compute eight separate intercorrelation matrices, one for each sex, for freshmen through seniors.

To answer our fourth question we had to compute still another intercorrelation matrix on the total sample, disregarding grade and sex. With these matrices, all our questions could be answered by computing various multiple R^2's and testing the significance of the difference between various pairs of them. The R^2's significant to our questions are given in Table 2.

The first R^2 (full model) is between our criterion and the 10 predictors, plus sex by grade interaction terms. There were 8 grade by sex categories, so our prediction system in this full model contained 80 predictors. The second R^2 (restricted model) is between the same criterion and the 10 predictors, without the interaction terms. Comparing these two R^2's tells us whether or not class by sex interactions are important in predicting school grades. Question 4 was answered by computing the significance of the difference between R^2 for row A and R^2 for row B in Table 2. This difference is significant beyond the .001 level. Thus, it makes a very important difference whether or not we consider grade and sex in our prediction system.

Since grade and sex were important variables, we used a full model containing the interaction variables in making the rest of our comparisons.

Our first question was, "How well do creativity tests predict school performance, compared with the usual kind of aptitude predictors?" The creativity test battery yielded a multiple R^2 of .5067 against school grades, and from the aptitude battery we obtained a multiple R^2 of .6300. There was no convenient way to test the significance of this difference directly, but the next two questions indicate rather clearly that the aptitude test battery is very likely the more efficient of the two.

The second question, "How much is gained, in predicting school per-

TABLE 2

Multiple R's against School-Grade Average $(N = 225)$*

Creativity and Aptitude Predictors	Number of Predictors	R^2	R
A 1–10 (including sex and grade interactions)	80	.7445	.86
B 1–10 (sex and grade disregarded)	10	.5049	.71

NOTE: All following R^2's include grade and sex interactions.

C 7–10 (aptitude)	32	.6300	.79
D 1–6 (creativity)	48	.5067	.71
E 7–10 plus 2, 3, 4	56	.7062	.84
F 7–10 plus 1	40	.6457	.80
G 7–10 plus 2	40	.6594	.81
H 7–10 plus 3	40	.6474	.80
I 7–10 plus 4	40	.6555	.81
J 7–10 plus 5	40	.6398	.80
K 7–10 plus 6	40	.6515	.81

* Significance of difference results between R^2's were as follows: A minus D (question 2) at .001 level; A minus C (question 3) at .10 level; A minus B (question 4) at .001 level; and E minus C (question 5) at .02 level. The remaining comparisons, all for question 6, yielded the following results: F minus C not significant even at the .10 level; G minus C significant at .05 level; H minus C not significant; I minus C significant at .10 level; J minus C not significant; and K minus C not significant

formance, by adding aptitude tests to a battery of creativity tests?'', was answered by comparing the prediction obtained by using the full model (variables 1–10) with that obtained by using only the creativity battery (variables 1–6). As we can see from Table 2, the multiple R^2 obtained by the full model is .7445. The creativity battery alone yields a multiple R^2 of .5067. The difference between these two (A minus D in Table 2) is significant beyond the .001 level. Therefore, the aptitude battery does add very significantly to the predictive efficiency of the creativity battery.

The answer to the third question, "How much is gained, in predicting school performance, by adding creativity tests to a standard aptitude battery?'', is obtained by comparing the prediction obtained ($R^2 = .7445$) by using the full model (variables 1–10) with that obtained ($R^2 = .6300$)

by using only the aptitude battery (variables 7–10). The difference is significant only at the 10% level. Therefore we can be sure of improving the predictive efficiency of this aptitude battery by adding to it this creativity battery only 90 times out of 100. The improvement obtained by adding these creativity tests to an aptitude battery is considerably less certain than that obtained by adding aptitude tests to this creativity battery. These results provide us with some indirect answers to our first question.

C   You are talking about school grades as the criterion, and you are analyzing what is in school grades, aren't you?

S   That is correct. We have another section later on creativity ratings of originality.

C   So you are suggesting that school grades don't have much creativity in them as measured by this battery.

S   No! They have some, but grades are more heavily loaded with the standard aptitude battery. It seems in this particular instance that the creativity tests are not working for predicting school grades as well as the aptitude tests.

C   What are the comparative reliabilities of the two classes of tests? Many of the creative tests tend to have lower reliabilities, don't they?

S   I can tell you the reliabilities of some of them. Others are almost impossible to obtain reliabilities on without testing and retesting, which is very difficult for us at Lackland. For one of them, the Word Meanings C (that is, the categories test), if you take the first five categories and correlate them with the second five (there is no reason to expect any serial disturbance there) you usually get a correlation of .85 to .90. I can't say anything at the moment about the Omnibus Opinion Survey. The Color-Form C is one of the tests for which a test-retest would be required. The Project Talent booklet gives the reliabilities for the Project Talent tests.

C   The nature of the question, if I understand it, is that if you equated the two types of tests on reliability, would there be as much difference in validity?

C   Yes, that is the question.

S   That is possible, but I don't know—I haven't done that.

C   Have you mentioned intercorrelations between the creativity battery and the standard aptitude battery?

S   We have eight different intercorrelation matrices by grade and by sex, and these correlations across samples bounced around very badly. In some of these groups the intercorrelations between the creativity tests and the aptitude tests were pretty high, and in some of them there was almost nothing. There didn't even seem to be any serial order in going, say, from eighth grade to twelfth grade. It would go up, then down, and with the girls you might get a complete switch. I examined these things for two or three weeks trying to find some trends in it, but I couldn't. There was nothing obvious that I could see.

C   Was your criterion of school grades, as given by teachers, based upon achievement tests or upon their own examination?

S   Their own examinations.

C   Their examinations probably don't reflect the amount of creativity that one might find in achievement by using other types of examinations of the right kind.

S   Well, that is very possibly true. We were interested in the fact that at an earlier conference Getzels and Jackson indicated that their results are from achievement tests only. We wondered whether these results applied to grades also.

C   Part of the issue here, of course, is the criterion problem. If we held up a different criterion in our present schools, we might be in quite a different predictive situation. Or if school were constituted quite differently with different criteria, we might be in a quite different situation, dealing with quite different phenomena.

S   That's true.

C   Is there anything in your knowledge of the particular culture of Hondo High School that might help here?

S   It might. It is an excellent high school, and in feedback from the colleges the graduates go to, Hondo High School usually rates pretty high. (Now this is according to the principal of Hondo High School.) The average Hondo High School student who goes away to college averages something like a B in college. It is fantastic.

C   Do Mexicans go to the school?

S   Not many. Well, no more so than to most schools of the area. There seems to be a very unusual type of student, military children, because there is a base there. They are unusual students, and it is an unusual type of school system.

C   The reason I asked is that we find these relationships working differently in different high schools and different elementary schools, too. And usually the kind of hunches that we get about the culture of the school helps us to explain some of these differences. The schools worship different things.

C   Did Flanagan's test correlate with the other creative tests?

S   Flanagan's test correlated more with the aptitude tests than any of the others.

C   We found at the 1959 conference that this test (which Flanagan then called an Ingenuity Test) was highly correlated with verbal ability. In some cases, in comparison with the verbal ability scores, its profile of correlations consistently went down, which suggested that the non-vocabulary part of his Ingenuity (Creativity) Test may have correlated in a negative direction with the criterion of school grades. In other words, the unique, nonvocabulary, and also the nonreasoning parts of the Ingenuity Test seemed to be negatively related to school grades— a fascinating positive finding (Flanagan, 1959, pp. 117–118).

S   Most of the creativity tests were quite new, and we had little prior information on them. Therefore, we felt justified in taking an a posteriori look at the basic regression data (regression weights, iterative sequence, etc.), to see if we could tell whether a few of the creative tests were bearing the major prediction load, whereas some were contributing little more than error variance. We spotted three of the tests, Word Meanings C, Brick Uses, and the Omnibus Opinion Survey—Complexity Scale, which appeared to be doing yeoman duty in the prediction systems. Consequently, we added to our original four questions another, namely:

5. Do the three creativity tests mentioned in the previous paragraph add significantly to aptitude tests in predicting school grades?

As we can see from comparison E minus C in Table 2, these three tests do add significantly (beyond the .02 level) to aptitude tests in predicting school grades.

Still another question arose from the consideration that in the practical school situation it may sometimes be necessary to know which *one* of a set of creativity tests will work best in conjunction with aptitude tests in predicting grades. Therefore, we asked:

6. Which of the six creativity tests, when added singly to a battery of aptitude tests, contributes most to prediction of school grades?

The appropriate comparisons in Table 2 answer this question rather definitively. Only one test, Word Meanings C, adds to the predictive efficiency of a battery of aptitude tests at or beyond the .05 level. Another, the Omnibus Opinion Survey—Complexity Scale, contributes to the aptitude battery at the .10 level. None of the other four is significant at or beyond the .10 level.

Summary and conclusion

Getzels and Jackson have shown that there is some relationship between the creativity measures they used in their study and their criterion of school performance, which was a composite of achievement tests. This study was concerned largely with clarifying to some extent the nature of the relationship between creativity tests and our criterion of school performance (grades), especially when considered in conjunction with the more venerable aptitude battery.

The one test which was used in both studies was Brick Uses. In the present study Brick Uses did not appear to have any significant relationship with that part of school grades left after conventional aptitude tests have accounted for as much of the variance as possible. Two other creativity measures, Word Meanings C and the Omnibus Opinion Survey, however, did appear to hold promise for adding validity to an aptitude battery in predicting grades. It is of some interest to note that both these tests were designed as tests of complexity.

Adding selected creativity tests to a battery of standard aptitude tests improves the prediction of school grades significantly. However, in general, it appears that adding standard aptitude tests to a battery of creativity tests improves prediction much more significantly than the other way around.

STUDY 3. PREDICTION OF HIGH SCHOOL PEER RATINGS OF ORIGINALITY

As part of the Hondo High School study, we collected peer ratings of originality. We suspected that there may be some effect attributable to interaction of the sex of the raters and ratees. It could be that, at this age, boys were better raters of boys and girls were better raters of girls. We knew of no way to investigate this problem directly, so we tried an inversion of the usual predictor-criterion relationship. We took each creativity test in turn as a criterion and predicted the test first with the aptitude measures and then with the aptitude measures plus the originality ratings, separately and in combination for each of our eight groups (freshman boys, freshman girls, sophomore boys, etc.).

First, we had obtained all the prediction we could with the aptitude measures. Then we computed multiple R^2's on the total sample in turn for same-sex rating combinations (boys rating boys, girls rating girls), for opposite-sex rating combinations, and for both taken together against each creativity test as a criterion.

For each of the six criteria, the R^2's generally increased across the following four sets of predictors: aptitude measures, aptitude measures plus same-sex ratings, aptitude measures plus opposite-sex ratings, and aptitude measures plus both same and opposite ratings.[2] In comparing the R^2's for the first and the fourth of these combinations, in turn, for

---

[2] For criterion 1 across these four combinations the R^2's were .436, .499, .479, and .514; for criterion 2, .439, .448, .447, and .455; for criterion 3, .306, .367, .368, and .399; for criterion 4, .195, .232, .241, and .270; for criterion 5, .157, .202, .210 and .241; and for criterion 6, .558, .586, .610 and .624.

each of the six criteria only three of the differences were significant at the .05 level, and those only barely so. Comparisons between the R^2's involving only aptitude measures with those involving only one set of ratings would have been futile. It is obvious that no differences attributable to rater-ratee sex interactions are present in the study.

With our worry about sex interactions dispelled, we went back to our eight groups and computed multiple R^2's, using originality peer ratings assigned by boys as one criterion and originality peer ratings assigned by girls as another criterion, and the four aptitude variables as our basic set of predictors. Then we computed more multiple R^2's, adding each of the six creativity tests to the aptitude battery, singly and in combination. Finally, these R^2's were combined, automatically controlling for sex by class interaction effects.[3]

In predicting originality ratings made by the boys, Color-Form C adds to the aptitude variables at the .01 level. Brick Uses adds to the aptitude battery at the .05 level.

In predicting originality ratings made by the girls, Color-Form C again adds to the efficiency of the aptitude battery at the .01 level. With this criterion, however, there is a slight switch. Brick Uses no longer adds significantly, but Flanagan's Creativity Test does (at the .05 level).

At this point, we wondered whether Color-Form C, added to the usual aptitude battery, would give us all the useful prediction we could get from the aptitude variables plus *all* the creativity tests. The answer is that it does not.[4] Even when we include all the aptitude tests and Color-Form C in our battery, there is something more to be gained from adding the other creativity tests.

It appears, then, that Color-Form C, Flanagan's Creativity Test, and Brick Uses were the only creativity instruments in this battery which added useful prediction to a set of standard aptitude measures, and all three appear to offer promise in predicting peer ratings of originality at the high school level.

C How good are they?

[3] For the two criteria of ratings by boys and of ratings by girls these R^2's were .372 and .372, respectively, for the four aptitudes; .442 and .445 for the aptitudes plus Color-Form C; .382 and .380 for the aptitudes plus Word Meaning C; .423 and .399 for the aptitudes plus Brick Uses; .420 and .413 for the aptitudes plus the Omnibus Opinion Survey—Complexity Scale; .400 and .403 for the aptitudes plus Imagery Clearness; .417 and .429 for the aptitudes plus the Flanagan Creativity Test; and .619 and .622 for the four aptitude tests plus all six creativity tests.

[4] The differences were significant at the .05 level between the R^2 of .372 for the aptitude tests and of .619 for all ten tests against the criterion of ratings by boys. Essentially the same results were obtained against the criterion of ratings by girls.

S   In predicting the ratings made by the boys, the aptitude battery gives multiple R^2's of .37. The aptitude battery plus Color-Form C brings us up to .44. When you add all the creativity measures to the aptitude measures, you get a multiple R^2 of .62. So they do add quite a bit. In predicting ratings by the girls we can get almost exactly the same results. The aptitude battery alone is .37, the aptitude battery plus Color-Form C is .45 instead of .44, and the whole works again is .62.

C   What was your peer-rating question?

S   The students were to pick the third of their class best described by the statement, "Very original. Comes up with unusual and creative ideas." They were also to pick the third of their class best described by the opposite statement, "Unoriginal. Seldom comes up with unusual or creative ideas."

C   I think that your ratings probably are ratings of intelligence or IQ—of aptitude rather than originality. We have asked teachers to rate students on different qualities, such as flexibility and fluency, and no matter what we ask them to rate, it correlates with IQ.

C   Yes, you have to do something to get teachers to change their "set" so they think about children in different ways from just the IQ, before you can get good differentiation in different characteristics. We find that when we do this kind of thing, when we ask them to really take this change of set seriously, then we get such a change. They say almost apologetically when you ask them to pick out the five top and five bottom children, "I hate to put some of my students down here at the bottom. But they don't do any of the things you have in that definition, even though they're the best I have in long division." It's almost a pained response to rate some of their "best" students toward the bottom. However, the halo effect operates quite predominantly if you don't do this.

C   We had some experience in working on the ratings on the confidential reports of the National Scholarship Foundation fellowship program. We found something like this. If you want certain things other than what teachers are likely to give you, you must ask them first for the traditional things they tend to give you and have them give you these several times in several ways to get them off their chest; then you can start asking for other items. We had to run across several ratings before we started getting any new dimensions of information from them. So if you want three or four new dimensions, you might have to ask them to give 17 to 20 ratings. Otherwise, the first few ratings will turn out to be essentially one single (halo) dimension.

S   I think we have some indirect evidence that something besides just intelligence is being rated. If what we are having rated here is intelligence, then the aptitude measures would give us most of the prediction that we can get. However, since these particular creativity tests do add considerably to the aptitude measures, it seems to me that is evidence of something predictable beyond intelligence, unless the intelligence tests are not measuring the intelligence that is being rated.

C I inquired about the instructions to your raters because the idea theory underlying your measures emphasized complexity rather than unusualness of ideas or departure from the obvious.

S We were not only looking for complexity in Word Meanings C and in the Complexity Scale of the Omnibus Opinion Survey, but we were also interested in originality as measured by Brick Uses and, we felt, as measured by Color-Form C.

C It seems to me that none of these get at this unusualness or departure from the obvious.

S Brick Uses does this as well as anything I know of, at least on the surface.

C But you were using the different categories rather than the unusualness of the Brick Uses responses. We find by our analysis of that score that it has a trace of originality, but mostly it measures spontaneous flexibility. This is the shift of categories score in the Brick Uses test. You could have measured originality by infrequency of response.

S By a statistical count—it could have been done that way, but I have not been too fond of that measure. I sometimes think that when you use that scheme you get a measure of originality, perhaps, but it is a useless originality. You give a strong weight to some pretty bizarre responses.

C This could be argued. One can say, "Here is the original person, but really I don't like him. He is no good because he comes up with wild ideas." Originality as such need not have anything to do with a value dimension. But you don't seem to like a person with just originality; you want value in there too, and that might be a separate thing.

C You can still eliminate your irrelevant responses and just not count them in scoring for originality.

C We may be talking from another point of view than that of the Air Force, which is interested in what can predict school grades and so on. How did this originality measure relate to the Air Force's needs, and why was it in there? Why was the Air Force interested in originality?

S Because previous work indicated that this measure might help predict school grades in the Air Force and performance of research and development officers in the field. The Air Force wouldn't care whether it is called creativity or whatever if it adds useful prediction to measurable qualities in which the Air Force is interested. If it works, of course, the Air Force can use it in its battery of predictors.

C We found that scores for originality, not saying how the test was used, from Plot Titles does predict achievement scores in addition to the prediction obtained from aptitude tests.

S The first study reported in this chapter indicates that these instruments do add to the prediction of school grades. They don't seem to do as much as the usual aptitude measures, but they do add significantly.

STUDY 4. AN ATTEMPT TO IDENTIFY ACCURATE RATERS OF ORIGINALITY

Studies involving ratings as criteria typically use the mean of a number of assigned ratings as the number against which predictor scores are correlated. If we assume that there are individual differences in the ability to rate—that is, that people differ in their objectivity, in their susceptibility to the halo effect, in their leniency, and so on—then our usual practice of taking the mean of a group of ratings to represent our criterion may have a built-in logical fallacy. It may well be that exactly those ratings which are farthest from the mean in a distribution of rating scores are the ones which are most accurate, and that by using the mean of this distribution of scores we weaken considerably the power of the criterion measure. All the foregoing, of course, assumes that we can identify the accurate raters in a group. This study is an attempt to do just that.

When we talk of the accuracy of a rater, we mean his accuracy in terms of something else. In other words, we need an outside anchor for establishing a rater's accuracy. In this study, the anchor was provided by a set of vocabulary test scores. The test was taken by everyone in the group, and then at a later date each person in the group estimated the score that each other person made on that test. By working with difference scores between actual and estimated performance on the vocabulary test, we can locate the persons in each rating group who are the most accurate at estimating their peers' vocabulary.

If we can assume that whatever quality makes for accuracy in guessing peer performance in vocabulary is generalizable to rating originality, then we can expect correlations between originality tests and ratings assigned by more accurate vocabulary estimators to be higher than similar correlations between the same originality tests and ratings assigned by less accurate vocabulary estimators, since the magnitude of a validity coefficient depends upon the "goodness" of both the predictor and the criterion.

The originality tests in this study were the following:

1. Guilford's Consequences Test.
2. Guilford's Brick Uses Test.
3. Word Meanings C.

The sample is 425 aviation cadets. The study is now in the final stages of analysis, and we should have some results soon. If these results are favorable, we will launch a much more ambitious study of the variance in rating scores.

I might add just a few words on this last thing that I mentioned. We ran a very simple little preliminary study in which we were investigating the same problem of goodness of ratings. Following about the same design, we found, using basic airmen who were rating "carefulness" and giving carefulness tests to these same airmen, that when we separated their ratings according to goodness and badness, again based on their estimate of pure vocabulary, the set of correlations between the five tests we used and the ratings went up in every instance in the good rating group. So we have some confidence in what we are going to get from this other study.

C Do I understand correctly that when you identify the raters who judge this vocabulary ability effectively, you will assume that these people can also more effectively rate creativity?

S Yes! We are assuming this because we feel that much of what goes into a rating or an estimate is a person's ability to perceive another person in the first place. He has to be able to observe other people and understand them. He must be less susceptible to halo effect and other rating errors.

C Isn't this empathy that you are trying to measure in your raters?

C Yes, but it seems to me that the creativity area itself is so nebulous compared to something like rating someone's vocabulary ability that I just wonder how related these two rating faculties would be.

S We have given up any hope of getting ratings of creativity. Creativity is something which is so dependent upon factors other than originality—upon the circumstances and many other things. Ours are ratings of originality. Originality, I think, can be defined as unusualness. Creativity would be almost impossible to define. This is one reason why we gave it up.

C In dealing with vocabulary, a very specific thing, there is not much question whether a person knows a word—it is more like a mathematical comparison in contrast to the open-ended, divergent type of thing. But even though you narrow down to originality, originality to you and to me is different.

S It is defined in the rating scale.

C   But for each individual there are differences, so I am very doubtful about the degree of correlation between the two rating abilities.

S   If we can get positive results from our study, they will indicate still more the power of this particular approach. Let me again emphasize that we have a little pilot study already completed which indicates that the people who best estimate vocabulary score (a very objective score) can also best rate carefulness, which is another nebulous concept. So we have quite a bit of hope for this last study.

C   In this pilot study is there a difference between those who are careful and those who have high vocabularies? That would be a crucial consideration, I think, because you are saying that there is no halo effect or that it is not a very strong one, because people can be differential. People can be good at rating this and be good at rating something else, separately. On the other hand, some people may be described as good at rating but this only means that they are reliable. If you ask them to pick people who are good, you can use the word "careful," "intelligent," "creative," "original," or "unusual," but they will name the same people all the time.

S   We looked into that. In the pilot study that we did there was no relationship between vocabulary and carefulness.

C   What kinds of raters were eliminated—the ones with low variance who simply did not perceive individual differences in the group? Did you compare the variance of good raters with the variance of poor raters?

S   Not in the pilot study. We plan this for the complete analysis that we are going to do. We are going to get into every possible phase if this one works.

C   I suspect that some people simply do not see individual differences and rate everybody about the same, in contrast to other raters who spread out their ratings.

S   This is a very important part of rating variance. It may be that you can train people to observe a little more carefully, train them to see people differentially.

C   Some raters stick their necks out by giving extreme ratings, while others are cautious.

C   Even if there are differences in the ability to rate in various areas, there might be a general rating ability, such as you are postulating.

C   I think the evidence is against a universal ability for rating. In the Woodworth and Thorndike experiments on judgments and perceptual phenomena, rating abilities were found to be very specific.

S   These were perceptions across different sense modalities. We are talking about only one perception. I wouldn't expect visual perception to generalize to "people perception," or anything like that. We are using one perceptual ability in this: the ability to perceive other people, complex though it may be.

C   We have hypothesized six different abilities to cognize social behavioral events. If we are right, there will be six different, relatively independent factors, plus a lot of specifics.

S   We are going to look into that.

C   There was a little research on the F scale wherein people were trying to predict F-scale scores on other people whom they talked to briefly. The one finding I remember is that people tend to predict that other people are like what they themselves are. If they are high F-scale people, they tend to think other people are. If they are low F-scale people, they tend to think others are low on the F scale.

C   Our results may be contrary to what other people have found. They do indicate that there is some generality in ratings, so maybe your approach will prove to be all right after all.

S   So far the discussion has sounded as if this were highly unlikely.

C   Aren't these questions being raised now the things that you are going to try to find the answers to? You said that you were assuming there was a general factor. Someone said you were postulating it. Aren't you hypothesizing it?

S   Yes. We are testing this hypothesis. It is not a rigorous statistical test, but to me it is a test. If all the correlations go up when they should go up (according to the hypothesis), and go down when they should go down, to me this is a test. We're making a prediction and then seeing whether the results come out.

C   This doesn't test for how many dimensions there may be in this field.

S   Not in this study, but in our forthcoming, larger study we are going to go into all kinds of phases of it. We're going to factor-analyze several different sets of data we get from it. We have even figured out a measure of the "halo effect," and we're going across several different kinds of human characteristics. We're going to get tests, estimates, and ratings on these characteristics, back and forth.

C   So you think that you will have more basis for interpreting than some of us felt you did when you started out by calling this a creativity rating.

S   A creativity rating? I think that I called it an originality rating.

C   There is an important point behind this investigation whether or not this particular method of analysis yields it. Recognizing the difference among raters and their ability to discern originality is very important. As an aside, at one point when we were preparing manuals for the scoring of the Unusual Uses and Plot Titles tests, we decided to make up what we called a recognition-of-originality test. We simply took the responses on Unusual Uses and Plot Titles scored as 5's versus those scored as 1's, made various pairings of them, and put them into a format which could be objectively scored. The subject's task was to say which of the two responses was more original, so that we had a subjectively scored test for measuring the ability of raters to recognize the original responses. I attribute part of the relative success of some of our studies in using this test to the fact that we picked raters who themselves were highly original. Emerson remarked that the next thing to an original person is the person who recognizes an original person. I think that this is quite an important point. In studies where one is putting a lot of effort into the prediction end in the data analysis, frequently the real weak point is the criterion. What that boils down to is your ability to select raters who are going to tell you when a genuine instance of the thing you are looking for is occurring.

C   This has been a provocative paper which has stirred discussion on many of the important issues in creativity research.

APPENDIX. DESCRIPTION OF VARIABLES IN THE HONDO STUDY

CREATIVITY BATTERY

1. *Color-Form C.*   This is a modified version of the original Stroop test. Each item of this test is the word "red," "yellow," "blue," or "green" printed in some color other than the color spelled out. For instance, the first item is the word "yellow," printed in blue ink. The subject is required to respond by checking on an answer sheet the color of the ink in which the word is printed, regardless of what the word says. We feel that performance on this test is related to a flexibility which is a likely component of originality. No reliability estimate.

2. *Word Meanings C.*   This test is composed of ten items such as "Which of the following are carpentry terms?" Each item is followed by fifteen alternatives, at least one of which is obviously a carpentry term (such as "hammer") and at least one of which is not a carpentry term (such as "tiger"). The other alternatives could be interpreted either way (such as "oak"). The subject is required to mark all the alternatives which he feels belong in the stated category. His score is the total number of alternatives marked. We believe that this test indicates a subject's conceptual complexity, which has been demonstrated by Barron to be related to originality. Odds-evens reliability, corrected by Spearman-Brown formula, is .87.

3. *Brick Uses.*   One of the Guilford creativity instruments, this test requires the subject to list as many uses for a brick as he can think of in 10 minutes. The test can be scored in a number of ways. The score used in this study was the number of different categories (construction, ballast, etc.) the subject mentioned. We consider this to be an originality measure. No reliability estimate.

4. *Omnibus Opinion Survey—Complexity Scale.*   This instrument is an inven-

tory-type test requiring the subject to agree or disagree with 150 statements. Six scores are derived, one of which is "complexity." The complexity key consists of 22 items. Odds-evens reliability, corrected by Spearman-Brown formula, is .44.

5. *Imagery Clearness.* Each of the 36 items on this test requires the subject to compare the strength of a visual image with that of a tactual or kinaesthetic image (for instance, he may be required to indicate which image is stronger, "a red rose" or "the feel of running your fingers over a towel"). The tendency to choose the tactual or kinaesthetic image is supposed to be indicative of ego strength, which, in turn, should be an important component of the creative personality, in its continuing struggle with more conservative opinion. No reliability estimate.

6. *Flanagan Creativity Test.* A multiple-choice test of ingenuity in solving stated problems.

APTITUDE BATTERY

  7. *Vocabulary* (Project Talent #102).
  8. *Visualization 2* (Project Talent #281).
  9. *Arithmetic Reasoning* (Project Talent #311).
  10. *Clerical Checking* (Project Talent #430).

(Reliabilities for ninth- and twelfth-grade boys and girls for these tests and for the Flanagan Creativity Test can be obtained from page 38, *Project Talent, Counselors' Technical Manual for Interpreting Test Scores.* Reliabilities range from .638 for ninth-grade girls on the Flanagan Creativity Test to .815 for twelfth-grade boys on Visualization 2.)

CRITERION

School-grade average for the school year 1959–60.

chapter 20 Creativity and Individual Differences in Criteria

Thomas B. Sprecher, Engineering Research Center, Western Electric Company

S   The title of my report, "Creativity and Individual Differences in Criteria," has a significant omission: it is *not* yet "Creativity and *Patterns* of Individual Differences in Criteria." In the near future, I hope to find out what kinds of patterns there are in these individual differences among criteria as measured by different approaches. At present, all that I am showing is the individual differences in criteria which exist, and some of the consistencies and inconsistencies in them. To answer Hyman's and Mednick's question to Calvin Taylor on the latter's presentation of the criterion problem, I anticipate that there are a few characteristics, perhaps in the order of 20 to 30, which can describe what individuals mean by creativity, effectiveness, success, what have you.   I believe that there will be some restriction in the number of concepts entering into the overall meanings of these various terms. When you get individuals combined, however, you obtain the complexity, and the wide range of things that can relate to criteria, which Taylor also showed amply in his studies.

Before I present the four kinds of data which I have collected and want to discuss, let me sketch briefly the background of the study. Western Electric has 130,000 employees, about 12 major plant locations, and thousands of engineers. Our study was conceived to help the Engineering Research Center devote some time to a study of its engineers in order to find out what effectiveness means. The company wants us to apply whatever tools psychology can contribute to discovering the meaning of effectiveness. With my background of interest in creativity, I have taken this opportunity to collect information which is related both to effectiveness, the company's general concern, and to creativity, to see what the contrast between these terms can show by shedding light on each other.

Let me now switch to the data, which have been obtained on approximately 70 engineers (in some cases we have more and some less), and describe our four different kinds of data. The first data are concerned with peer descriptions on 12 characteristics which I reported at the 1959 conference (Sprecher, 1963) and which are intended to identify many of the major kinds of behavior contributed by outstanding engineers. This following list is not all inclusive, certainly, but it is intended to include most of the major variables: (1) shows skill in reporting results to others, (2) persists in his attempts to get results, (3) likes to work on unusual and challenging problems, (4) tries to analyze a situation into its factors, (5) is able to reach a decision on his own, (6) seems to have many ideas for any given problem, (7) usually carries out his work energetically, (8) generally shows that he knows his subject matter, (9) maintains friendly relations with his co-workers, (10) sees what may happen and is ready for it, (11) often develops original approaches to problems, (12) develops valuable and worth-while ideas.

Each of the above twelve behavioral characteristics used in describing engineers was typed on a separate page, and below it each man in a department was given a list of his peers. On the first page he was asked to rate them on a scale from 0 to 10 as to how much of the characteristic "shows skill in reporting results to others" each of these men had. He could use any part of the 11-point scale he wanted to, and he could rate everyone high or everyone low or spread the scores out. On the second page, again a scrambled list of his peers was given, this time to be rated from 0 to 10 on "persistence," and so forth. Months later we went back to the same men who had described their peers on these 12 ratings and asked them to describe their peers on two separate pages: on the first, "How effective are these engineers on their jobs?" and on the second, "How creative are these engineers?" These global criteria on effectiveness and creativity were deliberately not defined. Specifically we wanted to find out what these engineers meant by the two words, "effectiveness" and "creativity."

A third kind of "job description" data was collected, essentially in the same form as above only in this case the words, "Creativity on my job needs a man who . . ." were substituted. A man is describing his own job only, not the jobs of others in his department. The supervisors of these engineers were also asked to describe their men's jobs on the same forms, but these supervisors described the jobs not from the point of view of creativity (because we had already asked too much from them), but solely from the point of view of effectiveness. We first asked each supervisor to say how many jobs there were in his department, and then asked him to describe job A on one page, job B on the next page, and so on.

The fourth kind of data is "critical incidents," which were extremely difficult to collect, by the way. We have ended up with only four supervisors, whom we have contacted over a period of two to four months, sometimes as often as once a week, sometimes as infrequently as once every four weeks. No more instructions were given than, "What are some of the things that have pleased you or displeased you about the men who report to you?" For two or three of these men, we recorded incidents just by writing down their answers; for one in particular we had a tape recorder so that we could get more accurate descriptions of his actual words in reporting these incidents. The incidents were then classified by me to point out the individual differences I saw among supervisors.

The first kinds of data to report are reliabilities. For the "job description" form readministered over intervals of two to five months, the test-retest reliabilities generally ranged from the .30's into the .80's.[1] Some of these reliabilities are not as poor as they might seem because the jobs change over a period of two or three months, and these reliabilities involved a period of four months. Also the number of variables was only 12, so that if one variable changed significantly, this would markedly lower the correlation. I am not contending that these reliabilities are good, because one of my conclusions will be that we need more reliability in our data in order to work with individuals.

Test-retest reliabilities for global ratings are better, as we might expect, generally ranging from the .50's to the .90's.[2] Although these are more stable measures, this does not necessarily mean that they are good, because perhaps the raters are stubborn or blind, rather than admitting new data to affect their perceptions.

The reliabilities for the "description of engineers" form were not high.

---

[1] The distribution of the reliabilities for effectiveness scores were 3 in the .80's, 1 in the .70's, 1 in the .60's, 4 in the .50's, 2 in the .40's, 1 in the .30's, and 1 approximately zero. The reliabilities for creativity scores were 2 in the .80's, 4 in the .60's, 2 in the .50's, 1 in the .40's, 2 in the .30's, and 1 in the .10's.

[2] The distribution of reliabilities for global ratings of effectiveness consisted of 1 in the .90's, 2 in the .80's, 8 in the .70's, 2 in the .60's, 1 in the .40's, and 1 in the .10's. For global ratings of creativity, there were 2 reliability coefficients in the .90's, 3 in the .80's, 4 in the .70's, 3 in the .60's, and 1 in the .50's.

The modal point here is in the .50's for peer ratings of engineers.[3]   Supervisors as a group were not much better, which is surprising but, I think, important.[4]   The total number of men who reported to supervisors was no more than 16 for any one supervisor.   Even with groups of as few as 6 to 10 men, a supervisor may not know his men reliably.   Interestingly enough, we can find out *where* the low reliabilities occur on the "description of engineers" form.   Do they fall down on specific variables such as "planning," "personal relations," or what have you?   These data will be interesting to us in our further work.

The next coefficients are correlations within each man's ratings of his own job on effectiveness and creativity.   John Doe rated his own job on effectiveness, and John Doe also rated his job on creativity.   Does he see these concepts the same on his job?   For some people the correlations are .90; the concepts are highly similar.   In contrast, others (five of them) had correlations of −.40.   Since the rest varied all up and down,[5] the obvious implications are that for some people these concepts are almost identical, whereas for others they are quite different or even negatively related and somewhat opposite in meaning.   We cannot assume either that creativity is different from effectiveness or that it is the same.   Any individual, since he is likely to be an "expert" on what he does in his job, may disagree with you.

Now, here is an interesting contrast.   When we switched from John Doe's ratings of his job to his ratings of other men on effectiveness and on creativity, does he see others in his group whom he rates high in effectiveness as also being creative people?   The answer is, by and large, yes.   We have already learned that when he considers his own job, where he knows most about what goes on, where he has his own intimate day-to-day knowledge of what he does and what these terms mean to him, he can generally discriminate between effectiveness and creativity. But when he switches to rating other people on their jobs, where he presumably knows less, these concepts tend to merge.[6]   This does not

[3] For peer ratings one reliability coefficient was found in the .80's, 2 in the .70's, 5 in the .60's, 6 in the .50's, 1 in the .40's, 3 in the .30's, 1 of approximately zero, and 1 negative reliability.

[4] For supervisory ratings of engineering, 1 of the reliabilities was in the .80's, 2 in the .60's, 1 in the .50's, and 1 in the .40's.

[5] There were 4 correlation coefficients in the .90's, 2 in the .80's, 5 in the .70's, 6 in the .60's, 14 in the .50's, 3 in the .40's, none in the .30's, 4 in the .20's, 4 in the .10's, 6 in the .00's, 1 between −.01 and −.09, 4 in the minus .10's, 2 in the minus .20's, 4 in the minus .30's, and 5 in the minus .40's.

[6] For peer ratings of engineers there were 9 correlations in the .90's, 12 in the .80's, 5 in the .70's, 11 in the .60's, 3 in the .50's, 4 in the .40's, 1 in the .20's, 4 in the .00's,

mean that they should merge but that they do merge in terms of these correlations, although, of course, there are exceptions.

C   When he rates other people, what we have isn't his estimate of other people's jobs but his estimate of other people, isn't it?

S   His estimate of their performance in global characteristics.

C   Well, that's a very different idea.

S   I'm not so sure that it is—I see your point, I think. But half the people said, "If I'm going to be creative on my job, it's an entirely different concept from being effective." Some of the correlations were zero or even negative, so we presume that these people mean, "If you want me to be effective in my job, I'll act this way; if you want me to be creative, I'll act this other way." Those are the results at one extreme, but most of the results were at the other end of the distribution, being .60 and above.

C   Yes, but you are still talking about people, and this is a much different idea, I believe, from speaking of their jobs and the characteristics the jobs require.

S   Oh, yes, the engineer could be doing two different things and doing both of them well simultaneously. This is a good point which I hadn't thought of.

C   Could he be thinking that way on his job—both rating other people and rating himself? The spread of correlations on the one is quite different from the spread of correlations on the other.

S   For instance, I might be highly creative, and I might be effective, but I've got to be creative in a different way on my job.

C   Yes, and the engineers could be saying the same things. They are not allowing so much of this opportunity in other people as they allow in themselves.

S   Yes, if I follow you correctly, I think that would be my original point. I think that Mullins is pointing out an alternative explanation.

C   My first reaction to this tremendous spread of correlations was that it's a defensive kind of thing. These are very different things, creativity and effectiveness. And when people are rating themselves and talking about their performances and their jobs with regard to these qualities, I wonder whether you'd get anywhere near the objectiveness of rating that you get when people are looking at other people.

S   People are not rating themselves here; they're rating their jobs. They say, "My supervisor doesn't want me to come up with new ideas,"

---

and 1 in the minus .40's. For supervisory ratings of engineers 2 correlations were in the .90's, 4 in the .80's, 1 in the .70's, 1 in the .40's, 1 in the .30's, 1 in the .20's, and 1 in the .10's.

and this varies with supervisors, from man to man. Some say, "My job is to be creative" (incidentally, the supervisor might not agree with them).

C   Do you know of any evidence of how much response sets enter into these ratings?

S   A single set of the mind could account for the person who says that effectiveness and creativity are the same thing on his job, because he does not discriminate. Such a mind set would not account for the person who says that creativity and effectiveness are quite different on his job and are independent concepts.

C   There are people who make wide distinctions between concepts and people who do not distinguish.

S   I don't think that this is necessarily a response bias. But I suppose that you could look at it that way.

C   Did you get any other information about these jobs and the extent to which people are accurately describing their jobs? That is, "My job requires creativity in order to be effective;" or "My job does not require creativity in order to be effective." Is there any way of looking at the different jobs that would tell you whether or not the people who made these evaluations are judging accurately?

S   You mean is there anything outside of this that would say whether they are right or wrong? There are supervisors to whom we have gone for such data. The supervisors may not agree with the men on these points, but I have not explored that as yet. In a couple of instances, I've gone back to these men, shown them their data, and said, "What do you think about this? Why do you agree that creativity and effectiveness are the same on your job?" One man said, "Because I am working in a new area that has never been explored before, and there is no literature. I have to be creative." The supervisor did not agree.

C   But what about the other one who says the opposite: "In order to be effective I must not be creative?" Have you gone back to him and asked him why?

S   I have gone back to one man who is—interestingly enough—judged by others to be creative, is judged to be outstandingly effective, and who on his job says that effectiveness and creativity are markedly different. He was a $-.40$ person in the correlations.

C   What did he say about this job that justified this psychology?

S   I didn't ask him. I just know that he recognizes the realities of the situation. Although, as I said, he is remarkably creative, he is surprisingly knowledgeable of what the supervisor wants and he gives it to him. He says, "The supervisor wants me, when he gives me instructions on Monday morning, to carry them out by Monday noon."

C This thoroughly describes the situation. Someone else would describe him as effective and creative, but he doesn't perform that way on the job.

S This man does not think that he is particularly creative. He says, "I'm just applying skills as anybody who has my particular background could do." Other people are impressed by his knowledge and creativity because he comes up with solutions they never thought of. He says he gets them right out of a textbook. Anybody who has any background or any specialty can do this, he claims.

Let us look at a few examples of how certain engineers rated their jobs on the 12 characteristics given at the beginning of this chapter. In the first case the engineer was describing his job in terms of the criterion variable of effectiveness.[7] This is a man who discriminates markedly in saying, "How important are these concepts for my job?" He says, "I need to be persistent and to be analytical in my job in order to be effective in my department. There's no need to be too interested in challenging problems or in original ideas, and I don't need to come up with a lot of valuable and practical answers." He does reject certain characteristics; in other words, he discriminates across job characteristics for effective performance.

Let us see how this same engineer described his job on creativity:[8] "If I'm going to be creative on my job [thank goodness he said this because it shows some consistency] I need to have original ideas, I need to have energy [which surprises me], I need challenging problems, I need to come up with many ideas, I don't need communication too much, I don't need job knowledge, and I don't need to plan—and valuable ideas is another need." Obviously this man discriminates markedly in these concepts on his job. If you are going to work with global impressions of other people or of the man himself, these individual differences in the rater and the ratee should be considered.

C Why did you say that "energy" surprised you? Because of the particular man or for some other reason?

S I may be wrong on this because energy relates to persistence. I don't think that necessarily the energetic person is the one who is creative. I've seen some creative people who look as if they're half

---

[7] On effectiveness on the 11-point scale this first engineer rated his job as 3 on "communication," 9 on "persistence," 2 on "challenging problems," 10 on "analyzes," 5 on "independence," 8 on "many ideas," 5 on "energy," 6 on "job knowledge," 10 on "personal relations," 7 on "plans," 5 on "original approaches," and 1 on "valuable ideas."

[8] In describing his job on creativity, the first engineer rated it across the same 12 characteristics listed above as 7, 8, 10, 8, 8, 10, 10, 5, 7, 5, 10, and 10.

asleep all the time, whereas others may be the hard-driving kind of individual.

C   Don't many engineers say that persistence to them is the essence of creativity?

S   Yes, and I would believe this, by the way. That is why I am starting to correct myself here in view of Parnes' comment, because energy is related to persistence.

C   Maybe it's the difference between energy and enthusiasm, the latter being an outward manifestation of energy—energy doesn't necessarily have to be visible. There is a mental energy in going about this work.

C   Are there elements in the pairs of patterns for a person which come out consistently the same?

S   There are some patterns with the same high points. Here are the results for a second engineer describing effectiveness on his job.[9] He is one of the outstanding people in the plant, rated high on creativity and effectiveness. "To be effective on my job," he seems to be saying, "all I need to do is to plan, to be persistent; I don't need to be energetic." This is one of the men who slouches around all the time—this is the way I would understand the dip on "energy."

In describing his job for creativity,[10] this second engineer said, "To be creative I need to come up with original ideas. Then I need to be analytical and to prefer challenging problems." Obviously, these concepts, creativity and effectiveness, are markedly different for this second engineer.

Now let me give the results for a third engineer who shows the more typical pattern—with one exception, which one of you asked about. "Everything is important for effectiveness on my job, except personal relations."[11] This man's career has been hampered (he is now fifty years old) because he does not get along with people. "Communication" is the one place where he is out of line in what might be the most typical of the patterns I see by inspection of the whole group of engineers. "Personal relations" is down, but everything else is high. In other words, most people do not discriminate except on "personal relations." I asked this man why personal relations are not important for effectiveness, and he said, "When I go down to X area and ask them to do some-

[9] This second engineer's effectiveness ratings across the above 12 characteristics are 8, 10, 8, 7, 8, 6, 5, 6, 8, 9, 5, and 5.

[10] This second engineer's 12 creativity ratings are 4, 5, 8, 8, 5, 7, 3, 8, 2, 5, 8, and 6.

[11] He rated his job in terms of effectiveness as 5, 8, 7, 7, 9, 8, 7, 7, 5, 6, 8, and 8. In terms of creativity he rated his job as 7, 9, 7, 7, 9, 7, 8, 7, 5, 7, 9, and 8, with his low spot again on 9, "personal relations."

thing for me, I'm an engineer; whether I'm a nice guy has nothing to do with what they do and with how effective I am in telling them what to do."

The second engineer, who is very creative and effective, thinks that personal relations *need* not be important. I asked him about this, and he said, "Well, there are some people who are effective, in spite of the fact that they do not get along with people. They are doing it the hard way."

C   When you speak about high and low on the patterns, are the various points on the scale departing at all? Or, for a given person, may using a rating of 7 be considered very high, whereas another person wouldn't consider the rating to be high unless it were 10?

S   Right. Most of these people are using the upper half of the scale, however. In comparison with the first engineer, who gave ratings as low as 3 and so on—not more than 20% of the men, if that many, ever dipped down that low in rating any aspect of their jobs. So these rating patterns have to be taken with a grain of salt.

Let me show you the supervisor of the third engineer, the one who has had his career hampered by lack of good personal relations. As the supervisor describes the third engineer's job in terms of effectiveness, he gives "personal relations" a rating of 9, as high as any in the job profile.[12]   On this job, the supervisor says, "The men have to be independent, have to know their job, and get along with people. They don't have to have many ideas, 'challenging problems' is down low, 'original ideas' tends to be low, and 'energy' is low." He stresses "independence," "job knowledge," and "getting along with people," and on all jobs under his supervision, "prefers challenging problems," "many ideas," and "original and valuable ideas" are low.

A supervisor is vitally important, then, in judging who is effective on his job; and when the above supervisor is approached by the psychologist, who will ask him which of his men are effective, the men who develop original ideas or who come up with many ideas are not going to be represented in the top group from his area. For the same type of jobs, another supervisor may disagree with him. Then, when the psychologist lumps together people in two different departments, disparate people are combined, and we have difficulty getting the kinds of correlation we would prefer. In spite of this, we do get correlations, we do get meaningful results. My thesis here is that we can get more and better results by working with the individuals who are doing the judging and the rating.

---

[12] The supervisor's ratings in terms of effectiveness of the third engineer's job were 7, 7, 6, 7, 9, 3, 5, 9, 9, 8, 6, and 7.

We usually wash out individual differences which, if kept separate by rater, would be very meaningful.

A fourth engineer's two descriptions of his job in terms of effectiveness and in terms of creativity were so similar that these two concepts mean nearly the same thing in terms of his job.[13]

For the last illustration on job differences, let me mention the man who is the bane of all psychologists: "Everything is important, sir!"[14] (*Laughter*)

C   In our study of Air Force scientists we have data similar to yours which have been partly but not fully analyzed. Among other things we are comparing four sets of profiles across a standard set of 17 characteristics: a scientist's ratings of his job, a scientist's ratings of himself, the supervisor's ratings of this same scientist's job, and the supervisor's ratings of the scientist.[15]

Let me go to the next kind of data. From each man in the study we gathered descriptions on these twelve "predictors" of the other ten (or so) men whom he knew. Later we got his rating of these same peers on effectiveness and then on creativity. Using these latter ratings as criteria, I can get multiple correlations, and obviously these multiple correlations will be high, because the number of observations I have approaches the number of variables. I am not interested here in multiple correlations, but I am interested in the individual differences in the beta weights (the best weights for each variable) that can be derived from this multiple-correlation paradigm. Indirectly and unknown to each engineer, he has given us a description of what he means by effectiveness as he rates his peers. Is it the same thing, or is it different from the description he was giving in rating his own job? Similarly, I can get these beta weights (standard partial regression coefficients) for creativity.

Let me first mention that I could do this on a *full* set of variables for only two supervisors, because only for those supervisors did I meet the minimum number of cases required in order to satisfy the mathematical requirements. In the beta weights for a full set of the 12 variables,[16]

---

[13] His twelve sets of ratings are as follows with each effectiveness rating being placed first followed by the corresponding creativity rating in parentheses: 5(7), 10(10), 10(10), 10(9), 9(8), 9(9), 8(9), 9(8), 10(9), and 10(9).

[14] All 12 of his ratings were 10, every one at the top of the scale.

[15] See Taylor, Smith, and Ghiselin, "The Creative and Other Contributions of One Sample of Research Scientists," in C. W. Taylor and F. Barron (Eds.), *Scientific Creativity: Its Recognition and Development*, John Wiley and Sons, 1963, p. 70.

[16] The beta weights in terms of effectiveness for supervisor B and supervisor D across the 12 characteristics in turn were: −.64 and −.47, −.62 and .72, .12 and .15, .35 and .03, .07 and −.68, −.37 and 1.43, .44 and −.08, .89 and .24, .46 and .08, .05 and −1.19, −.08 and 1.43, and .64 and −.80. Their beta weights in terms

there were several differences across supervisors. One immediate contrast is seen for "persistence." On effectiveness and on creativity for supervisor B, we have $-.62$ and $-.53$, respectively, while the figures are not minus but rather plus, as .72 and 1.21, for supervisor D. If we combine supervisors B and D, we would suspect that the people at the top for D would tend to be persistent, those at the top for B would tend to be not persistent, or at least not to emphasize this quality. By combining our data across supervisors, we would consequently wash out a difference that is differentially important, according to the supervisor. Maybe one way out is to get more individual estimates on these people. Let me belabor my point just once more. Variable 6, "many ideas," for supervisor B is $-.37$ on both effectiveness and creativity; for supervisor D it is 1.43 and 1.40 for effectiveness and creativity.

I'm not going to pretend that these results would be stable. We have noticed that there is unreliability in both of the measures that enter into these regression weights. But these are marked individual differences which might well account for some of the difficulties of using ratings effectively.

One more consideration is important, however. Some of these weights might be chance—not chance in the meaningless sense, but chance in the fact that supervisor D has an outstanding man working for him who comes up with ideas easily; consequently, the beta weight will be high for supervisor D. Maybe supervisor B has one man who is very effective, though he doesn't come up with many ideas yet, just a few good ones. So he throws the beta weight for "many ideas" down. Therefore these are empirical weights—the explanation is not necessarily that they are the supervisor's values or weights independently of the men—they might be situational.

Now let me describe a very interesting error that I made. You have all heard the story about the way you trap monkeys—in the field you put some food in a jar with a narrow neck and tie it there. The monkey sticks his hand inside and he gets a big handful of the food. But now he can't get it out because his fist is too big. He can't get away, so the hunter comes up and takes him. I was in that same situation, and I made like a monkey.

A statistician told me, "You have many men for whom you want to get these beta weights, but you don't have enough observations. Why don't you collapse some of your variables? In order to meet the mathematical requirements when your observations are only of 10 peers, you

of creativity were $-.23$ and $-.64$, $-.53$ and 1.21, .43 and -1.16, $-.49$ and $-.68$, $-.14$ and -3.20, $-.37$ and 1.40, $-.02$ and .81, .89 and .75, .45 and $-.30$, .12 and $-.82$, $-.62$ and .64, and $-.34$ and 1.50.

need to have only 8 variables, but you have 12. Why don't you throw out some variables?" I was the monkey; I couldn't throw any out but I combined some variables which I felt to be similar. I didn't want to throw away any of my numbers so I combined some, and I think that the lack of results which I got on those that I combined, versus the more instructive and meaningful results on those that I didn't combine, constitutes a very good lesson and perhaps an illustration of serendipity. In the case of creativity, I used 6 variables, the first 3 being combined ones and the last 3 being ones initially obtained in the list of 12 variables.

The first 3 are where I had my hand in the jar. I didn't want to throw away any of the three variables, so I combined here "communication," "analyzes," and "plans," put them all together, and called them "analyzes." Next under "drive" I combined "persistence" and "energy." Under "ideas" I combined four—"many ideas," "original ideas," "prefers challenging problems," and "valuable ideas." For "analyzes," the beta weights across 15 engineers ranged from $-.08$ to $+.21$; for "drive" they ranged from $-.29$ to $+.24$, and for "ideas" they ranged from $-.05$ to $+.17$. In contrast with the results for these three combined categories are those for the three variables where no combining was done (these are 3 of the 12 original variables which were left alone, untampered with). The beta weights for "independence" ranged from $-.67$ to $+.76$; for "job knowledge" they ranged from $-.95$ to $+1.77$; and for "personal relations" they ranged from $-.86$ to $+.82$. In the case of the first three beta weights for combined variables there were no individual differences that one would want to emphasize. But in the other three uncombined variables the individual differences emerge to show how important they are in the task of identifying creative men—or alternately to show the empirical weights for each characteristic in the men who were called creative.[17]

Let us now look at the test-retest reliabilities in coding and recoding the "critical incidents" data. These reliabilities are of interest for something other than the fact that their computation is a necessary psychometric demonstration. I initially coded these data into 16 categories and also more finely into 66 categories. For one supervisor I recoded these data after two days, for another after one month, and for two others two months later. Six of these eight reliability coefficients were in the .90's, one was .75, and one was .80. One reason that these reliabilities are generally in the .90's is that there was a marked spread

---

[17] Similarly, with effectiveness in mind, across 23 engineers the weights ranged from $-.03$ to $+.29$ for "analyzes," $-.48$ to $+.79$ for "drive," $-.11$ to $+.17$ for "ideas," -3.55 to $+1.36$ for "independence," -1.10 to $+1.47$ for "job knowledge," and -1.11 to $+2.12$ for "personal relations."

in the frequency of use of various categories of critical incidents. The more spread you have in your data, the higher your correlation can be, and I think this, indirectly, again illustrates my main point of individual differences.

My last set of data involves the percentage of the critical incidents classified into each of the 16 categories by each of the four supervisors. To highlight the findings I will present the results for only the 5 categories with the greatest differences among supervisors. For the "demands placed on the engineer by himself," supervisor A had 3%, B had 2%, C had 5%, and D had 6%. For "defining the problem," the range was from 9% to 3%. For "recognition of others, ethics, and social acceptance," the range was from 10% to 0%. For "quality of results" the range was from 5% to 17%. For "efficiency" the range was from 0% to 6%. Someone else might say these results show that there are consistencies across supervisors in how they see things. I prefer to emphasize the fact that these supervisors may well be looking for different characteristics in the men (these may be situational), but these differences in what is sought are going to affect the judgments they give of the men. For example, one supervisor may emphasize ethics, and a man who is highly rated has to be one who is fair, objective, and just.

In conclusion, I would like to draw some explicit points. I interpret these data as showing that:

Interpretation 1. Men differ widely in their *rational* descriptions of what is important on their own jobs (or on their subordinates' jobs).

Interpretation 2. Men differ widely in their empirical descriptions of what contributes to effectiveness and to creativity in other men's jobs.

Interpretation 3. Men differ widely in the extent to which they give equivalent descriptions to the terms "effectiveness" and "creativity."

I would expand these interpretations to say that:

A. Men should be allowed to define what such terms as "effectiveness" and "creativity" mean for them and for their particular situation.

B. Although the differences among men in such descriptions may be marked, the potential differences are even greater and indicate a need for a more inclusive list of variables which would permit more complex and varied meanings to be identified.

I also interpret the data to say that:

Interpretation 4. One man's *rational* and his *empirical* descriptions of what is important may not agree with each other, nor may two different empirical approaches agree.

Interpretation 5. The reliability of descriptions of others needs to be taken into account and improved.

My overall conclusion is that more *thorough* data on each *individual* rater need to be gathered to enable us to use accurately what he knows and for him to communicate to others.

The title of my report, I think, actually summarizes the point that I want to make now—simply that there are marked individual differences in several kinds of data: job descriptions, empirical regression weights, and critical incidents. I think that those are the three main kinds of data.

C   Does this suggest that ratings of people are bound to be complex? And that rating of products, perhaps anonymous products, may be a better way of getting at creativity?

S   We are doing an experiment on rating products, and I assure you that rating products is even worse than rating people. I have used examples of engineering products; I have shown these to 36 engineers and now to 16 supervisors in an analysis of variance design. The product which is rated lowest by one supervisor without any question is one about which another supervisor says, "Well, other people might not like this, but I can defend it because it is a real contribution to the company." The value systems which lie back of these judgments are markedly different. I think that they may be not too complex in the sense that only 20 variables can permit all the permutations that individuals wish, but the end results are markedly different.

C   May I make one suggestion: that perhaps there is confusion sometimes of value and perception. I did something like this a long time ago, and finally when we separated out at least the crude distinctions along which people placed products—for example, whether this would take 12 years to complete or 5 years, and so on—they agreed on a lot of things, but where they disagreed was as to what combination of things would be worth while. Their disagreement was in values, but not in perception of certain attributes of the object.

S   Right, this is the kind of disagreement I am finding here. These judgments are based upon coherent value systems which differ, even though the people objectively realize what the situation is. However, one man says, "When you buy a machine instead of building it yourself, this is very poor engineering." Another man says, "When you buy a machine instead of building it yourself, this is good engineering, because look how quick and easy it is. Why reinvent the wheel?" These are two different points of view, two value systems.

C   These are some of the products . . . ?

S   These are engineering products—machines, tools, equipment, material things that can be seen.

C   I was thinking more of, say, a series of ten different inventions that ten different people may have—put these together and have them rated for their creativity.

S   Well, I think that the same kind of thing would come up, really.

C   Even if you told the function that these things served?

S   Yes.

chapter 21 Types of Variables for Creativity Research

Alexander W. Astin, National Merit Scholarship Corporation

S I want first to talk very briefly about the kinds of variables that are being studied. It has occurred to me that there is a pattern to the sorts of operations which are being used by the different investigators to represent or measure creativity. I have drawn up a little table in which I try to portray these types of variables. This will not be any final word, but it seems to be one way of organizing or conceptualizing the kinds of research which have been discussed at the conference.

When we say we are studying "creativity," what is the nature of the variable we have in mind? I think that maybe these dependent variables can be classified in two ways (Table 1). One dimension is the

TABLE 1

Types of Dependent Variables

	Naturalistic	Manufactured
High social relevance (criteria)	I. Income, graduating from college, being hospitalized, etc.	II. Ratings (of job performance, social adjustment, etc.)
Low social relevance	III. Skin temperature, eyeblink rate, etc.	IV. Test scores (measures of traits, abilities, etc.)

"social relevance" of the variable. To what extent does the behavior (or product of behavior) which we are studying have intrinsic value or social relevance of some kind? In the criterion-centered approach we select for our focus of study a variable that is a socially relevant one. Social relevance is, of course, not so much of a dichotomy as I have portrayed it here (Table 1), but more of a continuum. Certainly we call criteria more socially relevant than other variables.

The second dimension for the variable is what I call "naturalistic" versus "manufactured" (Table 1). Psychologists are experts at manufacturing variables. In fact, it is my impression that psychologists overwhelmingly favor "manufactured, nonsocially relevant variables," and I'm speaking primarily here of "tests." Now certain exceptions to this would be achievement tests (where a high score would have some intrinsic social value), and tests which already have demonstrated predictive validity to socially relevant variables. In general, though, I think that tests can be considered both as manufactured and as having relatively low social relevance.

Examples of manufactured, socially relevant variables might be peer or supervisory ratings. That is, we don't have any creative product that exists in a form in which we can readily study it, so we manufacture what we think is a socially relevant variable through the use of observers or judges.

Concerning naturalistic variables, there are, again, two kinds: relevant and nonrelevant (Table 1). A naturalistic, socially relevant variable might be living or dying, dropping out of school or going on to graduate, winning a prize or not winning a prize, etc. Now the naturalistic, nonrelevant variables are more difficult to conceive of. Perhaps some constitutional characteristic, such as weight or body type, or some physiological response, such as eyeblink rate, would be less relevant than most variables. However, any naturalistic variable can probably be construed as socially relevant. We might add here that social relevance is, of course, nothing more than a value judgment. Bechtoldt (1959) said that by assigning "status" to a variable, it becomes a criterion. You can't "validate" a criterion in any empirical way; its validity is simply a matter of the value that you attach to it (Astin, 1964).

There is another classification which you could use to extend the table into another dimension: the method used to study the variable. We are all familiar with the distinction between correlational and experimental studies. Cronbach (1957) has discussed in detail the differences and similarities in these two approaches. However, there is a third category in between here that I would like to discuss: the "quasi-experimental" study. These are studies in which we attempt to draw experimental-like conclusions from correlational data. The possibilities here have, I think, never been exploited fully. We are, at National Merit, just beginning to see some of the potentialities in quasi-experimental designs.

Unfortunately most of the truly experimental work discussed at the conference has been done with "nonsocially relevant" variables. The reason is probably that it is very hard to assess socially relevant variables. Jablonski's work is perhaps an attempt to manipulate socially relevant variables, but I am inclined to wish that he would employ some control groups to evaluate the effects of his manipulations.

C Richardson, Bellows, and Henry did this and reported it in the 1959 evaluation of the National Science Foundation programs. The youngsters who were in the program were compared to those who were not. The ones in the program produced significantly higher than those who were not.

S As he describes it, Jablonski's program sounds like a kind of Skinnerian ideal where the manipulation has such an easily observed effect that you really don't have to worry about experimentation with controls.

I think that the method used has a great deal to do with the relevance of the results for practice. Certainly about the only immediate application to be made of the results of correlational studies is in selection and classification. This is so because correlations ordinarily cannot tell us very much about what can be done to people to change or manipulate their creativity.

The point that I am trying to make in raising the question of method, along with these observations about types of variables, is that the quasi-experimental designs make it possible to study socially relevant variables *in situ*. It is not necessary to mock up the dependent variable. Harmon, I suppose, is trying to draw some quasi-experimental inferences about his data; Drevdahl in the same way is attempting to make some experimental inferences about some nonexperimental data. Our college studies fall here, too.

Our concern, at National Merit, has been: how do we make quasi-experimental inferences? That is, how, without being able either to manipulate our subjects or to assign them randomly, do we assess what the college has done to the student? We have developed, we think, an experimental design which has the advantages of a matching design but does not at the same time suffer the consequences of regression effects, which are inevitable in matching designs (Astin, 1962b, 1963). Harmon and I, by the way, have an argument about this: he thinks that we still have regression effects.

We have been concerned with four problems in assessing the effects of colleges on students. The first and most important aspect is the criterion—what do young people do during and after college that is important and relevant, and how do we measure this? Holland has already discussed at some length our criteria of achievement.

A second problem concerns the fact that different colleges attract different kinds of students (Astin and Holland, 1962; Holland, 1959a). We have to find out, then, how colleges differ in their student "inputs."

A third problem is to define the college environment; that is, to define the salient features of the college which we might expect to affect the student behavior in question. We have done a factor analysis of college characteristics (Astin, 1962a), and Holland has already described our work with the Environmental Assessment Technique.

The final problem concerns the experimental design: how do we evaluate the effects of the environment on the student's behavior and at the same time control for differences in student input? So, in a sense, what we are trying to do is to put together information on student-input variables, socially relevant student performances, and the college environment, in such a way that we can learn something not only about what different colleges do, but also about how they do it and to whom they do it (the interaction problem). I won't go beyond that, but I think that there is a great deal of potential value in doing these quasi-experimental studies, primarily because they make it possible to investigate environmental influences on behavior more or less as the behavior occurs in its natural context. In other words, these designs make it easier to study naturalistic variables of relatively high social relevance.

C   Your presentation has reminded me of something that most people have forgotten if they ever knew about it, and that's a very important paper by Brunswick (1949) on representative design of experiments.

C   Your separation of variables into naturalistic and manufactured is intriguing. In science, in one sense all variables are manufactured by man. But maybe the crucial point is whether the manufactured variable very closely ties into, and thereby helps man to approximate, a particular natural phenomenon in which he is interested.

C   A lot of these things are extremely difficult to measure. We encounter this problem all the time in conducting creative seminars. How do you justify them if someone asks you?

C   How many patents, or what?

C   Right. We do not yet have any adequate way of actually measuring results. But those of us who are involved in these programs—and I'm sure the others will verify this—feel very sure that we are obtaining results because we get the feedback on an individual basis.

C   I like to disagree because I think that you can do both—can hit both ends of your problem.

C   I have seen a lot of creative programs in action. I have no doubts qualitatively that they get tremendous results. But because they are so effective, and because people who are immediately there think that they are so effective, it blocks almost any *attempt* to break down to find out the reasons why, because I am also sure that many other possible programs could be equally effective. Where it comes to a question of evaluation, I sometimes think that there is almost a dichotomy of interests. The experimenter would like to break the program down piecemeal and see what are the real contributing factors. I think that the other people who are offering the program and are sure it is going well resent certain kinds of piecemeal evaluations which might not actually give out the full flavor, so to speak, of the program.

C   I don't resent any evaluation, but I like it to be a realistic measure of what we are trying to do.

part V Creativity in Special Fields and Settings

chapter 22 The Creativity of Architects[1]

Donald W. MacKinnon, Institute of Personality Assessment and Research, University of California, Berkeley

S   In planning the study of creative persons made at the Institute of Personality Assessment and Research, architects were chosen for inclusion on the grounds that they might, as a professional group, reveal that which is most generally characteristic of the creative person. If an architect's designs are to give delight, the architect must be something of an artist; if they are to be technologically sound and efficiently planned, he must also be something of a scientist, at least an applied scientist. Yet, clearly, if one studies architects, he soon becomes aware that it does not suffice that an architect be at one and the same time artist and scientist if he is to be highly creative in the practice of his profession. He must also be to some extent businessman, engineer, advertiser, psychologist, author-journalist, psychiatrist, and educator.

To identify the most creative architects in the country for our study we turned to experts, first to five professors of architecture at the University of California (Berkeley), each of whom, working independently, nominated the 40 most outstandingly creative architects in the country. If there had been perfect agreement among the nominators, the panel would have supplied us with 40 names, the same 40 being

[1] The study of architects here reported has been jointly directed by Wallace B. Hall and the present author. This research has been supported in part by funds granted by the Carnegie Corporation of New York. The statements made and views expressed here are, however, solely the responsibility of the author.

nominated by each panel member. Actually we were given 86 names. Of the 86, 13 were nominated by all five members, 9 were nominated by four, 11 were nominated by three, and 13 by two, while 40 were individual nominations by single panel members. Subsequently, each panel member rated the creativity of those not nominated by him originally, provided that he knew them well enough to do so. In many cases panel members knew these other architects and were able to rate them.

In making their nominations, panel members agreed upon the following definition of creativity: originality of thinking and freshness of approaches to architectural problems; constructive ingenuity; ability to set aside established conventions and procedures when appropriate; a flair for devising effective and original fulfillments of the major demands of architecture, namely, (1) technology (firmness), (2) visual form (delight), (3) planning (commodity), and (4) human awareness and social purpose. The first three of this list were from Sir Henry Wooton in architecture and the fourth was from Maslow, a psychologist.

Each panel member rated, on a five-point scale, the creativeness of each nominated architect in meeting each of these four conceptualized demands of architecture, and wrote a summary evaluation of the architect's work, indicating why he had nominated him. On the basis of their mean ratings on these dimensions and the summary evaluations of their work, the nominated architects (known to us at this stage only by disguising code numbers) were listed in the order in which we would invite them to participate in the study. To get 40 acceptances 64 invitations had to be sent out.

Were the 40 who were willing to be assessed more or less creative than the 24 who declined, or were they indistinguishable in their level of creativeness? When the nominating panel's mean ratings of creativity for each of the 64 architects were converted to normalized standard scores and the means for the 24 versus the 40 were compared, they were found to be identical: 50.0 (S.D. 9.9) for the 24 not assessed, as against 50.1 (S.D. 9.5) for the 40 assessed architects.

As a further check on this point, 11 editors of the major American architectural journals, *Architectural Forum*, *Architectural Record*, *Journal of the American Institute of Architects*, and *Progressive Architecture*, ranked the 64 invited architects from the most to the least creative. In doing so, however, they used a different overall definition of architectural creativity. When their rankings were converted to normalized standard scores, the mean of 51.9 (S.D. 8.0) for the nonassessed 24 was slightly higher than that of 48.7 (S.D. 6.1) for the assessed sample, but the difference is not statistically significant.

We make no claim to have studied the 40 most creative architects in the country. We are assured, however, that the 40 whom we did assess are, as a group, indistinguishable in the level of their creativeness from the 24 who declined to be studied.

Having asked editors as well as professors to estimate the level of creativeness with which our assessed architects worked, we thought it only fair to let the architects themselves judge one another's creativity. The circles of Figure 1 show that the editors' ratings of the creativity

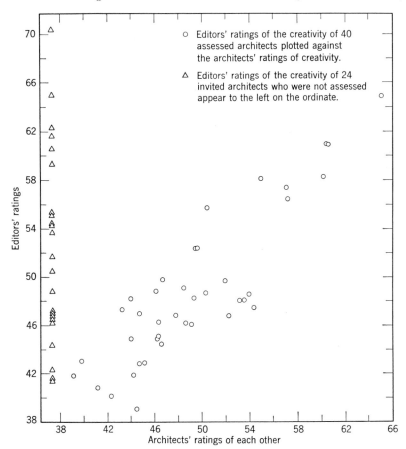

Figure 1 Scatter plot of relationships between editors' ratings of architects and architects' ratings of each other.

of the 40 assessed architects correlate +.88 with the architects' ratings. The 24 triangles at the left, each representing one of the architects who did not choose to be assessed, compared with the circles, show how the editors rated the creativity of the nonassessed architects relative to the

40 who were assessed. You will not be surprised to learn that the architect who towers head and shoulders above all others and regrettably chose not to be studied (the triangle at 70) was Frank Lloyd Wright. Of the 24 architects who escaped us, 13 were above the mean of 50 for all 64, while 11 were below. The distribution of the triangles graphically illustrates what I have already reported, namely, that though the mean rating of creativity of the nonassessed creatives is slightly higher, it is not significantly different from the mean rating of the creatives whom we were able to study.

To have limited our study to the assessment of 40 architects each of whom was recognized as highly creative would not have permitted us to say anything with confidence about the personality correlates of creativity, for the distinguishing characteristics of this sample—and there were many that we found—might well have nothing to do with their creativity. Obviously the design of our study required that the profession of architecture be widely sampled beyond the assessed 40 in order to discover whether and to what extent the traits of creative architects are characteristic of architects in general or peculiar to those who are highly creative.

To this end the *Directory of Architects*, published in 1955, was searched in order to select two additional samples of architects both of which would match with respect to age and geographic location of practice the assessed sample of 40. The assessed sample I shall now call Architects I. The first of the supplementary samples, which I shall call Architects II, is composed of 43 architects each of whom met the additional requirement that he had had at least two years of work experience and association with one of the 64 originally nominated and invited creative architects. The other additional sample, which I shall label Architects III, is composed of 41 architects none of whom had ever worked with any of the nominated creative architects.

By selecting three samples in this manner we hoped to tap a range of talent sufficiently wide to be fairly representative of the profession as a whole. In a first attempt to determine whether we had achieved this goal, it seemed reasonable to assume that an approximate and rough measure of an architect's creativeness might be the amount of space devoted to his work in the architectural literature. Accordingly two indices of publicity or prominence, and by inference also indices of creativity, were computed: (1) a weighted index of the number of articles by or about each architect and his work referenced in the *Architectural Index* of the literature for the years 1950–58, and (2) a weighted index of the number of pages devoted to each architect and his work during the same period.

C I'm not sure there's an analogy here, but we had a factor called "visibility" for our scientists concerning how well known one was by name and in person among scientists. I wonder to what degree your publicity index is really along this line. We never quite thought of this item as an index of creativity, and it was a separate factor from our four or five creative-like factors.

S I'm going to point out that this leaves much to be desired as a measure of creativity, and we went on to get what we thought were valid criteria measures. However, in the first instance it seemed to us of some interest to determine the extent to which the architects in the three samples had received a good deal of attention and space in the architectural literature. It is certainly visibility, but I would, myself, be inclined to think that it is also at least a very crude index of creativity because the architectural journals are devoted to describing the innovations and the original work of people in the field. I'm not sure that this would be equally true for people in other professions, but I think in architecture it is particularly true.

Mean scores were computed on these two indices of publicity or prominence for each of the three samples. The mean score for the weighted index of articles by or about each architect was 131 for Architects I, 20 for Architects II, and 3 for Architects III. The mean score for the weighted index of the pages devoted to each architect and his work was 97 for Architects I, 13 for Architects II, and 2 for Architects III. On both indices Architects I are clearly superior to the other two samples. Architects II on both measures are between Architects I and III, but much closer to the latter than to the former.

Because of restriction of range of the indices in the other two samples, the next analysis is limited to Architects I. The editors' estimates of creativity correlate $+.59$ with the number of articles and $+.69$ with the number of pages devoted to the architects' work. The architects' estimates of their own creativity correlate $+.50$ with number of articles and $+.62$ with number of pages about them in the literature. The data leave no doubt that there is a high positive relation between the amount of publicity an architect gets and the judged creativeness of his work. One may wonder whether architects are judged to be creative because their work gets a lot of attention, or whether it is the true creativity of an architect that determines the amount of publicity he gets in the architectural journals. Whichever way it is, the question must certainly be a sobering one for architects and editors alike.

Valuable as the indices of publicity and prominence may be as first approximations, as I said above, they leave a good deal to be desired as criteria of the creativity of architects. In search of a better criterion for the total sample of 124, six groups of architects and experts on architecture were asked finally to rate on a seven-point scale the creativity of each of the architects comprising the total sample of Architects I, II, and III whom they knew well enough to judge. Ratings of creativity were made for varying numbers of architects by the 5 members of the original nominating panel at Berkeley, by 6 editors of the major architectural journals, by 19 professors of architecture distributed nationwide, by 32 Architects I, 36 Architects II, and 28 Architects III.

John Burchard at MIT suggested that the professors at Berkeley were probably a rather provincial group and that their judgments would not correlate very highly with the judgments of professors nationwide, so I suggested to him that he send me a list of professors of architecture whose judgment he valued (he's a very great authority in the field, as you know), and I sent off letters to his nominees. Nineteen of them undertook the task of rating the creativity of the architects.

The mean rating of creativity and the standard deviation for each of the three groups of architects were as follows: Architects I, 5.46 and 0.43; Architects II, 4.25 and 0.56; and Architects III, 3.54 and 0.74. The mean differences in rated creativity between groups I and II and groups II and III were significant beyond the .001 level and, of course, were even more highly significant between I and III.

Having demonstrated that the three groups do indeed represent significantly different levels of creativity, and that the entire sample shows a wide range of creativeness, we can examine data obtained in the study to discover the correlates of creativity and, more specifically for our concerns in this conference, the concurrent validities of the variables that are more highly correlated with the criterion.

Now unfortunately our data are not so extensive for Architects II and III as for Architects I. It's a pretty expensive operation to bring people from all over the country to Berkeley, put them up in a hotel, pay them an honorarium, and do everything else that is involved in a full assessment. So in the case of Architects II and III we merely asked them if they would participate in our study while remaining at home. We mailed them a battery of procedures which took some six or seven hours of their time to complete, and they returned it completed to us. Under these conditions, unfortunately, some tests—tests of performance, including intelligence tests and the like—could not be administered to Architects II and III. That is a most unfortunate shortcoming of our research. I wish that we could have administered all our tests to all three samples. Where the Architect I group experienced a three-day-long assessment, the other two groups, working independently and at home, spent some six or seven hours completing a selection of tests questionnaires, and inventories from our total assessment battery.

There is space to do no more than sketch a few of the highlights of our findings. We may note first that the self-images of the more creative and the less creative architects are markedly different. The adjectives checked as self-descriptive by 80% or more of one sample but by less than 80% of a contrasting sample are revealing. Architects I, in contrast to both Architects II and III, more often see themselves as inventive, determined, independent, individualistic, enthusiastic, and industrious. More often than Architects II, Architects I also describe themselves as having wide interests, and more often than Architects III they see themselves as artistic, progressive, and appreciative.

In striking contrast more than 80% of both Architects II and III, but less than 80% of Architects I, describe themselves as responsible, sincere, reliable, dependable, clear-thinking, tolerant, and understanding. In addition Architects II, more often than Architects I, see themselves as forgiving, kind, sensitive, rational, and alert; and Architects III more often than Architects I describe themselves as peaceable, good-natured, moderate, steady, practical, and logical.

C   This is going to make stinkers out of all of us.

S   It is clear that creative architects more often stress their inventiveness, independence, and individuality, their enthusiasm, determination, and industry. Less creative architects are more often impressed by their virtue and good character and by their rationality and sympathetic concern for others.

Not only do the more creative architects more often say they are inventive; they also more often claim to have made innovations in architecture. The number of innovations reported by architects for our total sample correlates +.36 with their rated creativity.

The self-assertive confidence which is so clearly reflected in the more creative architects' image of themselves is also seen in their performance on two of the IPAR scales: one, measuring self-assertiveness, the other, independence, correlate +.34 and +.43 with rated creativity in the total sample of 124.

Turning now to the self-reports which our architects have given us on structured inventories and questionnaires, let us consider the group profiles on the California Psychological Inventory (CPI) of Architects I, Architects II, and Architects III.

The profile for Architects III, the least creative architects, is a remarkably favorable one, and an unusually even one, too, with scores above the mean on all scales save one, Sy (sociability), which is just at the mean. The high points are on Ai (the drive to achieve in an independent fashion), Do (indicating dominance, persistence, and social initiative), and Py (indicative of interest in and responsiveness to the inner needs, motives, and experiences of others). The impression which the profile for Architects III conveys is of men who are good citizens, responsible, productive, sensitive, and effective.

In contrast, the profile of the highly creative Architects I is a much more uneven one, with striking dips as well as peaks. Eight of the 18 scores are at or below the mean of 50, while 10 are above the mean of 50.[2]

From left to right those scales on which Architects I score differently from Architects III (at or beyond the .05 level of significance) are as follows: the highly creative architects score higher on Sp (social presence), and higher on Sa (self-acceptance); lower on Wb (sense of well-being), lower on Re (responsibility), lower on So (socialization), lower on Sc (self-control), lower on To (tolerance), lower on Gi (good impression), lower on Cm (communality), and lower on Ac (achievement via conformance); but higher on Py (psychological-mindedness), Fx (flexibility), and Fe (femininity).

On the first cluster of scales, which are measures of poise, ascendance, and self-assurance, creative architects reveal themselves as dominant (Do); possessed of those qualities and attributes which underlie and lead to the achievement of social status (Cs); poised, spontaneous, and self-confident in personal and social interaction (Sp), though not of an especially sociable or participative temperament (low Sy); intelligent, outspoken, sharp-witted, demanding, aggressive, and self-centered; persuasive and verbally fluent, self-confident and self-assured (Sa); and relatively uninhibited in expressing their worries and complaints (low Wb).

But it is on the second cluster of scores, those having to do with responsibility, socialization, and self-control, that creative architects differ most widely from their less creative colleagues. Their scores reveal the creative architects to be relatively free from conventional restraints and inhibitions (low So and Sc), not preoccupied with the impression which they make on others and thus perhaps capable of greater independence and autonomy (low Gi), and relatively ready to recognize and admit self-views which are unusual and unconventional (low Cm).

C   Which distribution of scores did you have on the ratings for creativity for the total sample—bimodal or what?

---

[2] Out of the 18 scales in the CPI, in every case but one the mean score for Architects II fell between the means of Architects I and Architects III or equaled one of these two means.

S It was unimodal, almost symmetric, showing a slight negative skew.

C Were the majority of these differences significant?

S I've read the ones that were significant.

C I was going to ask the same question, as I was looking for a batting average. Since you indicated we should have tried this test in our study, what percentage of the validity coefficients or of the mean differences were significant?

S I'll repeat those scales on which the mean scores for Architects I are significantly different ($\leq.05$) from those of Architects III: Sp, Sa, Wb, Re, So, Sc, To, Gi, Cm, Ac, Py, Fx, and Fe. In other words, 13 of the 18 scales, 72% of them, discriminate between Architects I and III.

C One of the things that interests me here is that the syndrome which you report is indeed quite consistent with what Barron and Gough and you have been describing for years and with some of the stuff we and other people have found; that is, the impulsivity, the irresponsibility, the self-acceptance, and so on. Aside from what is an effective test and what maybe you thought should have been done in someone else's study (which I think is very debatable, frankly), there is this other very positive thing.

C We have a lot of common findings which at some time we ought to discuss.

C Whether the tests are efficient or not, there are two things, I think, which are very important that we tend to neglect. One is, What can be predicted effectively, efficiently? This is one kind of issue. Another kind of issue is, What does it seem to mean? Even if the tests are not very efficient, I would argue that we all ought to be a little more broadminded about using instruments concerning which we have a dim view at the time, especially when doing so can tie together everybody's work. I think that we tend to overlook this and focus solely in our own areas of interest a little more than we should.

C I might rise to my defense on our studies because probably the most convincing check in science is for different investigators to use different approaches and yet find the same thing.

S As for the next cluster of scales, creative architects, like architects in general, are strongly motivated to achieve in situations in which independence in thought and action is called for (Ai). But, unlike their colleagues, creative architects are less inclined to strive for achievement in settings where conforming behavior is expected or required or rewarded (Ac). In efficiency and steadiness of intellectual effort (Ie), however, they do not differ from their fellow workers.

Their scores on the last three scales reveal the creative architects as definitely more psychologically minded (Py), more flexible (Fx), and having more femininity of interests (Fe) than architects in general.

All but two of the scales that differentiate Architects I from Architects III are also significantly correlated with the criterion in the total sample of 124. The correlations of the following CPI scales were significant[3] with the rated creativity of 124 architects: Sp (social presence), +.18; Sa (self-acceptance), +.19; Wb (sense of well being), −.20; Re (responsibility), −.20; Sc (self-control), −.31; To (tolerance), −.21; Gi (good impression), −.23; Cm (communality), −.31; Ac (achievement via conformance), −.24; Fx (flexibility), +.24; and Fe (femininity), +.24.

C   Are the correlations between the CPI scores pretty high? If so, you have a rather general thing instead of several separate things that differentiate.

S   The median coefficient of the 11 × 11 matrix of scales which correlate significantly with the criterion was +.115.

If I may be permitted an explicit example, take Sc (self-control), Cm (communality), and Fe (femininity), which were the three scales having the highest correlation with the criterion, respectively, −.31, −.31, and +.24. The intercorrelations of these scales, contrary to the implication of the question, were Sc versus Cm, .00; Sc versus Fe, −.01; and Cm versus Fe, −.07. Clearly there is at least some independence among these three CPI predictors of the criterion.

Hypothesizing that certain combinations of scales might predict the criterion better than simple scores, several CPI indices were computed and their correlation with the criterion determined, but only one of these did a better job than the best single scale. The only two combinations that will be mentioned are those that best predict the criterion. The scale combination of Py (psychological-mindedness) minus Sc (self-control) plus Fx (flexibility) correlated +.36 with the criterion, and the combination of Sa (self-acceptance) plus inverted Gi (good impression) correlated +.28 with the criterion.

Finally, for the total sample of 124 architects the 18 CPI scales were selected for derivation of the best multiple-regression equation to predict solely from the CPI the criterion of the architects' rated creativity. The program employed, using the 704 IBM computer, was an iterative search in which a variable was added to the equation if the increment in predictive accuracy was significant at or beyond the .05 probability point, and in a like fashion any variable was dropped if by so doing the accuracy was not reduced by more than this amount. Thirteen of the 18

[3] A correlation of .18 is significant at the .05 level, and one of .23 is significant at the .01 level.

CPI scales were selected for retention in the multiple-regression equation. Scores yielded by the equation correlated $+.67$ with the criterion.[4]

C This, I think, is obvious from what you said, but I want to make it explicit. You used all 18 scales in the machine, so you're including some nonsignificant validities that came along some way or another (suppressor, etc.) and added a significant difference.

S That's right. We did the other thing, too—using only those scales that showed significant validities, and we got almost as high a value. We thought that it was a fairer test, though, to try out the entire set of scales.

The Myers-Briggs Type Indicator (Myers, 1958), as many of you know, is a test based largely upon Jung's (1923) theory of psychological functions and types. About two-thirds of the entire sample is identified by this test as introverts: 65% of Architects I, 67% of Architects II, and 63% of Architects III. As for their preferences for thinking or feeling, the three samples show no significant differences. Each splits close to 50-50, approximately half preferring thinking, the other half preferring feeling, as the function with which they evaluate experience. It is not surprising, then, to find that scores on the extroversion and introversion scales and on the scales for thinking and for feeling are not significantly correlated with the criterion, nor do they significantly differentiate the three samples of architects.

The three groups are, however, markedly different in their preferences for judging and perceiving and in their preferred perceptual modes: sensation versus intuition.

The majority of Architects I (58%) are perceptive rather than judging types. In contrast, 44% of Architects II, and only 17% of Architects III, show a preference for perception. Conversely, the percentage of judgmental types increases from 40% of Architects I, to 53% of Architects II, to 80% of Architects III. Mean scores on judgment and perception show a corresponding progression from group to group.

The three groups are even more strikingly different with respect to their preference for one or the other of the two perceptual functions: sensation and intuition. It may first be noted that, although only 25% of the general population score as intuitive on this test, more than half

[4] The beta weights in the multiple-regression equation for the CPI scales which predict rated creativity of 124 architects were as follows: $+.138$ for Do (dominance); $+.231$ for Cs (capacity for status); $-.390$ for Sy (sociability); $+.324$ for Sa (self-acceptance); $-.167$ for Re (responsibility); $+.190$ for So (socialization); $-.301$ for Sc (self-control); $-.172$ for To (tolerance); $+.218$ for Gi (good impression); $-.267$ for Cm (communality); $-.193$ for Ac (achievement via conformance); $+.215$ for Py (psychological-mindedness); and $+.257$ for Fe (femininity).

of each of the subgroups are intuitive types. But despite the fact that more than 50% of each sample are intuitive, the three samples are still markedly different from each other in the frequency with which they show a preference for intuition: 100% of Architects I, 84% of Architects II, 59% of Architects III. Conversely, the percentage of sensation types in the three samples increases from 0% of Architects I, to 14% of Architects II, to 39% of Architects III. Mean scores on sensation and intuition show corresponding progressions from group to group.

It is not surprising, then, to find that preference scores for judgment and perception and for sensation and intuition are significantly correlated with the criterion: S (sensation) $-.41$, N (intuition) $+.45$, J (judgmental) $-.29$, and P (perceptive) $+.41$.

The best multiple-regression equation to predict the criterion solely from the eight scales of the Type Indicator retains four of them: with their beta weights they are $+.306$ N, $-.125$ F, $+.292$ J, $+.568$ P. Scores yielded by this equation predict the criterion less well than does the CPI solution, the correlation being $+.52$, only seven points higher than the correlation ($+.45$) of the best single scale, intuition, with the criterion.

C   Has this test shown the same kind of things on your samples from other fields?

S   We have found very much the same sort of correlations among our several groups. All our groups—and we've had writers, mathematicians, research scientists, architects, a small sample of painters—score as perceptive types with the exception of the research scientists, who are judgmental. It is interesting that even in the research-scientist sample the score on perception correlates $+.25$ with creativity; although the majority of the research scientists are on the side of judging, the more perceptive they are, the more creative they are.

C   Did the first four scales—introversion and this kind of thing—fail to discriminate on your other groups as they did here?

S   The validities of introversion and extroversion, and of thinking and feeling, were essentially zero in all our samples.

S   On the Allport-Vernon-Lindzey *Study of Values* (1951), Architects I score highest on aesthetic and theoretical.[5] (We have obtained this same finding with creative persons in other areas as well, with scientists

---

[5] For Architects I the mean scores on the Study of Values scales were 50.8 for theoretical, 28.4 for economic, 56.2 for aesthetic, 29.8 for social, 40.0 for political, and 34.8 for religious. For Architects II the mean scores across the same six scales were 47.8, 35.9, 52.9, 29.9, 39.0, and 34.5; and for Architects III the means were 47.0, 38.4, 47.7, 29.0, 39.4, and 38.8.

slightly higher on theoretical, artists a bit higher on aesthetic, and mathematicians equally high on both.) It is interesting to note that, despite the success with which, as entrepreneurs, architects carry out their professional practice, their lowest-rated value is the economic.

The aesthetic and theoretical are also the two highest values for Architects II and III, but these values are less pronounced for them. Furthermore, the economic value, the lowest of all values for highly creative architects, is held significantly higher (at the .01 level) by Architects III and also by Architects II. Indeed, in the total sample of 124, the theoretical value correlates with the rated creativity of the architects +.18, the aesthetic value +.35, and the economic value −.48.

C   Weren't all the creative architects doing all right, anyway?

S   No, they weren't. We were pleased that they weren't, because we were afraid that there would be some tendency for the judges to nominate those who were having great success, and indeed there were some in the creative group who were obviously very successful financially. But we had three who, while they were recognized by the profession as being creative, did not have large firms and were actually hanging on by the skin of their teeth, financially.

C   Do you have information on the relation of these same six value scores to intelligence for noncreative people?

S   I don't think that we have it. Does anyone else have it?

C   It's very low. It doesn't amount to much.

C   One thing that I'm very curious about is whether different individuals are contributing to the high rating on theoretical as opposed to aesthetic, or whether it is the same individual. I think that it would be quite difficult to tell on this test, but it would be more interesting if the same individual profiles were high on aesthetic and theoretical.

S   I can't say that everyone is high on both, but it's a clear majority trend. In the sample of architects theoretical and aesthetic values correlate +.26 (≤.01 level of significance).

C   Aren't they scored so that they're almost opposites?

S   No. The test is so scored that if a person goes up on some scales he has to go down on others.

C   I thought that the theoretical and the aesthetic groups were especially that way.

S   No, they're not. Allport and Vernon report that for males theoretical correlates with aesthetic −.10 and for females +.07, although in their manual they say that these two values are diametrically opposed. All I can say is that if these two values are in general opposed, as Allport and Vernon assert, then they're not opposed, or at least they're reconciled, in the case of our creative subjects, not only the architects but our other groups as well.   As I have already said, we find this elevation on these two scales in all our creative samples.

Only two scales were selected by the computer program for retention in the multiple-regression equation, and both with negative weights. The scores and weights are as follows: economic (−.516) and religious (−.171).   Scores yielded by the equation correlate +.50 with the criterion, doing less well than either the CPI or the Type Indicator.

Space permits mention of the predictive efficiency of only one more instrument, the phenomenal Strong Vocational Interest Blank (1959). Of the 57 regular and special scales of the SVIB which were scored, 40 are significantly correlated with the criterion, ranging from artist, which correlates +.59, to banker, which correlates −.66.

All scales of Group I (biological sciences), with the exception of veterinarian, are significantly correlated with the criterion: artist +.59, psychologist +.36, architect +.36, physician +.21, osteopath +.35, and dentist +.20.

Of the Group II (engineering and physical sciences) scales, two show significant correlations: physicist +.37 and chemist +.27.

Production manager (Group III) correlates −.31 with the criterion.

Every scale in Group IV (technical and/or skilled trades) shows a significant negative correlation with rated creativity: mathematics and physical science teacher −.18, printer −.19, industrial arts teacher −.25, farmer −.26, aviator −.27, carpenter −.27, vocational agricultural teacher −.28, forest service man −.28, and policeman −.52.

Only two scales of Group V (social service or welfare) show significant correlations and both are positive: city school superintendent +.18, and minister +.36.

Musician (Group VI) correlates +.40.

The single scale in Group VII (C.P.A.) did not correlate with the criterion, though the Senior C.P.A. scale in Group VIII did (−.46).

In Group VIII (business detail—administrative occupations in business) the significant correlates are: Senior C.P.A. −.46, purchasing agent −.50, accountant −.54, office man −.60, and banker −.66.

C   It all hangs together so nicely.

C   But from this you would wonder if the architects ever sit down at the drawing board at all.   Apparently they do.

C   I don't know much about the SVIB, but do you have any notion about the minister +.36 and religious, minus?   Is there any inconsistency there?

S   I think that the minister key probably picks up some interest in reforming people or educating them—changing them—and I think creative architects have a great desire to educate.

C A minister is a kind of entrepreneur of the soul. Social welfare is highly correlated with the persuasive, whereas religious value picks up a rather obvious thing, and this is a much more subtle scale.

S In Group IX (sales or business contact), sales manager correlates +.21 and real estate salesman −.32 with the criterion.

All scales of Groups X (verbal or linguistic) and XI (president— manufacturing concern) are significantly and positively correlated with rated creativity: advertising man +.42, lawyer +.44, author-journalist +.54, and president of manufacturing concern +.18.

Masculinity-femininity correlates −.48 with the criterion, and of the special scales the following show significant correlations: clinical psychologist +.35, and V.A. clinical psychologist +.34, but guidance psychologist −.27, industrial psychologist −.32, psychiatrist +.39, army officer −.23, and specialization level +.30.

The iterative search for best predictors among the SVIB scales selected 18 variables for retention in the multiple-regression equation. Scores yielded by the equation for SVIB scores correlated +.86 with the criterion of rated creativity.[6]

In this presentation I have had to limit myself to an overall description of our study of architects, discussing in detail only the nature of the criterion and the predictive efficiency of four structured personality inventories. I have chosen to stress the latter, since our findings suggest that personality inventories may not always run a poor third in the race to predict creativity, as Taylor and Holland (1963) have reported. (*Laughter*)

C Aren't these results about as favorable as have ever been found for the SVIB?

S I don't know. I'm not an SVIB expert.

C These are the best figures I have ever seen or heard of for predicting anything with the SVIB.

S We really had a most unusual sample, if I may say so. I'm prejudiced in favor of the architects, since this is the group I worked with and I have a strong feeling for them. I think that architects do have to be many things, not only artists and scientists, but also educators, businessmen, and what not. This may be one reason why we get so many

[6] The beta weights in the multiple-regression equation for the SVIB scales which predict rated creativity of 124 architects were −.59 for artist, −.70 for mathematician, −.26 for engineer, −.39 for policeman, +.31 for osteopath, +.86 for physicist, −.22 for mathematics-physics-science teacher, +.33 for social science high school teacher, +.13 for minister, −.34 for purchasing agent, +.13 for pharmacist, +.56 for sales manager, −.49 for life insurance salesman, −.24 for masculinity, −.19 for clinical psychologist, +.12 for experimental psychologist, −.24 for industrial psychologist, and −.29 for vocational counselor.

significant correlations with the SVIB. But more important, I think, is the fact that we really did get a good range of creative ability in this total sample.

C Let me say something both positive and negative. Our data with the SVIB and with my own instruments corroborate this right down the line, but we get smaller correlations because this is one of our best predictors. On the negative side, I would say that there is a lot of redundancy in the SVIB. There are only about five or six or seven factors at the most, so that the total number of things that we're talking about here that are really working is relatively small in terms of unique variance. Nevertheless our stuff gives very strong support to this— every finding and every trend—and it's very reassuring, because we are using a different population with a different set of criteria.

C I might mention in a very small voice that in taking people who were high on the Remote Associates Tests we had differences between them on the SVIB that are very similar to what you have referred. We find that the high scorers are characteristically high on artist, psychologist, mathematician, and the like, and the lows are characteristically high on farmer, high school teacher, office man, pharmacist, banker, carpenter, and policeman, which is something like what you were saying. The reason I mention this point is that one thing that we did do was to relate associative communality. We found that all these keys are very infrequent in the population in terms of being chosen very much, and that if you simply score this inventory for how probable it is for a person to get high scores on these keys, it becomes very improbable. You might want to look at it just in terms of what a person's tendency is to do something improbable, to choose things, or to end up on keys which are not frequent in the population, to do the original thing on the test. Perhaps this underlies a lot of the results.

S Throughout our protocols, these individuals describe themselves in an unusual fashion. They do the unusual thing, and that's why they're creative.

C In some ways these are verbal habits coming out in the assessments. Maybe we shouldn't interpret the content as much as the probabilities that are involved—or maybe both.

C One thing that seems to be very important here is the method of selection, which would give you a much greater spread than you would get in any normal sample drawn at random. You picked the very top people, and then you saw to it that you got some that were probably below average, so that your spread is probably greater on creativity or in most anything else than you would get in a random sample of all architects. It is thereby more difficult to interpret the magnitude of your correlations.

S I don't know that you can call our Architects III such a poor sample. They're all in business. But we did accentuate the distribution, I quite agree.

C Did you go to Architects III after looking at the data on Architects I and II first?

S No, we picked Architects II and III after I but before the data on the first group had been analyzed. We had Architects I from persons who were nominated as highly creative, and we didn't want to go back to the nominators and trouble them again. The requirement we set ourselves was to pick architects who matched the persons in the original sample with respect to age (within five years) and geographical location of practice. This was just a lot of clerical work to be done by searching the *Directory of Architects*.

C Would you think that not working with one of the creative people would make a person an Architect III, which turns out to be lower?

S That was the hypothesis that we made. It might have been an entirely false one, but if we wanted to get a good range, we wondered how best to proceed with this. Every person in Architects II had had two years of work association with one of the nominated creative persons—some experience, probably some learning in this situation. But you can't say it's only that. Probably the most creative students—the students who seem to have the most promise—get recommended for their apprenticeship in the offices of very, very good or highly creative architects. So we figured, without knowing which of these factors, ability or experience, was the more determining, that we would get architects of a sort of intermediate degree of creativity. And if we picked for Architects III those who had never had any work association with creative architects, we figured we'd get a lower order of creative persons.

C How did the three groups compare on age and on number of years of practice?

S They were matched on age, which indirectly would partly control years of practice.

C I wanted to ask you whether there was any pattern in why people declined.

S I think that the reasons varied from sample to sample. Barron, who is much braver than I and chose to work with writers, got some pretty emotional, angry letters rejecting the whole enterprise. These writers were offended by what we were doing in the study. I think that the architects declined for the most part, as far as we could determine, just because they were busy. They declined courteously. Maybe they have to do this in their business.

C   You don't feel that such refusals in any way altered your principal sample?

S   No. Two or three people accepted, and then at the last minute canceled out because they had developing opportunities, for example, a commission to do a building in India. One poor guy said, "If you need me I'll come, but it's going to cost me a lot of money."

C   How many rejections did you get among Architects II and III?

S   The rejection rate was a little bit higher, but I can't give you the exact figures. In the first place, these people weren't being offered a free trip to California, etc.

C   How long were Architects I there?

S   A week-end. We began on Friday afternoon after lunch and worked with them until Sunday afternoon.

C   Did you think of sending the same materials to Architects I who refused as you sent to Architects II and III?

S   I thought of it. I also thought long and hard about trying actually to see in person Architects II and III because it is very, very frustrating that we don't have intelligence scores for them as we have for Architects I.

C   Is there any study at all showing what the effect is of taking tests like these by mail versus taking them in some kind of institutional setting?

S   I don't know of any evidence on this. Does anyone else know?

C   I've done it under both circumstances and have gotten identical results.

C   We had a little experience that is not entirely directly on this point. We collected criterion data and administered some training-needs tests ourselves at military installations. Later we mailed another set of criterion forms as well as tests to be administered by their testing officers. We found evidence that they probably administered the tests as well as or even better than we did, but we collected a lot better criterion data than they did, possibly partly because, as outsiders, our criterion data were more obviously going to be used for research purposes only.

S   I might point out that, even with our creative Architects I, because we wanted to plan a very heavy week-end in which we would observe them, interview them, and do other things, we sent them a fairly sizable packet of tests and forms to be completed before they came. Certainly on those we haven't made a systematic study.

C I am pleasantly surprised to find efforts put into the criterion problem in several studies reported at this conference, together with so many attempts to put combinations of things together. I am also quite surprised, and pleasantly again, to see that this approach is working well in many places. I want to recall to you that we have also nearly always been able to get initial validities in the high .70's, the .80's, or the .90's for our empirical biographical keys on our initial samples, and we have obtained multiple correlations usually in the high .70's or in the .80's for a battery of test scores weighted in turn against each of our 17 factored criteria of creative and other scientific contributions. But we always expect some shrinkage in the validity of these best weighted combinations in cross-validation studies. And we are pleased at how well the validities for our biographical scores have held up on large cross-validation samples.

One question I have is that all your multiple correlations are for scores within instruments. Have you combined scores across instruments to see how they will come out, since this should give you even better initial results?

S We did a great big multiple correlation with 100 variables, but that was too many, obviously. What we plan to do is to go back and take three or four of our scales from each instrument to see what multiple-regression predictions we get.

C Did any of your highs or lows—your Architects I or III—have any biasing in the direction of geography or school or anything of this kind?

S No strong biasing as far as schools are concerned. Of course, there are areas around the country where creative architects congregate. In the nominations that we got, most of the architects were in these areas— Boston, New York, Philadelphia, Texas, Chicago, San Francisco, Los Angeles, Portland, Seattle.

C The same places where the general population is, and where you're likely to find the most creative in any field.

C What did the architects think of this report? Have you given it to the National Institute of Architects?

S They think it's wonderful. They're very pleased, quite intrigued, quite interested.

C Do they think that they should begin to use these instruments to select those to whom they give scholarships?

S I've been in communication with several deans, heads of schools of architecture, and they are pushing me to do a pilot study with them in selection. I don't think that we have anything to offer operationally, but we're very eager to develop such a program and see how it goes.

C   Was there any specific area of architectural design that yo r creative group was engaging in as compared with your noncreative group, or were they all in a wide spectrum of architectural work?

S   A pretty wide spectrum. Some of them are specializing almost entirely in private homes. Some of them are doing great big jobs. One of them had done a great deal of work with school buildings. They were pretty varied with respect to the kind of architecture they were doing in each group.

C   I have a red-hot letter from one of these deans. They all contributed to a total fund and financed a test with which they are quite displeased because they don't think the test is selecting the kind of people that they want, after they have spent that money. They wrote and asked whether we have tests for selecting the creative type of person. I don't know whether they have any more funds. But they might be willing to make a fresh start with this.

May I announce that we have a new program called Architectural Psychology, together with NIMH fellowships for graduate trainees. We think that it is a very rich field. We already have two trainees en route, and others will be starting next year. These trainees may be some of the most refreshing and creative graduate students we have ever had in psychology.

chapter *23* Creativity in the Visual Arts in Higher Education: *Criteria, Predictors, Experimentation, and Their Interactions*

Kenneth R. Beittel, The Pennsylvania State University

S   There are many reasons to consider the arts in any discussion of creativity, and the visual arts in particular. Although no one can ignore his environment, there is a tradition of independence and institutional disregard in art. Even in popular terms, the artist is known as a "loner." There is the "Bohemian syndrome," as I believe Cattell called it, and the attic—now the loft—studio. There is the feeling, probably a well-founded one, that instruction may kill talent. In popular terms, progressive education, the child study movement, and powerful spokesmen for art education have all done much to remove the fear laymen usually have of such specialized activities, even though cultural rewards for art are low.

More positively, the artist, especially the visual artist, turns out many products. Typically these are close in time to each other. These products are tangible, shippable, "judgable." Although many influences may intervene, a sample of products from Utah is apt to overlap pretty well a comparable sample from New Jersey.

Recent writings suggest revision of extreme positions on cultural relativism in the interpretation of art and argue for at least a balance between the attribution of aesthetic value to in-the-subject and to stimulus-bound variables (Pratt, 1961). In general, this will be the position taken in this paper. Berlyne's writing (Berlyne, 1960) is pro-

379

vocative, although he probably greatly oversimplifies the stimulus variables thought to influence aesthetic behavior. Other current germinal ideas come from Gombrich (1960), theories that the artist works according to "schema and correction" and that "making precedes matching." Finally, because I have decided to work with "art things at their livest," I like the sound of Barron's "perceptual choice" (Barron, 1952) and Bruner's "strategies" (Bruner, 1962). Perhaps my brightest and most creative students will be able soon to break down my global and still organismic language into more precise constructs and their relations and effects.

It may be important to point to the dialogue-like nature of the creative process in the visual arts. After the symbolic transformation effected through content-medium interactions, traces of process remain physically in the finished object for those who can to read. This may be much more the case than where the outcome is a discursive product, where the route is properly removed in the elegance of the final formula, theory, etc. Much modern art values its unique history and leaves it showing.

EARLIER PENNSYLVANIA STATE STUDIES

I have been uninclined to conclude too readily about the existence of interdisciplinary criteria of creativity common to the arts and sciences. I therefore did not completely share Lowenfeld's views about correlations observed between subtests drawn together by Brittain for his thesis at Pennsylvania State University (Brittain, 1952) and certain tests representing factors of creativity found by Guilford. Tests developed in similar ways and quite comparable in form and content often do correlate rather well. Later usage of such tests, however, indicated that their concurrent validities were low when they were assessed against three (demand or "work sample") art performances (Lowenfeld and Beittel, 1959; Brittain and Beittel, 1961) and against faculty creativity ratings, in a population of 50 upperclass, graduate art, and art education students. A test representative of spatial activity (Thurstone's Punched Holes) did relate significantly ($r = .395$). The only other significant correlation was with the Kieselbach Test of Aesthetic Discrimination in the unexpected direction ($r = -.333$). We used eight tests from the Guilford battery, three tests related to aptitudes felt to be relevant to art performances (Punched Holes, Hidden Figures, and Mutilated Words), the Kieselbach Test mentioned above, and three art performances which were designated as the criterion.

Several observations should be made at this point.

1. Judge ($N = 10$) intercorrelation was high (average $r = .830$).

Typically, "art expert" judges are used. Such judges are required to do blind analyses, as a rule, on five-, seven-, or nine-point scales. Expertness is usually defined in terms of amount of formal training (graduate art students or faculty). Where products from a certain educational level are involved, experience with that level is a further requirement. On the basis of further evidence (Linderman, 1960; Beittel, 1963), I would pick judges who are nonauthoritarian and, if possible, who had judged before.

I must digress still further at this point because of the importance of the topic of judging art products. I have commented elsewhere on this problem (Beittel, 1959, 1960). So-called separate verbal criteria for judging quality or creativity do not operate independently (Lansing, 1956). Only when criteria other than evaluative are included does the dimensionality of aesthetic judgment appear. In this, our work checks directly with Osgood's "semantic space" (Osgood, Suci, and Tannenbaum, 1957). On several factor studies, I have found criteria grouping under three major dimensions (Beittel, 1962b, and 1963). These I have called (1) evaluative (typically accounting for about half the variance and led by a simple "good-bad" scale), (2) process or spontaneity, and (3) descriptive (best represented by masculine-feminine). I will have more to say about process and descriptive dimensions later.

Judges may not always be sure of what is good, but they agree on average and poor works quite well. This is indicated by increased frequencies on the "below average" steps of a scale in almost every art-judging distribution I have seen. There are often a few works, judged high on a creativity criterion, which split the judges apart on a quality criterion. When it can be done, ranking all objects through progressive discriminations still "feels" like the best way of judging art products.

2. Going back to the first Pennsylvania State creativity study, the average relationship of the three demand performances used as the criterion was not high ($r = .379$). They were combined because the correlation of the faculty creativity rating of these students with the students' performance increased with the number of performances ($r = .348$ with one to $r = .508$ with three).

3. Although not related directly to the Lowenfeld-Beittel study, it needs to be pointed out that intelligence tests do not correlate significantly with art performance judgments (Burkhart, 1957, 1958). In a high school sample of 80 students, the number of works done in an "open" environment, where freedom of choice was encouraged, correlated .598 with a final judgment of the quality of a year's work (Burkhart, 1957). In this same study Burkhart, whose name I will use often in this report, had the insight to adapt Gough's adjective check list

to the specific description of a student's attitudes and feelings *while he works*. In the visual arts, concurrent validities of .30 to .60 have been yielded by such check lists.

4. For homogeneous experienced populations, prediction of performance criteria is good. This is especially true of graduate populations (but not with general creativity tests of the Guilford type). Since a later study shows a similar tendency for experience to strengthen the bond with predictors (Burkhart and Nitschke, 1962), a problem arises in the early identification of the creative individual in longitudinal predictive studies. This occurs because apparently there are those who have the desired traits early but who do not perform well, and vice versa, and because time seems to be needed to bring these two more into line. Evidence (Burkhart and Nitschke, 1962) leads us to believe that it is not the selection process which brings only certain kinds of people into the arts, which in turn strengthens criterion-predictor bonds; but rather experience itself—especially of certain kinds to be discussed later —which clarifies the good as good, the poor as poor, and reveals the emergent and recessive trends in producers.

5. A test designed to discriminate between art and nonart samples on the basis of aesthetic sensitivity was found to be negatively related to the creativity of products of a homogeneous group of art students in the Lowenfeld-Beittel (1959) study; this negative relationship has also occurred elsewhere (Hoffa, 1959; Giopolus, 1959). The Kieselbach Test, the Graves Design Test, and the Barron-Welsh Art Scale all have gone negative within a homogeneous art population with art performance judgments. Those "way out" rebel against such norms.

Michael (1959) studied the effect of intrinsic influences (awards and adult and peer standards) upon the art works and creative self-concepts of high school students, finding that "while the art work of the control group advanced in aesthetic quality, all three experimental groups . . . showed a significant decrease in aesthetic quality" in a four-week post-experimental period, as opposed to a four-week pre-experimental period (treatments occupying a middle six-week period). Among the dependent variables were (1) art works and (2) self-report, using the adjective check list developed by Burkhart (1957) and a self-matching by the student against a visual peer art scale (an extension of Burkhart's thesis). Analysis of students' statements revealed a clear distinction between "trial-and-error" and "preconceived" approaches to the working process, with significantly more trial-and-error approaches occurring in the control group.

Capitalizing on this approach-style difference, Burkhart began his studies of "spontaneous" and "deliberate" working methods in the arts (Burkhart, 1960). His original descriptions of high, average, and low art-producing levels of high school and college students had revealed that aesthetic quality did not discriminate between all students who worked freely and experimentally (more as artists say they work—see Pappas, 1957) and those who worked rather tightly and rigidly. For a while, I tried to get Burkhart to use another word for "deliberate," feeling that in the arts it has a negative connotation. But perhaps his intuition was correct, since the two style tendencies suggest the existence of creative and perhaps less creative approaches which are reflections of strong differences in personality structure. Burkhart uses "spontaneous high," "spontaneous low," "deliberate high," and "deliberate low" as his classification system. This system suggests that aesthetic quality may be uncorrelated with spontaneity of process, as it is indeed often found to be. Over time, however, evidence is accumulating (Mattil, *et al.*, 1961; Burkhart and Nitschke, 1962) that, where progress in art is made, it is related to an increase in spontaneity.

Spontaneous highs describe themselves as feeling "distinctive, self-confident, involved, uninhibited, loose, and versatile" when working, while deliberate highs feel "clever, conservative, moderate, practical, fussy, organized, etc." The spontaneous are more complex persons, are more open perceptually, see more movement in unstructured stimuli, score higher on scales of aestheticism and theoretical interest, are less authoritarian, and tend to come from permissive homes.[1] The ratio of spontaneous to deliberate students, especially the "highs," increases at upper levels (graduates, faculty, and artists). In an undergraduate college nonart major group, there may be 1 in 20, as compared to 8 in 20 among graduate art students.

Judgments on a spontaneous-deliberate continuum can be made reliably from finished art products. Interjudge agreement, in fact, is usually better than with aesthetic quality. Thus, there has been tapped a process-in-product criterion which has significant connections to predictors in the personality domain. Burkhart has developed these useful constructs on the production side. Barron (1952), Linderman (1960), Cardinet (1952), and Beittel (1963) have demonstrated similar connections on the response or aesthetic judgment side. What this means in the studying of creativity in the arts is that we predict for aesthetic quality and spontaneity of products separately. As an instance of this distinction, spatial aptitude tests usually relate at about .30 with aesthetic quality judgments of products, but not with spontaneity judg-

---

[1] Burkhart's description of the spontaneous high student matches quite closely Westcott's description of successful intuitive problem solvers (Chapter 4) and MacKinnon's highly creative architects (Chapter 22).

ments.   Conversely, creative personality predictor scales often relate
to spontaneity judgments, but not to aesthetic quality.

In passing, I should say that, although general creativity tests of the
Guilford type have not related to performance judgments, they have
shown significant differences under courses where a creative set or philosophy exists and those where it does not.   Algalee Meinz (1960) studied
the general creativity of elementary education majors as influenced by
courses in industrial arts, where ends are typically technique mastery
and tool application, as compared with art education, where a permissive
atmosphere and encouragement toward experimentation and expression
are the rule.   She found significant gains in several general creativity
tests in the art setting, as compared with significant losses on two such
measures in the industrial arts setting.   Such a study tells us little in a
firm way about what is operating, but at least it does state that something is and that the tests are sensitive to it.

RECENT STUDIES

During the 1960–61 school year, the Art Education Department at
Pennsylvania State undertook a study of "depth" versus "breadth"
methods of art instruction at the ninth-grade level.   (See Mattil *et al.*,
1961.)   "Depth" here refers to sustained concentration in the curriculum
(in this instance, painting), as opposed to dispersal, variety, and cov-
erage ("breadth").   The latter is most commonly used.

The study was done in a middle-sized Pennsylvania city 60 miles
from Pennsylvania State.   The instruction was handled by a highly
experienced art teacher having no ties with the university.   Comparable
depth, breadth, and control sections were set up.   An extensive battery
of pre- and posttests was administered, and three art works from the
beginning and the end of the year were collected and judged for spontaneity and quality.   The teacher was accustomed to what might be
termed an unenriched breadth approach.   The experimental breadth
group was given enrichment in materials, visual aids, and curriculum
planning.

Results showed depth > breadth > control groups in aesthetic quality and spontaneity and on predictors relating to creative thinking,
creative personality, and openness of perception.   Breadth and control
groups actually got worse on these measures.   This was true even though
students preferred breadth approaches, and the teacher remained skepti-
cal of "depth" until late in the year.   Marguerite Lienard (1960) did a
study at the same grade level and found a connection between dissatisfaction with one's art and progress in art.

Concurrently with the study just described, Burgart[2] and I began to collect measures of generalized personality traits related to creativity tests and criteria. Fourteen such tests were taken from existing sources (Gough, 1957; Bales and Couch, The Value Profile; Cattell, The Sixteen Personality Factors Questionnaire), while nine remaining scales were composed by Burgart and me. In all, there were 415 items in our first research version. Factor analysis on a variety of art and nonart college and graduate populations indicated that the major dimensions dealt with were the following: (*a*) flexibility, (*b*) spontaneity, (*c*) nonconformity, (*d*) rich internal life, and (*e*) independence and self-sufficiency.

Burkhart found in a study with art and nonart college students (Burkhart, 1961) that many of these scales correlated with judgments of spontaneity in art products. They did not, however, except in one instance, correlate with a criterion of creativeness in teaching for beginning student teachers which Burkhart set up, as he put it, "to cross from the art area to the teaching area through a comparative analysis of creative performance and personality structure." Space does not allow detailed discussion of Burkhart's early effort at studying criteria and predictors across disciplines. In passing, it might be mentioned that the student teachers were not in the arts and that Burkhart developed a beginning objective criterion of creativeness in teaching. He and two other raters counted the number of divergent versus factual questions and relative versus absolute evaluations in a given time period for a unit of instruction chosen by the student teacher, and given without grading before student teaching had begun under the critic teacher. The point I wish to stress is that again it was the spontaneity criterion in art which related to the personality scales. Six tests predicted spontaneity with a multiple R of .80. Of these, three were personality scales, of which the strongest was a word-pair scale developed by Burgart and me ($r = .640$ with spontaneity of art products). ($N = .80$ for the art group.)

Burgart and I have changed and revised our creative personality exploratory battery twice since. It has dropped from 415 to 233 to 130 items. The latest version contains 15 "content" scales, and controls for acquiescence set have been built in. This version is currently on trial in two concurrent validity studies in which it is also being matched against earlier and longer versions.

On the response or judging side, spontaneity or sensitivity to process

[2] Note that these are different co-researchers—namely, Robert C. Burkhart, Research Associate in Art Education, The Pennsylvania State University, and Herbert J. Burgart of the University of Georgia.

characteristics seems to be equally as important as in the production of art. As a result of factor analyses on judging criteria (Beittel, 1963) the dimensions of (*a*) evaluative, (*b*) process-centered, and (*c*) purely descriptive criteria were identified. It appeared that judges (graduate art students) differed in their ability to use process criteria (e.g., formal-informal, rational-intuitive, and controlled-accidental). Two judge clusters from an inverse factor analysis, based on the original exploratory personality battery, identified a more creative and a less creative (authoritarian) group differing on 15 of the 23 personality scales. The authoritarian group saw no relationship among various process criteria and gave evidence of a significantly lower mean on these criteria, regardless of the works being judged. In a cross validation of these judge differences, 24 graduate judges were matched for academic level, years of teaching experience, and age; and a descriptive analysis was made of the influence of sex, high or low aesthetic performance (based on products judged for spontaneity and aesthetic quality), and authoritarianism of personality. Separate analyses were performed for usage of evaluative, process, and descriptive criteria. Only on the process criteria did any difference appear, and that was associated with authoritarian personality structure. Since progress in art relates to progress in spontaneity, and since spontaneity is a process judgment of products, the importance of this sensitivity in judges is self-apparent.

I have developed a test called Visual Magila: An Experimental Exercise for Visual Preference Patterns. This test consists of 32 items, each of which contains five pictures from which the respondent is to choose two on the basis of his choice value pattern. These pictures, on 5 in. × 8 in. cards, were chosen from over 500 designs. They have the flavor of nonrepresentational experiments in black and white media.

Behind the collection of these cards was a desire to move further into an analysis of judging patterns, guided by my feelings of the dimensionality of the domain from the factor-analytic studies. I wished to tease out the major dimensions nonverbally. We scaled the 500 or so cards on (1) aesthetic quality, (2) spontaneity (process), and (3) masculine-feminine characteristics. My desire was not to use the aesthetic-quality dimension, since I knew it to be an overwhelming factor in choice, but to group examples on the same quality level and let them swing free on combinations of the remaining two clear dimensions. Thus, there would be what I called a process plus (P+) which was feminine; a P+, masculine; a P−, F; and a P−, M. Because of the "magic number 7 plus or minus 1 or 2," I added a fifth card to each set. This fifth card I called the "sport," because it was unique, more "difficult" or more unexpected in each set.

What is the evidence on the Magila? First, the dimensions scorable are distinct. Simplified, these are originality (sport), process (spontaneity), aesthetic sophistication, and femininity. A factor analysis over a large diversified adult population ($N = 712$) revealed the relative clarity of process, femininity, aesthetic sophistication, and "sport" dimensions.

The "sport" score is the percentage of original or novel choices. The other three scores are ratios of choices along bipolar scales, the ratio of positive, favorable choices for that type of score to negative, unfavorable choices. Thus, each type of score is stated in terms of a percentage score. For example, P% is the ratio of P+/P− choices.

The trends for these four Visual Magila scores from seventh grade through graduate school suggest indeed that one must consider both stimulus properties and population classifications in the description of judging behavior. The samples studied were the following three groups of *non-art* students: 180 seventh and eighth graders, 259 college freshmen and sophomores, and 34 college juniors and seniors. The following groups of *art majors* were also studied: 95 college freshmen and sophomores, 72 juniors and seniors, 42 masters students, 35 doctoral students, and 10 faculty members. When trends across the sequence of 8 samples listed above were sought, I found that the curve for the femininity score decreased rather regularly from scores of about 65% to nearly 25% at the masters level and then rose upward for doctorates and faculty toward 35%. The curves for the other three scores all showed rising trends, starting between 20 and 30% and rising to 60 to 70% in each case. The spontaneity score showed the most rapidly rising curve, and the other two scores for "sport" and aesthetic sophistication tended not to rise much until after the masters group of art majors, with a final steep rise across the doctoral and faculty groups.

Currently I am extending this study back to earlier elementary grades. My hunch is that some of the curves will reverse direction as we move backward through these earlier elementary grades.

As a predictor of creativity criteria in the arts, the Magila has compared favorably with the five strongest predictors in a follow-up study of 50 graduate art students (Beittel, 1962b; Burkhart, 1962) and has added to the predictive power of our batteries in a methods experiment (Burkhart and Nitschke, 1962).

In the summer of 1961, we amassed on a general education population of 69 students 80 variables based on 32 tests and 8 art criterion measures. We originally dealt with these 80 scores in a 30×30 criterion and criterion-related matrix and a 50×50 predictor matrix. In the predictor battery were 9 tests of general creativity (including Guilford's

Brick Uses, Unusual Uses, and Plot Titles). There were 23 personality scales from the original exploratory battery which Burgart and I collected. There were 7 art criterion measures (including work independent of class) and a composite. After observing our separate matrices, we drew up a new 40 × 40 matrix, composed of the 8 criterion measures and 32 selected predictors. We performed a factor analysis and were enlightened to find that the results made little sense. Examination of the 40 × 40 matrix revealed that personality, general creativity, and art criterion measures had high intercorrelations within their own sets but had virtually no overlap (with a few exceptions between personality and general creativity). In computing multiple R's, the highest was found with the criterion "class art achievement" ($R = .693$), but several predictors worked in reverse fashion.

At about this time, we brought Calvin Taylor to Pennsylvania State as a consultant. We then resolved to (1) work first with a graduate art-major group, (2) expand the criterion measures then in use, and (3) make use of predictors applicable in any discipline. The purpose of the third resolve was to permit us to extend any findings we made to other populations and other disciplines and into experimentation.

In the graduate art creativity study (Beittel, 1962b; Burkhart, 1962), $N = 50$, we set up seven criterion measures, performance tasks or products of one type or another, as targets for a carefully selected set of predictors. Among the latter were self-ratings, descriptive personality scales, word pairs, evaluative and judgmental tasks, a divergent question test, and others. We began with 116 separate scores, but many of these were variations and combinations of each other. We cut back first to 24 predictors, then dropped some of these and tried a second time with a new set of 23, and finally ended up with 12 strong predictors. Seventy-nine per cent of the intercorrelations of these predictors and the seven criterion measures were significant. The average multiple R obtained on the seven criterion measures was .81.

Seven out of the 12 strong predictors are termed "hierarchies." By this we refer to an admittedly gross and exploratory device based on the assumption that, in the prediction of creativity, traits and abilities are hierarchically ordered and are not additive combinations on only one level of measurement. What we do, in effect, is to ruthlessly convert a test into a binary variable by cutting at the median score for a given population. Then we combine, a priori, according to hunch, theory, or empirical evidence, a series of such tests in a fixed value order. When four tests are so combined, we arrive at 16 hierarchy types (2^n, where $n =$ the number of scales in the hierarchy). The hierarchy numbers order the population in a more rectilinear fashion which nevertheless correlates around .90 with the unordered total of "high" or "plus" or "1" scores, which are normally distributed. The hierarchy numbers, however, are unambiguous; a 16, for example, always means, on a four-test hierarchy, that the person is above the cut-off on all four tests; a 5, similarly, up on the most important test only; a 2 up on only the least important test. Although we do not think that we have solved the problem which such a technique attacks, we believe the idea that creativity is more than a linear combination of test scores merits further study and are encouraged that our simple device aids prediction.

We have constructed two tests in which the ascendance of one response set over another is built in. One of these is the Visual Magila Test mentioned previously, in which five pictures are presented in each item but only two are to be chosen. The five different pictures in each item repeat five dimensions of choice each time. In another test (SDT-1), five words are presented to the subject on each item and again he is asked to choose only two. The five words represent choices labeled (1) abstract, (2) process oriented, (3) theory oriented, (4) impulsive, (5) nonconventional.

Space does not allow great detail here; but the twelve useful predictors in the graduate art education group are (1) an art self-rating hierarchy; (2) a hierarchy from an inventory measuring complexity, aestheticism, theoretical interest, and nonauthoritarianism, (3) an abstract thinking hierarchy; (4) a score on the number of divergent questions asked on a "word question" test; (5) a single score on the complexity dimension alone; (6) an abstract orientation hierarchy made up of scales from four different sources (personality and otherwise); (7) a spontaneity hierarchy from scales originated by Beittel and Burgart in the personality inventory described above; (8) a separate word-pair test of flexibility, also originated by us; (9) a preference for words which are abstract, process oriented, impulsive, theory oriented, and nonconventional; (10) a nonauthoritarian hierarchy (from three separate scales); (11) a score representing the ratio of divergent to factual questions on the "word-question" test; and (12) what we called the "spontaneous abstract creative personality hierarchy" (a kind of superhierarchy merging the two major areas of spontaneity and abstract thinking.

In brief, high self-rating as a creative artist in comparison with one's peers, ideational and social self-determination, abstract thinking, divergent power, spontaneity, and nonauthoritarianism account for about 66% of the variance of our criterion measures.

Two of the criterion measures in this study were independent art works produced away from the school setting; another product was made at a testing session; and a fourth was a test requiring 15 thumbnail sketches on the basis of five stimulus line arrangements. Judgments of these four performances determined the aesthetic quality and the spontaneity during working (as rated from the product). Judgments of spontaneity (process judgments) appear to be somewhat more easily predicted (.84 average R) than those of quality (.78 average R).

A first, small, cross-validation sample of 15 graduate art education majors has been analyzed. Predicted aesthetic quality and spontaneity scores for the criterion art works of these 15 students were correlated with their actual (judged) scores. Although the sample was small, predictions were very good under the strongest three, four, five, or six positive predictors (predictors 1, 2, 3, 4, 5, and 7 described above). The highest r's were obtained for spontaneity predictions. The strongest positive predictors functioned well, predicting as highly as .843 (rho between predictors 1, 2, 3, 4, and 5 and the spontaneity judgment).

An extension of these studies has been made to undergraduate nonart populations. In a cooperative study with us, Burkhart and Nitschke (1962) carried out a combined prediction study and teaching experiment. In a report Burkhart refers to this study as one in which progress in art appears to be significantly related to opportunities for the student to learn through self-evaluation under a depth approach. Ninety-five students under two instructors were involved in a semester's work under (1) a self-reflective depth approach, (2) a fine arts depth approach, and (3) a breadth approach. In the first two groups, students did over a dozen works in any medium they chose, whereas in the breadth groups students did on the average three works per medium and typically worked in six different media. In the depth approach the student was looked upon as an "artist learning." In the breadth approach the student received formal instruction in the use of materials. In the breadth classes evaluations of individual progress in art were not undertaken, although in class discussion emphasis was placed upon general evaluative considerations relating to progress in art. In self-matching procedures in which the student chose from a pictorial scale a sample which he felt matched his own working style and level, posttest expert judgments of spontaneity of products related .475 to students' ratings in depth groups. There was a near-zero relationship in breadth groups. On a spontaneity criterion (based on class work and the quick drawing sample test mentioned in the graduate study), 25 out of 40 predictors (pre- and post-) related significantly. The predictors here referred to are measures developed for the graduate study and applied in the same or improved versions on this study. Since Burkhart and I had met in December 1961 and drawn up a theoretical framework covering evidence from past studies, we quantified crudely a predicted order of instructional effects variable. Out of 20 predictors, all related significantly to this variable (which covers five classes).

It thus appears that the more media used, the less is the progress in spontaneity and aesthetic quality of products. Conversely, the more products per medium, the greater is the progress in both spontaneity and quality. Teacher differences are ruled out to an extent because even within the depth groups, where there was freedom of choice in number of media used and in number of works done, these relationships persisted.

This is not spoken of, at this stage, as a formally controlled experiment. Rather, it is the pilot venture for efforts at more rigorous delineation of factors operative in learning *in* and *through art*. *Through art* signifies changes in one's creative thought and in his personality, in addition to improvement in his products. A generalized description of the instructional tactics employed in the above study follows.

Two *Depth* Classes (35 students):

Unstructured
Using self-evaluation
(Self-reflective learning
　approach)

Free choice of materials under individualized instruction; at least 12 works in a single medium. Course-evaluation procedure emphasized:
(1) The way students work (risk, etc.).
(2) Quality (level) of work and progress.
(3) Student's self-evaluative involvement.
Mostly procedural instruction given (e.g., ordering works, making distinctions of good to poor).
No formalized instruction on criteria, content categories, etc.

One *Depth* Class (19 students):

Structured
Using visual stimuli
(Fine arts approach)

Group instruction of art-interested students using two materials, black and white conté crayon on tone papers, and black and white cut paper. Assigned outside classwork, with the teacher as the evaluator of progress in art.

Two *Breadth* Classes (41 students):

(Typical "introduction to
　art approach")

Group instruction using six media: poster paint, crayon sgraffito, block printing, line and wash, paper cutting, and charcoal. The students had approximately 3 weeks to work in each of these media.

They had formalized instruction in
the use of materials, but evaluation
concerning progress in the art of the
individual student's work was not
undertaken by the teacher.

In summarizing a review of educational and psychological testing,
Harris (1962) raises an issue much to the fore in my own thinking:
"The paradigm of 'test, teach, then test again' puts predictors, learning
experiences, and the criterion into the same system; but to understand
the system adequately demands that attention be focused on the interactions of all three components." As an example of this interaction in
the study just mentioned, 77% of predictor-criterion relationships were
significant at posttest, 48% at pretest. Thus the generalization arises
that art experience (apart from treatment group differences) strengthens
criterion-predictor bonds.

In the above study, for spontaneity-of-product criteria, predictor
relationships ranged from .30 to .40 on pretests and .40 to .50 on posttests, while multiple correlations went to .90 on posttest product judgments. It thus appears that the predictors developed on the graduate
art education majors are useful with undergraduate non-art students or
general populations. Furthermore, these same predictors are sensitive
to improvement and change in art performance over a sustained instructional period and are sensitive in an hypothesized order of effects.

In order to observe in more clarity and detail some of the global
factors we find operative in creative learning in art, Bernard Schwartz,
a former graduate assistant in research with me, experimentally studied
the effect of working time and instruction on aesthetic quality and
spontaneity of an art product, with general education undergraduate
students grouped in randomized blocks according to their predicted
creative potential. In a carefully controlled experiment, students designated as high, average, and low in their creative potential, as identified
by an abbreviated 75-minute creativity predictor battery, were randomly
assigned to four treatment groups for which the independent variables
were working time (two 40- or two 20-minute periods) and instruction
(unstructured or structured). There were 144 subjects in the experiment
(123 of whom completed it appropriately). At the end of the first session,
a random half of each treatment group left, while the other half went
through some self-reflection concerning their feelings while working,
after which they evaluated their products (using structured check lists
in both instances). Eight expert judges evaluated all works, in their
half-finished state, for quality and process characteristics.

At the end of the second experimental session all students went through self-evaluations of their working feelings and their products. The same eight judges made final judgments paralleling their earlier in-process judgments. Again, analysis is incomplete, but on the aesthetic-quality judgment only (final judgment), certain corroborating trends appear. Remember that these were not art students and that only one product was involved as the criterion. The unstructured treatment groups significantly outscored the structured groups. The clarity of this finding surprised me because the taped instruction called "structured" was, to my ear, merely an extended discussion in general terms of what artists try to do under such conditions, etc. The students who were thrown on their own resources did significantly better. The group working for a longer time did better than those under short duration. Predicted creativity levels were also significant and in the expected order.

Apart from the treatment and classification differences, we were much interested in the fact that the random half of each treatment group who were forced to undertake self-evaluation of their feelings and products at the midpoint of the experiment made significant gains in the spontaneity and quality of their finished products over those who did not undertake such self-evaluation. Thus in a controlled brief experiment we found evidence supporting Burkhart's self-reflective depth findings.

The main purpose of experiments presently under way (Beittel and Burkhart, 1962) is to determine whether specific methods designed for self-reflective (or self-evaluative) training will increase the capacity of spontaneous and deliberate students for creative action, as determined by increases in tests of their creative potential in art and beyond, and their progress in spontaneity and quality in art, both in class and independently. Our generalized hypothesis is: *Methods designed to increase self-reflectiveness in art will bring about greater progress in art (on a variety of criterion products judged for quality and spontaneity) and cause concurrent gains on related general creativity, creative personality, and self-rating measures.*

THEORETICAL CONSIDERATIONS

I. There are four *dimensions of depth* related to the development through art of the capacity for creative action, as we can deduce them from our present evidence.

A. *Continuity in productivity:* at least a dozen works in a single medium; ongoing image of the self as learning; personal base established for comparison and change; symbolizes the self as emerging or becoming; provides framework for self-knowledge and self-evaluation; provides a base from which departures can be appraised; symbolizes fluency and productivity.

B. Self-evaluation of art products: a natural outgrowth of continuity; teacher evaluation of lesser effectiveness; energizing force of self-activity in evaluation; encourages depth of commitment; symbolizes sensitivity to value problems.

C. Divergent tasks: perceptual, formal, expressive, and ideational shifts; break from stereotypes; changed orientation; symbolizes need for personal viewpoint; self-discovery of changed orientation most effective; symbolizes original thought.

D. Process self-reflection: selective feedback of working process samples; conceptualization of the self in action; construction of process strategy plan; interactions of risk and control dimensions in vital inquiry methods; power and freedom from concern over heuristics of discovery; symbolizes flexibility and intuitive thought; aids transfer.

These four dimensions are seen as essentially cumulative in character. That teaching which utilizes all four should be the most effective.

II. *Classification of students* according to creative potential relates to treatment effects. Classifications are seen as mobile and as points along a continuum.

A. Spontaneous highs: gain most from independent work; resistant to training; can learn under a variety of methods; open to indirect influence; autonomy, discovery, and integration and instructional concerns; hit ceiling on our tests; statistically the smallest group.

B. Spontaneous lows: no clear findings; egocentric and nonevaluative, which makes methods a problem; may need sustained and large products; discipline, control, enrichment of impoverished viewpoint, and productivity are instructional concerns.

C. Deliberate highs: mixed findings; art improves under (*a*) continuity in productivity, (*b*) self-evaluation of art products, (*c*) divergent orientations, (*d*) process self-reflection; personality and creativity affected by a diversified depth where the environment forces a change in viewpoint; suggestion that a combination of depth-breadth is needed, or simultaneous depth treatments.

D. Deliberate lows: findings clearest; benefit from (*a*) continuity in productivity, (*b*) self-evaluation of art products, (*c*) divergent perceptual tasks, (*d*) process self-reflection; cumulative effect of four depth dimensions needs study.

III. *Experimental questions* now under study are as follows:

A. Number of depth dimensions beneficial (continuity in productivity, self-evaluation of art works, divergent orientation, process self-reflection).

B. *Values of completely individualized instruction* (reapportionment of contact conditions within same contact hours).

C. *Climate variables:* dominative-integrative, teacher-centered versus learner-centered, hostile-supportive, direct-indirect influence, divergent-factual orientation.

D. Type of *teacher* or *authority evaluation* or criticism.

E. *Transfer* from art learning and art process discoveries *to life-related tasks.*

IV. *Assumptions about creativity experiments in art in educational settings.* We view research as a process transacted under researchable conditions and environments. Art education is ideally situated for inquiry into creative aspects of the educative process because students typically work individually at specific products which can be stored and studied. Art products, however, must be seen in terms of their known relationships to teaching, treatment, student, and environmental variables to be understood—in other words, products in themselves can be misleading. Also, as our current investigations are demonstrating, the processes leading to final products are educationally and theoretically more important than the products themselves.

Underlying present efforts to develop a model for learning and teaching in the arts is the further assumption that it is ultimately most useful to study first individual learners of known classification under specific experimental treatments and proceed gradually to treatment interactions, to teacher and student interactions, to group phenomena, and eventually to teacher-training methods and the work of application in various school settings. It is important to keep in mind, also, the concern within art education for that learning which not only improves one's art but also gives evidence of transfer to other learning or life-related tasks.

C I want to comment about Beittel and his work. I am impressed by a fellow in art education who makes excellent pottery and who also has learned to talk like a psychologist and to work as a researcher and statistician—a true scientist.

chapter 24 Measuring Creative Abilities in Public Relations and in Advertising Work

John M. Elliott, The Richardson Foundation[1]

S   One of my responsibilities in the Richardson Foundation is the area of creativity, so I am here to find out what is going on.
The Foundation is just beginning to embark on a survey of the field with
specific interest in the most promising psychological tests for identifying
creative talent in business, government, and research.   Later, I hope
that the Foundation will take a broad interest in the field of creativity
in general, through appropriate grants and other forms of encouragement.

Annual reports of some of our leading corporations have pointed out
that 50% or more of the products marketed by them today were not
even in the test market stage as recently as ten years ago.   This almost
unbelievable concentration on the creation of new consumer products
has placed a high premium on innovation in product development and
marketing.

Nor is this search for creative talent confined to the business world.
Creativeness can make a crucial difference in any activity, as it did in
the World War II race for the atomic bomb.   The thoughtful person
loses his complacency when he realizes that some of the most important
brains behind our atomic research were those of men like Einstein,
Fermi, and Hans Bethe, who were citizens of Germany and Italy before
the war and found their way, possibly by chance, to our country.   What

[1] Now Manager of Recruitment and Manpower Development, Continental Baking
Company, Rye, N.Y.

importance should we attach to the creativeness of the man who thought of mounting eight guns, instead of two, on the wings of the Spitfire, which turned the tide in the Battle of Britain? Or the man who thought up the degaussing and asdic apparatus on merchant ships at a time when we were losing from 100 to 190 ships per month—many more than were being built? Now we are involved in the missile and satellite race, and, to quote the late President Kennedy, "the issue is undecided." He also said:

> The human mind is our fundamental resource. The success of the United States as a civilized society will be largely judged by the creative activities of its citizens. Today we must give priority to those aspects of science and technology which will increase our military strength through our creative activities.

Creativity has many definitions, which may differ in the art field, in the scientific area, and in business and industry. Most business executives are concerned less with the creative genius of an Einstein or a Michelangelo than with creativeness as demonstrated in the day-to-day production of useful new ideas.

From a businessman's viewpoint, creativity can be defined as the capacity to produce fresh, original, and valuable ideas on a continuous basis. In the business world men of proven creative ability are being sought not only for the scientific research end of business but also for communications areas, particularly advertising and promotion.

I will now give you a brief report of my own small, exploratory research in creativity, which has generally dealt with creativity in two fields other than science, namely, public relations and advertising. To the best of my knowledge, this study is the first attempt that has shown some degree of success in measuring creative ability in these two fields.[2]

Creativity, as we know it from factor-analytic studies of Guilford and others, appears to comprise at least six to eight unique intellectual factors or components, each of which can be measured with a reasonable degree of accuracy. These studies have revealed such factors as "originality," "awareness of implications in a given situation," "associational fluency," "expressional fluency," and "ideational fluency."

Most of the "creativity" tests used in our own studies are Guilford's factor-analyzed tests. They are all paper-and-pencil tests with time limits. Test questions are of the following types:

1. What would be the possible consequences if everyone grew at the rate of two inches a year between the ages of 20 and 30? (The furniture and garment businesses would boom, for example.)

---

[2] This work was accomplished in the New York management consulting firm of Dale, Elliott and Company, Inc.

2. Name as many games and sports as you can in the time allowed (e.g., football, backgammon).

3. Write words similar in meaning to the word "fair." Work as rapidly as you can. (An imaginative person will interpret the word "fair" in a number of ways. It can mean "blonde," "just or impartial," "county carnival," and so on.)

4. List vehicles used for transporting (e.g., train, wheelbarrow).

5. List as many alternate uses as you can for a penny (e.g., as a temporary fuse).

6. List as many reasons as you can for purchasing the following articles: (*a*) pyrex dishes, (*b*) loose-leaf binders, etc.

In explaining these tests to management personnel I have pointed out that the answers to none of these questions require specialized education, training, or experience. Thus a younger, inexperienced person may have as good a chance of obtaining a high score on these particular creativeness tests as one with some years of experience. The tests in this sense appear to measure creative potential, as well as ability.

In carrying out our studies we first obtained the collaboration of two prominent New York public relations consulting firms. The top executives in each firm were asked to select one group judged to represent their most creative individuals and another their least creative people, all of whom had at least several years on the job to demonstrate creativeness or the lack of it. No group in the middle range was used.

One interesting thing we found at these firms was that, although the intelligence test scores averaged well above the population mean, the less creative people actually averaged slightly higher on an intelligence test than did the more creative individuals. In another study it was found that, by restricting selection of creative people to those who scored in the top 20% of an intelligence test, 68% of the creative people were eliminated in the process.

By combining the men in both public relations firms into two groups we had a total of 25 individuals in the "most creative" group and 17 in the "least creative" group. All 42 were engaged in work involving client contacts, either directly or indirectly.

Five of the eight tests we administered showed significant group differences. Of the five tests found to separate the two groups successfully, two of them did the job even more effectively than the other three tests. Accordingly, if a person scored in the favorable range on either of these two tests, he was given two points toward a total score, whereas if he scored favorably on one of the other three tests he was given one point. On this "multiple-cutoff" scoring plan, then, if a person scored in the favorable range on all five tests, he would make a total score of seven.

Using this scoring plan we obtained results as follows: 23 of the 25 individuals (92%) rated as the most creative public relations people scored in the favorable range (five points or higher), whereas only one of the 17 (6%) in the least creative group scored favorably.

After this encouraging experience in the public relations area, we then obtained the collaboration of one of the country's leading advertising agencies. Seventy-five individuals in this agency, consisting of 40 members of the Copy Department and 35 persons on noncreative assignments, took our test battery—the same eight tests used in the public relations firms.

Of the 40 individuals in the Copy Department, four different raters (rating independently) agreed on 14 individuals as being the most creative people, and 14 as representing the least creative. Twelve of the 14 individuals rated as most creative in the Copy Department scored in the favorable range (6 of the group obtained favorable scores on four of the tests and the other 6 scored favorably on all five tests), whereas only 1 of the 14 persons in the least creative group scored in the favorable range. Similar results were found if we used the top half (the top 20) versus the bottom half (the bottom 20) in the Copy Department. We found that 16 of the top 20 (80%) in the more creative group obtained scores in the favorable range, whereas only 4 of the 20 (20%) in the less creative group scored favorably. This represented a phi coefficient of approximately .60 for the relationship between test battery performance and composites of several of management's "rank order" ratings on creativity of persons in the Copy Department. The interesting thing here is that the tests show potential for separating the more creative from the less creative people *within* the Copy Department, all of whom are relatively creative individuals.

Our next step was to compare the most creative 25 individuals in the Copy Department with a group of 24 individuals from other departments who were considered to be *the least creative people in the agency.* Using a cutoff score below 4, our results were that 22 of the 25 in the highly creative group, in comparison with only 3 of the 24 in the least creative group, were identified by the test battery.

Finally we compared four groups in the agency, selected on the basis of their relative creativeness. The first group consisted of the 14 top creative people in the Copy Department; the second group, the 14 least creative members of the Copy Department; the third group, the 11 most creative members of the so-called noncreative group from other departments; and the fourth group, the 24 men regarded as the least creative people in the agency.

The percentages above a cutoff score of 4 consistently decreased across the four groups as follows: 93%, 79%, 45%, and 12%. Thus, if a relatively uncreative individual applied for a job in which creativeness was important, for example, in the Copy Department, and took the tests, his chances of obtaining a favorable score would be about one in eight.

Although we were highly gratified with the results obtained in these test research studies, let me end on a note of caution. Our work was done with relatively small groups, so that there is some margin for error in our findings. Before we can predict creativeness with the desired degree of confidence, additional research will need to be undertaken, centering in follow-up studies of individuals whose creativeness has been predicted at the time of their employment. However, our findings to date certainly indicate that this new tool can, even in its present form, be of real help in spotting truly creative young people among candidates for advertising and public relations jobs, and it should be used, with the necessary safeguards, as a step in the employment process. Or, viewed at the other end of the creativity scale, the test battery appears to have good promise, at this stage, for spotting applicants with below-average potential to be creative in advertising and public relations work.

C In comparing your promising results with the somewhat disappointing results that we found on our scientists for these "creativity" tests of the intellectual type, I have a general observation to report. These highly verbal, quick-response "creativity" aptitude tests appear to have much more promise in discriminating between levels of creativity in the communications areas of public relations and advertising work than they do in scientific research work. Perhaps the former activities are truly much more verbal in nature than is creative work at the scientific frontiers. And perhaps the highly verbal "creativity" training programs will prove to be more valid for public relations and advertising than for scientific research work. The clue for us here may be that the essence of creative scientific research work entails more nonverbal learning and thinking and producing than we have realized, so that we may need nonverbal intellectual tests of creativity of a more prolonged response type in order to get more valid predictions of creativeness in science.

C Yes, I agree with your comment—it really hits the nail on the head.

chapter 25 The Effect of Group Climate on the Leader's Influence on Creative Group Performance[1]

Fred E. Fiedler, University of Illinois

S The past two decades have seen a dramatic rise in a wide variety of professional work performed by teams, not only in the sciences, but also in other professional activities such as architecture, city planning, the theater arts, and engineering. This is shown by the increase in multiple-authorship papers and large research laboratories, as well as the growing concern with problems which arise as a consequence of interdisciplinary research.

A number of papers have appeared in the literature which deal with various aspects of this problem. Among them have been the work of Maier and Hoffman (1960), Ghiselli and Lodahl (1958), Pepinsky (1959), Torrance (1959), Ziller and Exline (1958), D. W. Taylor and Faust (1952), Parnes and Meadow (1959), and Bush and Hattery (1956). These and other studies have been predicated on the hypothesis that creative group interaction is more than the summation of individual member abilities. In other words, aggregating creative and able individuals does not automatically ensure creative teamwork.

This paper examines the influence which the group climate has on the relation between leader attitudes and intelligence, on the one hand, and on the group's creativity, on the other.

[1] This report summarizes one part of a research program, supported by the Group Psychology Branch of the Office of Naval Research (Contract NR 177–472, Nonr 1834(36), Project on Group and Organizational Factors Influencing Creativity, Fred E. Fiedler, L. M. Stolurow, and H. C. Triandis, Co-Investigators).

The measures which have been of especial importance in our work are based on commonly used intelligence scales and the leader's descriptions of his "least preferred co-worker" (LPC). This description of LPC is typically obtained before the leader participates in the experiment, and it therefore does not necessarily represent his description of one of his group members. Rather, the leader is asked to think of all the individuals he has ever known, and then to describe someone with whom he could work least well.[2] These descriptions are made on simple eight-point bipolar adjective scales similar in form to the semantic differential (Osgood, Suci, and Tannenbaum, 1957), such as:

Friendly :—8—:—7—:—6—:—5—:—4—:—3—:—2—:—1—:   Unfriendly
Rejecting :—1—:—2—:—3—:—4—:—5—:—6—:—7—:—8—:   Accepting
Unhelpful:—1—:—2—:—3—:—4—:—5—:—6—:—7—:—8—:   Helpful

All scales are heavily loaded on an evaluative factor which indicates the favorableness with which the individual sees his LPC. The LPC score is obtained by simply summing the item scores. A series of studies in our laboratory have determined some of the personality, attitudinal, and behavioral characteristics of the individual with a high or a low LPC score. A person with a high LPC score, one who describes his LPC in a relatively favorable manner, tends to be relatively person-oriented, compliant, considerate, permissive, and passive in his leadership behavior. A low LPC leader, one who describes his LPC in a very unfavorable manner, tends to be more task-oriented, directive, controlling, managing, and business-like. These and related scores have been important predictors of performance in previous studies (Fiedler, 1962), and they were applied here to research on group creativity.

We have completed one series of four investigations of leader attitudes and group creativity, using leader LPC scores, which will be summarized first. The relation of leader intelligence to group performance will be discussed in the second part of the paper. The main point will be how the role played by the leader in the interaction is affected by the group's climate or the leader's perception of it.

---

[2] The leader is also asked to describe his most-preferred co-worker. A comparison between the profiles of most- and least-preferred co-workers yields the "assumed similarity between opposites" (ASo) score, which has been extensively utilized in previous studies of task groups (Fiedler, 1958). Usually ASo and LPC correlate .70 to .90, and both scores tend to be practically uncorrelated with usual personality and biographical indices.

LEADER ATTITUDES AND GROUP CREATIVITY

The "Dutch" study

The first investigation in the series was conducted in the Netherlands (Fiedler, Meuwese, and Oonk, 1961). It dealt with three major variables, namely (a) the homogeneity or heterogeneity in cultural and religious backgrounds of team members, (b) the leadership structure of the group, and (c) the leader's perception of his co-workers, as measured by LPC.

The subjects were 64 male Dutch university students. Thirty-two of them were Northern Dutch Calvinists, while the other 32 were Southern Dutch Catholics. All subjects were given interpersonal perception tests before the experiment proper. From these we obtained LPC scores, indicating the leader's attitude toward poor co-workers.

The men were assembled into four-man teams. Half the groups had an appointed chairman (the "formal" groups); the other groups were given no instruction about the chairmanship (the "informal" groups). In addition, the groups were divided in such a way that half the formal and informal groups were homogeneous in respect to religion, whereas the other groups were heterogeneous, consisting of two men from each faith. Each person participated in two teams, once in a homogeneous group and once in a religiously heterogeneous group.

The tasks given to these four-man teams consisted of devising three original stories from the same Thematic Apperception Test, or TAT, card within a 20-minute period, and of completing, as a group, Guilford's Plot Titles or Alternative Uses Test within a 15-minute period (Guilford, Berger, and Christensen, 1954). The criterion of group creativity on the TAT task was based on ratings by two independent judges; the scores for Plot Titles and Alternative Methods were based on Guilford's manual.

There were no significant differences in main effects between formal and informal, or homogeneous and heterogeneous groups, as far as overall task performance was concerned. However, we found a high positive rank-order correlation (.75) between the leader's LPC and his group's creativity in seven homogeneous formal groups, but negative correlations in six homogeneous informal groups, in eight heterogeneous formal groups, and in eight heterogeneous informal groups (correlations of −.67, −.72, and −.21, respectively).

In view of the well-known social strains between Calvinists and Catholics in Holland, it seemed reasonable to assume that homogeneous groups would tend to be more relaxed and pleasant than heterogeneous groups. Formal groups also tend to be less stressful, since there is no competition for leadership status. This suggested that the homogeneous groups with formal leadership would be most pleasant and relaxed, a hypothesis which was supported by content analysis of the tape-recorded sessions (Meuwese and Oonk, 1960). It appeared, therefore, that a compliant, passive, person-oriented leader is more effective in groups which are, themselves, relaxed and pleasant. A more task-oriented leader seemed to be better for groups which operate under conditions of greater tension.

The hypnosis study

The hypothesis which emerged from this first study was tested in an experiment in which leader attitudes were modified by means of hypnosis. Subjects were 12 highly hypnotizable and 12 very unhypnotizable women. All were treated in the identical manner throughout the experiment, and all were assured that they were hypnotizable. This study had several purposes discussed in detail elsewhere (Fiedler, London, and Nemo, 1961), and, as it turned out, the hypnotic manipulations themselves were relatively unimportant as far as the group creativity problem was concerned.

Briefly, the procedure relevant to this report was as follows. Each subject worked with two other women who were introduced to her as fellow participants, but who were actually the experimenters' accomplices. The group was then asked to elect a chairman (who always turned out to be the subject). They were given the same task which had been used in the Dutch study, namely, to make up three different stories from each of the TAT cards they were given. All sessions were tape-recorded and later analyzed by means of Bales' system.

To test the hypothesis from the Dutch study, the subject and the confederates described the group atmosphere after the sessions. These group-atmosphere ratings were made on scales similar to those from which LPC scores were derived (e.g., friendly-unfriendly, accepting-rejecting, helpful-unhelpful). These scores presumablp indicate the pleasantness and satisfaction or unpleasantness and frustration which the subject and the confederates felt with the interpersonal relations in the group. The analysis of these data revealed that one of the major factors in the leader's group-atmosphere score is related to the leader's lack of tension and of feeling accepted by his group members.

The results of this experiment clearly supported the findings of the Dutch creativity study. In groups which the leader rated as pleasant, the correlations between her LPC score and group creativity were positive (.64). In groups seen by the leader as unpleasant, the correlation was negative $(-.72)$. An analysis of the group interaction, based on Bales' system, showed that the high LPC leader tended to be at ease in pleasant groups but tense in groups she saw as relatively unpleasant. However, the low LPC leader was more relaxed than the high LPC leader in groups she saw as less pleasant.

The criterion scores of both the Dutch study and the hypnosis study were based on TAT card stories. Moreover, since the hypnosis study had confederates as members, it was of importance to determine whether the same results would occur when we used more natural groups and criteria.

The church leadership study

A third investigation was conducted within the context of a national church leadership training conference (Fiedler, Bass, and Fiedler, 1961). This conference brought together 108 Unitarian church leaders and laymen from various parts of the United States for one week of training. The participants were, thus, adults who had had generally broad leadership experience, either as church administrators or as leaders of various lay organizations affiliated with the church.

The workshops, which covered a period of five days, dealt with leadership problems related to group creativity during the first four days of the week. The number of participants averaged 95. The conference members were organized into teams of four persons plus one observer. Teams were reshuffled each day so that every person served as leader one day, as observer one day, and as group member three days, and so that no more than two group members would serve twice in the same team. In other words, the groups on successive days can be considered reasonably independent cases, for each of the four creativity days and for the one noncreativity day.

As before, LPC scores were obtained before the group sessions. After each session, the observer collected group-atmosphere ratings and other research information.

There were 18 to 20 groups on each of the four days. On each of these days the groups were given a different problem which was to be completed within a 35-minute period.

These problems were as follows:

On the first day: to write a justification for a decision taken by the minister of the church not to divulge the intent of a local physician— a nonparishioner—to commit a mercy killing.

On the second day: to write a Sunday School parable for six- to eight-year-olds illustrating the desirability of the doctrine of separation of church and state.

On the third day: to develop an appeal for funds to send a ministerial student through school.

On the fourth day: to plan a three-minute skit, for presentation that evening, to illustrate the need for better music in the worship service.

In all cases, the members of the conference were asked to rate or judge each group's product excluding their own. Criterion reliabilities could be obtained for all but the Fund Appeal Problem. Agreement between raters was high, i.e., correlations of .91, .76, and .90.

For each of the problems, we divided the groups into the third in which the leader and the other group members indicated a relaxed, pleasant atmosphere, a middle third, and the third in which groups were rated as having relatively unpleasant atmosphere. The results of this third investigation were again consonant with those of the first two studies.

Although the correlations were not uniformly high for each day (that is, for each different problem), positive correlations were found between leader's LPC and group creativity scores in groups rated as pleasant, while negative correlations tended to occur in groups which were rated as less pleasant. This trend was most pronounced when we utilized the leader's rating of group atmosphere as the basis of splitting the groups,[3] a finding which was observed in the hypnosis study as well. Therefore, it appeared that the degree to which the leader sees the group as pleasant and accepting of him determines in part whether his style of leadership will contribute to, or facilitate, collaborative thinking on the part of the group members.

These three studies utilized laboratory groups and criteria which were quite artificial in the hypnosis study, and only moderately realistic in the investigation of church leaders. To what extent are these results generalizable to real-life situations?

Investigation of farm supply company boards

We had previously conducted a major investigation of 32 small co-operative corporations (Godfrey, Fiedler, and Hall, 1959). The companies, which were very similar to each other, sold the same products and had the same personnel and organizational policies. The criteria of success consisted of the percentage of company net income and operating efficiency over a three-year period. The boards of directors are policy-

---

[3] In detail, correlations were obtained for the groups after subdivision into thirds according to the leader's group-atmosphere score. For the highest third, the correlations between the leader's LPC score and group creativity were .28, .89, .49, and .37, respectively, for the four problems. For the middle third, the correlations were .10, .67, .19, and −.08 across the four problems. For the lowest third, the four correlations were .03, −.03, −.14, and −.60. (Only the correlation of .89 was significant at the .025 level.)

and decision-making bodies and are, therefore, engaged to some extent in creative tasks.

From the 32 companies were selected the 10 in which the board of directors sociometrically expressed strong liking and confidence for the general manager. Presumably these would be pleasant groups with smooth interpersonal relations between key personnel. The ten in which the boards liked their general managers least well would probably be groups in which relations would be relatively strained. Similarly, companies were selected where board leaders and managers highly chose or highly rejected each other. There is very little overlap in these samples.

Here again, we found that the informal or sociometric leaders with high LPC scores who were nondirective, dependent, and relaxed were most successful where pleasant board-management relations existed.[4] The directive, task-oriented and distant leaders of boards with low LPC scores had more effective companies under strained board-management relations.[5]

LEADER INTELLIGENCE AND GROUP CREATIVITY

The four investigations which have been reported present consistent evidence that the most effective interaction between leader and group depends to a substantial degree on group climate. Thus, where the leader-group interactions were pleasant or were seen in this manner by the leader, the relaxed, passive, and somewhat compliant leader obtained the best results. Where the group seemed less pleasant and harmonious, the more directive, task-oriented leader obtained better results. This was the case even though all groups here described were relatively pleasant and nonstressful.

It seems reasonable to wonder in light of our findings whether the same relations obtain when we are dealing with other types of attributes, such as the leader's intelligence. One would expect that the leader who must concentrate on maintaining group harmony would be able to contribute less to the group's task than a leader whose group is relaxed and harmonious to begin with, and who feels accepted. This suggests that the

---

[4] In five companies where the board president and the general manager endorsed each other sociometrically, the correlation between the LPC score of the board president and the net income of the company was .67. In ten companies where the entire board of directors sociometrically chose the general manager, the correlation between the board president's LPC score and the company's net income was .21.

[5] In eight companies where the board president and the general manager did *not* endorse each other, the correlation between the LPC score of the board president and the net income of the company was −.40. In ten companies in which the entire board of directors did *not* sociometrically choose the general manager, the same type of correlation was −.60 (significant at the .05 level).

leader's own ability and intelligence scores should correlate with group performance under pleasant conditions but not under conditions of group stress. One series of analyses clearly substantiated this hypothesis (Fiedler and Meuwese, 1963).

In the previously described Dutch study, the leader's ability was measured by means of an abbreviated, 14-item intelligence score similar in form to the Miller Analogies Test. We then compared groups which were relatively pleasant (having no one in the group who was singled out as destructively critical) with groups in which such a critical person was named. As shown by a content analysis, the former were more harmonious than the latter. The leader's intelligence score correlated more highly with group performance under the more harmonious ($\rho = .69$) than under the more stressful condition ($\rho = .26$).

A more definitive test of this hypothesis was undertaken in a study in which stress was experimentally introduced. This investigation by Meuwese (1964) utilized 54 three-man groups of ROTC Army cadets and Navy midshipmen. Eighteen groups were assigned to each of three conditions. A "control" condition was made relatively free of stress. The men were told to come in street clothes, and they were assured that their performance would not become part of their ROTC record. A second set of 18 groups each consisted of two Army cadets and one midshipman in uniform, participating in an "internal stress" condition. The lower-ranking Army cadet was named as the chairman. The problems (to propose a method for equalizing Navy and Army ROTC pay, and to tell a fable stressing the need for a strong army in a small country located on a seacoast) were designed in the hope that they would create some dissension between Army and Navy participants. The third condition was made externally stressful. Three Army cadets, again in uniform, participated, with the highest-ranking cadet as group chairman. To introduce realistic stress, a high-ranking Army officer, either a colonel, a lieutenant colonel, or a major, sat across the table from the group members and rated them at five-minute intervals. This last condition was clearly the most stressful, as indicated by the members' group-atmosphere scores as well as their comments after the experiment.

Correlations were computed between leader intelligence scores and group performance under these three conditions, as well as between member scores and group performance. In general, the intelligence scores of the leaders correlated significantly with group performance primarily under the control condition, while intelligence scores of the members did so only under the external stress condition.

DISCUSSION

The major purpose of this paper was to show the effect of group climate on the relationship between leader attributes and group performance. The investigations which are here reported present a very consistent picture of these interactions. A harmonious, cohesive group presents a favorable working climate for the permissive, considerate person-oriented leader, and it permits the leader to contribute to group performance according to his intelligence. A less pleasant, disharmonious group climate requires a more task-oriented, active, controlling leader. Moreover, where stress becomes relatively great, or where the group is not harmonious, the leader's intelligence does not contribute to group performance, whereas the members' intellectual abilities do contribute to a substantial degree.

These findings suggest that the maintenance functions of the leader absorb his energies under stressful conditions, throwing the burden of creative group performance upon the group members. Similar results were obtained by Fiedler and Meuwese (1963), who conducted an analysis of military crews for which leader ability and intelligence scores as well as group performance measures were available. These analyses demonstrated that leader ability scores correlate highly with group performance only when either the leader is sociometrically accepted by the members of his group or the group is cohesive and harmonious.

The findings which relate the leader's LPC scores to group performance have recently been incorporated in a more general model of leadership effectiveness (Fiedler, 1964). These studies have shown that the nature of the task, as well as the power structure of the group, also determines in part the type of leader attitudes which are conducive to creative group interaction. Research on the specific determinants of this interaction is currently under way.

chapter 26 NASA's Efforts and Interest in Creativity

Allen O. Gamble, National Aeronautics and Space Administration

S   With reference to the considerable discussion we have been having about process versus product, my first point is that we in the National Aeronautics and Space Administration (NASA) are product oriented. In fact, we almost have to be, since ours is a very practical mission. Second, I will describe briefly the NASA manpower picture; third, discuss our interest at NASA in creativity and creativity research; fourth, make an offer; and fifth, present a plea.

First let me relate the following incident, which occurred a long time ago. Back in 1946 Robert J. Lacklen and Paul G. Dembling, who were, respectively, Personnel Officer and Classification Officer for the National Advisory Committee for Aeronautics (NACA), went to the NACA Langley Aeronautical Research Laboratory near Norfolk, Va., with the mission of classifying the positions or jobs of the research scientists in the laboratory. They were presented with a special challenge, which others before them had tried to meet and failed. This challenge consisted of classifying the jobs of a group of men who were in a large room engaged in studious writing, sketching, or formulating on the blackboard, using slide rules, looking out the window, or just sitting. Lacklen and Dembling soon found that these men were thinking. This was their business, thinking about problems of aeronautical structures and coming up with theoretical and practical solutions.

Now thinking is a process, internal to the individual and thus hard to measure and evaluate. But problem solutions are concrete, with identifiable characteristics to serve as the basis for evaluation. And the evaluation can relate to both the work done and the doer thereof. By taking this approach, Lacklen and Dembling discovered that, if the solution to a research problem answered only the specific problem to which it was directed, it was not a very creative solution. But if it answered other problems as well, and thus had a wider breadth of applicability, the work was more creative and the doer's position therefore should rank higher on the classification and salary scale. As an example at one end of this scale of values, one scientist's problem on structures concerned a landing gear strut on a particular aircraft, but his solution solved only that particular problem. This research product was judged to be narrow in applicability and thus low in creativity. At the other end of the scale, the solution by one of the scientists of a problem concerning aerodynamic pressures on plates provided an elegant theoretical answer to a recurring difficulty which, up to this point, had been soluble only by empirical testing in wind tunnels. His generalized solution answered not only specific problems in all types of aircraft but also an array of problems concerning bridges, buildings, and other structures.

By using this innovative (and in itself creative) approach, Lacklen and Dembling were able not only to determine the proper grade level of all the scientists and engineers in the Theoretical Structures Division at Langley, but also to identify several of the younger men who were about to be promoted on merit. Ever since, NACA and thereafter NASA have continued to use this approach as an integral part of the position classification system for scientific and engineering positions, particularly to provide higher salary levels for talented scientists who are not in supervisory positions.

This breadth-of-applicability approach was soon applied in the process of selecting scientists and engineers for NACA. In April 1947 the following paragraph appeared in the Aeronautical Research Scientist examination, which I developed for qualifying scientists and engineers for research positions in NACA:

Applicants who have achieved the distinction of making a creative research contribution to the field may be eligible for a higher grade than the grade for which they would otherwise be eligible. Such research must have been on a hitherto unsolved problem related to aeronautics. It must have been creative research, in that it must have produced a basic principle, concept, method, approach, or technique that not only solves the specific research problem at hand, but also is directly applicable to the solution of other research problems, and may open a new area of research. On the one hand, such creative research characteristically involves the introduction of unorthodox assumptions, idealizations, approaches, physical concepts, mathematical developments, or relationships which are not obvious but correct, and which have not previously been made even by authorities in the field. On the other hand, it may also characteristically involve the rejection of assumptions, idealizations, approaches, physical concepts, mathematical techniques, or relationships hitherto held valid but which, for obscure reasons, do not hold when applied to the problem.

It should be emphasized that this definition of creative research written in the examination refers explicitly to the end product of research, that is, to the solution of a research problem. The definition is applied to something concrete, a product of research. The evaluation does not attempt to go behind this end product to determine how it was made, only whether the man himself produced it.

This was the first time that a federal examination for Civil Service positions provided a means for an applicant with evidence of superior achievement in research to become eligible for the next higher grade and salary level. The "breadth-of-applicability" concept thus had its second practical application. Incidentally, the 1947 definition quoted above has now been broadened to cover inventions in my recent NASA examination for Aero-Space Technology, the successor to the old Aeronautical Research Scientist examination.

The third use of this concept has been made by Calvin Taylor and Robert Ellison, who developed a "breadth-of-applicability" rating scale for criterion use. This was applied as one of the key measures in developing the Biographical Inventory they have been working on for us since 1959. They have already described this to you and discussed its use (see Chapter 16).

My second topic is a very quick view of the NASA manpower picture. We have changed much from the National Advisory Committee for Aeronautics, which had about 8,000 total employees when absorbed by NASA in October 1958. Now in June 1962 we have grown to about 21,000 people. As in the old days of NACA, about 35% of our people are research scientists and engineers, including practically all the varieties. We even have life scientists now. But the major change is that now about 90% of our funds flow out into industry, universities, and nonprofit institutions. This means that we are having to develop new contract monitoring skills in addition to continuing our in-house research work.

This leads into my third point, which is NASA's interest in creativity. We clearly need—in fact, we must have—a generous proportion of highly creative scientists and engineers if we are to achieve our mission of exploring space. The National Aeronautics and Space Administration has given a solid demonstration of both official and grass-roots interest in research on creativity. Some 1,400 of our scientists and engineers at three Research Centers have willingly filled out Taylor and Ellison's experimental forms of the Biographical Inventory, and their supervisors have taken time to rate them on several scales. At our Langley Research Center, the last one visited, 98% of the forms distributed were accounted for, and failure to complete questionnaires was due mostly to travel or absences for other reasons.

This NASA interest leads in turn to my fourth point, which I called at the beginning an "offer." Probably NASA's nearly 8,000 scientists and engineers comprise the largest and most varied group of research and development professionals in the free world. They are uniquely categorized as to fields of work, as distinct from fields of academic training. There is, to my knowledge, no better criterion group for study of large numbers of scientists and engineers. They have already demonstrated their willingness to give of their valuable time for research on creativity, and they could do so again. So we are in a sense "offering" them to serve in future research. But all this depends upon the nature and intent of the research, as judged by the laboratory director. First, the work would have to be planned so as not to take too many people at once and not too much time of any person. Second and even more important, the type of research would have to lead toward practical usefulness, such as improved methods for selection, for training and development, for increased organizational and managerial effectiveness, and the like. Taylor and Ellison's work on the Biographical Inventory fulfilled both these requirements.

Finally, I want to make a plea. This plea is for money, not from you but from others. I have been very much impressed with this conference, by the quality of research and the distance we have come since the first one in 1955, and since Lacklen first attended in 1957 and I attended in 1959. We cannot support much research on creativity. Our mission won't let us. The mission given to NASA by Congress is to do research for the benefit of all mankind in the exploration of space. We have a mission in the life sciences, but it does not include personnel or psychological research on creativity itself. We have only this one small contract with Calvin Taylor to develop the Biographical Inventory, but that is about as far as we can go. But we in NASA who are concerned with scientific and engineering manpower believe that research in creativity should be supported heavily—at the level of hundreds of thousands of dollars—by federal agencies and private foundations who do have a mission involving research in creativity, and by industry which has much to gain. This should become a matter of high priority to the nation.

chapter 27 Prospects for Future Creativity Research in Industry

J. H. McPherson, The Dow Chemical Company

S Efforts to apply what we already know about creative individuals, the creative process, and the creative environment in an industrial setting can take a variety of directions. The success of whatever directions are set will depend partially upon the dominant philosophy held by the top management of the organization. Ascertaining this philosophy is difficult, especially when it seems to be in the process of rapid change. When an organization is moving from what might be called a state of "benevolent autocracy" to a state of "maturity," a state where aggressive action is expected, there will be obvious effects on the emergence of creative behaviors. When an organization is in such a state of change there is often some ambivalence in the minds of individuals at both "close to top management" levels and subordinate levels about how much aggressive action the system can tolerate. A shift from benevolent autocracy toward maturity can be assessed by noting an increase in the attention given to suggestion programs or operation improvement programs and by an increase in the expectations for aggressive action by staff groups. Such changes are in general favorable for creativity but carry with them also some urgencies that may not be so favorable.

Another attribute of such a change is an increase in the number of methods and systems being used to measure rate of progress, using a host of what might be called "end-result" variables. Too much attention on "end-result" variables without concomitant attention to the intervening variables of group morale, feelings of pressure, etc., might result in short-range achievements at the sacrifice of conditions that might lead to greater long-range achievements. It is my hope that we can increase our efforts to measure organizational philosophy and climate and relate these measures to indices of creativity. It is part of our plan for the next year to bring to our various levels of management an increased appreciation of the relationships between participative leadership and productivity (creativity).

It is also our hope that we can consolidate in a more forthright manner our evidence about the relationship between the various behaviors of supervisors and the creativity of their subordinates. When will we have a good statement describing creative managerial behavior? What aspects of originality must a manager possess in order to nurture the originality of others? How and what kind of support should be given to a scientist who mouths a need for independence but who is obviously dependent?

Recognition that the dominant philosophy of the organization will affect efforts to create an environment where creative individuals can thrive is useful; waiting for an exact understanding of this philosophy is futile, especially if it is in a state of rapid change. Consequently, it is wise to settle on one's own philosophy of management as it relates to creativity and proceed.

At this moment it is fortunate that Maslow's (1950) description of the self-actualizing person, Marie Jahoda's (1958) description of positive mental health, and the common attributes of the creative person as derived from previous Utah conferences are so congruent because these common elements permit the organization of the goals, objectives, and plans for our program. Briefly stated, our efforts are to help individuals move from:

Dependency to independence.
Few ways to behave to many ways.
Passivity to activity.
Superficial interests to deep interests.
Short-term perspective to long-term perspective.
Subordinate positions to equal positions.
Lack of awareness of self as an infant to awareness of and control over self as an adult.

These goals require us to be aware of the variety of individual blocks to creativity, the ways groups support or inhibit creativity, and the effects of organizational policy on creativity.

We define creativity in such a way that it can be expected from everyone in the corporation. We hope not to define it in such a way that many professions can assume it to be the private domain of another rather than an activity toward which they should aspire.

Some of our plans require an increase in the activity of what we call the Employee Review Board. The action of this board is directed to finding high-potential persons at both the hourly and the salary levels, considering the adequacy of their placement, and taking the appropriate action required to give them a chance to transfer to jobs of greater potential if this seems indicated. This activity has been partially successful so far. Current gains in this area are represented by a specific statement of corporate policy encouraging transfer and critical of supervisors who hold on to their personnel. I wish we could have some specific research projects indicating what can happen when a talent search is conducted among the 25- to 35-year-old hourly personnel who have for various reasons given up the hope for opportunity to use their talents in the occupational world.

Our long-range and short-range plans call for an increase in the development of test requirements for entering chemical operating jobs, laboratory technician jobs, etc., which will permit us to provide other methods for advancement besides seniority.

Our current labor contract contains many clauses which ensure opportunity to our personnel. I am sure that various labor contracts could be analyzed to determine whether they tend to create conditions favorable or unfavorable to creativity. In this context, I believe that we should do much more about educating union leaders concerning the nature of the creative process and the needs of creative individuals.

I would like to refer to a paper titled, "The Predictive Value of Unreduced Tension as Related to Creativity," by L. C. Repucci (1962) of our staff. He computed a productivity index for 94 of our technical personnel (this index is derived by adding the total number of patents, patent disclosures, and patents pending and dividing this total by the number of years of professional experience at Dow). All 94 subjects were given three tests: a word discrimination test, for which there were no right answers, a chemistry test, and a progressive addition test. Scores on these tests were not important. After taking them each subject was asked to make up (in 10 minutes) additional test items. Repucci developed methods for giving each subject a "test item production score." He had hypothesized that the word discrimination test would produce more tension and that the more creative scientists would tend to make up items like the ones in this test, rather than items like those in the chemistry test. This hypothesis was not confirmed. But his more creative scientists did produce more test items than his less creative ones. He also received peer and superior overall creativity rankings for this sample. The top-ranked high-creative scientists received a significantly higher "test item production score."

His last two paragraphs are interesting:

> If educators were to present to students each semester a list of unsolved problems in a given field and ask the students to volunteer one solution for each problem before the course was completed and if a count was kept of the number of problems offered, the number of subjects who attempted to solve the problems, and the number of solutions attempted by each student, then by the end of each academic year and by the end of each educational milestone, be it high school or the Ph.D. degree, a rank ordering of the data should indicate which students have a chance of meeting the minimum requirements of creativity.

> Such an approach might minimize the need for psychological tests or "creativity" tests and might throw a different perspective on the environmental issue. Furthermore, such an approach need not be limited to educators. Laboratory directors could follow much the same procedure.

A second paper by Repucci (1961), on the biographical differences between high and low creative subjects is the next report of interest. In one study he examined biographical differences between a group of nine chemists who had a patent rate of one or more per year (the average was in fact, 2.91 patents per year) and compared them with a group of seven chemists who had a patent rate of .00 per year. The mean number of years of professional experience for the high group was 9.6, and for the low group, 10.7. With respect to age, the mean for the high group was 39.7 years, and for the low group, an even 40.0 years. So you see, Repucci is not talking about newly graduated chemists but rather people who have been in the field for some time. All subjects had a Ph.D. in chemistry.

This study revealed many interesting differences. I will not try to cover all of them. But you might be interested in knowing that 33% of the high group read seven or more scientific journals regularly, while 0% of the low group did so. Seventy-seven per cent of the high group had assistantships in graduate school, while 0% of the low group did so. Forty-four per cent of the high group were *not* interested in administrative work, but 0% of the low group were *not* interested in administrative work.

Some items which are often held to differentiate between groups did not prevail in this study. Familial eminence in science, geographical location, and democratic versus authoritarian home environments were not found to be different for the two groups.

Repucci then studied 29 subjects who were rated on the dimension of creativity by both supervisors and peers. He found 16 subjects whom both supervisors and peers rated as high creative and 13 subjects whom both supervisors and peers rated as low creative.

Not only did these results differ from the previous study but also a comparison of the two studies reveals some interesting differences which may reflect on the need to keep our criteria clearly in mind when we speak of creativity. Briefly, the major differences seem to be that the high patent people are more aggressive, more self-sufficient, more unsocial, and less given to joining either organizations or social units than are the subjects who are *rated* high creative. This suggests that part of the picture involved in being rated high creative is based upon successful social interaction.

I will give one last comparison. Seventy-seven per cent of the high patent producers belonged to one or more honor societies, but 66% of the high rated subjects belonged to *no* honor societies.

These data are rich. We do not have time to explore the results concerning the low patent producers versus the low rated subjects.

The third area of exploration that Repucci has engaged in concerns personality. He has developed from an item analysis of the MMPI profiles of the high versus low patent producers a technical exceptional success scale which he is presently trying to validate.

We hope to select from the various tests discussed at these four Utah conferences a battery to give to our technical employees after they are hired and to relate their test performance to their subsequent productivity.

We also hope to devise some group methods for examining the characteristics of our high patent productive groups as compared to our low-producing groups.

Another activity that we are currently engaged in is a three-step program involving research group leaders. The first step in this program is the evaluation of the group leader in research. Three sources of data are used for this purpose: (1) a special set of questions for the group leader's use in his evaluation of his own behavior, (2) a battery of tests (MMPI, Strong, MAT, and Edwards), and (3) his subordinate's evaluation of him. The group leader distributes to his subordinates an evaluation sheet of the Osgood Semantic Differential variety which is completed (anonymously) and returned to me. A session with each individual group leader will be held to review the information from these three sources.

The second step in the program is an evaluation of each subordinate. All the subordinates have taken a similar battery of tests. Each group leader will evaluate each of his subordinates, using the Supervisor's Evaluation of Research Personnel (forced-choice device) developed by William D. Buel and published by Science Research Associates.

The third step will involve looking at the group operations as a whole. We have not decided what measures we will use at this stage.

This three-step program is a pilot study. We hope that it will be successful so we can learn from it.

In conformity with our premise that we expect creativity from everyone, we run a one-day session on creativity for salesmen. Some of you may recall that studies of the adjectives salesmen use to describe themselves indicate that they do not use such terms as creative and original in their self-descriptions. It seems most appropriate that they begin to see themselves as creative. On the training days devoted to creativity, the blocks to creativity are discussed and the salesmen experiment with brainstorming new uses for our products. We are finding that individuals working alone under the standard brainstorming instruction produce a greater number of product uses than does the group effort. One interesting observation from the last experience was that the shape of the object (in this case, pieces of Ethafoam) regulated in some degree the nature of the uses given. Those who had flat sheets of the foam thought up a preponderance of sheeting uses, for example.

On these creativity days the salesmen also take 10 of Guilford's tests (Consequences, Unusual Uses, etc.). We have tests on a sample of over 100 salesmen now. We will relate performance on these measures to the rest of the sales battery and to performance in the field. Sales managers are helping out by providing examples of creativity in the field.

In the training area, enough interest is developing in creativity to permit us to expect a good reception for a course. Gordon's book, *Synectics* (Gordon, 1961) has received a certain popularity. I hope that we can manage to do a reasonable facsimile of "synectics" training. One reaction to this book has been that, of course, we already use analogy and metaphor in our creative process. Repucci has arranged with one of our creative laboratory groups to record group problem-solving discussions so that we can see actually what happens.

During the past one and one-half years we have been conducting a special training course on Job Performance Review. This course is based primarily on Maier's (1958) book, *The Appraisal Interview;* and the supervisors in training, including many research group leaders, receive guided practice in conducting review sessions with employees. During this course, the self-actualizing personality is discussed and the conditions that help people in such development are reviewed.

There is also a gradual movement of research management toward participation in a course called Management II or, *sotto voce,* "sensitivity" training, which is really bringing to industry the kind of training received at the National Training Laboratories held in Bethel, Maine, each summer. I have had sufficient participation in this course to know that some of the most capable research supervisors have gained insights into themselves that will contribute greatly to their ability to provide a creative environment for their subordinates.

Of course, it is impossible to avoid thinking about how training in counseling, or changes in supervisor's behavior, etc., can help promote some of the emotional attributes of the creative. How can adults be helped to become more independent and more able to be persistent in getting a hearing for their ideas?

The next paper to be discussed is entitled, "Independence: an Important Variable in the Description of the Creative Individual" (McPherson, 1962). This paper pursues four purposes: (1) a description of the personality characteristics of the creative person, (2) a comparison of this description with descriptions of our local scientific population, (3) a description of dependency, one of the emotional characteristics, and (4) some suggestions that might prove useful in helping persons become more independent.

It is to the fourth purpose that the next remarks will be directed.

Since moving from the dependent or counterdependent pole is necessary for human growth and apparently positively related to successful job performance, the last issue to be explored has to do with how to help dependent people move toward independence.

A way of analyzing the helping relationship, a way that seems to make very good sense, has been suggested by Glidewell (1962).

In situations where a person with a problem asks for help, and/or the person in a helping role offers or gives information, orientation, opinion, suggestion, or direction and the person accepts *without* clarification, elaboration, giving his own opinion, or own suggestion or modification, then there is *dependency*. This dependency may be realistic or unrealistic, but dependency is involved in the relationship.

In situations where the person with a problem rejects a supervisory idea *without* clarification, elaboration, own opinion, or modification, then there is *counterdependency*.

This counterdependency may be realistic or unrealistic. The person with a problem is bending over backward to try to demonstrate that he is not dependent.

In situations where a person with a problem asks for help and/or the person in the consultative role offers information, opinion, direction, etc., and the person accepts or rejects *only after* clarification, elaboration, or modification, then there is in process an action that reduces dependency.

Helping people become more independent should also tend to help them counteract depression and anxiety, and should aid them in developing their ego strength.

The provision of a psychologically significant climate, one where efforts are made to reduce dependency, will be more beneficial to the development of some of our scientific personnel than the manipulation of the physical environment in which they live.

The laboratory supervisor's decision to help his personnel become more independent depends upon many factors: his own needs for independence, his desire to enjoy the illusionary comfort provided by dependent people, his ability to endure the counterdependents, and his skill in handling dependent people.

For those of you who are still struggling with the definition of "creativity," I refer you to a third paper by Repucci (1960), "Definitions of Creativity."

Since it is often difficult to arrange to test the highly-sought-after scientist in today's society, I have prepared a manual for interviewers of applicants for technical positions. This manual contains recommendations for interviewing for sensitivity to problems, originality, etc. The manual is crude but provides a base for further development.

In various other ways we have begun to apply the results coming from these creativity research conferences. In addition, our Medical Department has recently become interested in experimenting with psilocybin, so I can say that we are doing some research in this area, and we have plans for more.

And, finally, we will, of course, continue to publish the *Creativity Review*, which so many of you already receive.

C   An interviewing procedure for selecting creative scientists is one of the things we felt was badly needed when we reported our study of Air Force scientists at the previous conferences. So many organizations are using interviewing techniques as they search for scientists throughout the country.

C   What plans do you have for organizational follow-up on the effects of the "sensitivity program"? How do you go about doing that? Are you sending people to a program at the National Training Laboratory?

S   We have in mind a collection of "before" and "after" measures. Some of our people have attended the NTL at Bethel; others have gone to Arden House. But we have our own sensitivity training within the company.

C   By family units or straight equating or what?

S   Our own people do the training, and the participants come from various levels of various departments in the corporation, not family units at this time.

C   What do you mean by family units?

C   The supervisor and his immediate subordinate group.

S   Our training department is quite dedicated to doing research. There are only two staff members, and they do all the Job Performance Review training, the "sensitivity training," and other training, so that their time for research is limited. The Job Performance Review course has pleased me greatly. The instructors don't talk about "what's average" or how many lines should be on a rating scale or the "sandwich technique." They really talk about the actual interaction between two people.

C   Have you found any way to utilize Gordon's mechanisms?

S   No, but I feel that if I don't in another year or so, it will be a major kind of failure. Parnes, how are you using the mechanisms?

C   We have used them in special seminars in evenings, but we've never gone extensively into them because of the time factor. You really need a whole separate program if you are going to do this in detail, other than just explaining these things.

S   I bought ten copies of *Synectics* (Gordon, 1961) and circulated it to top management people. In general, I've had a pretty good response, with some negative reactions. One person didn't like it at all. He's a really good fellow and is going to give me suggestions on how to build a better training program.

My evaluation of the book is very high. I don't know what the rest of you think of it. Have you read it, Barron?

C   I'm reviewing it for *Contemporary Psychology*, but I am not yet ready to comment.

C   I think that it is a first-rate book. The language at the beginning is apt to put psychologists off, and some people will resist because Gordon uses rather unusual words in a way that we're not used to. But I think that he has a great deal of insight, and I would be very much surprised if you do not find his operational procedure valuable.

S   Didn't you feel during the discussion of the effects of drug therapy the relationship between the mental states induced by drugs and the mental states sought after in synectics groups?

C   Yes.

C   May I put in a negative point? I think that most psychologists will react adversely to one part of the book where Gordon goes into a very long, detailed, dogmatic description of what you have to do in order to select the right people.

S   Oh.

C Using the definitions used in this conference, I think that he's selecting noncreative people by his selection techniques.

S Do you?

C No, no.

C Yes, he wants them to be a member of a team. Well, read it over again in terms of our conference.

C Yes, but the curious thing is that the people in this group have 132 patents to their names. So they're not noncreative. They are quite creative.

C You mean that this is a function not of the selection but of the treatment afterwards.

C No, Gordon is talking about the particular group he started with. He is talking about the procedures he *now* uses in selecting people for his training in various companies. I am willing to admit that his methods might be effective, but his evidence doesn't say that.

C Yes, but we've talked with him.

S I think that it is best for the health of the people I work with if I embrace his book with considerable enthusiasm.

chapter 28 Observations of a Committee from Industry on the Creativity Conference[1]

Lois-ellin Datta, General Electric Company[2]

      S   Before I present the report of our subcommittee, each member will comment briefly about his work and interests in creativity.

    Clark   For the past eight years, Management Development at Boeing has been teaching an 18-hour course in Creative Problem Solving in our off-hour programs for supervisors. Results were evaluated when a University of Washington graduate student made this the subject of his master's thesis. Copies are available from Dr. Jarold Niven, Management Research Chief, Boeing Company, Seattle 24, Wash.

    Recent classes report on a job problem they have solved, using one of the techniques taught in the class. We have reports on some startling specific results reached by graduates who ran brainstorms with their work associates. Brainstorming seems to be a quick way of collecting all the ideas a group has on a problem.

    McRae   The U.S. Army Management School at Ft. Belvoir is deeply interested in creativity and the creative process. The school is concerned with the complexity of problems encountered by its participants and wants to provide them with training and experience in a variety of

---

[1] Other observers in this subcommittee were Charles Clark of Boeing Aircraft Company, Colonel Robert B. McRae of the U.S. Army Management School, M. L. Roberts of Esso Research and Engineering Company, and Albert Wight of Aerojet-General Corporation.

[2] Now with the National Institute of Mental Health, Bethesda, Maryland.

operational concepts, methods, and techniques of creative problem solving.

Three Creative Problem Solving Seminars have been held at the school, and in the regular courses training in problem sensitivity, problem definition, creative attack of problems, and evaluation and use of alternatives has been provided.

The school is vitally concerned with the studies being presented at this conference and is especially anxious to keep abreast of not only the work in identification of creative people but also in tests, exercises, problems, etc., developed to provide experience in creative problem solving.

Roberts At the Esso Research Center we really have not yet done too much in this area of research on creativity. I guess that is the reason I am here. Most of the work we have been doing is in the area of organizational behavior, management training, trying to get a feel for organizational help—the interaction approach, I guess. We are at the brink now of this great interest in delving deeper into this area of creativity, predictors, environmental factors, and the like. Right now we have not really done much in this area, and I am here to find out what is going on.

Wight I joined the management development activity of Aerojet-General Corporation about a year ago to develop a creativity program. I had been teaching creativity classes in industrial design at the University of Utah for a couple of years and was doing graduate work in psychology under Calvin Taylor. I feel that this association of creativity with management development is a logical one, because although we try to develop the creative ability of the individual, he really can't be very creative if his supervisor doesn't allow him to be. So I feel that we have to get to the supervisor first and work to develop the proper climate, this area of freedom we were just talking about, and the recognition and appreciation of creativity. The more I get into this, the more I think what we are dealing with is not an abstract concept of creativity, but really the development of human potential.

As a result, I have started calling my seminars not just creativity seminars, but seminars on creativity and the development of human potential. I think that there is less resistance to this concept, too. The manager can't say that he isn't interested in the development of human potential, even though he might say that he isn't interested in creativity.

C I think that I can add something to that point you made. A few years ago, I had the opportunity to interview several managers of engineers in the General Electric Company. I was interviewing them to see what happened to people who graduated from GE's creative engineering program, and I asked these men whether they had hired graduates of the program. I then asked them if they were satisfied with these graduates, and the typical reaction was this: "Yes, these are the best men possible. I'm very happy I hired men from the program. The only thing is that it takes us two years to beat out all that creativity."

Wight Although I am in management development, I have not limited my seminars to management or supervisory personnel. I have taken them down through engineering, and in some cases to draftsmen. These people invariably say, "Well, this is all fine, this is great stuff, but you have the wrong people in these classes. We want to be creative, so why don't you tell our supervisor to let us?" So this is what we are doing, primarily, working with the supervisors.

C Wight is also bringing back some interesting interview information about working conditions that might be more ideal for creativity and human development.

Wight Right. I have conducted rather intensive interviews within one department of our engineering area in an attempt to identify the conditions that facilitate or inhibit creativity. The report was given to the plant manager, division managers, and some of the other key individuals. Then we held a meeting about two or three weeks ago in which we discussed its implications. The managers were told by the plant manager to cooperate with management development to correct the conditions reported to be interfering with the work. Many think our biggest problem is with the plant manager himself, but how do you tell him this? He is a very strong individual and is not aware of the effect he has on the entire organization.

C It sounds as though he is on your side, though.

Wight He is on our side—this is right. All these people are on our side, but most of them think that we can have creativity by edict.

Q Can't you document the results of creativity in action in dollars and cents in certain cases?

Wight This is done a great deal with value engineering, which is nothing but creativity actually.

C Do you come up with new ideas, though, say, $300,000 a year or something?

Wight This can be done and has been done. A great deal of it is done in the value engineering program, which is entirely separate from the creativity program at Aerojet, I might add, although we do coordinate and I have given a few lectures on creativity for that program.

C Well, some new idea may be created.

Wight I am now attempting to develop a questionnaire, based on the interview data, other questionnaires, and information extracted from creativity and psychology literature, to collect similar data from the remainder of the corporation. This, we hope, will give us a better picture of the climate for creativity within Aerojet and will point out specific problems to be dealt with in our management training programs.

Datta The General Electric Company's creative engineering program, begun in 1937, pioneered attempts to increase "original and worthwhile" behavior in professional personnel. One expression of the company's continuing interest in this area is the initiation of a creativity research effort in the Missile and Space Vehicle Department; I am here because we hope that the opportunity to hear about and personally discuss your most recent research will substantially contribute to our studies.

I find myself in a somewhat awkward position, speaking for a majority of which I am a minority. We are a subcommittee of observers which has been asked for a report on the conference, and we seem to be interestingly structured. It turns out that all members of this observer subgroup are concerned with management and organization development in industry and in the armed forces. We can't give you, as the other observers have, much feedback on what we are doing, because most of us are just beginning. We came here hoping it is as blessed to receive as it is to give much in the way of research results or possible ideas.

Our interests in creativity are front door and back door. Wight's is an example of front-door interest—he wants directly to increase creativity through such activities as brainstorming. An example of back-door interest is the work which Roberts has been doing in organization development, work which might be related somewhat to Brust's interests in how to get this kind of change in behavior accepted. Roberts has gone to many of the top-level personnel in his organization and asked, "Can I help you? What's hurting you? What are your problems essentially?" Many of the problems turned out to be needs similar to what Mackinnon and Barron have identified as characteristics of creative individuals—to be independent, to be flexible, and so on.

But front door or back door, most subcommittee members are interested in changing behavior. And we had hoped to get from the conference some information on the implications of current research for changing the behavior of many industrial and military personnel to be more like that of creative individuals. As a subcommittee we are not intensely interested in predicting behavior, nor are most of us intensely interested in identifying creative individuals. The personnel with whom we are concerned have the "intellectual prerequisites" for creative behavior—they are the survivors of tough schools and demanding jobs, and we think most of them could be quite creative. What can the results of recent experiments suggest to us about what factors in the industrial situation may inhibit creative behavior or may somehow foster it, factors which we realistically can expect to influence?

I will begin with a few convergent comments. The various observations fall into three groups. One group bears on the conference itself; the second is the extent to which our need for implications has been satisfied; and the third area is our reaction to the direction of research in creativity as we have perceived it from this 1962 conference.

For us, the greatest value of this conference has not been in the papers per se (we could eventually read them) but rather in the discussion, the opportunities to hear your reactions to the papers, most of which stem from very different viewpoints from ours. We wondered whether the papers could be read by the participants and observers beforehand, so that at sessions such as these the highlights could be presented and time would be available for longer and even more spirited open discussions. Perhaps the participants could write anonymously some of their reactions to the papers which would be circulated before the meeting so that the authors might have time to prepare a rebuttal.

C   Who would the authors send a rebuttal to? (*Laughter*)

S   Turning now to the second part, our need for implications has been only partially reduced. The discussion during Brust's remarks expressed this responsibility to bridge the gap between the research which is done for the sheer joy of it and the possible applications thereof. If the researchers don't state any implications, many of us have such a strong need for inferences in our daily work that we will make them for you, and we've found during this conference that we would be the wiser and the richer for your opinions.

I think that this responsibility rests both on those who want the implications and on those who have done the research—papers such as Harmon's, for example, speak very much to this need of ours. In other presentations, however, when a question such as, "How can this be related to the school system?" was raised, there was quite a long reaction time. The delay between the question and the answer perhaps indicated that the implications of the research results for our real and pressing problems in education and development had not been previously considered. I think that they ought to be.

You might ask, "Why should I be so concerned with pointing out implications for GE or the U.S. Army?" One possible reason is that you, too, are ultimately interested in changing behavior—if not now, then later. And this occurs to me even more strongly because so many of the variables which seem to describe creative people are those also which describe, in the studies of authoritarianism, the more liberal kind of people. The connection between creativity and psychological "goodness" also has been suggested by Maslow (1950), by Rogers (1959), and by Stein (1963), and there seems to be some evidence for the obverse. The less creative subjects seemed to be characterized by such authoritarian attributes as rigidity and low ego strength, providing an additional link between creativity and a psychologically good society. Some industrial situations might epitomize the pressures that are seen in the larger society as interfering with creative behavior. These industrial and military situations provide, perhaps, a stronger microcosm for checking out some of your ideas than does the college sophomore in introductory psychology.

C   You should realize in requesting implications that someone has to be willing to provide financial support or otherwise provide free time so that the interested researcher will be able to do this additional work of thinking and sketching what he feels are the various implications of his work. Maybe industry should give us, as basic researchers in the behavior sciences, partial support, say at least 10% added onto research budgets of interest to them, regardless of the major source of these budgets, so we will be more able to think through and add our implications to the other contributions of our research.

Let me remind you that in our earlier discussion about education, I said that people in the practical situations are asking us as basic researchers to do almost everything—the R work plus the implications plus the D work plus the communicating and the selling—they tend to put most, if not all, of the burden on us. I strongly argue that someone has to recognize that each of these demands places an added task requiring extra human effort on the backs of already fully occupied researchers.

Your comments also reminded me of an interesting suggestion that Sterling McMurrin made in a special meeting with our research group just before leaving for his new post as the U.S. Commissioner of Education. He felt that it might be possible to have researchers indicate at the conclusion of each project whether they felt their findings had important implications for educational practice. If a researcher felt that his results had potential practical implications, then a trailer project of a developmental nature could be considered, with the first opportunity being given to the researcher to undertake this trailer project. However, if he would prefer to continue in basic research, then another person or persons could have the opportunity to pick up this trailer project.

They could then accomplish the necessary "educational engineering" work of properly reshaping the fruits of the project to be more manageable, useful, and suitable for installation into educational practice. A similar procedure could be established for industry.

S   Point three concerns some directions for future research, as we see the needs. As I said, the majority of the group wants "something usable." We want to know what changes we can realistically expect to make in the environment which will help foster creative behavior. Excluding what had happened earlier in the conference series, we felt a certain current lack of interest in such kinds of studies, except in the work of Fiedler, Parnes, and Hyman. In addition, we would be very much interested in studies of group dynamics and creativity in the structure of the industrial and military milieus. Fostering creative behavior within the complex power structures of large organizations or across operations which are part of a checks and balances system offers problems whose solutions affect a large proportion of our population.

These comments fairly well summarize the suggestions which came from the group. A minority opinion on directions for research is that the difference between available and emitted responses may be what many of the studies on changing the conditions of creativity are getting at. To a large extent we may be able to influence the responses which are emitted by telling the subjects what our criterion of creativity is, either directly or through creativity training. But the pool of available responses from which the emitted response develops may be determined largely by certain value systems which the individual has. The effects of these value systems perhaps can also be traced in their relationship to certain cognitive strategies. Are these motivational structures going to be so resistant to change that we don't have much chance of effecting enduring changes in creative behavior? What cognitive/motivational systems are the crucial ones to creativity, linking characteristics of the creative individual and studies of productive thinking? Can we identify what in our society seems to influence the development of these value systems, using the tools of cross-cultural research?

In conclusion, thank you for the new orientations that your discussions have given us, for the generosity with which you have informally discussed our problems and explained your research, for the encounters which have left us indeed grateful for the opportunity to observe. Thank you also for listening to our observations.

C   Excellent.

C   We somewhat arbitrarily split the observers into two subgroups so that some of them presented individual reports while others formed the subcommittee for this collective report. Some of those who might have been more interested in identification and prediction of creativity at earlier stages were those who gave the individual reports. Not because of any specific planning, your subcommittee got only the industrial people.

S I'm very glad that it did because I think the industrial environment is a particularly critical one for studying changes in behavior. This need might otherwise not have been brought out so sharply.

C My experience with the requests for these Utah creativity conference reports was that after the Sputniks educators became more widely interested in creativity. The Sputniks put the pressure on the educators. Before the Sputniks it was mainly the industrialists who were writing for the reports.

S I think, as you say, that industrial management has for a long time had a vested interest in creativity. But how interested individual managers have been in changing situational factors is debatable—in fact, we spent much of last night debating it. I think Roberts' experience in Esso has pointed out some very effective ways in which we can somehow reconcile what management says it wants and what managers are willing to go along with.

C I would like to comment on our findings about bridging activities in some existing R and D programs. We discovered in agriculture that there are two distinctly different kinds of specialists (D people)—two distinct types of these "engineers"—who are manning the successive links across the bridge between basic researchers and practitioners. If education (and maybe industry) likewise built this same kind of bridge between behavioral sciences and practical applications, we might have tremendous changes and improvements in the future, as has been suggested in Harmon's report, in McPherson's report, in my report, and in the comments of various others here.

Let me again use agriculture as the example. The changes in agriculture have almost been unbelievable since Abraham Lincoln officially initiated the country agent as the second link across the bridge on which the technical specialist is the first link. A hundred years ago, 85% of our nation was occupied in producing food each day with only 15% not so engaged. The situation now is that about 10% is producing food so that the other 90% of us are thereby freed to do other things. This 10% figure in the nation is continuing to decrease. In the great agricultural state of California only 6% are now producing food. And yet both California and the rest of the nation are producing food in abundance. This is a tremendous change over the period of a few decades of serious utilization of research, of implementing basic research findings into practice across this bridge.

C   We do have some leads from social psychology, from some of the studies that have been done on modifying prejudice, changing food habits, and things of this nature, so that we do have some ideas on actually doing some work of this kind. We have some insights into changing behavior on a low, or should we say deep, level, on values. But of course changing values on a very deep level is extremely difficult. It is much easier to change behavior of individuals within groups than it is to change behaviors through the psychotherapy routine.

C   May I challenge that a little bit? For a while the literature and some of the things we have learned about attitude change suggested that the best we can do sometimes is to reinforce existing attitudes rather than change them. But in some of the newer work, where researchers are dealing with cognitive structure and needs, such as the Hovland project at Yale, including Abelson and Rosenberg and others, you find that sometimes changes in conduct do occur very drastically, a sort of reorganization, which I think is almost exactly what we mean by creativity. I think that what you said is no longer true. Sudden dramatic changes can occur and are lasting, and they happen just like that.

C   Right, I would second that.

C   I seem to be remembering things which I read that influenced me at the time but that I had forgotten. As you were talking I thought about a very great book, *Experiment in Autobiography*, by H. G. Wells. He saw clearly what was happening. He wrote in the late 1920's and 1930's a description of just what is occurring now. The last part of that book is especially interesting, because he went around and talked with world leaders including Stalin and F.D.R. He developed a phrase, "the open conspiracy," to describe what he foresaw as the direction in which the democratic society would move, and he identified industry, science, and education as the three critical elements in it. Particularly the alliance between industry and science he felt was important.

C   I would like to comment on the minority report, the aspect of the deeper, more basic kinds of changes in creativity that creative training programs or developmental programs are trying to accomplish. Sometimes in the all too brief reports that we are able to be given on programs of this kind, the idea might be gained that the person increases his ability, for example, to come up with x number of ideas or this or that without realizing the effect that this also has on the individual's attitude and behavior. As researchers, we have sensed and observed some of these changes, but we cannot yet report a great deal of systematically obtained evidence. One exception, however, is one of our studies, where we got significant changes on Gough's dominance scale. There are numerous of these apparent changes still to be measured, but I think that little evidence is yet available that this kind of thing has happened.

C   As a member of this subcommittee, I would like to make a few comments myself.   One is that I don't believe any of this discussion should be anonymous.   I think that this face-to-face contact, the interchange and exchange of opinions and ideas, is very healthy.   Differences of opinion are healthy.   If there is any conflict, it should be dealt with in the open.

C   May I comment on conflict briefly.   We exhibit a cordiality here at this conference, and I think it's genuine.   The reason why we don't argue, I think, about a lot of these things is that we know the other fellow's point of view and know that he can defend it very well.   There are certain orientations which I don't consider the best in the world, but I do know that one researcher may use a particular approach better than I would do.   I work in a certain way because that is the way I like to work.   Because someone else works in a different way doesn't mean his contribution is not valuable.   So I see a lot of these things as very academic and not worth arguing about.   I could go around and argue with everyone and they could all argue with me, but I see very little to gain from this academic chopping up, which can be done more easily informally and is done that way.   We know as a group what the weaknesses are in the various approaches we take, but we are willing to take a chance on moving ahead by each using his selected approach.

S   Speaking personally, in reading the research which many participants have reported elsewhere, I've tried to evaluate the implications of the results for the day-to-day work I do.   And I've also tried to take a longer view, to identify the positive contributions of a given approach to creativity and the areas where a different approach or interpretation might seem more valid.   Maybe you have hashed these matters out so much among yourselves that you all really know what the rest of you might see as strengths and weaknesses in the various approaches and have modified your own behavior just about as much as you are going to in this life.   But I said that we've come here for help, and while I know what I think, I haven't had the benefit of the earlier discussion you have participated in.   Yet, whenever I *have* heard what the rest of you think, it has broadened my opinion of the different approaches and it may change my own behavior.   Perhaps those who study the conference reports might also benefit by public availability of these comments.   The New York Academy of Sciences 1960 symposium is an example of what I mean, particularly Guilford's comments (Furness, 1960).

C   I think that we could go along with this, but we would add that we are not so sure what's good and what's bad.

C   I think that is a very important point. I'm sure most of you have had this reaction. I wonder whether it's valuable to suggest that people should do research in behavior change or to suggest that they do research in anything at all, since they are likely to do anything they please anyhow and they probably should. I think that Jablonski in his program with the high school students would affirm that it's probably not a good idea to tell everybody to do this or do that or to suggest exactly what the direction should be. I think that NSF has probably steered as clear from this as possible, and so has the Public Health Service and everybody else, and that is very good. I can understand that an expression of interest is worth while. But I think it should be clear that if you want people to do research that is going to be useful or creative, you probably just ought to leave them alone.

C   But if you spell out the areas of research for which there are felt needs, as has just been done by the subgroup, and make them known, each person can still take whatever role he wishes in the research he conducts. There will always be members of the research team who will look at this felt-need list and want to attack it. But unless it is made known, people may not do anything about it.

C   Not only this, but those engaged in basic research at the same time could be thinking of the implications. And this, I think, is a very important point.

C   Let me turn to another point. When I was invited to this meeting, I began to wonder what I would be doing at a conference on identification of creative talent. But the more I thought about it, the more I have come to believe that identification and behavior change are really separate sides of the same coin, and eventually we have to do both, of course. You can't handle identification in isolation, and you can't handle behavior change in isolation.

C   This brings up another point which I wanted to make. I wanted to object, too, to what the reporter said about our not being interested in prediction and identification. I think that we are very much interested in prediction and identification, but we are more interested in the immediate problem of environmental conditions, of trying to develop the potential that we already have on board. One objection was raised that this is a conference on the identification of creative scientific talent, not on environmental conditions. But I take issue and say that if we can create a climate where creativity can thrive, the creative people will identify themselves and will normally gravitate to the positions that require a higher degree of creativity. Another point that I wanted to make is that I noticed throughout the conference a tendency to speak of the creative or the noncreative as though we have two different things here entirely, that either a person is or he isn't creative. I think that this is dangerous because we see it a great deal in industry, where managers say, "I'm not so sure that I want creative people." Or they say, "We need a few creative people, and we'll put them over here to the side and give them special treatment. But the rest of these people we will treat the way we always have, with the club and what have you, forcing them to conform, controlling and directing them, observing them closely"—all the things which we think stifle creativity. If we are going to develop the creative potential, we have to apply across the board as much as possible those techniques which we feel allow creativity.

C   The one thing that I am interested in about this in industry pertains to the adjectives which the architects used to describe themselves as argumentative and forceful people and the comments that were made about courage. Back in 1916, I believe, David Sarnoff wrote a memo which he submitted to the Marconi Wireless people asking why they didn't have radio music boxes to be sold for reception of radio waves in every home. He predicted what the sales of these radio music boxes would be. This memo was kicked around in the Marconi Wireless Company, which was later taken over by RCA, GE, and Westinghouse. These companies kicked the memo around for five years and finally began to act on it. The first year that they produced and sold these radios, the sales came within a hundred thousand of Sarnoff's prediction. If that memo had gone through immediately, we might have had radio and all the electronics developments that have come out of it maybe five years earlier.

The one thing that I am curious about is what do people do with their creative products in industry after they create them, because nobody is necessarily waiting there with open arms. Some additional factor—salesmanship, persuasiveness, push, get-up-and-go, initiative—is needed to push an idea into an organization.

C   Plus the need on the public's part to want it.

C   I'm thinking of right inside our own company. What could we do to prepare the way for better reception of creative ideas by selecting and developing wiser judges of these ideas and products?

C   Maybe we could change the title of these conferences to the Identification and Development of Scientific Creativity.

C   The title we decided to put on the Wiley volume of selected papers from the first three conferences is *Scientific Creativity: Its Recognition and Development.*

C   Which shortens down to R and D. (*Laughter*)

C   This might be an indication of the maturity of these conferences.

Taylor   As a closing remark, we do appreciate and are amazed at the great involvement of those who have been here. Let me illustrate my point by citing the comments of one of our university administrators, a physical scientist, who came to a previous conference in this series. Some local people were mingling in the lodge lobby outside the conference room, and he chatted with them briefly during a break. Someone who knew him asked what was going on. He said, "It is a meeting mainly of psychologists." One of our participants then heard him hurriedly add, "But they really aren't much like psychologists; they are much more like scientists." (*Laughter*) It is this deep involvement in scientific research which has been impressive.

I also want to comment on the notion of the observers' sitting back, as their graduate training had taught them, and listing the good features and the features that are not so good in each report. I am becoming more and more convinced that we have overdone such training, in what amounts usually to destructive criticism, at the expense of needed training in productive, creative, and other constructive activities. May I then add the important observation that one positive thing about all the research that each of you has reported is that *you did it*—you did not let the destructive criticism within yourself or from others stop you from doing your research in creativity. *You found some way to do it and you did it.*

And because all of you did your research and because it was of such wide variety, we have been treated, in almost boundary-free mental space, to a rich and abundant feast upon which our minds have fed and grown during the past three days.

As you all realize, my strong belief is that the most vital elements in such research conferences are the people—their work and their ideas. So we do most truly appreciate your many fine contributions—in your reports and in your lively discussions—in this most challenging area of creativity. We also appreciate the financial support for this conference and for the entire conference series that has been provided by the National Science Foundation. And we are very happy that Milton Levine has again so well served as the NSF representative throughout this 1962 conference.

chapter 29 NSF's Efforts and Interests in Creative Talent

Milton Levine, National Science Foundation

S   I have been asked to provide the entire group during this formal part of the conference with some comments which several of us have made informally.

I would like to suggest a way to develop test items on "creativity" which might well fall within the approach of McPherson in Chapter 27 and also might have some reference to Astin's Table 1 in Chapter 21. Perhaps a socially related way of developing test items to measure creativity might be to try the direct approach with the individual who has already been identified as creative—the architect, psychologist, artist, musician, or anyone else.   After you have identified the "creative" individual, in addition to going through the predictor and criterion sessions with him, you might ask him directly, as McPherson pointed out, to give you a test item or a series of test items on an open-ended base. Since you have already identified him as creative, why not ask this "creative" person to develop the test item or items which he feels would identify a creative person?   This pretty much suggests that we use the same technique that the Strong Inventory uses—namely, that it takes one to identify one.   Perhaps those of you working in this area might experiment with this technique and develop it.

I have been asked throughout the past few days about my role within the National Science Foundation and how the NSF fits in the area of "creativity" and its support of the conference.   I would like to give you a very quick overview of the Foundation and where we fit.   The NSF has several divisions.   The Division of Scientific Personnel and Education is the one within which we work and the one which supports this conference. In addition to Scientific Personnel and Education, there are several other major organizational elements: Mathematical, Physical, and Engineering Sciences Division, Biological and Medical Sciences Division, and the Social Sciences Division. Within the Scientific Personnel and Education Division, there are a number of sections with which some of you are familiar: Course Content, Institutes, Fellowships, Special Projects, and Scientific Personnel and Education Studies Section. It is from this last Section that specific funds are provided to the University of Utah to support these conferences. Within the Scientific Manpower Section, there are two major activities—Scientific Manpower Studies and the National Register of Scientific and Technical Personnel. My position is Program Director of the National Register.

I might point out that the National Register works through the scientific communities specifically and supports the professional scientific societies in the collection of information. At present, we have data on over 200,000 scientists who reported to the National Register in 1960. We are currently in the process of collecting information for 1962. I would just like to give one piece of information out of the National Register data in an attempt to answer the subcommittee report that Lois-ellin Datta just gave as to why we should be interested in the creative behavior of scientists in industry. Since some 45% of the total scientific and technical personnel who have been registered are employed in industry and business, I think that you have some indication where almost half our scientific talent is employed, so there is definitely a reason to give some attention to scientists in industry. The kinds of data that we collect and report from the National Register include highest degree level, age, type of employer, kind of work performed, and years of professional experience. These data represent items which apparently everyone is interested in for one reason or another.

We also support, with the U.S. Office of Education, the Doctorate Survey conducted for the Federal Government by the National Research Council. Lindsey Harmon is responsible for this project, and we think that this is a greatly-needed research area to be supported.

I would like to give my personal evaluation of this conference. I come away perhaps more enthusiastic and excited than I was at the last conference, and I get this same general feeling from those of you with whom I have spoken who were also at the last conference. There seems to be a "jelling" of some progress toward a seeable goal. We are pleased to hear that selected papers of the last three conferences, for which numerous requests have been made both to the University of Utah and to the National Science Foundation, have been published. Since no more copies of the first three conference reports are available for distribution, the book of these selected papers, *Scientific Creativity: Its Recognition and Development* (Taylor and Barron, 1963), is very welcome. The Foundation's current support to the University of Utah was primarily for two phases of work: for the conference that we're all at now, and, as has been mentioned, for the preparation of a stock-taking report, a synthesis of what we have learned to date—what has come out of the 1955, 1957, and 1959 conferences. This stock-taking report (Taylor, 1964b) contains a discussion of promising areas of creativity research. I think that this report will be most welcomed by all individuals either currently in the field of creativity or looking for new areas to challenge their research efforts. The report of this present conference, as well as the earlier reports, will be in demand; and perhaps we can anticipate this demand by having more copies produced so that we don't run out so quickly. I believe that all these papers and reports are needed to satisfy a basic communication problem. We in this room have had the advantage of discussing creativity research face to face. The 200 nominees who wished to attend this 1962 conference and are not sitting here would very much like to get the same information as we have received. I think what is really needed is a wider dissemination across all disciplines. The present knowledge of creativity should be disseminated to other groups—chemists, biologists, physicists, artists, and educators. Individuals in different areas of specialization might well push the movement of better defining, identifying, and recognizing creativity, as well as implementing programs of creativity.

A common thread of discussion throughout this session has been the implications of creativity in different settings. What are the implications to the educative process? What does this really mean to educational institutions? What could they do; what should they do? What does it mean, and what are the implications in terms of productivity in industry, in the educational institution, in government? What are the implications to the scientific community? Once we distribute information on creativity widely, across all disciplines, what will be the reaction of the scientific community among the several disciplines? What will be the implications to our national goals? And I think that we should never forget (I know this group won't) that as we start moving to wider circles of dissemination of this information, what will be the implications for the individual? How will he be utilized? What happens to the individuals who are now correctly or incorrectly identified or who are not identified as creative? What problems have been caused, or may be caused in the future, by the emphasis on the creative individual? We look to those of you in this group, and to all the persons that each of you individually and collectively will influence by your research, to ensure that these issues will not be overlooked. The specific enthusiasm that has been expressed by each of the speakers on the panel and the type of activity reported gives one the feeling that the breakthroughs in the area of creativity seem to be a little closer.

I cannot help but echo the need for greater support for research in the field of creativity. The support which has been given by the NSF should be supplemented, I believe, by industry, by private foundations, and by universities. And I think that the support should come from the groups that have expressed needs, from those groups that are asking questions of implication. I think it is healthy that the support come from a variety of sources. The Federal Government has kicked it off; the government may continue it, but the critical thing is that "creativity" should get wide support rather than solely support from government agencies. The point made about the individual's freedom in getting his research done is a good one; having many more groups supporting this research is one way of assuring this freedom.

Finally, I would express our sincere thanks to the chairman, the steering committee members, and the many local assistants for having put together a very successful conference. I think that as a result of the difficult work that has been accomplished during the past several years by many good researchers in creativity, we are really at the threshold of moving in a positive direction. Thank you.

C   May I ask a question about this long register form which we are asked to fill out and which looks like lots of questionnaires. Could you tell us how the information we all provide is used in times of urgent need?

S   The National Register of Scientific and Technical Personnel, a comprehensive program for registration of United States scientists, is maintained so that timely information will always be available on the supply and professional characteristics of qualified personnel in critical science fields.

As first conceived, the primary purpose was to provide a means for identifying and locating individuals with special scientific and engineering skills during periods of full or limited mobilization. The current National Register serves also as a source of statistical information useful in estimating supply, level of training, type of work performed, and related data on scientific and technical personnel.

The information on individual scientists in the National Register is considered privileged and is not available for placement purposes or other private uses. Individuals are identified only where an urgent need clearly in the national interest exists. I will give two examples of when we identify individuals. It is important that scientists in the United States be aware of research that is being done in foreign countries, so the

NSF supports the translation of scientific literature. Since the information we collect on all the scientists in the United States includes their foreign language proficiencies, we do identify selected people in critical scientific fields who can then be contacted to assist in the translations of foreign journals.

On another occasion we received an urgent request for a physiologist who had a high proficiency in Russian and lived or was available within the Washington, D.C., area; also, it would be most desirable if this individual were engaged in government activity. This scientist would accompany a Russian delegation scheduled to arrive within two days. Within 45 minutes, six names were identified, and from this list one individual was able to assist materially. I would like to repeat that the National Register releases data on the characteristics of the scientific and technical personnel and identifies key personnel only when in the national interest. The National Register is not used for recruiting, placement, or other private uses.

Bibliography

Adkins, D. C., and S. B. Lyerly. *Factor analysis of reasoning tests.* Chapel Hill: Univer. of North Carolina, 1951.

Allport, G. W., P. E. Vernon, and G. Lindzey. *Study of values: manual of directions* (rev. ed.). Boston: Houghton Mifflin, 1951.

Andrews, E. G. The development of imagination in the pre-school child. *Univer. of Iowa studies in character*, 1939, 3 (4).

Astin, A. W. An empirical characterization of higher educational institutions. *J. educ. Psychol.*, 1962a, 53, 224–225.

Astin, A. W. "Productivity" of undergraduate institutions. *Science*, 1962b, 136, 129–135.

Astin, A. W. An empirical characterization of higher educational institutions. *J. educ. Psychol.*, 1962c, 53, 224–235.

Astin, A. W. Differential college effects on the motivation of talented students to obtain the Ph.D. degree. *J. educ. Psychol.*, 1963.

Astin, A. W. Criterion-centered research. *Educ. psychol. Measml.*, 1964, 24, (No. 3), in press.

Astin, A. W., and J. L. Holland. The environmental assessment technique: a way to measure college environments. *J. educ. Psychol.*, 1961, 52, 308–316.

Astin, A. W., and J. L. Holland. The distribution of "wealth" in higher education. *Coll. Univer.*, 1962, 37, 113–125.

Bales, R. F., and A. S. Couch. *The value profile: a factor analytic study of value statements.* Harvard University. (Mimeographed)

Barron, F. Personality style and perceptual choice. *J. Pers.*, 1952, 20, 384–401.

Barron, F. Complexity-simplicity as a personality dimension. *J. abnorm. soc. Psychol.*, 1953a, 48, 163–172.

Barron, F. Some personality correlates of independence of judgment. *J. Pers.*, 1953b, 21, 287–297.

Barron, F. The disposition towards originality. *J. abnorm. soc. Psychol.*, 1955, 51, 478–485.

Barron, F. Originality in relation to personality and intellect. *J. Pers.*, 1957, 25, 730–742.

Barron, F. The psychology of imagination. *Sci. Amer.*, 1958, 199 (3), 150.

Barron, F. Current work at the Institute of Personality Assessment and Research. *In* C. W. Taylor (Ed.). *The third (1959) research conference on the identification of creative scientific talent.* Salt Lake City: Univer. of Utah Press, 1959, pp. 72–76.

Barron, F. Review of: Kubie, L. W. *Neurotic distortion of the creative process.* (Porter Lectures, Series 22.) Lawrence: Univers. of Kansas Press, 1958. Reviewed in: *Contemp. Psychol.*, 1960, 5, 170–171.

Barron, F. The creative writer. *Calif. Mon.*, 1962a, 72 (5), 11–14, 38–39.

Barron, F. Psychotherapy and creativity. *In* G. S. Nielsen (Ed.). *Proceedings of the XIV International Congress of Applied Psychology,* Copenhagen, 1961. Copenhagen: Munksgaard, 1962b. Vol. IV, pp. 36–49.

Barron, F. Creative vision and expression. *In* A. Frazier (Ed.). *New insights and the curriculum:* Yearbook 1963, Association for Supervision and Curriculum Development. Washington: National Education Assoc., 1963a. Pp. 285–305.

Barron, F. *Creativity and psychological health.* Princeton, N. J.: Van Nostrand, 1963b.

Barron, F. Diffusion, integration, and enduring attention in the creative process. *In* R. W. White (Ed.). *The study of lives: Essays on personality in honor of Henry A. Murray.* New York: Atherton Press, 1963c. Pp. 234–248.

Barron, F. Discovering the creative personality. In *College Admissions 10: The behavioral sciences and education.* Princeton, N. J.: College Entrance Examination Board, 1963d. Pp. 79–85.

Barron, F. The disposition toward originality. *In* C. W. Taylor and F. Barron (Eds.). *Scientific creativity: its recognition and development.* New York: Wiley, 1963e. Pp. 139–152.

Barron, F. The needs for order and for disorder as motives in creative activity. *In* C. W. Taylor and F. Barron (Eds.). *Scientific creativity: its recognition and development.* New York: Wiley, 1963f. Pp. 153–160.

Barron, F., and T. Leary. *To find and foster creativity.* A report of the Rhode Island School of Design. Providence, R. I.: 1961.

Bechtoldt, H. P. Construct validity: a critique. *Amer. Psychologist,* 1959, 14, 619–629.

Beittel, K. R. A comparison of Brittain's and Guilford's tests of creativity and a factor analysis of ten measures thought to be useful for research in art education. Unpublished research studies sponsored by the Council on Research. The Pennsylvania State Univer., 1954–55 and 1956.

Beittel, K. R. The creativity complex in the visual arts. *Studies in art Educ.,* 1959, 1 (1), 26–37.

Beittel, K. R. Art. Review of research in art and art education. *In* Chester W. Harris (Ed.). *Encyclopedia of educational research.* (3rd ed.). 1960.

Beittel, K. R. (Ed.). Creativity, education, and art: interpretations. Research issue, *Eastern Arts Assoc. Bull.,* 1961, 18 (4).

Beittel, K. R. Construction and reconstruction of teaching methods through experimental research. *Eastern Arts Assoc. Bull.,* 1962a, 19 (4).

Beittel, K. R. Predictors and settings relating to the capacity for creative action in the visual arts. A progress report supported by the National Science Foundation GL-17984. Department of Art Education, The Pennsylvania State Univer., 1962b. P. 88.

Beittel, K. R. Factor analyses of three dimensions of the art judgment complex: criteria, art objects, and judges. *J. exp. Educ.,* 1963, 32 (2), 167–174.

Beittel, K. R., and R. C. Burkhart. The effect of self-reflective training in art on the capacity for creative action. Project No. 1874, U. S. Office of Education Cooperative Research Program. The Pennsylvania State Univer., 1962.

Berlyne, D. E. *Conflict, arousal, and curiosity.* New York: McGraw-Hill, 1960.

Blatt, S. Experimental evidence of preconscious functioning in efficient problem solving. Paper read at EPA meetings, New York, 1960.

Blatt, S. Patterns of cardiac arousal during complex mental activity. *J. abnorm. soc. Psychol.*, 1961, 63, 272–282.

Block, J., and P. Petersen. Some personality correlates of confidence, caution, and speed in a decision situation. *J. abnorm. soc. Psychol.*, 1955, 51, 34–41.

Bloom, B. S. Report on creativity research by the examiner's office of the University of Chicago. *In* C. W. Taylor and F. Barron (Eds.). *Scientific creativity: its recognition and development.* New York: Wiley, 1963.

Bouthilet, Lorraine. The measurement of intuitive thinking. Unpublished doctoral dissertation, Univer. of Chicago, 1948.

Brittain, W. L. Experiments for a possible test to determine some aspects of creativity in the visual arts. Unpublished doctoral dissertation, The Pennsylvania State Univer., 1952.

Brittain, W. L., and K. R. Beittel. Analyses of levels of creative performance in the visual arts. *J. Aesthetics and art Criticism*, 1960, 19 (1), 83–90.

Brittain, W. L., and K. R. Beittel. A study of some tests of creativity in relationship to performances in the visual arts. *Studies in art Educ.*, 1961, 2 (2).

Bruner, J. S. *On knowing.* Cambridge: Harvard Press, 1962.

Brunswick, E. *Systematic and representative design of psychological experiments.* Berkeley: Univer. of California Press, 1949.

Buel, W. D. Supervisor's evaluation of research personnel. Chicago: Science Research Associates, 1960.

Burgart, H. Art in higher education: the relationship of art experience to personality, general creativity, and art performance. *Studies in art Educ.*, 1961, 2 (2), 14–35.

Burge, M. *Intuition and science.* Englewood Cliffs, N. J.: Prentice-Hall (Spectrum), 1962.

Burkhart, R. C. The relation of intelligence to art ability. *J. Aesthetics and art Criticism*, 1958, 17 (2).

Burkhart, R. C. An analysis of individuality of art expression at the senior high school level. Unpublished doctoral dissertation, The Pennsylvania State Univ., 1957.

Burkhart, R. C. The creativity-personality continuum based on spontaneity and deliberateness in art. *Studies in art Educ.*, 1960, 2 (1), 43–65.

Burkhart, R. C. The interrelationship of separate criteria for creativity in art and student teaching to four personality factors. *Studies in art Educ.*, 1961, 3 (1).

Burkhart, R. C. *Spontaneous and deliberate ways of learning in art.* Scranton: International Textbook Co., 1962.

Burkhart, R. C., and E. Nitschke. The effect of the depth vs. breadth method of instruction upon progress in art as self-reflective learning. Report to National Science Foundation. The Pennsylvania State Univer., 1962.

Burroughs, W., and B. Gysin. *The exterminator.* San Francisco: Auerhahan Press, 1960.

Bush, G. P., and L. H. Hattery. Teamwork and creativity in research. *Admin. Sci. Quart.*, 1956, 1, 361–372.

Cardinet, Jean. Esthetic preferences and personality. Unpublished doctoral dissertation, Univer. of Chicago, 1952.

Carroll, J. B. A factor analysis of verbal abilities. *Psychometrika*, 1941, 6, 279–307.

Cattell, R. B., *et al.* *The sixteen personality factors questionnaire.* Champaign, Ill.: Institute for Personality and Ability Testing.

Christal, R. E.   Factor analytic study of visual memory.   *Psychol. Monogr.*, 1958, 72 (Whole No. 466).

Christensen, P. R., and J. P. Guilford.   An experimental study of verbal fluency. *Brit. J. stat. Psychol.*, 1963, 16, 1–26.

Christensen, P. R., J. P. Guilford, and R. C. Wilson.   Relations of creative responses to working time and instructions.   *J. exp. Psychol.*, 1957, 53, 82–89.

Cowen, E. L.   Stress reduction and problem-solving rigidity.   *J. consult. Psychol.*, 1952, 16, 425–428.

Cronbach, L. J.   The two disciplines of scientific psychology.   *Amer. Psychologist*, 1957, 12, 671–684.

Crutchfield, R. S.   Conformity and character.   *Amer. Psychologist*, 1955, 10, 191–198.

Crutchfield, R. S.   Personal and situational factors in conformity to group pressure. Proceedings of the XVth International Congress of Psychology, Brussels, 1957. *Acta Psychologica*, 1959, 15, 386–388.

Crutchfield, R. S.   Conformity and creative thinking.   *In* H. E. Gruber, G. Terrell, and M. Wertheimer (Eds.).   *Contemporary approaches to creative thinking: a symposium held at the University of Colorado.*   New York: Atherton Press, 1962a. Pp. 120–140.

Crutchfield, R. S.   Detrimental effects of conformity pressures on creative thinking. *Psychol. Beit.*, 1962b, 6, 463–471.

Crutchfield, R. S.   Independent thought in a conformist world.   *In* S. M. Farber and R. H. L. Wilson (Eds.).   *Conflict and creativity. Control of the mind, Part 2.* New York: McGraw-Hill, 1963.   Pp. 208–228.

Ditman, K. S., M. Hayman, and J. R. B. Whittlesey.   Nature and frequency of claims following LSD.   *J. nerv. ment. Dis.*, 1962, 134, 346–352.

Doerter, J.   A study to determine the influence of college art instructors upon their students' painting.   Unpublished doctoral dissertation, The Pennsylvania State Univer., 1962.

Ellison, R. L.   The relationship of certain biographical information to success in science.   Unpublished master's thesis, Univer. of Utah, 1960.

Fiedler, F. E.   Leader attitudes and group effectiveness.   Urbana: Univer. of Illinois Press, 1958.

Fiedler, F. E.   Leader attitudes, group climate, and group creativity.   *J. abnorm. Psychol.*, 1962, 65, 308–318.

Fiedler, F. E.   A contingency model of leadership effectiveness.   *In* L. Berkowitz (Ed.).   *Advances in experimental social psychology.*   New York: Academic Press, 1964.

Fiedler, F. E., A. R. Bass, and Judith M. Fielder.   The leader's perception of co-workers, group climate, and group creativity: a cross validation.   Group Effectiveness Research Laboratory, Univer. of Illinois, 1961.   (Mimeographed)

Fiedler, F. E., P. London, and R. S. Nemo.   Hypnotically induced leader attitudes and group creativity.   Group Effectiveness Research Laboratory, Univer. of Illinois, 1961.   (Mimeographed)

Fiedler, F. E., and W. A. T. Meuwese.   Leader's contribution to task performance in cohesive and uncohesive groups.   *J. abnorm. soc. Psychol.*, 1963, 67, 83–87.

Fiedler, F. E., W. A. T. Meuwese, and Sophie Oonk.   Performance of laboratory tasks requiring group creativity.   *Acta Psychologica*, 1961, 18, 100–119.

Flanagan, J. C.   The relation of a new ingenuity measure to other variables.   *In* C. W. Taylor (Ed.).   *The third (1959) University of Utah research conference on the identification of creative scientific talent.*   Salt Lake City: Univer. of Utah Press, 1959.   Pp. 117–118.

Fleming, E. S., and S. Weintraub. Attitudinal rigidity as a measure of creativity in gifted children. *J. educ. Psychol.*, 1962, 53, 81–85.

French, J. W. *The description of personality measurement in terms of rotated factors.* Princeton, N. J.: Educational Testing Service, 1953.

Frost, R. Between prose and verse. *Atlantic Mon.*, April 1962.

Furness, F. F. Fundamentals of psychology; the psychology of thinking. *Annals N. Y. acad. Sci.*, 1960, 91.

Gershon, A., J. P. Guilford, and P. R. Merrifield. Figural and symbolic divergent-production abilities in adolescent and adult populations. *Rep. psychol. Lab.*, No. 29. Los Angeles: Univer. of Southern California, 1963. P. 27.

Getzels, J. W., and P. W. Jackson. *Creativity and intelligence.* New York: Wiley, 1962.

Getzels, J. W., and P. W. Jackson. The highly intelligent and the highly creative adolescent: a summary of some research findings. *In* C. W. Taylor and F. Barron (Eds.). *Scientific creativity: its recognition and development.* New York: Wiley, 1963. Pp. 161–172.

Ghiselin, B. *The creative process.* Berkeley: Univer. of California Press, 1952. Also New York: Mentor Books, 1955.

Ghiselin, B. (Ed.). Mathematical creation. *The creative process.* New York: The New American Library, 1955. P. 42.

Ghiselin, B. Ultimate criteria for two levels of creativity. *In* C. W. Taylor and F. Barron (Eds.). *Scientific creativity: its recognition and development.* New York: Wiley, 1963. Pp. 30–43.

Ghiselli, E. E., and T. L. Lodahl. Patterns of managerial traits and group effectiveness. *J. abnorm. soc. Psychol.*, 1958, 57, 61–66.

Giopolus, P. The relationship of tests and physical sensitivity to tests of aesthetic preference and performance. Unpublished master's thesis, The Pennsylvania State Univer., 1959.

Glidewell, J. C. Helping function. Paper presented at the Management Work Conference, Washington, D. C., 1962.

Godfrey, Eleanor P., F. E. Fiedler, and D. M. Hall. *Boards, management, and company success.* Danville: Interstate Publishers, 1959.

Gombrich, E. H. *Art and illusion.* New York: Pantheon Books, 1960.

Gordon, W. J. J. *Synectics: the development of creative capacity.* New York: Harper, 1961.

Gough, H. G. *California psychological inventory manual.* Palo Alto: Consulting Psychologists Press, 1957.

Gough, H. C. Imagination—undeveloped resource. In *Proceedings of the first annual conference on research developments in personnel management.* Los Angeles: Univer. of California, Institute of Industrial Relations, 1956. Pp. 4–10. *Reprinted in* S. J. Parnes and H. F. Harding. *A source book for creative thinking.* New York: Scribner's, 1962. Pp. 217–226.

Gough, H. G., and Woodworth, D. G. Stylistic variations among professional research scientists. *J. Psychol.*, 1960, 49, 87–98.

Guilford, J. P. Some lessons from aviation psychology. *Amer. Psychologist*, 1948, 3 (1), 3–11.

Guilford, J. P. An emerging view in learning theory. *Western Wash. coll. Bull.*, 1960a, 29–46.

Guilford, J. P. Basic conceptual problems in the psychology of thinking. *Ann. N. Y. acad. Sci.*, 1960b, 91 (1), 6–21.

Guilford, J. P.   Frontiers of thinking that teachers should know about.   *Reading Teacher*, 1960c, 13, 176–182.

Guilford, J. P.   The nature of creativity.   *Western Wash. coll. Bull.*, 1960d, 17–28.

Guilford, J. P.   The nature of intelligence.   *Western Wash. coll. Bull.*, 1960e, 3–16.

Guilford, J. P.   The psychology of creativity.   *Creative crafts*, 1960f, 1, 5–8.

Guilford, J. P.   Factorial angles to psychology.   *Psychol. Rev.*, 1961, 68, 1–20.

Guilford, J. P.   An informational view of mind.   *J. psychol. Researches*, 1962a, 6, 1–10.

Guilford, J. P.   Creativity in the visual arts.   *Creative Crafts*, 1962b, 3, 2–5.

Guilford, J. P.   Creativity: its measurement and development.   *In* S. J. Parnes and H. F. Harding (Eds.).   *A source book for creative thinking.*   New York: Scribners, 1962c, 151–168.

Guilford, J. P.   Factors that aid and hinder creativity.   *Teachers Coll. Rec.*, 1962d, 63, 380–392.

Guilford, J. P.   Parameters and categories of talent.   In *The Yearbook of Education.*   London: Evans Brothers, 1962e, 151–168.

Guilford, J. P.   Potentiality for creativity.   *Gifted Child Quart.*, 1962f, 6, 87–90.

Guilford, J. P.   Potentiality for creativity and its measurement.   In *Proceedings of the 1962 invitational conference on testing problems.*   Princeton: Educational Testing Service, 1962g, 31–39.

Guilford, J. P.   An informational theory of creative thinking.   *USAD Instructors' J.*, 1963a, 1, 28–33.

Guilford, J. P.   The nature of intellectual activity.   In *The behavioral sciences and education.*   New York: College Entrance Examination Board, 1963b, 65–73.

Guilford, J. P., M. S. Allen, and P. R. Merrifield.   The evaluation of selected intellectual factors by creative research scientists.   *Rep. psychol. Lab.*, No. 25.   Los Angeles: Univer. of Southern California, 1960.   P. 12.

Guilford, J. P., R. M. Berger, and P. R. Christensen.   A factor-analytic study of planning: I. Hypotheses and description of tests.   Los Angeles: Psychol. Lab., Univer. of Southern California, 1954.

Guilford, J. P., P. R. Christensen, J. W. Frick, and P. R. Merrifield.   Factors of interest in thinking.   *J. gen. Psychol.*, 1961, 75, 57–74.

Guilford, J. P., and P. R. Merrifield.   The structure-of-intellect model: its uses and implications.   *Rep. psychol. Lab.*, No. 24.   Los Angeles: Univer. of Southern California, 1960.   P. 28.

Guilford, J. P., P. R. Merrifield, P. R. Christensen, and J. W. Frick.   Some new symbolic factors of cognition and convergent production.   *Educ. psychol. Measmt.*, 1961a, 21, 515–541.

Guilford, J. P., P. R. Merrifield, P. R. Christensen, and J. W. Frick.   Interrelationships between certain abilities and certain traits of motivation and temperament.   *J. gen. Psychol.*, 1961b, 76, 37–74.

Guilford, J. P., P. R. Merrifield, P. R. Christensen, and J. W. Frick.   The role of intellectual factors in problem solving.   *Psychol. Monogr.*, 1962, 76 (Whole No. 529).

Guilford, J. P., P. R. Merrifield, and A. B. Cox.   Creative thinking in children at the junior high school levels.   *Rep. psychol. Lab.*, No. 26.   Los Angeles: Univer. of Southern California, 1961, p. 35.

Harris, C. W.   Review of this issue.   In *Educ. and psychol. testing, rev. of educ. res.*, 1962, 32 (1), 103–107.

Helson, Ravenna.   *Creative interest in women: its personality context and relation to creativity.*   Unpublished manuscript.

Hoffa, Harean. The relationship of art experience to some attributes of conformity. Unpublished doctoral dissertation, The Pennsylvania State Univer., 1959.

Holland, J. L. Undergraduate origins of American scientists. *Science*, 1957, 126, 433–437.

Holland, J. L. Determinants of college choice. *Coll. Univer.*, 1959a, 35, 11–28.

Holland, J. L. The prediction of college grades from the California Psychological Inventory and the Scholastic Aptitude Test. *J. educ. Psychol.*, 1959b, 50, 135–142.

Holland, J. L. The prediction of college grades from personality and aptitude variables. *J. educ. Psychol.*, 1960, 51, 245–254.

Holland, J. L. Creative and academic performance among talented adolescents. *J. educ. Psychol.*, 1961, 52, 136–147.

Holland, J. L. Explorations of a theory of vocational choice and achievement: II. A four year prediction study. *Psychol. Rep.*, 1963, 12, 547–594.

Holland, J. L. Some explorations of a theory of vocational choice: I. One and two year longitudinal studies. *Psychol. Monogr.*, 1962b, 76 (26 Whole No. 545).

Holland, J. L. The nature of student achievement: a summary and model for research and practice. Evanston: National Merit Scholarship Corp., 1962c. (Mimeographed)

Holland, J. L., and A. W. Astin. The prediction of the academic, artistic, scientific, and social achievement of undergraduates of superior scholastic aptitude. *J. educ. Psychol.*, 1962, 53, 132–143.

Holland, J. L., and R. C. Nichols. The prediction of academic and extra-curricular achievement in college. *J. educ. Psychol.*, 1964, 55, 55–65.

Houston, J. P., and S. A. Mednick. Creativity and the need for novelty. *J. abnorm. soc. Psychol.*, in press.

Hutchinson, W. L. Creative and productive thinking in the classroom. Unpublished doctoral dissertation, Univer. of Utah, 1963.

Huxley, A. *The doors of perception.* New York: Harper, 1954.

Huxley, A. *Heaven and hell.* New York: Harper, 1956.

Huxley, A. *Island.* New York: Viking, 1959.

Hyman, R. On prior information and creativity. *Psychol. Reps.*, 1961, 9, 151–161.

Hyman, R. Creativity. In *International science and technology*, 1963. P. 51.

Jacobsen, T. L., and J. J. Asher. Validity of the concept constancy measure of creative problem solving. *J. gen. Psychol.*, 1963, 68, 9–19.

Jahoda, Marie. *Current concepts of positive mental health.* Basic Books, 1958.

Johnson, D. M., R. C. Johnson, and A. D. Mark. A mathematical analysis of verbal fluency. *J. gen. Psychol.*, 1951, 44, 121–128.

Jones, C. A. Some relationships between creative writing and creative drawing of sixth grade children. Unpublished doctoral dissertation, The Pennsylvania State Univer., 1961.

Joyce, J. *Finnegan's wake.* New York: Viking, 1959.

Jung, C. *Psychological types.* New York: Harcourt Brace, 1923.

Jung, C. Psychological commentary. *In* W. Y. Evanswentz (Ed.). *The Tibetan book of the dead.* London: Oxford Univer. Press, 1960.

Karlin, J. E. A factorial study of auditory function. *Psychometrika*, 1942, 7, 251–279.

Kelley, H. P. *A factor analysis of memory ability.* Princeton; N. J.: Educational Testing Service, 1954.

Kincaid, Clarence. The determination and description of various creative attributes of children. Unpublished doctoral dissertation, The Pennsylvania State Univer., 1960.

Kirchwer, W. K., and M. D. Dunnette. The successful salesman—as he sees himself. *Personnel*, 1958, 35, 67–70.

Klaus, D. J., and A. A. Lumsdaine. *Some economic realities of teaching machine instruction.* Pittsburgh: American Institute of Research, 1960.

Kohler, W., and J. Fishback. The destruction of the Muller-Lyer illusion in repeated trials: II. Satiation patterns and memory traces. *J. exp. Psychol.*, 1950, 40, 398–410.

Lacklen, R., and L. R. Harmon. Criterion committee report. *In* C. W. Taylor (Ed.). *The second (1957) University of Utah research conference on the identification of creative scientific talent.* Salt Lake City: Univer. of Utah Press, 1958.

Lansing, K. M. The effect of class size and room size upon the creative drawings of fifth-grade children. Unpublished doctoral dissertation, The Pennsylvania State Univer., 1956.

Leary, T. *Multilevel measurement of interpersonal behavior.* Cambridge: Psychological Consultation Service, 1956.

Leary, T. *Interpersonal diagnosis of personality.* New York: Ronald Press, 1957.

Leary, T. Think, talk, act. Paper read at APA, Chicago, September 1960.

Leary, T. Helping the helpless. Paper read at Northwest Regional Conference of the American Public Welfare Assoc., Boston, 1961b.

Leary, T. How to change behavior. *In* G. S. Nielsen (Ed.). *Clinical psychology.* Copenhagen: Munksgaard, 1962a.

Leary, T. Interpersonal behavior and behaviorism. Harvard Univer., 1962b. (Dittoed)

Leary, T. Measuring verbal interaction in Freudian and Rogerian psychotherapy. Harvard Univer., 1962c. (Dittoed)

Leary, T., and W. Clark. Religious implications of consciousness-expanding drugs. *Religious Educ.*, 1963.

Leary, T., and M. Gill. The dimensions and a measure of the profess of psychotherapy. In E. Rubenstein (Ed.). *Research in psychotherapy.* Amer. Psych. Assoc., 1959.

Leary, T., and R. Metzner. *The ecstatic experience.* Cambridge: Psychedelic Monographs, 1964.

Leary, T., G. H. Litwin, and R. Metzner. Reactions to psilocybin administered in a supportive environment. *J. nerv. ment. Diseases*, 1963, 137 (6).

Leary, T., R. Metzner, and R. Alpert. *The psychedelic experience.* New Hyde Park: University Books, 1964.

Leary, T., R. Metzner, M. Presnell, W. Weil, R. Schwitzgebel, and S. Kinne. A change program for adult offenders using psilocybin. Cambridge: Psychedelic Review Service, 1963.

Lienard, Marguerite. What is the relationship of children's satisfaction with their art products to improvement in art? *Studies in art Educ.*, 1960, 3 (1), 43–65.

Linderman, E. The relationship of specific aspects of art picture judging to some personality variables of the judges. Unpublished doctoral dissertation, The Pennsylvania State Univer., 1960.

Lowenfeld, V., and K. R. Beittel. Interdisciplinary criteria of creativity in the arts and sciences: a progress report. *Research in art Educ.*, 9th Yearbook of the NAEA, 1959. Pp. 35–44.

Loy, Lorraine. The effect of verbalization on transfer. Unpublished master's thesis, Univer. of Utah, 1961.

McGlothlin, W. W.   Long-lasting effects of LSD on certain attitudes in normals: an experimental proposal.   California: Rand Corp., 1962.   (Mimeographed)

McHale, W. J.   Some variables relating to three-dimensional and two-dimensional performances: a comparative study.   Unpublished doctoral thesis, The Pennsylvania State Univer., 1962.

MacKinnon, D. W.   The creative mind: contribution to a panel discussion.   *Northern Calif. Bull.*   (AIA), 1958, 11, 6–7, 10.

MacKinnon, D. W.   The creative worker in engineering.   In *Proceedings of the eleventh annual industrial engineering institute*, Univer. of California, Los Angeles, Feb. 6, 1959, and Berkeley, Feb. 7, 1959.   Pp. 88–96.

MacKinnon, D. W.   Genus architecturs creator varietas Americanus.   *AIA J.*, September, 1960a, 31–35.

MacKinnon, D. W.   The highly effective individual.   *Teachers coll. Rec.*, 1960b, 61, 367–378.

MacKinnon, D. W.   Identifying and developing creativity.   In *Selection and educational differentiation*.   Field Service Center and Center for the Study of Higher Education, Univer. of California, Berkeley, 1960c,   Pp. 75–89.

MacKinnon, D. W.   What do we mean by talent and how do we test for it?   In *The search for talent*.   New York: College Entrance Examination Board, 1960d.   Pp. 20–29.

MacKinnon, D. W.   Characteristics of the creative person: Implications for the teaching-learning process.   In *Current issues in higher education*.   Washington, D. C.: National Education Assoc., 1961a.   Pp. 89–92.

MacKinnon, D. W.   Fostering creativity in students of engineering.   *J. Engrg. Educ.*, 1961b, 52, 129–142.

MacKinnon, D. W.   Intellect and motive in scientific inventors: Implications for supply.   In *The rate and direction of inventive activity: economic and social factors*.   A conference of the universities-national bureau committee for economic research and the committee on economic growth of the Social Science Research Council.   Princeton: Princeton Univer. Press, 1962a.   Pp. 361–384.

MacKinnon, D. W.   The identification and utilization of talent: a symposium.   Introduction.   In G. S. Nielson (Ed.).   *Proceedings of the XIV international congress of applied psychology*, Copenhagen, 1961.   Copenhagen: Munksgaard, 1962b.   Vol. 5, pp. 48–52.

MacKinnon, D. W.   The nature and nurture of creative talent.   *Amer. Psychologist*, 1962c, 17, 484–495.

MacKinnon, D. W.   The personality correlates of creativity: a study of American architects.   In G. S. Nielsen (Ed.).   *Proceedings of the XIV international congress of applied psychology*, Copenhagen, 1961.   Copenhagen: Munksgaard, 1962d.   Vol. 2, pp. 11–39.

MacKinnon, D. W.   What makes a person creative?   *Sat. Rev.*, Feb. 10, 1962e, 15–17, 69.

MacKinnon, D. W.   Contribution to panel discussion: Prediction of creativity and success.   In S. M. Farber and R. H. L. Wilson (Eds.).   *Conflict and creativity. Control of the mind, Part 2*.   New York: McGraw-Hill, 1963a, Pp. 59–69.

MacKinnon, D. W.   Creativity and images of the self.   In R. W. White (Ed.).   *The study of lives: essays on personality in honor of Henry A. Murray*.   New York: Atherton Press, 1963b.   Pp. 250–278.

MacKinnon, D. W.   The identification of creativity (Ie recherche de la creativite).   In English and in French.   *Bull. de l' Assoc. internat. de Psychol. appliquee*, 1963c, 12 (1), 24–47.

MacKinnon, D. W. Identifying and developing creativity. *J. secondary Educ.*, 1963d, 38, 166–174. Abbreviated and slightly modified version of an earlier paper by the same title (1960c, q.v.).

McPherson, J. H. *Manual for interviewers of applicants for technical positions.* Midland: The Dow Chemical Co., 1955.

McPherson, J. H. *Independence: an important variable in the description of the creative individual.* Midland: The Dow Chemical Co., 1962.

Maier, N. R. F. *The appraisal interview.* New York: Wiley, 1958.

Maier, N. R. F., and L. R. Hoffman. Quality of first and second solutions in group problem-solving. *J. appl. Psychol.*, 1960, 44, 278–283.

Maltzman, I. On the training of originality. *Psychol. Rev.*, 1960, 67, 229–242.

Maltzman, I., W. Bogartz, and L. Breger. A procedure for increasing word association originality and its transfer effects. *J. exp. Psychol.*, 1958, 56, 392–398.

Maltzman, I., S. Simon, and L. Licht. The persistence of originality training effects. *Tech. Rep.* No. 4, Contract Nonr 233 (50). Berkeley: Univer. of California and Office of Naval Research, 1959.

Maslow, A. H. Self-actualizing people. A study of psychological health. *Reprinted from* W. Wolff (Ed.). *Personality symposium.* Grune and Stratton, 1950. Pp. 11–34.

Maslow, A. H. *Motivation and personality.* New York: Harper, 1954.

Mattil, E. L., *et al.* The effect of a "depth" vs. a "breadth" method of art instruction at the ninth grade level. *Studies in art Educ.*, 1961, 3 (1), 75–87.

Maw, W., and Ethel W. Maw. Establishing criterion groups for evaluating measures of curiosity. *J. exp. Educ.*, 1961, 29, 299–305.

Meadow, A., and S. J. Parnes. Evaluation of training in creative problem-solving. *J. appl. Psychol.*, 1959, 43, 189–194.

Meadow, A., S. J. Parnes, and H. Reese. Influence of brainstorming instructions and problem sequence on a creative problem-solving test. *J. appl. Psychol.*, 1959, 43, 413–416.

Meinz, Algalee P. General creativity of elementary majors as influenced by courses in industrial arts and art education. Unpublished doctoral dissertation, The Pennsylvania State Univer., 1960.

Merrifield, P. R., J. P. Guilford, and A. Gershon. The differentiation of divergent-production abilities at the sixth-grade level. *Rep. psychol. Lab.*, No. 27. Los Angeles: Univer. of Southern California, 1963, 15.

Meuwese, W. The effect of the leader's ability and interpersonal attitudes on group creativity under varying conditions of stress. Unpublished doctoral dissertation, Univer. of Amsterdam, 1964.

Meuwese, W., and Sophie Oonk. Enkele determinanten von creativiteit, structuur en proces in kleine experimentele groepen. Unpublished doctoral dissertation, Univer. of Amsterdam, 1960.

Meyers, W. Creativity as a set or role. Unpublished doctoral dissertation, Harvard Univer., 1963.

Michael, J. A. The effect of awards, adult standard, and peer standard upon the creativeness in art of high school pupils. Unpublished doctoral dissertation, the Pennsylvania State Univer., 1959.

Miller, Barbara. A study of creativity in college students and teaching method types. Senior honor thesis, Univer. of Michigan, 1960.

Miller, G. A., E. Galanter, and K. H. Pribram. *Plans and the structure of behavior.* New York: Holt, 1960.

Miller, H. Reflections on writing. *In* B. Ghiselin (Ed.). *The creative process.* New York: The New American Library, 1955. P. 178.

Moore, Marianne. The monkey puzzle. In *Collected poems of Marianne Moore.* New York: Macmillan, 1951.

Morley, F. C. Creative behavior in the elementary school. Unpublished doctoral dissertation, Columbia Univer., 1958.

Mosher, F. Strategies for information gathering. Paper read at symposium on processes of cognitive growth, EPA meetings, Atlantic City, 1962.

Myers, I. B. *Some findings with regard to type and manual for Myers-Briggs Type Indicator, Form E.* Swarthmore: privately printed, 1958.

Myers, I. B. *The Myers-Briggs Type Indicator.* Princeton, N. J.: Educational Testing Service, 1962.

Myers, R. E., and E. P. Torrance. *Invitations to thinking and doing.* Minneapolis: Perceptive Publishing Co., 1961.

Myers, R. E., and E. P. Torrance. *Invitations to speaking and writing creatively.* Minneapolis: Perceptive Publishing Co., 1962.

Nichols, R. C., and J. L. Holland. The prediction of first year college performance of high aptitude students. *Psychol. Monagr.,* 1963 (No. 570).

Nicholson, P. J., III. An experimental investigation of the effects of training upon creativity. Unpublished doctoral dissertation, Univer. of Houston, 1959.

Nielsen, E. C. Factor analysis of a biographical information inventory. Unpublished doctoral dissertation. Salt Lake City: Univer. of Utah, 1963.

O'Casey, Sean. *Inishfallen, fare thee well,* Scranton, Pa.: Haddon Craftsmen, 1949.

Osborn, A. F. *Applied imagination* (3rd ed.). New York: Scribner's, 1957.

Osgood, C. E., G. J. Suci, and P. Tannenbaum. *The measurement of meaning.* Urbana: Univer. of Illinois Press, 1957.

Pappas, G. An analysis of the process of beginning and developing works of art. Unpublished doctoral thesis, The Pennsylvania State Univer., 1957.

Parnes, S. J. (Ed.). Compendium of research on creative imagination. Creative Education Foundation, Buffalo, 1958.

Parnes, S. J. (Ed.). Compendium no. 2 of research on creative imagination. Creative Education Foundation, Buffalo, 1960.

Parnes, S. J. Can creativity be increased? *Studies in art Educ.,* 1961a, 3, 39–46.

Parnes, S. J. Effects of extended effort in creative problem-solving. *J. educ. Psychol.,* 1961b, 52, 117–122.

Parnes, S. J. Education and creativity. *Teachers coll. Rec.,* 1963a, 64, 331–339.

Parnes, S. J. *Instructors' manual for semester courses in creative problem solving* (rev. ed.). Creative Education Foundation, 1963b.

Parnes, S. J. *Student workbook for creative problem-solving courses and institutes* (rev. ed.). Univer. of Buffalo Bookstore, 1963c.

Parnes, S. J. The deferment-of-judgment principle: a clarification of the literature. *Psychol. Rep.,* 1963d, 12, 521–522.

Parnes, S. J., and H. F. Harding (Eds.). *A source book for creative thinking.* New York: Scribner's, 1962.

Parnes, S. J., and A. Meadow. Effects of "brainstorming" instructions on creative problem-solving by trained and untrained subjects. *J. educ. Psychol.,* 1959a, 50, 171–176.

Parnes, S. J., and A. Meadow. University of Buffalo research regarding development of creative talent. *Research conference on the identification of creative scientific talent,* Univer. of Utah, 1959b.

Parnes, S. J., and A. Meadow. Evaluation of persistence of effects produced by a creative problem-solving course. *Psychol. Rep.*, 1960, 7, 357–361.

Pepinsky, Pauline N. Originality in group productivity: I. Productive independence in three natural situations. Columbus, Ohio: Personnel Research Board, Ohio State Univer., 1959.

Pickford, R. An experiment on insight. *Brit. J. Psychol.*, 1938, 28, 412, 422.

Pratt, Carroll C. Aesthetics. *Ann. rev. Psychol.*, 1961, 12, 71–92.

Repucci, L. C. *Definitions and criteria of creativity.* Midland: The Dow Chemical Co., 1960. (Mimeographed).

Repucci, L. C. *Biographical differences between hi and lo creative subjects.* Midland: The Dow Chemical Co., 1961. (Mimeographed)

Repucci, L. C. *The predictive value of unreduced tension as related to creativity.* Midland: The Dow Chemical Co., 1962. (Mimeographed)

Rogers, C. R. Toward a theory of creativity. *In* H. H. Anderson (Ed.). *Creativity and its cultivation.* New York: Harper, 1959. Pp. 69–82.

Rompel, R. W. Validities of the creative process check list for the prediction of 22 criteria. Unpublished master's thesis, Univer. of Utah, 1962.

Russell, W. A., and J. J. Jenkins. The complete Minnesota norms for responses to 100 words from the Kent-Rosanoff Word Association Test. *Tech. Rep.* No. 11, Contract N8onr 66216. Univer. of Minnesota, 1954.

Sanford, N., H. Webster, and M. Freedman. Impulse expression as a variable of personality. *Psychol. Monogr.*, 1957, 71 (11 Whole No. 440).

Schimek, J. G. Creative originality: its evaluation by the use of free expression tests. Doctoral dissertation, Univer. of California Library, Berkeley. (Obtainable on microfilm)

Snapper, A. Mediating verbal responses in transfer of training. Unpublished A.B. honors thesis, Harvard Univer., 1956.

Sommers, W. S. The influence of selected teaching methods on the development of creative thinking. Doctoral dissertation, Univer. of Minnesota, 1961.

Sprecher, T. B. Criteria of creativity. *In* C. W. Taylor (Ed.). *The third (1959) University of Utah research conference on the identification of creative scientific talent.* Salt Lake City: Univer. of Utah Press, 1959.

Springbett, B. An approach to the measurement of creative thinking. *Canad. J. Psychol.*, 1957, 11, 9–20.

Stein, M. I. A transactional approach to creativity. *In* C. W. Taylor and F. Barron (Eds.). *Scientific creativity: its recognition and development.* New York: Wiley, 1963. Pp. 217–227.

Stein, M. I., and S. J. Heinze. *Creativity and the individual.* Glencoe, Ill.: The Free Press, 1960.

Stewart, W. R. The interaction of certain variables in the apperception of painting. Unpublished doctoral dissertation, The Pennsylvania State Univer., 1961.

Strong, E. K., Jr. *Manual for Strong vocational interest blanks for men and women, revised blanks (Form M and W).* Palo Alto: Consulting Psychologists Press, 1959.

Suchman, J. Inquiry training in the elementary school. *The sci. teacher*, 1960, 26 (7), 42–47.

Suchman, J. *Inquiry training: building skills for autonomous discovery.* Urbana, Ill.: College of Education, Univer. of Illinois, 1961. (Mimeographed)

Suchman, J. *The elementary school training program in scientific inquiry.* Report of title VII project No. 216, National Defense Education Act of 1958, Grant 7–11–038. Univer. of Illinois, 1962.

Taylor, C. W. (Ed.). *The 1955 University of Utah research conference on the identification of creative scientific talent.* Salt Lake City: Univer. of Utah Press, 1956.

Taylor, C. W. (Ed.). *The second (1957) University of Utah research conference on the identification of creative scientific talent.* Salt Lake City: Univer. of Utah Press, 1958.

Taylor, C. W. (Ed.). *The third (1959) University of Utah research conference on the identification of creative scientific talent.* Salt Lake City: Univer. of Utah Press, 1959.

Taylor, C. W. The creative individual: a new portrait in giftedness. *Educ. Leadership,* 1960, 18(1), 7–12.

Taylor, C. W. A tentative description of the creative individual. *In* W. B. Waetjen (Ed.). *Human variability and learning.* Washington, D. C.: Association for Supervision and Curriculum Development, 1961, 62–79. Also Chapter 15 *in* S. J. Parnes and H. F. Harding (Eds.). *A source book for creative thinking.* New York: Scribner, 1962.

Taylor, C. W. Effects of instructional media on creativity: a look at possible positive and negative effects. *Educ. Leadership,* 1962a, 19 (7), 453–548.

Taylor, C. W. The criterion-oriented approach to the development of creativity tests. *Proceedings of ETS Western invitational testing conference,* Los Angeles, 1962b, 32–45.

Taylor, C. W. Are we utilizing our creative potentials? *Nursing outlook,* February 1963a, 11 (2).

Taylor, C. W. Bridges from creativity to research (*in* Clues to Creative Teaching series). *The Instructor,* Dansville, N. Y., September 1963b, 5, 132b.

Taylor, C. W. Different approaches to creativity (*in* Clues to Creative Teaching series). *The Instructor,* October 1963c, 5, 62, 70.

Taylor, C. W. Intelligence vs. other intellectual talents: current confusions. *Childhood Educ.,* April 1963d, 364–366.

Taylor, C. W. Knowledge and creativity (*in* Clues to Creative Teaching series). *The Instructor,* Dansville, N. Y., December, 1963e, 5, 66.

Taylor, C. W. The creative process and education (*in* Clues to Creative Teaching series). *The Instructor,* Dansville, N. Y., November 1963f, 5, 112.

Taylor, C. W. Creativity and expression (*in* Clues to Creative Teaching series). *The Instructor,* Dansville, N. Y., March, 1964a, 5, 13.

Taylor, C. W. (Ed.). *Creativity: progress and potential.* New York: McGraw-Hill, 1964b.

Taylor, C. W. Developing creative characteristics (*in* Clues to Creative Teaching series). *The Instructor,* Dansville, N. Y., May, 1964c, 5, 99, 100.

Taylor, C. W. Developing creative thinking (*in* Clues to Creative Teaching series). *The Instructor,* Dansville, N. Y., April, 1964d, 7, 71, 72.

Taylor, C. W. Evoking creativity (*in* Clues to Creative Teaching series). *The Instructor,* Dansville, N. Y., June, 1964e, forthcoming.

Taylor, C. W. Learning and reading creatively (*in* Clues to Creative Teaching series). *The Instructor,* Dansville, N. Y., January, 1964f, 5, 113.

Taylor, C. W. Listening creatively (*in* Clues to Creative Teaching series). *The Instructor,* Dansville, N. Y., February, 1964g, 5, 103, 104.

Taylor, C. W., and F. Barron (Eds.). *Scientific creativity: its recognition and development.* New York: Wiley, 1963.

Taylor, C. W., G. M. Cooley, and E. C. Nielsen. Identifying high school students with characteristics needed in research work. Supported by National Science Foundation, contract NSF–G17543, 1963. (Mimeographed)

Taylor, C. W., B. Ghiselin, and J. A. Wolfer. Bridging the gap between basic research and educational practice. *NEA J.*, January 1962, 23–25.

Taylor, C. W., and J. Holland. Development and application of tests of creativity. *Rev. Educ. Res.*, Feb., 1962, 32 (1), 91–102. (See also Chapter 2 *in* C. W. Taylor (Ed.). *Creativity: progress and potential.* New York: McGraw-Hill, 1964. Pp. 14–48.)

Taylor, C. W., W. R. Smith, B. Ghiselin, and R. L. Ellison. Explorations in the measurement and prediction of contributions of one sample of scientists. *Tech. Rep.* ASD-TR-61-96, Aeronautical Systems Division, Personnel Laboratory, Lackland Air Force Base, Texas: April, 1961.

Taylor, C. W., W. R. Smith, B. Ghiselin, B. V. Sheets, and J. R. Cochran. Communication abilities in military situations. *Tech. Rep.* WADC-TR-58-92, Lackland Air Force Base, Texas: Wright Air Development Center, Personnel Laboratory, 1958.

Taylor, D. W. Variables related to creativity and productivity among men in two research laboratories. *In* C. W. Taylor (Ed.). *The second (1957) University of Utah research conference on the identification of creative scientific talent.* Salt Lake City: Univer. of Utah Press, 1958.

Taylor, D. W., P. C. Berry, and C. H. Block. Does group participation when using brainstorming facilitate or inhibit creative thinking? *Admin. Sci. Quart.*, 1958, 3, 23–47.

Taylor, D. W., and W. L. Faust. Twenty questions: efficiency in problem-solving as a function of size of group. *J. exp. Psychol.*, 1952, 44, 360–368.

Taylor, Janet. A personality scale of manifest anxiety. *J. abnorm. soc. Psychol.*, 1953, 48, 285–290.

Thurstone, K. L. A factorial study of perception. *Psychometric Monogr.*, 1944, 4.

Torrance, E. P. Explorations in creative thinking in the early school years: VI. Highly intelligent and highly creative children in a laboratory school. *Research Mem.* BER-59-7. Minneapolis: Bureau of Educational Research, Univer. of Minnesota, 1959.

Torrance, E. P. Conditions for creative growth. Minneapolis: Bureau of Educational Research, Univer. of Minnesota, November 1960. (Mimeographed)

Torrance, E. P. *Guiding creative talent.* Englewood Cliffs, N. J.: Prentice-Hall, 1962.

Toynbee, A. Has America neglected her creative minority? *Utah Alumnus*, February 1962, 10.

Vafeas, W. P. The effect of barriers on the creative development and aesthetic quality of three-dimensional art forms. Unpublished doctoral dissertation, The Pennsylvania State Univer., 1961.

Walker, H. Relationships between predicted school behavior and measures of creative potential. Doctoral dissertation, Univer. of Michigan, 1962.

Wallace, H. R. Creative thinking: a factor in sales productivity. *Vocational Guidance Quart.*, 1961, 223–226.

Weisberg, P. S., and J. S. Kayla. Environmental factors in creative function. *Arch. gen. Psychiatry*, 1961, 5, 554–564.

Weisberg, P. S., and K. R. Springer. Environmental factors influencing creative function in gifted children. Cincinnati: Department of Psychiatry, Cincinnati General Hospital, 1961. (Mimeographed)

Westcott, M. A new approach to productive thinking; basic theory and methodology. Unpublished manuscript, Univer. of Oxford, Institute of Experimental Psychology, 1955.

Westcott, M. A method for the study of creativity as a special case of problem solving. Paper read at EPA meetings, New York, April 1960.

Westcott, M. On the measurement of intuitive leaps. *Psychol. Reps.*, 1961, 9, 267–274.

Westcott, M. Inference, guesswork, and creativity. Final report of Project 684, Cooperative Research Program, U. S. Office of Education, 1962.

Westcott, M., and Jane Ranzoni. Personality correlates of intuitive thinking. Paper read at EPA meetings, Atlantic City, April 1962.

Westcott, M., and Jane Ranzoni. Correlates of intuitive thinking. *Psychol. Reps.*, 12, 595–613. (Also as Monograph Supplement 5-V12)

Wild, K. *Intuition.* New York: Macmillan, 1938.

Withers, Maida R. Measuring the creativity of modern dancers. Unpublished master's thesis, Univer. of Utah, 1960.

Yamamoto, K. *Revised scoring manual for tests of creativity thinking (Forms VA and NVA).* Minneapolis: Bureau of Educational Research, Univer. of Minnesota, 1962.

Ziller, R. C., and R. Exline. Some consequences of age heterogeneity in decision-making groups. *Sociometry*, 1958, 21, 198–211.

Index